Founding Visions

FOUNDING VISIONS

The Ideas, Individuals, and Intersections that Created America

LANCE BANNING

Edited and with an Introduction by
TODD ESTES

Foreword by GORDON S. WOOD

UNIVERSITY PRESS OF KENTUCKY

Copyright © 2014 by The University Press of Kentucky

Scholarly publisher for the Commonwealth,
serving Bellarmine University, Berea College, Centre College of Kentucky,
Eastern Kentucky University, The Filson Historical Society, Georgetown
College, Kentucky Historical Society, Kentucky State University, Morehead
State University, Murray State University, Northern Kentucky University,
Transylvania University, University of Kentucky, University of Louisville,
and Western Kentucky University.
All rights reserved.

Editorial and Sales Offices: The University Press of Kentucky
663 South Limestone Street, Lexington, Kentucky 40508-4008
www.kentuckypress.com

Frontispiece: Lance Banning (Courtesy of the University of Kentucky History
Department).

Cataloging-in-Publication data is available from the Library of Congress.

ISBN 978-0-8131-5284-4 (hardcover : alk. paper)
ISBN 978-0-8131-5286-8 (epub)
ISBN 978-0-8131-5285-1 (pdf)

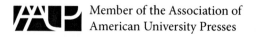

Contents

Foreword

Gordon S. Wood

Lance Banning was no ordinary historian. Indeed, he was one of the most distinguished American historians of his generation. Not only has he had an important and lasting effect on our understanding of the ideas and politics of the early Republic, but, more important, his writings (the best of which are collected in this book) have become a model of what historical scholarship ought to be. In his approach to the past he had no present-minded political agenda, no desire to browbeat the past for the sake of reforming an oppressive present. All he sought to do in his scholarship was explain as carefully and as scrupulously as possible what the ideas and politics of the early Republic were like.

Not that he was uninterested in the present. Nor did he deny any connection between then and now. In fact, he always believed that the discussions that the Founders had among themselves were worth listening to. Perhaps if we listened closely enough to the past, he said, we might be able to see our present problems from fresh perspectives. He was convinced that we could learn something from the Founders, that their ideas and values, though coming from a different world, still had relevance for us. He realized that the Founders he studied and admired, especially James Madison, knew only too well that political power was dangerous and that it had to be separated and balanced but not repudiated. Ultimately, however, Lance respected the integrity and separateness of the past. He was a historian's historian; he took the fears and fantasies of the participants in the past seriously and always sought to be objective and fair to the figures he studied. And he never wrote his history with any crude didactic purpose in mind.

I first met Lance in the early 1970s when he became executive director of the American Civilization Program at Brown University, where I had been teaching since 1969. He had just received his Ph.D. from Washington University, where he had encountered two of the most stimulating scholars of the early modern Anglo-American world, John Murrin and J. G. A. Pocock. Interacting with those scholars helped prepare him for a fresh approach to intellectual history in the writing of his dissertation, "The Quarrel with Federalism: A Study in the Origins and Character of Republican Thought"(1971). He soon developed that dissertation into his book *The Jeffersonian Persuasion: Evolution of a Party Ideology* (1978). In this work Lance did not neglect the great minds of political theory. James Harrington, John Locke, and David Hume were present. But his work was not a traditional study of the influence of the ideas of these great thinkers; it was not a history of ideas abstracted from their social and political circumstances. Instead, his work moved along the borderland between ideas and politics, where ideas interacted with politics and became what he labeled ideology. His book was the cultural history of politics at its best, and it profoundly influenced our understanding of the early Republic.

Since in the early 1970s when we first met Lance was preparing his dissertation for publication and I had recently published my book *The Creation of the American Republic, 1776–1787* (1969), we discovered that we had a lot in common. Indeed, we could scarcely keep from seeking out opportunities to talk about the history of the early Republic. I still recall our many conversations with excitement and pleasure. We marveled at the emergence of what was already being called the "republican synthesis," little realizing at the time what a monster that "hypothesis," as Lance labeled it, would become. It was an intellectually stimulating time for me, and I only wish that Lance could have stayed at Brown. But his administrative position at Brown was temporary and carried no tenure. In 1973 he became an assistant professor at the University of Kentucky, where he spent the rest of his career.

We kept up our intellectual relationship, of course, but it was more hit or miss. Because we were interested in the same material, our scholarly paths crossed more often than most. We were invited to nearly every conference on republicanism or the Founding and had many opportunities at these meetings to renew our conversations about the early Republic. Although we occasionally differed on some points (I thought he played down Madison's nationalism in the 1780s too much, which he needed to do in order to make sense of Madison's states' rights position of the 1790s), we both agreed that the supposed opposition between a republican tradition and a liberal tradition maintained by many historians, political theorists, and law professors was wrongheaded. We both believed that a sharp dichotomy between two clearly identifiable intellectual traditions could not be supported by the complicated reality of the Founding era. But it was Lance who produced the series of articles that undermined that dichotomy. In his work, much of which is collected in this book, he showed the scholarly world how the Founders, grappling with an ever-changing political reality, linked and blended together the two seemingly incompatible traditions. Few bodies of scholarship have had as great an impact on the study of the political thought of early America as has Lance's.

What in my mind is most impressive about Lance's scholarship is the care and honesty he brought to it. Nothing for him was ever simple about the past. He thought through every problem and wrestled with every issue concerned with the ideas and politics of the early Republic. For him, everything about the era of the Founding was more complicated, more nuanced, more filled with tension than most scholars were willing to admit. Where others saw simplicity, he saw complexity. Where others lumped things together, he drew distinctions. He had a subtle and scrupulous mind. No one in my opinion was a more painstaking scholar than Lance.

Lance always worried that he was too slow in bringing his work to press, that he was not productive enough. He should not have worried. When the works of other scholars will be long forgotten, Lance's scholarship on the era of the Founding will continue to be discussed and plumbed. We are indeed fortunate to have much of that important and insightful scholarship brought together in this book.

Introduction

Todd Estes

Lance Banning was one of the best historians of his generation. He was also one of the most modest and self-effacing, which is why this book of his collected essays is only now in your hands. This introduction will deal briefly with his modesty and narrate how the collection finally came into being, many years after its conception. But its primary purpose is to establish Banning's significance as a historian of early America and to elucidate the ways that his body of work—much of it collected in these pages—served to reshape the historiographical landscape by challenging the received wisdom, offering bold new interpretations, refereeing disputes and controversies among specialists, and doing all of it with a remarkable fairness and evenhandedness that was at least as prominent as his modesty and certainly more important. Above all else, Banning was absolutely dedicated to doing history as carefully and meticulously as possible. He believed the most important thing was to get it right, to do history with a thoroughness and dedication to accuracy and fairness. He believed we historians owed that to our discipline and to the past.

He practiced what he preached, too, right up until his untimely death in 2006. For a long time, Banning declined to gather his fugitive work into one volume even as some of his peers were doing so with theirs. When he finally approached a university press about the possibility in 1995, the same year his remarkable work *The Sacred Fire of Liberty* appeared, he did so with great reluctance, almost apologetically. He did not sign a contract for an essay collection for ten more years, until March 2005. Less than a year later he was dead, felled by complications from lung surgery in January 2006. He had gone into the hospital with symptoms at Thanksgiving and lingered for a

time. As death neared he reflected on his career, regretting less the work he
left behind uncompleted than the graduate students he had not yet finished
mentoring, and worrying that he somehow was abandoning them. As word
of his death spread to and from many different quarters of the academic (and
nonacademic) world, his students, friends, and colleagues across the globe
mourned the loss of a kind, generous, unassuming, and unpretentious man
of towering and lasting intellectual accomplishments. Banning was an academic star who never acted like one.

Perhaps it was the unconscious effect that James Madison seems to have
had on many of the scholars who write about him. Just as Madison was
regarded in his day as kind, quiet, thoughtful, and considerate, those words
have been used to describe some of the scholars who study him. Something
in the subject seems to draw congenial people. Marvin Meyers, who prepared an outstanding volume of Madison's political thought, wrote in the
acknowledgments to that book: "The best scholars, I find, are often the most
generous. The late Douglass Adair offered friendship, counsel, and, above
all, the model of a Madisonian gentleman and scholar."[1] Lance Banning, too,
was a Madisonian gentleman and scholar in all ways, as numerous students,
friends, and colleagues will attest.

In fact, Banning had to overcome his Madisonian modesty before broach-
ing the subject of compiling his various works into a collection. When he first
posed the idea to an editor, he did so in a purely exploratory fashion, wanting
to gauge interest and share some "musings" about such a project.[2] Three years
passed before Banning wrote again in June 1998 with some updated thoughts
in which he made clear that he had been "rethinking" the organization of the
project and had dropped the idea of writing any wholly new chapters. Ultimately, even as his thinking had evolved about the organization and contents
of such a volume, Banning still had other work and writing deadlines compelling his attention, and so the potential volume lay idle.

Then, in December 2004, Banning returned to the project a third time.
"I've been giving some thought, long overdue and too often promised, to the
possibility of the essay collection," he wrote.[3] By the next spring, Banning
had in hand an encouraging set of six referee reports on his proposed volume and was finally ready to go. "My key consideration . . . is finding a way
to keep some of the good essays from getting permanently buried in obscure
places," he noted.[4]

And there things stood at the time of his death. Lance worked on the collection during 2005 along with other projects, but it had to be abandoned
when he went into the hospital. The project lay dormant until Lance's widow,

Lana, told me in 2011—not for the first time—that one of her great hopes was that his collected essays might somehow appear in print and that Lance had talked about this during his last weeks. After discussions and correspondence between various parties, the project found its present home with the University Press of Kentucky, whose editor, Stephen Wrinn, expressed very strong enthusiasm for the book. Once secured, Kentucky moved quickly to fast-track the project and move it toward publication, a process nearly two decades in the making from Banning's first initiatives to final fruition.[5]

It is important, however, not to let the vagaries of the editorial and publishing processes detailed above—nor his well-documented reputation for modesty and kindness—obscure the central purpose of this collection: to establish firmly Lance Banning's lasting significance as a scholar of early American history. His personal qualities, as important and ingratiating as they were for colleagues and students, are not the reason for this collection. Only the importance of Banning's work can justify publication now, nearly a decade after his death. Not only was he an influential and important historian during his career, Banning's scholarly work still has great significance. His interpretations have become part of the enduring historiographical literature on early U.S. history, to be read and studied by current and future generations of graduate students, young professors, and established scholars in at least three key fields of inquiry.

In the mid-1960s, Bernard Bailyn demonstrated the crucial significance of opposition ideology to the American Revolution, showing how fears of corruption and tyranny from the English past resonated so powerfully with American colonists then struggling against a powerful, distant, consolidated government that seemed to them bent on using political and military power to subvert liberty. The constellation of ideas that formed opposition thought was often labeled "republicanism." Bailyn's student Gordon S. Wood extended the explanatory power of republicanism into the 1780s in his work—but he suggested an end to classical republican politics with the adoption of the Constitution. Banning, however, suggested very powerfully that republican ideology did not die off with the new frame of government. Instead, the values and fears that animated the Revolution also explained the rise of opposition in the 1790s to the Hamiltonian Federalist program. Banning demonstrated—first in his dissertation, then in a 1974 *William and Mary Quarterly* article, and finally with his 1978 book—the ideological origins of the Jeffersonian persuasion.

By showing the ways that republican principles influenced the rise of political parties in the 1790s and articulating the conceptual understandings of what and why the participants in the drama acted as they did, Banning revolutionized historiographical interpretations of the Jeffersonian Republicans. His interpretation transformed them from simplistic riders of the democratic wave who swept into power against the undemocratic, elitist Federalists into principled opponents of a Federalist governing ideology and economic and cultural infrastructure that Jeffersonians understood to be a threat to the basic values of the American Revolution. He showed that the Jeffersonians were just as much backward-looking as forward-looking, and that their ideology was an amalgam of both elements. Jefferson's self-proclaimed "Revolution of 1800" was not just empty campaign rhetoric but, Banning contended, a ringing declaration of a restoration of Revolutionary principles that Jefferson and others feared would be snuffed out by the Anglophile Federalists if they prevailed. Although Banning confronted the dilemmas, contradictions, and shortcomings of the Jeffersonian persuasion quite ably, his essential contribution was to show conclusively the persistence of the contest over the meaning of the Revolution, the ways in which it lingered long after the Revolution, and the deep resonance that the ideology and conflicts of that earlier era continued to hold for the new nation in its infant decades. In short, he linked the first party conflict to the Revolutionary past, demonstrating an essential connection between the two, and extending chronologically the republicanism identified by Bailyn and Wood.

Having helped establish the republican interpretation (or "hypothesis," as he often phrased it), Banning then distanced himself from some of the ends and uses to which that idea was applied. He became not only an active and central participant in the republicanism-liberalism debates that flourished in the 1970s and 1980s, but also a thoughtful analyst, synthesizer, and referee of those contests. His 1986 *William and Mary Quarterly* article was one of the critical texts in these often contentious exchanges. But the other three pieces contained in that section of this volume all include some very shrewd commentary by Banning on the debates in which he took part, revealing a scholar who could step back to assess the debate itself, locating both his own contributions and others' in relation to the field as a whole, and remarking on the key readings (and some serious misreadings) that delineated the field and shaped the course of the dispute. In these, he showed himself to be scrupulously fair while also holding himself and the profession to the highest standards, reminding everyone of how hard it is to do serious historical inquiry and why that difficult, painstaking work is so important. Banning intervened in these debates not in a partisan way but with restraint and respect toward others. As such, his involvement was widely seen as being in the pursuit of knowledge, and it was generally received in that spirit of collegiality.

Even as he had just made a major historiographical contribution to our understanding of Jeffersonian political thought in the late 1970s, by the early 1980s Banning was beginning a research project that ultimately produced a third strikingly original, revisionist intervention, this time regarding the political thought of James Madison, often called America's preeminent political theorist. When Banning started in on this project, Irving Brant, one of Madison's biographers, cast a huge shadow over the field. Brant portrayed Madison as a thorough-going nationalist during the 1780s, a thinker whose attraction to a powerful, consolidated, national government knew few bounds. According to Brant, Madison then made a sharp U-turn in the 1790s, abandoning Alexander Hamilton and falling back on a doctrine that made the case for the rights of states against a consolidated national government. Brant's interpretation—which actually echoed Hamilton's own charges against Madison at the time—quickly took root in the literature. Soon, scholars presumed the existence of a "James Madison problem": namely, how to understand and explain how the Virginian moved from nationalist to states' rights advocate in a decade's time.[6]

As was his typical practice, Banning started with no preconceptions and went back to the documentary record. As he read Madison's own work and reread the extant scholarship, he identified various ways in which Madison had been misread, the ways those misreadings had worked themselves into the literature, and how those misperceptions, with each new iteration, took on a life of their own. Banning offered a patient, careful correction to the received wisdom on Madison, showing how dilemmas or mysteries about Madison's actions and writings could be resolved once they were properly understood and contextualized. As Banning shaped his revisionist account into published scholarship, the result was not a single big breakthrough in understanding but rather, as Alan Gibson put it, "a series of specific revisions that cumulatively create[d] a fundamentally new understanding of the path of Madison's political career and the character of his political thought."[7] Reaching fullest form in *The Sacred Fire of Liberty,* this series of revisions developed initially in many articles, chapters, and essays, such as those that appear in this volume.

Beyond these three critical interpretive interventions and historiographical contributions, Banning's work is significant for two other reasons as well—and ones just as worthy of study and emulation by both established and beginning scholars. He was as meticulous a scholar as there was, as Gordon Wood appreciatively notes in his foreword. Lance worked at an admittedly and self-consciously slow pace, yet still produced a tremendous *quantity* of high-quality scholarship, as the appendix to this volume shows. But the reason his work took time had nothing to do with being dilatory or with procrastination. Rather, it stemmed from the enormous care he invested in reading his sources closely and carefully and also from reading the work of other historians with that same care and attention. His scholarship, especially the pieces reprinted in this collection, is a model of careful, meticulous research, fair-minded and even-handed interpretations, and precise, carefully calibrated writing.

One of the reasons he wrote so precisely was because of his irritation and frustration when others misread (or superficially read) his own work. Thus, he was careful not to make those mistakes himself with the work of other scholars. Ever the careful student and fair-minded arbiter, Banning traced several historiographical debates to their origins in hasty reading and faulty comprehension by historians of the work of other scholars. Speaking specifically of the republicanism-liberalism debate, Lance observed that "many readers were collecting their impression of the republican interpretations not from careful reading of the major works themselves but from misleading summaries by others." Then, Banning spoke frankly, if parenthetically, about the larger malady of which this misreading of republicanism was a symptom. "(If there is anything, in fact, that tends to disillusion me about our business, this would surely be the great degree to which our universal struggle to remain abreast of an exploding literature is leading to a huge amount of careless reading or to even poorer strategies for keeping up.)"[8] Note that Banning did not name names, did not cast aspersions, and did not make this point in a hostile or score-settling manner. Instead, he identified what is still a major problem of contemporary scholarship—the problem has arguably grown even worse in the two decades since he wrote that passage—diagnosed its cause, and reminded scholars of the necessity of slowing down, reading carefully, and comprehending fully. Such reminders are useful to scholars and students at any stage of a career since the pressures that Banning described can create problems for us all.

Second, Banning's role in historiographical controversies was often to do what James Madison himself had done—to mediate by finding a legitimate middle position between polar opposites and by showing that few historical phenomena have ever been wholly one thing or another. Banning's work challenged oversimplifications and false dichotomies, particularly when those interpretations were constructed on misreadings of documents or misunderstandings of the history of events themselves. Lance's mind gravitated toward subtlety and nuance. As he was always reminding those of us who were his students, the past was complicated and any viable historical treatment of the past must take that complexity into account and faithfully reproduce it if a scholarly work is to help us understand complex ideas and developments. By challenging not only superficial readings of the works of others—whether those of historical actors or other historians—Banning's work offers regular reminders against sloppiness, oversimplification, and exaggeration. He provides a model for how to dig deeply into a historical problem, how to find the richness of a past that does not reduce to ready-made categories or glib scholarly constructions that tend to divide and separate what historical figures frequently combined themselves. He was always on guard against this in his own writing as well as in considering the works of others. Taken together, his body of scholarship provides plentiful examples of the real insights and deeper understandings that can come from careful, nuanced, and painstaking scholarship that rejects facile categories or polarities, does not hide behind received authority, or cloak itself in the realm of the purely theoretical. In all this, Banning never lost sight of the actual history of events and never forgot the basic lesson that historians must not simply analyze events but should also be certain to tell readers what actually happened.

The contents of this volume follow, as closely as possible, the editorial decisions and organization that Banning sketched out in his evolving conceptions of the book. Banning originally planned to draft some new essays and to update or add postscripts to older pieces. Although he later dropped the idea of writing anything new for the collection, he did still plan to provide his own retrospective assessments of his publications. Still, even as he changed his mind about how much to do with them, his original format for the volume—which pieces to include, how to group those pieces—remained constant, and that is the outline I have followed here. I have made some additions or deletions of individual articles as needed, but I have maintained the basic structure and outline of the volume that Banning developed during the planning stage. The sections are organized thematically, with the readings grouped accordingly. The chapter headnotes continue and elaborate on many of the themes sketched out in this introduction, applied to the specific writings contained in that part.

The collection begins with his thoughtful essay on the problem that power posed for the Revolutionary generation, a piece that very ably sketches out what he called some of his long-held central concerns about the intersections between political theory and political practice as they appeared in the enduring struggles shaped by the American Revolution. This selection will serve as a conceptual framework for the essays that follow. Next comes a section on the republicanism-liberalism debate, with a select set of his most significant writings of nicely varied lengths.

Those two parts are followed by two more dealing with Banning's work on the Constitution and then James Madison. They collect his short treatments of the Constitutional Convention and *The Federalist Papers*. Both are brilliant illustrations of Lance's ability to distill in a short treatment a tremendous amount of information on large, complex topics in essays that also make significant interpretive and analytical points. He considered these pieces to be as good as any shorter treatments then in print on the Convention and ratification. In the early 1980s he began publishing the first iterations of the revisionist portrait of Madison that emerged in mature form in *The Sacred Fire of Liberty*. Three of the most important early statements of Banning's quarrel with the extant literature are reprinted here, and they suggest that he discovered very early in his work the different perspective and insight on Madison that shaped his interpretations.

Finally, although Banning is perhaps best known as a scholar of Madison and the Founding, he made his reputation initially as a sensitive and careful student of Jeffersonian political ideology, as his first book demonstrated. He never fully left that interest behind, particularly the ways in which political thought connected to party development. The last section of this volume reprints two articles Banning wrote in the 1990s that addressed political economy and the development and early history of the Jeffersonian political party.

One of the major contributions of this collection will be to make widely available a book chapter that Banning considered "certainly one of my best pieces": his "1787 and 1776" essay that appeared in an obscurely published collection of essays on the Constitution. Banning believed that this work, on the relationship of the Constitution to the Declaration of Independence, was "as good a piece as I've ever written."[9] Without a doubt, this was the essay at the top of Banning's list of those he hoped would be rescued from obscurity and given a wider exposure through a collection of his work. Readers will see why as they savor the elegant writing and thoughtful, careful analysis that illuminates one of the classic questions of early American history. If asked to pinpoint a single essay that demonstrates simultaneously all of Banning's skills as an historian, this is the one to which I would beckon readers.

Ultimately, the reason for bringing this volume to print after Lance's death is the very fundamental reason he began the project in the beginning:

to keep the excellent work of a leading historian from being lost to posterity. By making available in one location many of the significant works of a master historian, this volume will aid scholars, students, and researchers for years to come. It will also serve as a tribute to a fine man, a wonderful mentor and teacher, and an even better historian. Those of us who knew Lance Banning will always miss him. But now, even those who never met him can discover in these pages the richness of his life's work and the many lessons it has to teach us all.

Notes

1. Marvin Meyers, ed., *The Mind of the Founder: Sources of the Political Thought of James Madison* (New York, 1973), vii. In addition to this Madison volume, Meyers is best known for his superb book *The Jacksonian Persuasion: Politics and Belief* (New York, 1957). Of his own first book, entitled *The Jeffersonian Persuasion,* and of Meyers himself, Lance used to joke in seminars, "I stole that title from a good man."

2. Lance Banning to Fred Woodward, senior editor at the University Press of Kansas, July 1, 1995, correspondence in the possession of the editor. Banning's relationship with the Kansas Press was strong and of long standing. He was coeditor (with Wilson Carey McWilliams) of the American Political Thought series for the press and saw approximately thirty-five books through to publication in that series since the 1980s. I am indebted to Fred Woodward for many long discussions over email regarding the Banning collection, and for graciously sharing with me his correspondence with Banning along with the outside readers' reports. All of this proved enormously helpful to the drafting of this introduction and to the organization of the volume itself.

3. Banning to Woodward, December 2, 2004, email communication in the possession of the editor. His old ambivalence had not receded. "I still can't help feeling anything but seriously torn about the idea." Again he worried about letting good, important pieces go "lost," and he feared that there might be little interest in "the more theoretical pieces." Above all, however, he was conflicted and ambivalent. "I worry that the whole idea of doing a collection is basically a piece of insufferable vanity. Gordon Wood, who's a far more important historian than I am, has never put his essays together like this, and I'm not at all sure that mine are important enough that there'd be any real demand." Of course, Gordon Wood did eventually collect his various articles, chapters, and essays in three edited collections. See Wood's *Revolutionary Characters: What Made the Founders Different* (New York, 2006); *The Purpose of the Past: Reflections on the Uses of History* (New York, 2008); and *The Idea of America: Reflections on the Birth of the United States* (New York, 2011).

4. Banning to Woodward, March 14, 2005, email communication in the possession of the editor.

5. After due consideration, the University Press of Kansas (with whom the book had been contracted) ultimately decided to relinquish its claim on the volume and, with gracious good wishes, allowed the project to migrate to Kentucky, where it was warmly received.

6. For a discussion, see Gordon Wood, "Is There a 'James Madison Problem'?," in *Liberty and American Experience in the Eighteenth Century,* ed. David Womersley (Indianapolis, 2006), 425–447.

7. Alan Gibson, "Lance Banning's Interpretation of James Madison: An Appreciation and Critique," in *Political Science Reviewer* 32 (2003): 269–317. Gibson's article is a sympathetic yet rigorous analysis of the totality of Banning's scholarship on Madison that provides many thoughtful and subtle assessments of the body of work.

8. Lance Banning, "The Republican Interpretation: Retrospect and Prospect," in *The Republican Synthesis Revisited: Essays in Honor of George Athan Billias,* ed. Milton M. Klein, Richard D. Brown, and John B. Hench (Worcester, Mass., 1992), 92.

9. Banning to Woodward, June 22, 1998, and July 1, 1995, correspondence in the possession of the editor.

PART 1

The Enduring Issues of the American Revolution, 1776–1815

At its core, expressed in the broadest terms, most of Lance Banning's scholarship in one way or another addresses the challenges that the American Revolution created but did not resolve. From his work on the Jeffersonians and their creation of a party ideology based on adaptations of Revolutionary principles, to his studies of James Madison's efforts to create and implement a Constitution capable of fulfilling the promise of the Revolution by dealing with some of its perceived excesses, to his other more focused examinations of related historical problems, Banning's work revolves around this theme. At the heart of many of those issues is the problem of power—how to distribute it, how to divide it, how to restrain it, but also how to enable its use for pursuing good ends.

"The Problem of Power" appeared in a 1987 collection of essays on the American Revolution edited by Jack P. Greene. The entire essay is a model of succinct writing. The first paragraph may be as elegant and eloquent as any Banning ever penned. While his prose was graceful and unlabored, it also was never fussy or impenetrable, even when dealing with complex material. All those traits are displayed here. Note how easily yet effectively he summarizes complex bodies of political thought (Locke, Sidney) and historiographical treatments (Bailyn, Weston, Colbourn). The ability to simplify complex ideas without dumbing them down or losing sophistication was one of his hallmarks as a writer. Likewise, note how well he frames the discussion of the problem of power for American Revolutionaries not in abstract theoretical terms but in a grounded historical consideration, revealing not only what early Americans thought but what they did, and focusing always on the intersections between theory and practice.

Power proved among the most difficult matters faced by early national Americans, Banning demonstrates, because it was embedded in so many issues. If the American Revolution was fueled by a rejection of the abuses of power that the colonists blamed on Great Britain, how could Americans establish new governments of their own that placed power in safe hands so as to prevent such abuses in the future? As Banning shows, the Revolutionaries overcorrected for the problem, forgetting that power was not always abused, that it was in fact essential to good government, and that it was often necessary for reaching productive ends. The Constitution, written and ratified in 1787–1788, was the Revolutionary generation's great contribution to political theory. It divided power in various ways, simultaneously creating safeguards while also enabling active, energetic government. But the Constitution did not resolve the problem of power. Implementing the new system proved complex and difficult, spawning numerous controversies on Constitutional interpretation and ultimately giving rise to political parties (a development wholly unanticipated by the Founders) and the contentious battles spawned in the 1790s and beyond. In each period Banning traces the particular historical problems concerning the use of power, locates their evolution and development across time, shows how some matters produced shared agreement while other sparked endless disputes, and suggests that many of the thorniest issues the founding generation grappled with have persisted through all of U.S. history right down to the present.

This essay demonstrates Banning's skill as a historian in maintaining analytical and narrative command of the material and also exemplifies his ability to synthesize without losing particularity. It also shows, in short, his ability to take large issues and vast bodies of historical knowledge and render them not only comprehendible but also revelatory of larger patterns and themes both in history and in the historical literature. For all those reasons, "The Problem of Power" serves as an accessible yet sophisticated general introduction to this collection of Banning's work, as it displays so many of his trademark qualities as a writer and historian.

The Problem of Power

Parties, Aristocracy, and Democracy in Revolutionary Thought

Power is a hand that can caress as well as crush, provide as well as punish. It cannot say yes to some without denying others. It may lack capacity to nourish if it cannot also grip. Properly directed, nonetheless, the might of a community, concentrated in its government, can increase the happiness and nurture the prosperity of the society it shields. If it were otherwise—if the fist could not be opened, if everyone possessed the same ideas and interests, or if the revolutionary generation had not expected government to promote the general welfare as well as to protect the citizenry from lawlessness within and dangers from without—power might have proved a less persistent problem than it did.

Power puzzled revolutionary leaders longer and more deeply than older histories suggested because the revolutionaries did not consistently conceive of government as no more than a necessary evil, which should be limited to the protection of the individual in his pursuit of private goods. Nor did they always think of their society in terms of the relationships between an aggregate of solitary social atoms.[1] Living in an age of commerce, the revolutionary generation wanted benefits, not just protection, from their governments. Heirs to neo-classical and civic-humanist political ideas, as well as to the English libertarian tradition, they were accustomed to regarding man both as an individual involved in a relationship with other individuals and as a member of persistent social groups. In consequence, although the Revolution started with a fear of unresponsive central power, it produced a general government whose reach and grasp were more impressive than the claims that generated the American rebellion, and it involved the revolutionaries in a lifelong argument not only over ways in which great power might be rendered safe, but also over ways in which it could be shared and exercised so as to take advantage of its positive potential. Recent histories have focused scholarly attention on dimensions of the revolutionaries' thinking that were long neglected. A better understanding of the sources of their thought has thrown new light on how it changed and made it possible to see the federal Constitution as an incident in an extended effort to resolve a set of problems that the Founders redefined, but neither solved nor ceased debating.[2]

From this new perspective, it is helpful to approach the Revolution as a moment in our past when circumstances forced the nation's leaders to consider fundamentals. The moment was a long one. Historians today seem more and more inclined to think of this consideration of the fundamentals as a process that began as early as 1763 and may have reached a partial resolution only after the conclusion of the War of 1812.[3] The circumstances were the sort that pressed the revolutionaries to probe continuously deeper into all the basic concepts: virtue and self-interest; the many and the few; parties and the public good; liberty and power. The institution of our present federal government came roughly halfway through the course of this collective effort. The writing and approval of the Constitution ultimately altered nearly all the terms of the continuing debate, but it did not do so at once, nor did it solve all of the problems that the argument involved.

In 1763, most articulate American colonials identified themselves as English and shared with other Englishmen a reasonably coherent way of thinking about political society and power. Government, they thought, originated in the consent of the society it served and exercised a legitimate authority only when it faithfully protected the indefeasible rights of those it sheltered. But as power naturally inclined to turn against the liberties it was intended to defend and individuals were equal only in their right to hold their lives and property secure, the most effective way to guarantee that all would be protected and that government would stay within its proper bounds was to divide the sovereign authority (or legislative power) among three different branches, each representing different segments of society and all combining to provide the three essential characteristics that just, enduring governments require.[4] On both sides of the ocean, the history of seventeenth-century England was remembered as the story of the nation's struggle to confine the government within due limits and to forge effective links between the exercise of power and society's consent.[5] On both sides, by the middle of the eighteenth century, Englishmen complacently and boastfully agreed that their complicated government of king-in-parliament had solved this problem in a manner that was properly the envy of the enlightened world.[6] With power shared among the Crown, the House of Lords, and the House of Commons, every major segment of society possessed sufficient power to protect its vital interests, and the state reflected all the finest qualities of every simpler form of government without the risks and limitations which simpler governments entailed: the unity and vigor of a monarch; the wisdom commonly associated with a leisured, well-born few; and the responsiveness to common good that flows from the participation of the body of the people.[7]

Coherent as it seemed, eighteenth-century thinking was in fact a very complicated blend of elements that did not blend as smoothly as contemporaries thought. When British thinkers asked about the origins and limits of governmental power, their reasoning began with individuals. In the manner of John Locke, they emphasized a natural equality of rights, the limitations of legitimate authority, and the logical necessity that any aggregate of equals must be guided by the largest number.[8] When they thought about *good* government, by contrast, eighteenth-century Englishmen and their colonial cousins concerned themselves primarily with the relationships between two fundamentally *unequal* social groups: the many, and the few who are distinguishable from the majority by their greater leisure, better birth, and superior possessions.[9] This second line of reasoning, which may be traced back through the Renaissance to ancient Greek and Roman thinkers, was more preoccupied with the achievement of a stable mixture of the virtues of two social groups than with the rights of individuals. Where Locke assumed a sharp distinction between society and government, the neo-classical tradition was inclined to merge the two, conceiving of society as *embodied in* the different parts of government and worrying less frequently about the limits of governmental power than about the maintenance of its internal equilibrium.

Logically, these different modes of thought involved some rather contradictory assumptions and suggested inconsistent attitudes toward power. Historically, they had converged so neatly during the seventeenth-century struggle to confine the Stuart kings that eighteenth-century Englishmen were seldom conscious of the tensions.[10] Men had sometimes to be thought of in their individual capacities and sometimes as constituents of persistent and potentially conflicting groups. Regarded either way, their liberties seemed safest when power was divided among the few, the many, and the one. The governmental equilibrium that guaranteed security for every segment of society seemed simultaneously to shield the individual from grasping power. This seemed more certainly the case because the course of English history suggested that dangers to the governmental balance and the liberties of subjects both ordinarily issued from the usurpations of the one (or the executive) and because habitual association of liberty with property encouraged an assumption that the whole political society was present in the Lords and Commons, which confined the Crown and linked the exercise of power with consent.[11]

For colonials, however, the crisis in imperial relations which ground its way inexorably toward independence in the decade after 1765, severely shook this integrated way of thinking. The Revolution pitted its constituent ideas against each other, wrenched them into different shapes, and forced the altered elements into a new configuration. Half a century later, power was a different sort of problem. If this was less apparent to contemporaries than it seems to us, that was in part because Americans still feared the possibility of its abuse and still expressed this fear in eighteenth-century language, condemning "aristocracy" and "influence" and the like, employing terms that were increasingly ill-suited to contemporary practices and needs. But the persistence of such terms was also a reflection of the fact that older structures of ideas had not abruptly crumbled. While the Revolution and the Constitution rapidly produced a new consensus about the character and limits of legitimate authority, the problem of good government was not so readily resolved; newer worries over parties and the public good could not be easily disjoined from more traditional concerns about relationships between the many and the few. Aristocracy, democracy, and parties troubled revolutionary leaders in succession. Successive grapplings with these problems significantly reshaped the country's thought and institutions, but the hardest questions raised by the determination of the Founders to secure a government at once responsible and wise were not so much resolved as thoroughly rephrased.

Crisis came upon the empire in the aftermath of Britain's brilliant victory in the last and largest of four eighteenth-century wars with France. Struggling with a swollen national debt, obliged to govern conquered Canada, and conscious of a gathering concern with the irrationality and looseness of imperial relations, the ministry began to tighten its control and initiated parliamentary legislation intended to require the older colonies to pay a portion of the costs of their administration and defense. The colonies rebelled, proclaiming that it was the right of English peoples to be taxed only by their own elected representatives and that it was the custom of the British empire to confide internal regulation of the colonies' affairs to their provincial governments, in all of which the people's representative assemblies had come to hold the largest share of power. So serious and uniform was the colonial resistance that the Stamp Act had to be repealed. Yet Parliament insisted on its sovereign right to legislate in every case for all the British peoples, and the need for a colonial revenue remained. Different taxes followed. More colonial resistance ensued. In 1774, the spiral of resistance and reaction culminated in the punitive Coercive Acts, the meeting of a Continental Congress, and the ministry's decision to resort to force.

Independence, in a sense, resulted from the empire's inability to reach agreement on the character and limits of legitimate authority. Not directly represented in the British Parliament (and aware from the beginning that even the admission of a few colonial representatives would not make Parliament responsive to colonial desires), Americans repeatedly attempted in the decade after 1765 to pressure and persuade the English to accept new definitions of the limits of its power. Early in the crisis, it was not unreasonable for them to think they could succeed. From their perspective, Parliament's attempt to levy taxes obviously threatened not only the accepted right of Englishmen to hold their property secure, but all of the traditional (or "constitutional") arrangements linking power with consent. The House of Commons, they conceded, guarded liberty "at home." Parliament was rightfully the ultimate authority within the empire. But Parliament's encroachment on the local legislatures' customary right to hold the purse strings challenged the assemblies' very place within the governmental structure, disputing their control of just the power that the Commons had itself employed to win a vital and continuous role within the central government. Colonials expected Englishmen to recognize that they were asking only for security against the claims of arbitrary, irresponsive power, which was no more than Englishmen demanded for themselves. The arguments they wielded were grounded firmly in the English libertarian tradition. The limits they insisted on were moderate at first: Parliament should leave taxation in the hands of the colonials' own representatives, which would continue to protect their other rights; the central government should check its growing inclination to intrude on the provincial governments' conventional or "constitutional" autonomy in local matters.[12]

These arguments, of course, did not persuade the English. Parliament would not agree that its authority was constitutionally limited by the traditional prerogatives of the colonial assemblies. The ministry decided to respond to extra-legal pressure with coercion, and coercion drove the Continental Congress to deny that the colonials were obligated to submit to *any* legislation to which they had not assented. From this point, the path ran straight to arms and independence. And when Americans had reached its end, they found themselves committed to a revolution. Although a decade's argument had not convinced the English, it had radically transformed their own ideas.

It did so in two ways. First, the lengthy effort to define the "constitutional" extent of parliamentary control resulted in a powerful new emphasis upon an active and continuous relationship between legitimate authority and popular approval, as well as on a newly literal insistence on inherent, equal rights, which governments could challenge only at their peril.[13] In their attempt to bind a distant, unresponsive central government, colonials recurred repeatedly to Locke and other theorists who traced the purposes and limits of political authority to pre-governmental compacts. Thousands of colonials became accustomed to assuming that, as individuals were the parties to these compacts, every individual (or, as the eighteenth century conceived it, each responsible, white male) is equally entitled to protection and personally entitled to an active voice in political decisions. Although some English writers tried to argue that colonials were "virtually" represented in the House of Commons, along with other Englishmen who lacked the right to vote, the confrontation with an uncontrollable imperial authority hammered home the lesson that power-wielders will respond primarily to those to whom they owe their places and with whom they share a fundamental unity of interests. In the colonies, where unprecedented numbers had the right to vote, the governmental officers and branches most immediately dependent on the people were valiant in the defense of liberty, while the appointive branches often lagged behind. Meanwhile, the distant House of Commons, which rested on a more restricted franchise, seemed ever more apparently a feeble guardian of liberty, or even part of the increasing danger. Popular election and political responsibility, accountability and a direct dependence on the body of the people, increasingly appeared as one.[14]

They seemed the more identical, by 1776, because colonials no longer trusted that the House of Commons genuinely protected even the majority in England. This was the second way in which the crisis had disrupted older modes of thinking. Compelled to understand why the imperial government, which was supposed to be ideally designed for the defense of freedom, repeatedly refused to stay within its limits—and more and more inclined to link responsibility with popular election—colonials immersed themselves in English writers who believed that recent economic and political developments had undermined the equilibrium between the parts of government and washed away the barriers against abuse. Emphasizing the dependence of the Lords (and bishops) on the Crown, together with the ministry's control of rotten boroughs and ability to influence independently elected members of the Commons through awards of offices or pensions, English opposition writers warned that all effective power was devolving on an uncontrollable executive. The apparent danger to the independence of the House of Commons was particularly disturbing to writers whose ideas still carried traces of their origins in the republican assumptions of the English interregnum—and to Americans, who had no native aristocracy, decreasing trust in nonelective officers, a rising inclination to insist on individual equality, and growing reason to associate their unity in the defense of liberty with uncorrupted local houses of assembly and the uniformity of interests among the equals on whose votes these representatives depended.[15]

Common Sense became the most effective pamphlet the world had ever witnessed because it joined and made explicit both of the conclusions toward which thinking had begun to point. If independence was the only logical response to failure to compel the mother country to accept the limitations necessary for colonial security, that failure was a consequence in turn, Paine argued, of England's governmental structure. The vaunted English constitution actually combined "the base remains of two ancient tyrannies," aristocracy and monarchy, with "some new republican materials." Mixed of such discordant elements, it functioned only when the Crown corrupted its republican component, rendered it a hidden tyranny, and issued English freedom "warning to depart." In order to "receive the fugitive," the pamphlet finished, America would have to link its separation from the peril with destruction of the remnants of those tyrannies, creating a new order in which power would depend entirely on the people and liberty might permanently endure.[16]

To Paine, creation of a revolutionary order seemed a relatively simple task: power should be limited by written charters and made to rest exclusively on popular election. To the majority of revolutionary leaders, though, the reconstruction never seemed that easy; and time revealed additional dimensions of the problem. Power, it developed, was a many-headed creature, and as soon as it seemed tamed, another fearsome head escaped the bonds. Indeed, the earliest attempts to make it safe were cause for rising worry before the war was through.

The early theater of the American Revolution was the thirteen states. Distant, unresponsive power had proved dangerous, so power was brought home and grounded firmly on the democratic body of the people. The Continental Congress, which did not receive a formal charter of authority until 1781, was trusted only with responsibilities that Parliament had not abused: it did the nation's diplomatic business and oversaw the war, but was denied an independent power of taxation or even the authority to regulate external trade. The general government, in practice, became the instrument of thirteen wary, revolutionary states, and all these states except Rhode Island and Connecticut (whose governments had always been entirely elective) formalized the lessons of the recent crisis by preparing new, more democratic frames of government. Written constitutions, usually including bills of rights, expressed the revolutionary understanding that governments were servants of the people, attempted to define the limits of their power, and distributed responsibilities among their different parts.

Separate parts for different functions. Although they shared Paine's opposition to hereditary privilege and contrasted the identity of interests between the people and their democratic representatives with the irresponsibility of aristocrats and kings, most revolutionary leaders disagreed with Paine's conclusion that the simplest form of government was best. Chartered limitations of authority, they argued, would not be automatically and universally respected. Power tended naturally to overflow its proper limits and could not be safely trusted to a single set of servants, not even to the annually elected representatives of an undifferentiated people. Good government, moreover, demanded qualities not found in representative assemblies: unity, consistency, and wisdom, as well as a reflection of majority demands and needs. And even in societies without hereditary ranks, there were still differences between the many and the few, each of whom required protection. Therefore, nearly all the states established complex governments, and most of them attempted, by various expedients, to make the upper house of legislature counterpoise the popular assembly, assuming that the wisdom and stability imparted by a second branch would counterbalance the impetuosity of the people's immediate representatives. Many revolutionary leaders hoped to make the second house the special guardian—if not the representative—of property. All insisted on a rigid separation of executive and legislative powers.[17]

The new state constitutions were the written evidence of the ambivalence of revolutionary minds. Most revolutionary leaders were natural aristocrats, products of a deferential world who simultaneously gloried in their unity with lesser people and continually betrayed their caution in the face of revolutionary agitation. A train of thought as old as Aristotle reinforced their consciousness of the potentially conflicting interests of the great and small and justified their feeling that a sound and stable polity demanded qualities which they could not associate with governments invariably responsive to majority demands. They had resisted British measures in order to protect their liberties, their property, and their traditional ability to make most day-to-day political decisions. They knew that these could also be endangered from below. Although they were beginning to believe that even the unpropertied had rights—a genuine respect for the essential dignity of every individual was among the most important contributions of the Revolution— they did not forget that their societies were made up of distinctive groups, among which men of property and talents (they themselves) comprised the most conspicuous minority. Thus, bills of rights and written constitutions, which derived all power from the people, also demonstrated a conviction that no government should be entirely sovereign, and constitutional divisions of governmental power were meant to guarantee that even the majority would be restrained.

It is easy to exaggerate these reservations. It is clear, in fact, that older histories unduly minimized the transformation that accompanied independence. Most revolutionary leaders were emotionally, irrevocably committed to a democratic social order, to the eradication of hereditary privilege in favor of a reconstructed world where power would derive from talent and public service. Most were not more fearful of the people than they were committed to the concept that legitimate authority can have no other source than popular election. Recent scholarship has shown that revolutionary thinking called not merely for a distant, abstract social contract, but for continuous and active, vigilant participation by the body of the people, for governments not only limited but genuinely responsive to popular control. The crisis of the empire had suggested that liberty was safest where power rested most immediately upon the people. Accordingly, the new state constitutions all provided for annual elections of the popular assemblies and usually for annual elections of the senates and executives as well. Many lowered the amount of property required to exercise the franchise. Nearly all placed stringent limitations on the powers of executives, which were almost always to be chosen by the legislative branch. Most revolutionaries traced the origins of the imperial dispute—and the subversion of the British constitution—to bloated, grasping ministries and a corrupted House of Commons. Severe restrictions on appointive powers and a denial of the right to veto legislation were intended to exclude executives from legislative matters and put an end to their capacity to wedge themselves between the people and their representatives. In all the states but two, the only institutional restraint on the assembly was the second house of legislature, and the second house was commonly inclined to let the first assume the lead.[18] On balance, the departures from colonial tradition were as striking as the continuities and more impressive than the reservations evident in the establishment of bicameral regimes.

The reservations warrant serious attention because they did so much to shape and render comprehensible the discontents that characterized the middle 1780s and prepared the way for truly sweeping constitutional reform. A constitutional convention met, of course, primarily because of the debility of the confederation government. By 1786, a huge majority of revolutionary leaders recognized a crisis of the union. Few denied that power had been inappropriately divided between the states and general government or that the Articles of Confederation were inadequate to national needs. But constitutional reform assumed the character it did because the Constitutional Convention refused to limit its attention to the weaknesses of the confederation. Most members of the great Convention were equally dissatisfied with the way in which the problem of power had been handled in the revolutionary states. And once they had decided that amendment of the Articles could not suffice to cure the nation's ills, they turned their minds as well to thorough reconsideration of the structure of a sound republic.

The framers' discontents can be described in a variety of ways. The Revolution, we might say, had solved the problem of the character and sources of political authority. America's rejection of hereditary power was permanent and fierce. So was the conviction that government should have its origins in a literal agreement of the people, embodied in a written charter. Nearly all the members of the Constitutional Convention shared the popular revulsion with aristocrats and kings, and the tiny number who did not immediately admitted that even a revival of lifetime terms of office was impracticable in the United States. Monarchy and aristocracy, in any literal definition of those terms, no longer posed real dangers. On the other hand, nearly all the delegates agreed that, everywhere, the country suffered from "an excess of democracy."[19] There was a general consensus that the revolutionary constitutions had confided too much power to the lower houses of assembly, which could not effectively be checked by governmental branches less immediately responsive to popular demands. Rule by the assemblies seemed to demonstrate that unrestrained majorities were dangerous custodians of private rights and public good. Liberty, defined as popular control of power, no longer seemed a certain guarantee of liberty defined as the inherent rights of all—or even of the well-considered, long-term interests of the whole community. Good government, in short, appeared to have been sacrificed to revolutionary fear of unresponsive power.[20]

As its members understood it, then, the Constitutional Convention was confronted with two fundamental problems, not just one. The first and more apparent was the revolutionary fear of concentrated, central power, which had resulted in a general government unable to advance the nation's interests or even to fulfill its legal obligations. This problem the Convention sought to solve by reconstructing the confederation as a federal republic. In a sense, the delegates decided to attack the problem that had wrecked the empire and was on the verge of wrecking the new union by calling on the people to create a limited, safe substitute for Parliament and King: a general government that might be trusted with taxation, regulation of the country's commerce, and other positive responsibilities because all of its officers would owe their places to the people or the states, with whom political responsibilities would be carefully divided. But the decision to erect a great republic was accompanied by a determination to avoid the vices that the delegates associated with the structure of power in the revolutionary states, and this immediately involved them in a second problem, which demanded every bit as much imagination as the first. The members meant to build into their great republic additional security for the few against the powers and the passions of the many, but most of them remained unwilling to confide authority to officers entirely independent of the many. All believed that any such expedient would be rejected by the public. The delegates could not entrust the powers they intended for the new regime to nonelected agents, and yet they were determined to create a government that would display the virtues they considered lacking in the states: consistency, the wisdom to discern the long-term interests of the community, and the vigor to defend the greater good whenever it appeared at odds with partial or more immediate considerations.

Once again, the great Convention's ingenuity was equal to the task. It provided that the three great branches of the federal government would derive in different ways, for different terms, and sometimes more and sometimes less directly from the people: the House of Representatives would be elected every other year by all those qualified to vote for members of the lower houses in the states; the senators would be selected by the local legislatures; and the president, rearmed with several of the powers commonly denied to state executives, would also be elected indirectly. No branch would be dependent on another. Different duties, varied terms of office, and different degrees of distance from the people would guarantee the equilibrium between the parts, provide security for both the many and the few, and assure attention to the long-term public good as well as to the people's current needs. In effect, the Constitution was intended to secure the characteristic qualities or "principles" of aristocracy and monarchy, but without resorting to hereditary power or departing from the democratic principle that, in the end, the majority must rule.[21]

Not everyone, of course, admired the framers' ingenuity. The Constitution was approved by hairsbreadth margins in the larger states, and only after its supporters promised subsequent amendments, which became the Bill of Rights.[22] Nor was this narrow victory merely an expectable result of fear of change and popular distrust of central government. Rather, the opponents of the Constitution recognized the framers' fear of popular majorities, understood that the Convention had deliberately attempted to distance power from the people, and at once condemned the "squinting" of the plan toward aristocracy and monarchy. George Mason, who attended till the end and then refused to sign, insisted from the first that the Convention would not have its cake and eat it too, that the attempt to introduce the benefits of aristocracy and monarchy would sooner or later result in the real thing.[23] Anti-Federalists generally maintained that so much power, so well shielded from majority demands, would quickly prove unsafe for both the people and the states. Most believed the plan was inconsistent with democracy, and many claimed that it had been deliberately concocted by a conclave of aspiring lords to lay the groundwork for a gradual reintroduction of hereditary rule.[24] Federalists could denounce extravagant suspicions and insist that the new government was both republican and safely limited to tasks that did not call for intimate familiarity with the people's local needs and situations.[25] Such arguments by no means conquered Anti-Federalist fears of unresponsive power.

Neither did the quick addition of a bill of rights. While it is true that absence of the guarantees afforded by the first amendments had been among the loudest, most consistent Anti-Federalist complaints, most Federalists regarded the amendments as redundant: they denied the federal government powers it had not been granted in the first place: they effected no substantial alteration of the federal system. The Bill of Rights, it can be said in hindsight, confirmed a preexisting understanding that the Constitution transferred only limited authority to the general government from the states and people. It thus contributed importantly to rapid, general recognition of the legitimacy of the new regime. But its adoption left abundant room for further argument about the limits of federal powers, and this argument immediately became entangled with an equally important controversy that the Bill of Rights did not address. During the ratification controversy, Federalists and Anti-Federalists had generally agreed that governments can be created or abolished by the people, that the people have a right at any time to redistribute power as they please, that popular approval of a written constitution represents an exercise of this authority, and even that a federal republic should incorporate effective checks and balances between the branches of the general government, together with a rational division of responsibilities between the federal government and states. But Federalists and Anti-Federalists had disagreed profoundly over how much power could be placed at a considerable remove from popular control without encountering an unacceptable risk that rulers would entirely slip their bonds, becoming—first in fact, but then perhaps in form as well—entirely independent of the people. The amended Constitution did not settle this dispute. It rearranged the parties and moved it to a different ground.

In 1787 and 1788, the ratification contest divided revolutionary leaders who condemned an excess of democracy and a crippling fear of central power from those who were more fearful of a concentration of authority in distant officers who would be subject only indirectly or infrequently to popular election. Concerned that power so remote from popular control might be monopolized by an elite, manipulated by the great at the majority's expense, and turned in time against the liberties as well as the interests of ordinary people, Anti-Federalists entered on the federal experiment with apprehensions that were only partly eased by the adoption of the Bill of Rights.[26] And while most Federalists had favored constitutional devices intended to restrain tyrannical majorities, not all of them dismissed the dangers that transfixed the opposition. Among the most important advocates of constitutional reform were leaders who had never meant to place as much authority as possible in rulers only distantly responsive to majority demands, men whose fear of interested majorities was fully counterbalanced by the revolutionary memory of rulers whose independence from the people had released a governing minority to pursue ambitions of its own. For Federalists like these, whose most important spokesman was James Madison, the Constitution was a necessary, democratic remedy for democratic ills, but the multiple divisions of authority established by the charter were as critical to preservation of the Revolution as any other feature of the great reform.[27] After 1789, such Federalists soon joined with former Anti-Federalists to identify the Constitution as a threatened boundary beyond which further concentration of authority would indeed prove inconsistent with a democratic sympathy of interests between the rulers and the ruled. Within three years, revolutionary leaders had divided once again, this time into warring parties whose appearance had been unanticipated by the framers of the Constitution and whose disagreement reached an ideological intensity without real parallel in subsequent American history.

The policy disputes and sectional antagonisms which divided the first political parties cannot be covered in this chapter.[28] What bears remarking is the very great degree to which their bitter argument about the use of power was inseparably entangled with continuing disputes about its proper distribution. The rapid triumph of the Constitution was accompanied and even speeded by a fierce debate about its meaning,[29] an argument compounded almost equally of new concerns about relationships between the nation's economic groups and sections and of old, unanswered questions about liberty and power.

Parties had their origins within the infant federal government, when congressmen and cabinet members quarreled sharply over the morality and social consequences of Alexander Hamilton's political economy. Madison and Thomas Jefferson, as well as many former Anti-Federalists, realized that Hamilton's proposals for managing the revolutionary debt would involve a major shift of wealth from South to North, from West to East, and from the many to a few whose fortunes would expand dramatically as a result of federal largesse—all of which seemed inconsistent with republican morality, with harmony between the nation's sections, with a sound commercial policy, and with the relatively modest distances between the rich and poor that seemed most consonant with political democracy. No less importantly, however, Hamilton's proposals, together with the broad construction of the Constitution advanced in their defense, threatened to entail a major shift of power from the states to the general government and from the House of Representatives to the federal executive. The economic program and the disregard of constitutional restraints both seemed to center power at a level and in governmental branches least responsive to the people, while creating in the congressmen and private citizens who were enriched by governmental payments an interest fundamentally at odds with the majority's.[30] In this direction, many warned, lay an eventual reintroduction of hereditary privilege and the immediate oppression of the body of the people.[31]

How much power, of what sort, had been confided to the general government? Which responsibilities could safely be entrusted to a government so distant from the people, and which would have to stay within the firm control of their immediate representatives in the several states? What degree of leadership should be permitted to the federal executive? How intimate should be the link between the rulers and the ruled? Throughout the long, uncompromising course of their ferocious party war, the Federalists and Jeffersonian Republicans struggled with the problems that the Revolution had not solved, and none of these divided them more clearly than the effort to define a level of continuing popular involvement in political decisions that would be sufficient to assure a government responsive to the people's needs without reintroducing popular misrule.[32]

The clashing groups within the infant government both quickly pledged allegiance to the Constitution. Each accused the other of a settled wish to see it overturned. Madison and Jefferson and their supporters detected an increasing danger to the constitutional devices that controlled the risks associated with great power, along with an increasing danger to the social foundations of democracy. The Hamiltonians, still preoccupied with localism and an excess of democracy, denounced the opposition's efforts to arouse the people and accused the Jeffersonians of trying to reverse the recent constitutional reform. After 1793, the choices forced upon the country by the wars of the French Revolution, together with conflicting sympathies about the Revolution itself, polarized the national electorate behind the contending governmental factions and encouraged both emerging parties to regard the other in virtually apocalyptic terms. The Jeffersonian Republicans condemned a Federalist conspiracy to undermine the balance of the federal system, revive hereditary privilege, and prepare the way for a reunion with Great Britain. Federalists charged the Jeffersonians with slavish admiration of the atheistic, levelling democracy being pioneered in France, insisting that continual suspicion of elected rulers was incompatible with liberty and order.[33]

These accusations were sincere expressions of the deepest fears of the contending parties. They were also efforts to contend with more immediate developments and issues that could not be easily encompassed by familiar ways of thinking. Persistent party conflict was itself a new phenomenon, for which contemporaries had no ready, well-developed justification.[34] The absence of a concept of a party system, of a theory of the public benefits of party competition, favored a conspiratorial interpretation of opponents' motives. So did the country's peripheral involvement in Europe's revolutionary wars, which reminded both new parties of the immediacy and fragility of America's own revolutionary settlement. Only gradually, therefore, were old preoccupations with relationships between the many and the few distinguished more consistently from newer arguments about the nature of a sound relationship, in a republic, between the rulers and the ruled.

Over time, the stubborn presence of competing parties and the lengthening experience with federal institutions did encourage a rephrasing of traditional concerns. Condemnations of aristocratic plots or radical democracy were joined and partially displaced by newer worries over the relationship between the whole and the parts in an established federal republic. In the years between the great embargo and the declaration of the War of 1812, the really urgent questions were those concerning the relationship between the nation and its sections, between political parties and the public good; it began to be a bit more common for issues to be stated in such language. But the first years of the new republic were an age of difficult transition, never quite complete. The old concerns did not entirely lose their urgency until the revolutionary generation was replaced by younger leaders and party conflict temporarily disappeared. Even then, the newer questions, concerning the relationship between the people and their agents, party loyalty and public interest, or the nature of a sound division of responsibilities between the federal government and states, would reappear within the context of a new legitimation of two-party conflict. Through a civil war and many other changes, most of them persist today.

Notes

1. Classic statements of the older view include Louis Hartz, *The Liberal Tradition in America: An Interpretation of American Political Thought since the Revolution* (New York, 1955) and Daniel J. Boorstin, *The Lost World of Thomas Jefferson* (Boston, 1948).

2. Useful reviews of the recent literature are Robert E. Shalhope, "Toward a Republican Synthesis: The Emergence of an Understanding of Republicanism in American Historiography," *William and Mary Quarterly*, 3rd ser., 29 (1972): 49–80; Shalhope, "Republicanism and Early American Historiography," ibid., 39 (1982): 334–356; and Daniel Walker Howe, "European Sources of Political Ideas in Jeffersonian America," *Reviews in American History* 10 (1982): 28–44.

3. A particularly good, recent argument that the revolutionary era extended through the War of 1812 is John M. Murrin, "The Great Inversion, or Court versus Country: A Comparison of the Revolution Settlements in England (1688–1721) and America (1776–1816)," in J. G. A. Pocock, ed., *Three British Revolutions: 1641, 1688, 1776* (Princeton, 1980), 368–453.

4. Classic statements of this eighteenth-century synthesis included, in order of their appearance: Algernon Sidney, *Discourses Concerning Government* (London, 1698); [John Trenchard and Thomas Gordon], *Cato's Letters: or Essays on Liberty, Civil and Religious, and other Important Subjects,* 4 vols. (London, 1733 [Org. pub., 1720–23]); and [James Burgh], *Political Disquisitions,* 3 vols. (London, 1774–1775).

5. For the dominance of Whiggish views of history, see H. Trevor Colbourn, *The Lamp of Experience: Whig History and the Intellectual Origins of the American Revolution* (Chapel Hill, N.C., 1965).

6. Corinne Comstock Weston, *English Constitutional Theory and the House of Lords, 1556–1832* (New York, 1965); Bernard Bailyn, *The Ideological Origins of the American Revolution* (Cambridge, Mass., 1967).

7. "As with us the executive power of the laws is lodged in a single person, they have all the advantages of strength and dispatch that are to be found in the most absolute monarchy; and as the legislature of the kingdom is entrusted to three distinct powers . . . actuated by different springs and attentive to different interests, . . . there can be no inconvenience be attempted by either of the three branches but will be withstood by one of the other two.

Here then is lodged the sovereignty of the British constitution, and lodged as beneficially as is possible for society. For in no other shape could we be so certain of finding the three great qualities of government [wisdom, virtue, and strength] so well and so happily united. . . . Like three distinct powers in mechanics, they jointly impel the machine of government in a direction different from what either, acting by itself, would have done, but at the same time in a direction which constitutes the true line of the liberty and happiness of the community." William Blackstone, *Commentaries on the Laws of England,* John Taylor Coleridge, ed., 4 vols. (16th ed.; London, 1825), I, 49–50, 154–155.

8. John Locke, *Two Treatises of Government,* Peter Laslett, ed., rev. ed. (New York, 1965).

9. J. G. A. Pocock, *The Machiavellian Moment: Florentine Political Thought and the Atlantic Republican Tradition* (Princeton, 1975).

10. Locke and Sidney contributed alike to the development of a contractual philosophy and to the English modification of classical ideas. The blending of the two was complete by the time of *Cato's Letters.* For the persistence and transmission to the colonies of this blend, see Caroline Robbins, *The Eighteenth Century Commonwealthman: Studies in the Transmission, Development, and Circumstance of English Liberal Thought from the Restoration of Charles II until the War with the Thirteen Colonies* (Cambridge, Mass., 1959).

11. Libertarian philosophers regarded men as owners, both of property and of their other rights. Civic humanists regarded ownership, especially of land, as the prerequisite for the independence of will that was the precondition for participation with other owners in political relationships. In both England and the colonies, the right to vote ordinarily rested on property qualifications. On the link between liberty and property, besides Pocock, see C. B. Macpherson, *The Political Theory of Possessive Individualism: Hobbes to Locke* (Oxford, 1962) and H. T. Dickinson, *Liberty and Property: Political Ideology in Eighteenth-Century Britain* (New York, 1977).

12. My discussion of the Revolution rests throughout on the body of recent literature reviewed in the articles cited in note 2 above. But for the argument over sovereignty, see particularly Edmund S. Morgan, "Colonial Ideas of Parliamentary Power, 1764–1766," *William and Mary Quarterly,* 3rd ser., 5 (1948), and Edmund S. and Helen M. Morgan, *The Stamp Act Crisis: Prologue to Revolution,* rev. ed. (New York, 1963). Older, but also useful in this respect, is Charles Howard McIlwain, *The American Revolution: A Constitutional Interpretation* (New York, 1923). For the rise of the assemblies and their attempt to replicate the powers of the House of Commons, see

Jack P. Greene, *The Quest for Power: The Lower House of Assembly in the Southern Royal Colonies, 1689–1776* (Chapel Hill, N.C., 1963) and "Political Mimesis: A Consideration of the Historical and Cultural Roots of Legislative Behavior in the British Colonies in the Eighteenth Century," *American Historical Review* 75 (1969): 337–367.

13. The transforming effect of an individualistic, natural-rights philosophy is a major theme for Bailyn, *Ideological Origins of the American Revolution,* and Gordon S. Wood, *The Creation of the American Republic, 1776–1787* (Chapel Hill, N.C., 1969), the two works that have become the starting points for current views of revolutionary thinking.

14. When British proponents of the theory of virtual representation pointed out that a majority in England also lacked the right to participate in parliamentary elections, colonials were quick to answer that two wrongs did not make a right. English radicals, who supported the colonials, increasingly agreed. For evidence that English radical thinking was moving in similar directions, see John Brewer, *Party Ideology and Popular Politics at the Accession of George III* (Cambridge, 1976) and Colin Bonwick, *English Radicals and the American Revolution* (Chapel Hill, N.C., 1977).

15. This is a major theme of Bailyn as modified in Pauline Maier, *From Resistance to Revolution: Colonial Radicals and the Development of American Opposition to Britain, 1765–1776* (New York, 1972).

16. *The Complete Writings of Thomas Paine,* Philip S. Foner, ed., 2 vols. (New York, 1945), I, 6–9 and below. A superb discussion of the pamphlet is Bernard Bailyn, "Common Sense," in *Fundamental Testaments of the American Revolution,* Library of Congress Symposia on the American Revolution, no. 2 (Washington, D.C., 1973), 7–22.

17. The provisions of the revolutionary constitutions are discussed most fully in Willi Paul Adams, *The First American Constitutions: Republican Ideology and the Making of the State Constitutions in the Revolutionary Era,* trans. Rita and Robert Kimber (Chapel Hill, N.C., 1980). But my discussion of constitutional thought and developments from 1776 to 1787 rests especially on Wood and my own reading in primary and secondary sources. As in *The Jeffersonian Persuasion: Evolution of a Party Ideology* (Ithaca, 1978), I do suggest that American thinking departed more slowly from its British sources than Wood believes.

18. Revolutionary hostility to privilege, the role played by the assemblies in resisting Britain, and many other factors contributed to this result, but annual elections, similar electoral bases, similar property qualifications for members, and (in several states) clauses giving the origination of money bills to the lower house were particularly influential in making the second house a pale reflection of the first. Massachusetts (followed by New Hampshire after 1784) was the only state to grant its governor a provisional veto. New York's governor participated in the exercise of a similar power as a member of a special council of revision.

19. Elbridge Gerry's phrase. Max Farrand, ed., *The Records of the Federal Convention of 1787,* 4 vols. (1937 ed.; New Haven, 1966), I, 48.

20. The last three sentences paraphrase the major argument of "Vices of the Political System of the United States," in *The Papers of James Madison*, Robert A. Rutland, et al., eds., 14 vols. (Chicago and Charlottesville, Va., 1962–), 9:354–357. See also Madison's speech of June 19 in Farrand, *Records*, 1:318–319.

21. In Britain, wrote Thomas Jefferson, who may have remembered the passage from Blackstone quoted in note 7 above, "their constitution [supposedly] relies on the House of Commons for honesty and the Lords for wisdom, which would be a rational reliance if honesty were to be bought with money and if wisdom were hereditary." Jefferson despised hereditary lords (and corrupted representatives), yet praised a system that attempted to produce a "proper complication of principles," contrasting it with the situation in Virginia, where "173 despots," the number in the lower house, ruled honestly but unwisely. *Notes on the State of Virginia* (1785; New York, 1964), 113–124. A reading of the records of the Convention or *The Federalist* leaves little doubt that the framers sought an executive and upper house that would impart the unity and wisdom traditionally associated with a king and an aristocracy.

22. Robert Allen Rutland, *The Ordeal of the Constitution: The Antifederalists and the Ratification Struggle of 1787–1788* (Norman, OK, 1966).

23. "Objections to the Proposed Federal Constitution," in Cecilia M. Kenyon, ed., *The Antifederalists* (Indianapolis, 1966), 195.

24. For Antifederalist thinking, see Kenyon's introduction to *The Antifederalists;* Jackson Turner Main, *The Antifederalists: Critics of the Constitution, 1781–1788* (Chicago, 1961); Herbert J. Storing, *What the Anti-Federalists were FOR: The Political Thought of the Opponents of the Constitution* (Chicago, 1981); James H. Hutson, "Country, Court, and Constitution: Antifederalism and the Historians," *William and Mary Quarterly* 38 (1981): 337–368.

25. These were the major themes of *The Federalist*, especially of Madison's numbers.

26. Banning, *The Jeffersonian Persuasion*, chap. 4.

27. I have elaborated a revisionary view of Madison's thought and conduct during the later 1780s and early 1790s in three recent essays: "James Madison and the Nationalists, 1780–1783," *William and Mary Quarterly*, 3rd ser., 40 (1983): 227–255; "The Hamiltonian Madison: A Reconsideration," *Virginia Magazine of History and Biography* 92 (1984), 3–28; and "The Practicable Sphere of a Republic: James Madison, the Constitutional Convention, and the Emergence of Revolutionary Federalism," in Richard Beeman, et al., eds., *Beyond Confederation: Origins of the Constitution and American National Identity* (Chapel Hill, N.C., 1987), 162–187.

28. The interpretation follows Banning, *The Jeffersonian Persuasion*, Murrin, "The Great Inversion," Drew R. McCoy, *The Elusive Republic: Political Economy in Jeffersonian America* (Chapel Hill, N.C., 1980), and other recent works emphasizing the parallels between the first party conflict and eighteenth-century British arguments between the Court and the Country. For a review of this literature and a response to its critics, see my "Jeffersonian Ideology Revisited: Liberal and Classical Ideas in

the New American Republic," *William and Mary Quarterly,* 3rd ser., 43 (1986): 3–19.

29. See also Banning, "Republican Ideology and the Triumph of the Constitution, 1789–1793," *William and Mary Quarterly,* 3rd ser., 31 (1974): 167–188.

30. This paraphrases remarks of Jefferson to George Washington recorded in "Anas," in Paul Leicester Ford, ed., *The Works of Thomas Jefferson,* 12 vols. (New York, 1904), 1:192–198 and above.

31. Among the most systematic explanations of the antidemocratic consequences of consolidation was Madison's report to the House of Delegates on the responses to the Virginia Resolutions of 1798. See Gaillard Hunt, ed., *The Writings of James Madison,* 9 vols. (New York, 1906), 6:357–359.

32. Also helpful for contrasting party attitudes toward a politically active population is Richard Buel, Jr., *Securing the Revolution: Ideology in American Politics, 1789–1815* (Ithaca, 1972).

33. On Federalist political thought, see also James M. Banner, Jr., *To the Hartford Convention: The Federalists and the Origins of Party Politics in Massachusetts, 1789–1815* (New York, 1970); Linda K. Kerber, *Federalists in Dissent: Imagery and Ideology in Jeffersonian America* (Ithaca, 1970); and Gerald Stourzh, *Alexander Hamilton and the Idea of Republican Government* (Stanford, 1970).

34. Richard Hofstadter, *The Idea of a Party System: The Rise of Legitimate Opposition in the United States, 1780–1840* (Berkeley, 1969).

PART 2

Republicanism, Liberalism, and the Great Transition

One of the great scholarly debates of the 1970s and 1980s was the question of whether classical republicanism or modern liberalism best characterized the organization of political and economic life in the early republic. Viewed from the perspective of a quarter century or more, the debate seems today almost quaint and overblown. But at the time it raged, it was a central organizing paradigm of scholarship, the source of frenzied debates in journals and at academic conferences, and a subject few could avoid if they worked in any field of U.S. history up through the Civil War. Lance Banning was front and center in this debate, although as a somewhat unwilling and increasingly disillusioned participant. As such, he had a front row seat for the republicanism-liberalism controversy, and he kept a keen eye on the contest unfolding around him even as he contributed fundamentally to the encounter himself.

In the series of essays that follow, we can see Banning engaging his scholarly colleagues in two ways. First, he did so as a widely acknowledged actor in the debate by penning some of the crucial landmark pieces himself. His 1986 *William and Mary Quarterly* essay advancing the "republican" interpretation was paired in the journal with one by Joyce Appleby advocating the "liberal" interpretation, and the two pieces, side by side, became core texts in the controversy. When Daniel T. Rodgers surveyed the republicanism debate in a famous 1992 *Journal of American History* historiographical essay, he cited Banning's article as one of the seminal works in the scholarly battle. Rodgers classified Banning as part of the "St. Louis republicanism" school since it centered on scholars affiliated with Washington University either directly (J. G. A. Pocock, John Murrin, Banning) or indirectly (Drew McCoy) and as distinct from "Harvard republicanism" associated with Bernard Bailyn and Gordon Wood. Rodgers's article made clear what was already widely recognized by specialists: that Banning was a central player in the controversy.

Second, and just as significant, Banning also acted as a shrewd, fair-minded, and level-headed observer of the historiographical wars in which he himself engaged. The remaining three selections included here show Banning at work as a critic of scholarship (his own included) on republicanism and liberalism. Here are cases of the author's scholarly life imitating his own research conclusions. For just as Banning argued at length that James Madison was influenced *by* the debates in the Constitutional Convention and the ratification process, Banning was himself influenced in his own thinking on republicanism by the contributions of other scholars. Banning reflected on and revealed his evolving thought both in longer pieces (such as "Some Second Thoughts on Virtue") and in short reviews ("Quid Transit?"). In these works Banning is superb in his ability to examine primary source works and the scholarship about them in retrospect and notice distinctions, contrasts, subtleties of interpretation, unexpected divergences, or unacknowledged convergences in the literature. Banning was also very good at tracing the evolution of these disputes over time through his close readings of the scholarship.

He was particularly shrewd in identifying misreadings of scholarly work by others as well as the corresponding misapplications of those works. In "Second Thoughts on Virtue," for example, he tracks the ways in which Gordon Wood's work has been misread in several influential works which, when then summarized in subsequent works, created a feedback loop of sorts that perpetuated the confusion. Banning stated that he wrote his 1986 *William and Mary Quarterly* essay because he was convinced that there had been far too much misreading (or citing of unread works) by scholars. In fact, in most of these selections Banning writes not as an advocate for one interpretation or the other—he states repeatedly that the Revolutionary generation "blended and combined" republican and liberal concepts—but rather as an impartial referee, looking for errors of reading and writing that hinder accurate, careful understanding.

Two last notes: his "Second Thoughts on Virtue" is a terrific investigation of the meaning of language and the changing concepts of words. It models the kind of closely considered treatment of a subject that Banning advocates and reveals how the meaning of the word "virtue" can change over time and mean different things to different people. It was through such careful clearing away of misreading and misunderstanding that the way toward scholarly comprehension lay. The final selection in this chapter, "The Republican Interpretation: Retrospect and Prospect," is a tour de force. It shows a scholar at the height of his powers, thinking out loud about his own work and where it fits with that of others, how it has been influenced and has shifted over time, and how his own contributions have both shaped, and been shaped by, the field. It is a powerful and sweeping self-assessment. What comes through in this piece (in all four selections, actually) is Banning's trademark fairness and intellectual honesty. He does not settle scores, engage in clever or snarky put-downs of others, or worry about advocating for his own positions. Rather, he engages these issues as impartially as a participant can, seeking honestly to advance the scholarly conversation, referee disputes, clarify points of knowledge, point out areas where scholars (including himself) have exaggerated claims or been imprecise in their use of language, and point the field in the direction of advancing knowledge. Recognizing that not all differences can be resolved, however, he helpfully clarifies respective positions and arguments, thus making a significant contribution through a seemingly small but helpful intervention.

There is some repetition and overlap in the articles that follow. But the value in including all four is that they show Banning at his best in bringing clarity and focus to the use of words, to the evolving meanings of language, and to the dense thicket of historiographical controversies (real and unresolvable ones as well as those that are exaggerated and created by misreadings of the material). I have not attempted to edit them. Speaking to his graduate seminars of the way his own work was sometimes treated, Banning once said he wished others would "read my work, and read it right!" Banning read the work of other scholars carefully and thoroughly, cutting through to the essential arguments, and always bringing light and insight rather than emotion and vitriol to scholarly debates. This careful, painstaking work of reading and taking the measure of others' writing as well as his own is shown to great effect in these selections.

Jeffersonian Ideology Revisited

Liberal and Classical Ideas
in the New American Republic

Recent studies of the Jeffersonian Republicans may leave some readers at a loss. The last fifteen years have brought a new interpretation of the character and sources of Jeffersonian ideas.[1] This "republican hypothesis" (to modify a term of Robert E. Shalhope's) is a consequence of previous reinterpretations of American Revolutionary thought.[2] Like them, it places major emphasis on the persistent influence in the new American republic of concepts, hopes, and fears that may be traced to England's seventeenth-century classical republicans and their eighteenth-century opposition heirs. As Shalhope tells us, though, the same fifteen years have also seen the rapid growth of a variegated criticism of revisionary views of Revolutionary thinking.[3] The reinterpretation of the Jeffersonians has been erected on unstable ground, and in several recent works Joyce Appleby has charged that it is simply wrong, urging a renewed attention to what might be called a "liberal hypothesis."[4] The specialists seem so at odds that general readers must be sorely puzzled and historians are faced with an imposing barrier to further study.

This article seeks to get beyond that barrier, which may not be as insurmountable as first appears. Appleby and those she criticizes are all concerned to come to closer grips with Jeffersonian opinion, an enterprise that has large stakes not only for our comprehension of the new republic but for efforts to reshape our understanding of America in the fifty years and more after the first party quarrel came to an end. There are major differences among these scholars, which can be clarified where they cannot be reconciled. When that is done, it should be evident that Appleby and her opponents have all grasped portions of important truths, that all have been incautious, and that insights from both camps must be combined for further progress. As things now stand, the literature appears to force a choice between mutually exclusive interpretations of Jeffersonian ideology—a choice we do not really have to make, and one that would impede a better understanding.

Current scholarship, writes Appleby—from Richard Hofstadter to J. G. A. Pocock, Lance Banning, John M. Murrin, and Drew R. McCoy—"points Jefferson and his party in the wrong direction," toward nostalgia for the past instead of enthusiasm for the future, toward admiration for "agrarian self-sufficiency" rather than acceptance of commercial development. This scholarship makes Jefferson "the heroic loser in a battle against modernity," whereas he was actually the "conspicuous winner in a contest over how the government should serve its citizens."[5]

Between 1755 and 1820, Appleby points out, European demand for the grain and other commodities produced by American farmers expanded dramatically, while West Indian demand continued strong. The resulting opportunity for ordinary people to prosper by producing for the Atlantic market was not viewed apprehensively by Jefferson and other Virginia nationalists. On the contrary, these changing circumstances became the material base for a new social vision that owed little to the past, that was "both democratic and capitalistic, agrarian and commercial."[6] The prospect of an expanding, improving, commercial mode of agriculture persuaded Jefferson and others that the bulk of the American people could enjoy a rising standard of living, unprecedented social and economic independence, and—with these—political freedom. From 1783, therefore, Virginia nationalists and Jeffersonian Republicans advocated policies of making new lands available to farmers, opening world markets, and developing internal improvements, while they opposed fiscal measures that would burden farmer-owners. Such policies were "neither regional nor, strictly speaking, agrarian."[7] They entailed "neither American isolation nor a slowed pace of growth." They represented, in fact, "a form of capitalism" that looked to free trade to create "the integrative network that social authority supplied elsewhere."[8] The Jeffersonians, in sum, did not pit "rich against poor, or the commercially inclined against the self-sufficient," but sought a freely developing economy that would benefit all, eradicate privilege, and "stimulate the natural harmony of interest" among the propertied that John Locke had assumed.[9] In Jeffersonian hands, expanding involvement in the Atlantic economy became the context for "the flowering of liberal thought in America."[10] It was hardly an occasion for revival of agrarian nostalgia and British opposition fears.

Proponents of the views attacked in "Commercial Farming and the 'Agrarian Myth' in the Early Republic" must first protest that they have not been carefully represented in the essay. Close examination of the article reveals that Appleby's target is fuzzier than first appears and that she seems to make a sharper challenge to recent work than is in fact the case. The essay opens with a summary of Hofstadter's portrayal of the Jeffersonians as celebrators of the self-sufficient yeoman, although none of the recent writers has been significantly influenced by Hofstadter's point of view. Appleby repeatedly objects to an interpretation that regards the Jeffersonians as spokesmen for the self-sufficient against the commercially inclined. Yet Pocock says that Jeffersonians derived from England's seventeenth-century republicans *both* a belief that men engaged in commerce are capable of republican citizenship *and* an archetype of the landed man as the ideal, autonomous citizen; they did not oppose commerce or technological improvements but "the alliance of government, finance and standing army."[11] Banning's *Jeffersonian Persuasion* specifically denies that either English oppositionists or Jeffersonian Republicans identified their enemies as those involved in manufacturing or commerce; both groups commonly contrasted the virtuous freeholder, not with merchants or manufacturers, but with government officers, public creditors, and stock-jobbers.[12] And the central theme of McCoy's *Elusive Republic* is the Jeffersonian attempt to reconcile received republican values with *rejection* of an isolated, Spartan mode of life.[13] Maintaining that the Jeffersonians conceived commercial growth as vital to the perpetuation of a virtuous citizenry, the latter book, indeed, has been our most important source for fuller understanding of the Republican commitment to free trade and to the acquisition of new lands on which American farmers would produce for the Atlantic market. Recent scholarship, in short, does not advance quite the interpretation that Appleby condemns. It may, in fact, claim some of the responsibility for arguments that she develops.

Similar objections can be raised, this time with louder voice, to the second article in which Professor Appleby elaborates her criticism of interpretations emphasizing British opposition sources of Republican ideas.[14] Jefferson's dislike of Montesquieu, she argues, hints further difficulties with recent views. Jefferson strongly favored commercial developments and economic innovations about which the civic-humanist tradition was suspicious; he also held a concept of human nature radically at odds with Montesquieu's. Montesquieu was essentially an advocate of aristocratic power who believed that republics must rest on commitment to the public good and must thus be small and founded on a frugal, homogeneous citizenry. Jefferson, by contrast, accepted James Madison's alternative to the small republic. His object was not to raise power to check power in a civic arena where men would attain fulfillment by rising above self-interest, but to secure a polity that would protect the private and personal realm where men would freely exercise their faculties. He praised Destutt de Tracy's critique of Montesquieu because Tracy's analysis began with individuals, not social orders, and because it sought to eradicate social injustice by eliminating privilege and protecting a natural equality of rights.

Appleby's Jefferson, in brief, espoused a "liberal economic order" incompatible with Country ideology. He was "temperamentally at odds with the reverence for the past nurtured by civic humanism" and "repeatedly insisted that his was the party of change."[15] Claims that Jefferson was under the influence of eighteenth-century opposition thought must thus result from a misreading. Banning and McCoy, Appleby charges, have *assumed* an influence of Country ideas on the Republicans without presenting "confirming evidence" for such an influence, presuming that a search for such was "unnecessary" in light of the work of Bernard Bailyn, Gordon S. Wood, and others.[16] After 1789, Appleby concludes, the Country-minded and the Court-minded, sharing a traditional vocabulary, both became Federalists. The Jeffersonians broke more completely with the past. Placing their faith in a limited rather than a balanced government, they sought to nurture capitalist development by freeing the private energies of equal men.

A reading of *The Jeffersonian Persuasion* or *The Elusive Republic* would suffice, I trust, to refute the surprising charge that neither offers solid evidence for opposition influences on Republican ideas. It is more important to remark that Appleby's criticism of these books would be more telling if either of them really argued what she says they do. Appleby objects to works that "have depicted the thought of Americans in the 1790s as *encapsulated in* the conceptual world of Montesquieu's civic humanism"; she condemns "the recent scholarly effort to *assimilate* Jefferson into the Country party tradition of eighteenth-century England."[17] No such effort was intended by most of the authors mentioned in her critiques, nor does it seem to me that recent scholarship is fairly taxed with leaving the impression that there were no significant differences between the Jeffersonians and their seventeenth- and eighteenth-century sources.

The implications of this point are too important to pass over. Both Appleby and Isaac Kramnick, who has endorsed her point of view, write as though the recent claims that Jeffersonians were strongly influenced by English opposition thought are equivalent to claims for the *identity* of Jeffersonian and opposition thinking, perhaps particularly for an identification of the thought of the Republicans with that of Bolingbroke or Montesquieu, who both defended a traditional hierarchical social order. Nearly everyone who has advanced these claims would certainly deny that this has been the point. Indeed, some might complain that critics have occasionally come close to standing arguments upon their heads.[18]

For example, Appleby maintains that "historians of the early national period have recently claimed that the classical" republicanism that can be found in the works of John Adams "dominated American politics well into the nineteenth century."[19] None of these historians has actually advanced this notion. As early as 1977 Pocock wrote, "It is notorious that classical republicanism was . . . transformed in the making of the Federal Constitution and the Federalist and Republican minds."[20] *The Jeffersonian Persuasion* explicitly accepts Wood's argument for an "end of classical politics" and the repudiation of Adams, while qualifying this by suggesting that rejection of the concept of a balance of social orders did not entail an end of other traditional concerns.[21] *The Elusive Republic,* accepting major arguments of Wood and Banning while transcending their concern with political and constitutional ideas, emphasizes the *ambivalence* of Republican attitudes toward manufacturing and commerce, rising from their struggle to combine a commitment to prosperity, active industry, and economic growth with a traditional distrust of the potential civic consequences of these things. Recent scholarship, in short, often actually *insists* on American departures from received ideas, most especially on American hostility to privilege and American rejection of "the distinctions of class and rank whose balancing played so central a role in classical republicanism."[22] This scholarship should not be condemned as though the authors claimed that an entire, unchanging, civic-humanist tradition persisted into the new republic. Such criticism charges it with errors never made and caricatures a thesis that requires a subtler reading.

The Jeffersonian Persuasion, The Elusive Republic, Murrin's "Great Inversion," and other titles mentioned in Appleby's critiques are all revisionary studies. All maintain that previous interpretations of America's first party quarrel were imperfect in the absence of the fuller understanding of eighteenth-century British thinking pioneered by Caroline Robbins, Pocock, Kramnick, Bailyn, and others. All argue that comprehension of the new republic's politics was incomplete without a recognition of the parallels between American disputes and the familiar exchanges between the English Court and Country, together with a fuller appreciation of the continuing American concern with concepts, hopes, and worries that may be traced to classical antiquity by way of James Harrington and Niccolo Machiavelli.

All these works display some of the characteristic weaknesses of a revisionary effort. Their authors sought to add a new dimension to existing knowledge. They attempted to revise and alter, without entirely overturning, the body of previous scholarship. In the manner of revisionists, however—emphasizing new materials and stressing differences from older views—most of them were less explicit than they might have been about received opinions they did not dispute. Most were also guilty of incautious use of language, which is the more regrettable when passages are separated from their qualifying context. Flaws such as these are certainly responsible for some of our current confusion. But this confusion will be radically compounded if we fail to see that the Country ideology or opposition thinking identified in the majority of recent studies is simply not the Country ideology described by Appleby, or if we read these works as though they have denied the major changes in received ideas effected by the Revolution.

Appleby has fastened her attention on one of several groups that together composed the eighteenth-century opposition as most recent writers have described it—the backward-looking, fearful country gentlemen and their great Tory spokesman, Viscount Bolingbroke. She identifies the opposition heritage exclusively with Bolingbroke's reactionary posture and condemns her scholarly opponents for associating the American Republicans with Bolingbroke's or Montesquieu's world view. Two misleading consequences follow. First, arguments that Jeffersonians were influenced by some of Bolingbroke's ideas by no means necessarily imply that the Republicans adopted other aspects of the viscount's Tory thought or that revisionists believe that ideology was unaffected by the Revolution.[23] Second, an exclusive emphasis on a single aspect of a complex heritage seriously distorts the major emphases of several recent works and loses sight of their most important contributions. Revisionists have drawn attention to the influence on the Jeffersonians of civic-humanist preoccupation with virtue and corruption, to eighteenth-century concern with standing armies, public debts, executive influence, and government by money. They have stressed the Country's condemnation, not of commerce, but of financialism, mercantilism, and all-absorbing luxury.[24] Somewhere, nearly all of this has disappeared from Appleby's summary of Country thought and of the republican hypothesis.

Appleby's critiques suggest that recent scholarship has traveled ever farther down a fundamentally false trail, placing ever-growing emphasis on this nostalgic, anti-modern, Country bent of Jeffersonian thinking and failing to detect a crucial change. Quite the contrary is in fact the case. *The Jeffersonian Persuasion* advanced the thesis that the emergence and character of an opposition to Federalism "was dependent to an important and unrecognized degree on an *Americanization* of eighteenth-century opposition thought."[25] It sought not just to demonstrate a lingering regard for old ideas but to explain how specific classical and opposition concepts were *altered* in such ways that they continued to exert a vital influence in a setting very different from the one in which they had originally appeared. Since 1978, historians have focused with increasing intensity on the question how the Jeffersonians accommodated and adjusted their heritage of British opposition and classical republican ideas to their perception that the world was characterized increasingly by complexity, commercialization, specialization, and professionalism.[26] Far from being false, this trail has been productive of increasing insight—the right one to pursue.

Yet this is not to say that Appleby is altogether wrong. Revisionists *have* stressed the central influence on the Jeffersonians of British opposition thought, which had been overlooked before. In doing so, they may have given so much space and stress to what was old, inherited, and hesitant about the future at the core of Jeffersonian belief that there was need for a revitalized insistence on what was progressive and new. To the degree that recent works have mistakenly or unintentionally overemphasized the conservative characteristics of Jeffersonian thought, Appleby's work should serve as a useful corrective. She helps us see more clearly the differences between the Jeffersonians and eighteenth-century British thinkers, among them differences that the revisionists themselves insisted on and differences that they neglected but would not deliberately deny. Her influence is already working to restore a better balance and to reinforce a growing emphasis on the varieties of Jeffersonian opinion.

Saying this, however, does not settle the dispute or even probe its depths. Thus far, I have suggested that the distance between Appleby and the revisionists will seem narrower if we recognize that most of the latter have neither argued nor deliberately implied that the Jeffersonians were wholly derivative or exclusively conservative in their thinking. Even so, the gap remains a large one. For Appleby does not intend a mere corrective. Rather, seconded by Kramnick, she rejects the major thesis of the recent work and calls for a renewed attention to the advent and influence of modern liberalism. Here—and not in classical republicanism or eighteenth-century opposition thought—we are to find a more appropriate beginning for studies of the origins and nature of the Jeffersonian impulse. No revisionist would wish to follow her to this extreme. Neither is it necessary that we choose between two such sharply irreconcilable points of view.

Analytically, of course, modern liberalism and classical republicanism are distinguishable philosophies. *Liberalism* is a label most would use for a political philosophy that regards man as possessed of inherent individual rights and the state as existing to protect these rights, deriving its authority from consent.[27] *Classical republicanism* is a term that scholars have employed to identify a mode of thinking about citizenship and the polity that may be traced from Aristotle through Machiavelli and Harrington to eighteenth-century Britain and her colonies. The two philosophies begin with different assumptions about human nature and develop a variety of different ideas. Their incompatibility will seem much more pronounced if we expand our use of *liberalism* to encompass capitalism or imply a bourgeois attitude and set of values.[28]

A full-blown, modern liberalism, as Appleby and Kramnick appear to use the term, posits a society of equal individuals who are motivated principally if not exclusively by their passions or self-interest; it identifies a proper government as one existing to protect these individuals' inherent rights and private pursuits. A fully classical republicanism, as Pocock may best explain, reasons from the diverse capacities and characteristics of different social groups, whose members are political by nature. No republicanism will still be "classical" if it is not concerned with the individual's participation with others in civic decisions where the needs and powers of those others must be taken into account.[29] Liberalism, thus defined, is comfortable with economic man, with the individual who is intent on maximizing private satisfactions and who needs to do no more in order to serve the general good. Classical republicanism regards this merely economic man as less than fully human. Assuming a certain tension between public good and private desires, it will identify the unrestrained pursuit of purely private interests as incompatible with preservation of a commonwealth.

Liberal and classical ideas were both available to eighteenth-century Englishmen and to America's Revolutionary generation. Distinguishing between them is a useful scholarly pursuit. Identifying contradictions, tensions, or confusions in the thought of any individual or group who may have held ideas derived from two ultimately irreconcilable philosophies can certainly improve our understanding. But major difficulties will arise if we suppose that the analytical distinctions we detect were evident to those we study, or if we suggest that, in America, one of two separate and competing modes of thinking displaced the other in the years before 1815.

Logically, it may be inconsistent to be simultaneously liberal and classical. Historically, it was not. Eighteenth-century opposition thought was always a complex blend of liberal and classical ideas. So was the thought of

America's Revolutionary generation. Jeffersonian Republicans inherited a way of thinking that accustomed men to move immediately from the concepts of a contractual origin of government and inherent individual rights to the assertion that a balanced form of government *and* sufficient virtue to preserve that form are necessary guarantees of liberty.[30] The major novelty and most important contribution of revisionary work has not been to deny that Revolutionary Americans and Jeffersonian Republicans were Lockean and liberal, but to demonstrate that liberal ideas were only part of their inheritance, to show that other parts of the inheritance assured that Jeffersonians could never be wholly comfortable with the increasing complexity and privatization of American life. Among the most important implications of this work is the suggestion that nineteenth-century America did not begin with and may never have achieved a liberal consensus.[31]

In developing this thesis, revisionists may well have overemphasized the similarities between the Jeffersonians and British oppositionists. They may have exaggerated the classical at the expense of the liberal dimensions of Jeffersonian thought, if only by assuming that the latter had received sufficient emphasis. They may thus have left an impression that the Jeffersonians were less progressive than they really were. This is the valid element in Appleby's protest. In recognizing this, however, let us take care not to tip the balance to an opposite extreme. While it is possible to throw a brilliant light on Jeffersonian ideology by emphasizing liberal and democratic ideas—consider Daniel J. Boorstin's classic book[32]—the benefits that have accrued from recent efforts to explain American disputes by reference to the exchanges between the English Court and Country are readily apparent when we measure how far we have come from Boorstin's point of view. While it is true that Jeffersonians were never strictly classical in their republicanism—no one has really argued that they were—neither were they merely liberal. Thus, although I would agree with Appleby that Federalism had both Court and Country wings, I would resist the rather contradictory suggestion that the party battles of the new republic can be described as contests pitting Federalist attachment to tradition against a liberal, Republican commitment to change. What do we do, on this hypothesis, with the substantial evidence that the cosmopolitan, most thoroughly commercial, and most aggressively capitalistic segments of new-republican society were Federalist in their politics?[33] What would we do with evidence, which remains persuasive to my mind, for the Country character of many Jeffersonian ideas? What, finally, would be the consequences of this thesis for our understanding of American developments in the years after 1815?

A premature discovery of a wholly liberal perspective holds risks beyond those most directly related to our understanding of the Jeffersonians. One of the most important consequences of the modern reinterpretation of Revolutionary republicanism has been the understanding that the Revolutionaries left to their successors a lasting and profound commitment to values and ideas that were not part of a liberal consensus, transmitting to their heirs a more complex political tradition whose rediscovery permits important reinterpretations of American developments and conflicts from the War of 1812 to Watergate.[34] This does not mean that the advent of a liberal perspective is without further value as an explanation of developments. It may mean, though, that we are well advised not to claim too much for its explanatory benefits. Like the concept of modernization, to which it seems to bear a resemblance, the rise of liberalism may explain too little if it is called upon to explain too much, too soon.

In the end, I would suggest, it is no longer possible to accept any analysis of the first American party struggle that describes the Republicans and Federalists in terms of left versus right, liberal or progressive versus conservative or reactionary. If revisionary work has taught us anything, it has surely taught us that both parties were a bit of each. Prepared to understand the Jeffersonians as neither unambiguously left nor unequivocably right, I find instructive Appleby's insistence that the desire to free the individual from formal restraints and to use the government to promote access to opportunity were major and essentially progressive elements of the Jeffersonian position, elements inadequately discussed in recent work. At the same time, I resist depiction of Jeffersonian Republicanism as a "flowering of liberal thought" or "a form of capitalism." We cannot simply shut our eyes to the abundant evidence that the Republicans had many reservations about the eager, unrestrained pursuit of economic opportunity and even stronger reservations about the use of government to speed the processes of economic change. Republicans *were* conservative compared to their Hamiltonian opponents *in several important respects.* Appleby is right to stress that they conceived themselves as a progressive force, as the party seeking to defend and perfect a revolutionary new order. In America, however, this new order was commonly defined as one that had escaped or rejected major political, commercial, industrial, and financial changes that had overtaken contemporary England. These novelties the Jeffersonians were determined to resist.[35]

Building on the work of Marvin Meyers and Major Wilson, Daniel Walker Howe has recently described the early nineteenth-century Whigs as neither of the left nor of the right.[36] Whigs were partial modernizers. They were comfortable with, and advocates for, economic changes about which the Jacksonians were anxious, yet they envisioned a process of modernization that would be directed, disciplined, and controlled. They were hesitant about dimensions of modernity and progress that Jacksonians were more inclined to accept: laissez-faire, equality, party competition, executive initiatives, secularization, and the like. A comparable analysis of the Federalists and Jeffersonians has yet to be achieved. Its benefits, however, may be hinted by the disagreement between Appleby and other scholars. Its development must draw from both.[37]

This seems to me entirely possible, for—to put a former point another way—the recent reconstructions of Revolutionary republicanism and of Jeffersonian opinion have always recognized and sometimes even emphasized the powerful impact in America of liberal ideas (provided that we do not use too broad a definition of this word). John Locke and Algernon Sidney contributed importantly *both* to the development of a contractual philosophy *and* to the English modification of the classical republican tradition.[38] English oppositionists included theoretical republicans and Protestant dissenters as well as country gentlemen and Tory politicians, whose role may have been unduly stressed of late by both the students of republicanism and their critics. Noting this, *The Jeffersonian Persuasion* argued that the eighteenth-century opposition was moving in a democratic direction (or returning to a Harringtonian condemnation of hereditary privilege) well before the American Revolution.[39] Bailyn and Wood both attributed a large part of the transformed and transforming character of Revolutionary thought to the influence of a democratic, individualistic, natural-rights philosophy. Subsequent interpreters have been consistently concerned with the continuing transformation, not simply the persistence, of eighteenth-century concepts, a transformation they have always understood as very much a consequence of individualistic and contractual dimensions of Revolutionary thinking. These interpreters need quarrel, not with further study of this transformation or with new attempts to analyze the liberal contribution, but only with arguments that seem to urge retreat to an older, more constricted interpretive perspective, one that might deny much of the newly rediscovered complexity of Revolutionary discourse and imply an easier American adjustment to modernity than the republican hypothesis suggests.

If liberalism connotes adherence to an individualistic and contractual theory of the origins and limits of government, then the Jeffersonians were certainly liberals—which, however, will not help explain how they differed from the Federalists. If liberalism suggests a conception of politics in which the general good will emerge if the state respects the rights of all and individuals attend to little or nothing more than improving their private lives and voting their self-interest, then Republicans (and Federalists) were something less or something more than liberals; most did not consider self-interest a sufficient basis for citizenship, and most did not, as Boorstin would have it, regard the state as existing solely to protect an individual pursuit of private satisfactions.[40] Finally, if liberalism implies unqualified acceptance of acquisitive behavior, "a wholehearted ideology of the market," redefinition of man as *"homo oeconomicus"* rather than *"homo civicus,"*[41] or unequivocal support of an emerging commercial, industrial, and capitalistic order, then it is simply not helpful to describe the Jeffersonians as liberals. Many of their opponents were more nearly comfortable with attitudes such as these.

Jeffersonian Republicans did not oppose business, commerce, manufacturing, or every variety of social change, much less technological or managerial improvements in agriculture and communications. Neither did most of the eighteenth-century oppositionists from whom many of their ideas derived. Both Republicans and oppositionists, however, were sharply aware of the ease with which a spirit of commerce becomes an avaricious desire for private gain and self-immersed enjoyment. Both were convinced that such a spirit, together with the inequality of fortunes that it can promote, is incompatible with preservation of a commonwealth. Both believed agriculturalists to be less subject to the transition from a spirit of virtuous industry to a spirit of avaricious enjoyment than other social groups. Both believed that dangers to virtue and to the moderate level of property-holding that supports it can be accelerated by mercantilism and financialism. While they were not opposed to commerce, they did fear commercialization, which they hoped could be contained and reconciled with traditional values. They distrusted urban crowding and were horrified by the political and social consequences of English industrialization. In these ways, and in so far as governmental intervention may actually have been required in order to encourage commercialization and industrialization, they stood against modernity.

In opposing mercantilism and financialism—"unnatural" economic policies and governmental rewards to "parasites"—Jeffersonians were in accord with later liberals. But they did not share the "liberal" desire to unleash the acquisitive spirit, the liberal denial of any tension between private enterprise and public good. Republicans, like nineteenth-century liberals, disapproved of governmental guidance of the economy; but, unlike liberals, they did not aim essentially at using government to nurture the conditions for a general race to get ahead. The Jeffersonians were not Jacksonians. They were still uncomfortable with the thought that uninhibited pursuit of market opportunities would automatically result in public happiness and harmony. They were even more uncomfortable with the notion that the role of the state is to facilitate the growth of capital and credit, hurrying the community into the marketplace. They held that individual improvement ought to be restrained by a residual regard for others, that private satisfactions must sometimes give way to public duties. And they suspected that this commitment to community would be endangered if commerce and manufacturing, which they accepted as the proper, narrow top of the pyramid of economic enterprise, should become too heavy for the pyramid's broad and equal agricultural base.

The irreducible difference between a strictly liberal interpretation of Jeffersonian ideology and a republican hypothesis may lie in our understanding of the way in which the Jeffersonians related the public and private spheres of life. On this point, proponents of the republican thesis can summon valuable assistance from Hannah Arendt. Arendt understood that American Revolutionaries "knew that public freedom consisted in having a share in public business, and that the activities connected with this business by no means constituted a burden but gave those who discharged them in public a feeling of happiness they could acquire nowhere else."[42] She shared the Revolutionaries' own sense of the tension between this active—and ultimately still classical—kind of liberty, and privatization. She saw, of course, that Revolutionary republicans desired the liberty to pursue their private welfare and that they sometimes even spoke as though happiness lay exclusively in the private realm. But Arendt saw, as well, that these republicans continued to define "liberty" as much in terms of freedom *to* participate actively and virtuously in politics as in terms of freedom *from* restraint. To them, she wrote, "Tyranny . . . was a form of government in which the ruler, even though he ruled according to the laws of the realm, had monopolized for himself the right of action, banished the citizens from the public realm into the privacy of their households, and demanded of them that they mind their own, private business. Tyranny, in other words, deprived of public happiness, though not necessarily of private well-being, while a republic granted to every citizen the right to become "a participator in the government of affairs," the right to be seen in action."[43]

Let us follow Arendt one more step, drawing also both from advocates of the republican hypothesis and from their critics, in order to apply these thoughts to the Jeffersonian Republicans. "The Declaration of Independence," Arendt said, "still intends us to hear the term 'pursuit of happiness' in its twofold meaning: private welfare as well as the right to public happiness, the pursuit of well-being as well as being a 'participator in public affairs.'" Even during the Revolutionary period itself, she suggested—and even within Thomas Jefferson himself, we might add—the classical-republican insistence on liberty in its participatory meaning "came into conflict with ruthless and fundamentally antipolitical desires to be rid of all public cares and duties; to establish a mechanism of government administration through which men could control their rulers and still enjoy" a mode of government that would release them to attend exclusively to their private concerns.[44] The Jeffersonian Republicans undoubtedly attracted many individuals whose concerns were essentially private. It seems certain, as well, that a fundamentally antipolitical spirit encroached increasingly on the participatory ideal in the years after 1789.[45] But the republican hypothesis has shown, I think, that the men who developed a Jeffersonian persuasion and who led the Republican Party into the War of 1812 were still sufficiently classical in their thought that they could not accept the antipolitical spirit as compatible with liberty. Indeed, these Jeffersonians quarreled with the Federalists, in no small part, because so many of the latter wished to banish ordinary people from the public realm.

American Revolutionaries and Jeffersonian Republicans attempted to combine (and probably confused) concepts of liberty deriving from a classical tradition—freedom *to*—with more modern or liberal concepts that associated liberty more exclusively with the private, pre-governmental realm—freedom *from*. Historians can usefully explore resulting tensions and confusions. They should consider whether different social groups and political factions mixed liberal and classical dimensions of their heritage in different ways.[46] They will certainly wish to study changes over time. But the question need not be which set of concepts most Jeffersonians ultimately preferred. The Jeffersonians, together with their rivals, may have drawn from a coherent—which is not to say consistent—universe of thought that could contain important elements of both philosophies in a persistent, fruitful tension.[47]

The Jeffersonians were very much concerned with freedom *from* and with replacement of a social and political order grounded on hereditary privilege by an order resting on individual equality and talent. They were not the eighteenth-century British opposition. And yet they never broke entirely free from an eighteenth-century concern with freedom *to*, from a continuing insistence on public duties as well as private rights, or from a humanistic fear of merely economic man. It is, in part, because they never did that "the revolutionary notions of *public* happiness and *political* freedom have never altogether vanished from the American scene." Because of this, their heirs continue to the present to distrust the "antics of a society intent upon affluence and consumption."[48] The Jeffersonian perspective—and even, perhaps, our own—was a product of a Revolutionary republican discourse whose parameters proved stubbornly resistant to complete transcendence.

Notes

Mr. Banning is a member of the Department of History at the University of Kentucky. A version of this article was presented at the convention of the Western Society for Eighteenth-Century Studies, Huntington Library, February 1984. He wishes to acknowledge an excellent commentary by Professor Appleby, which further clarified their differences, as well as sensitive readings by several friends.

1. The new interpretation emerged as a collective product, although there are significant differences in individual views. Lance Gilbert Banning's "The Quarrel with Federalism: A Study in the Origins and Character of Republican Thought" (Ph.D. diss., Washington University, 1971) was directed by John M. Murrin, who suggested that a major portion of the argument might be summarized in the form of "Republican Ideology and the Triumph of the Constitution, 1789 to 1793," *William and Mary Quarterly*, 3d Ser., 31 (1974): 167–188. J. G. A. Pocock, who served as second reader of the dissertation, drew upon its findings for portions of *The Machiavellian Moment: Florentine Political Thought and the Atlantic Republican Tradition* (Princeton, N.J., 1975) and for other works cited below. The dissertation also influenced Drew R. McCoy, "Republicanism and American Foreign Policy: James Madison and the Political Economy of Commercial Discrimination, 1789 to 1794," *WMQ*, 3d Ser., 31 (1974): 633–646, and "The Republican Revolution: Political Economy in Jeffersonian America, 1776 to 1817" (Ph.D. diss., University of Virginia, 1976). All these works, in turn, profoundly influenced Banning, *The Jeffersonian Persuasion: Evolution of a Party Ideology* (Ithaca, N.Y., 1978). A similar interpretation of Jeffersonian thought was independently advanced in Forrest McDonald, *The Presidency of Thomas Jefferson* (Lawrence, Kan., 1976). Murrin, "The Great Inversion, or Court versus Country: A Comparison of the Revolution Settlements in England (1688–1721) and America (1776–1816)," in J. G. A. Pocock, ed., *Three British Revolutions: 1641, 1688, 1776* (Princeton, N.J., 1980), 368–453, is an important recent addition.

2. Especially Bernard Bailyn, *The Ideological Origins of the American Revolution* (Cambridge, Mass., 1967), and Gordon S. Wood, *The Creation of the American Republic, 1776–1787* (Chapel Hill, N.C., 1969).

3. Robert E. Shalhope, "Republicanism and Early American Historiography," *WMQ*, 3d Ser., 39 (1982): 334–356. Also useful is Daniel Walker Howe, "European Sources of Political Ideas in Jeffersonian America," *Reviews in American History* 10 (December 1982): 28–44.

4. Joyce Appleby, "Commercial Farming and the 'Agrarian Myth' in the Early Republic," *Journal of American History* 68 (1982): 833–849; "What Is Still American in the Political Philosophy of Thomas Jefferson?" *WMQ*, 3d Ser., 39 (1982): 287–309; and *Capitalism and a New Social Order: The Republican Vision of the 1790s* (New York, 1984). See also Isaac Kramnick, "Republican Revisionism Revisited," *American Historical Review* 87 (1982): 629–664, and John Patrick Diggins, *The Lost Soul of American Politics: Virtue, Self-Interest, and the Foundations of Liberalism* (New York, 1985). Kramnick and Diggins both specifically endorse Appleby's interpretation, but neither discusses America between 1789 and 1815.

5. Appleby, "Commercial Farming and 'Agrarian Myth,'" *JAH* 68 (1982): 836–837.

6. Ibid., 844.

7. Ibid., 847.

8. Ibid., 848.

9. Ibid., 849.

10. Ibid.

11. J. G. A. Pocock, ed., *The Political Works of James Harrington* (Cambridge, 1977), 151.

12. Banning, *Jeffersonian Persuasion*, 68, 204–205, 269. See also Murrin, "Great Inversion," in Pocock, ed., *Three British Revolutions*, 417–418.

13. American Revolutionaries did not distrust "independent artisans and mechanics" but "poverty-stricken, landless laborers, and especially those [large-scale manufactories] dependent on government subsidy and promotion." "The Revolutionaries did not seek to reject a proper degree of civilization in the name of republicanism; they wished only to stop at the point where refinement became corruption" (Drew R. McCoy, *The Elusive Republic: Political Economy in Jeffersonian America* [Chapel Hill, N.C., 1980], 65, 73). Some recent works come closer than Banning or McCoy to advancing the view Appleby condemns, as will be discussed below. I single out these books because they are the fullest presentations of recent views and are similarly selected in Appleby's second article.

14. Appleby, "What Is Still American?" *WMQ*, 3d Ser., 39 (1982): 287–309.

15. Ibid., 308, 306.

16. Ibid., 302–303.

17. Ibid., 302, 288. My emphases.

18. An exception might be made for McDonald, *Presidency of Jefferson*, esp. 19–22: Jeffersonian ideology "was borrowed *in toto* from such Oppositionists as Charles Davenant, John Trenchard, Thomas Gordon, James Burgh, and most especially . . . Bolingbroke. As a well-rounded system, it is all to be found in the pages of the *Craftsman*. . . . The essence of [the Jeffersonian program was to] restore America to the pristine simplicity of an Arcadian past." McDonald obviously wrote this book with tongue sometimes in cheek, aiming for general readers and often seeking language designed to shock and rouse his fellow professionals. But McDonald's other

recent work presents Alexander Hamilton as a modernizing, liberal hero and suggests that he would characterize the first American parties in terms almost opposite to those of Appleby. This view is shared by none of the other recent writers.

19. Appleby, "What Is Still American?" *WMQ,* 3d Ser., 39 (1982): 293.

20. Pocock, ed., *Works of Harrington,* 147.

21. Banning, *Jeffersonian Persuasion,* 84–103. "Adams was an eighteenth-century classical republican. . . . His friends were living in a different mental world. . . . Adams' failing was his inability to comprehend the changes in the theory of a balanced constitution that the concept of a democratic social order introduced" (ibid., 97–98).

22. Appleby, "What Is Still American?" *WMQ,* 3d Ser., 39 (1982): 300.

23. Chapter 2 of *The Jeffersonian Persuasion* discusses Bolingbroke as one of several outstanding figures in an opposition tradition to which radical Whigs contributed fully as much as reactionary Tories. It contains only passing references to Montesquieu. Similarly, when J. G. A. Pocock writes that the stance of the 18th-century opposition was that of a "radical right," it is clear he is referring to the demand for a return to an uncorrupted constitution ("Machiavelli, Harrington, and English Political Ideologies in the Eighteenth Century," *WMQ,* 3d Ser., 22 [1965]: 572). Whig or Tory, all oppositionists regarded patronage, "government by money," and much else as undesirable innovations. But British acceptance of the opposition's demand for the excision of these innovations would scarcely have been conservative in practical effects, nor were all opposition writers on the right of the political spectrum when the spectrum is defined in broader terms.

24. It needs to be emphatically reemphasized that even in the writings of Pocock, which stress the antithesis of virtue and commerce, it is not commerce defined as exchange that is identified as a focus of 18th-century worries. Revisionists have repeatedly insisted that commerce becomes a problem in 18th-century minds when it produces luxury, enervation, and single-minded attention to acquisition and enjoyment. Similarly, it might be noted that in *Capitalism and a New Social Order* Appleby identifies the Republicans with a capitalist vision partly by defining *capitalism* in terms of buying and selling (especially among farmers). Although I do not like the rather anachronistic use of this word, I would readily agree that Jeffersonians endorsed free exchange. Different conclusions emerge, however, if we associate capitalism primarily with entrepreneurial activities and investment.

25. Banning, *Jeffersonian Persuasion,* 129. Emphasis added.

26. In addition to McCoy see, for example, Robert E. Shalhope, *John Taylor of Caroline: Pastoral Republican* (Columbia, S.C., 1980), Lawrence Delbert Cress, *Citizens in Arms: The Army and the Militia in American Society to the War of 1812* (Chapel Hill, N.C., 1982), and Ralph Ketcham, *Presidents above Party: The First American Presidency, 1789–1829* (Chapel Hill, N.C., 1984).

27. I have no objection to identifying liberalism, if defined *this* way, particularly with John Locke. American historians have not ordinarily gone as far as Pocock toward discounting Locke's influence.

28. As in C. B. Macpherson, *The Political Theory of Possessive Individualism: Hobbes to Locke* (Oxford, 1962).

29. Most helpful are Pocock, ed., *Works of Harrington*, 145–151; *Machiavellian Moment*, 115–116, 394–395, 523–527; and "Virtue and Commerce in the Eighteenth Century," *Journal of Interdisciplinary History* 3 (1972): 119–134.

30. For 18th-century blending of the two philosophies see *Jeffersonian Persuasion*, 55–69. The similarities between the two are as clear as their ultimate incompatibility, and the same thinkers often contributed to both. Liberalism and classical republicanism both insisted on a definition of the individual in terms of his autonomy. Both linked liberty with property. There were many points of contact and even of confusion.

31. Cf. Louis Hartz, *The Liberal Tradition in America: An Interpretation of American Political Thought since the Revolution* (New York, 1955).

32. Boorstin, *The Lost World of Thomas Jefferson* (Boston, 1948).

33. Murrin cites the most important studies, principally by authors not especially concerned with the history of ideas.

34. For a useful discussion of some benefits of the displacement of Hartz's thesis with a republican hypothesis see Dorothy Ross, "The Liberal Tradition Revisited and the Republican Tradition Addressed," in John Higham and Paul K. Conkin, eds., *New Directions in American Intellectual History* (Baltimore, 1979), 116–131.

35. Even the suggestion that both parties were conservative in some respects and progressive in others risks implying value judgments or assuming a teleological perspective. Like Appleby, I think we should avoid this, but it does seem helpful to point out that the future was hardly on the side of the independent craftsmen and small farmers whose advocates the Jeffersonians were. It was on the side of the entrepreneurial capitalists associated with Alexander Hamilton's Bank of the United States and Society for Useful Manufactures, corporations that were novel in American conditions.

36. Howe, *The Political Culture of the American Whigs* (Chicago, 1979).

37. A more sophisticated interpretation of the first party struggle must also link our growing understanding of party thought with our regrettably scanty information about the social sources of party division. The two most ambitious recent starts toward this are James H. Hutson, "Country, Court, and Constitution: Antifederalism and the Historians," *WMQ* 38 (1981): 337–368, and Murrin, "Great Inversion," in Pocock, ed., *Three British Revolutions*, 368–453. Both are valuable and impressive. Neither seems free from difficulties. The Federalists of 1787 included groups and individuals, most notably James Madison, who cannot be associated with a Court tradition. To compare the Federalists to the English Court and Antifederalists to the Country, while revealing, still seems to force materials into the misleading terms of left versus right. We should be careful, too, to avoid a definition of "Court" that would make the term nearly synonymous with pro-government or pro-commercial. Other useful attempts to link the findings of historians of party thought with those of stu-

dents of party behavior include H. James Henderson, *Party Politics in the Continental Congress* (New York, 1974), and Robert Kelley, "Ideology and Political Culture from Jefferson to Nixon," *AHR* 82 (1977): 531–562.

38. One of the earliest sourcebooks for current understanding of the sources of Revolutionary thinking emphasized the contribution of 18th-century opposition writers to the preservation and transmittal to America of both republican and liberal ideas. Caroline Robbins, *The Eighteenth-Century Commonwealthman: Studies in the Transmission, Development and Circumstance of English Liberal Thought from the Restoration of Charles II until the War with the Thirteen Colonies* (Cambridge, Mass., 1959).

39. Banning, *Jeffersonian Persuasion*, 63–64, 81. John Brewer's *Party Ideology and Popular Politics at the Accession of George III* (Cambridge, 1976) deals more fully with this issue.

40. Boorstin, *Lost World of Jefferson*, esp. 190–196.

41. Kramnick, "Republican Revisionism Revisited," *AHR* 87 (1982): 661–662.

42. Hannah Arendt, *On Revolution* (New York, 1963), 115.

43. Ibid., 127. Also helpful on these matters is Trevor Colbourn, ed., *Fame and the Founding Fathers: Essays by Douglass Adair* (Chapel Hill, N.C., 1974).

44. Arendt, *On Revolution*, 129, 133.

45. Jan Lewis, *The Pursuit of Happiness: Family and Values in Jefferson's Virginia* (Cambridge, 1983), is an interesting, although not entirely successful, consideration of this question. Lewis stresses privatization, especially in the period after 1812, yet it seems clear that the Virginia gentry did not massively withdraw from politics even in these years when nearly all historians would agree that the 18th-century heritage was fading. Lewis also emphasizes a continuing distrust of commerce, insisting that individual opportunity and self-reliance were not embraced but dreaded. See pages 115–116, 161–165.

46. Eric Foner, whose *Tom Paine and Revolutionary America* (New York, 1976) was published as I neared completion of *The Jeffersonian Persuasion,* suggests the presence of a distinctive and perhaps more completely liberal variety of Republicanism. Tench Coxe may have represented yet another variety of urban, cosmopolitan Republicanism. See Jacob E. Cooke, *Tench Coxe and the Early Republic* (Chapel Hill, N.C., 1978). John R. Nelson, Jr., "Alexander Hamilton and American Manufacturing: A Reexamination," *JAH,* 65 (1979): 971–995, is helpful for understanding the popular, urban appeal of Jeffersonian ideology, as, of course, is Appleby. Since 1978, it has become increasingly apparent that Jeffersonian opinion ranged across a broad spectrum. Spokesmen included reactionaries or conservatives such as John Randolph and John Taylor, together with radicals such as Joseph Priestley or Thomas Cooper, English émigrés who were far more acceptive of modernity. (For the range of this spectrum on the issue of a proper military force for a republic, see Cress, *Citizens in Arms,* 155–166.) The presence of such variety, however, does not exclude the possibility of identifying a core of belief that held Jeffersonians together, and I remain willing to

argue both that the Republicans were bound together by the concepts explored in *The Jeffersonian Persuasion* and *The Elusive Republic* and that the thought of the great party leaders should be placed somewhere toward the middle of the party's spectrum.

47. Some of the fruits of this tension are analyzed in Ketcham's *Presidents above Party,* which appeared after this passage was written. Ketcham, who begins by asking why Jefferson should have mentioned Bolingbroke and Thomas Paine in the same sentence as "advocates of human liberty," also offers a very useful discussion of the complementary but distinguishable contributions of Tories and radical Whigs to the opposition response to the "modern Whig" (or Court) tradition of Walpole, Mandeville, and Daniel Defoe. See pages 3 and 55–57, passim.

48. Arendt, *On Revolution,* 135. Published while the present article was in press, Richard K. Matthews, *The Radical Politics of Thomas Jefferson: A Revisionist View* (Lawrence, Kan., 1984), 84–91, also draws on Arendt for a criticism of the liberal interpretation. But Matthews is almost equally opposed to the republican hypothesis.

The Republican Interpretation

Retrospect and Prospect

Twenty years ago, when *The Creation of the American Republic* had just come off the press and I was still researching my doctoral dissertation, none of us had heard of a "republican interpretation" of the Revolution. As late as 1978, unless I misremember, I did not employ this term or any of its cognates in *The Jeffersonian Persuasion,* although the dissertation from which that book derived was finished just as Robert Shalhope was describing the emergence of a "republican synthesis" and calling for a reinterpretation of the new republic in its terms.[1] Modern scholarship develops with astounding speed. By 1982, when Shalhope's second article appeared, the republican hypothesis had been extended well into the nineteenth century; and it had exercised sufficient influence through the past ten years that it had also come to be a target for a great variety of critics.[2] If it had ever been a synthesis, it seemed to be a synthesis no more. Indeed, at least to the extent that the republican interpretation had been pushed beyond the ratification of the Constitution, there were signs of growing influence for a criticism which, I thought, was leading readers to mistake its contents and neglect its most important contributions.[3] At that point, I entered the notorious debate about the influence of "republican" and "liberal" ideas.[4]

If subsequent citations are a guide, I probably accomplished only part— and, from today's perspective, maybe not the most important part—of what I aimed at in the article of 1986. My controversy with Joyce Appleby had two dimensions. At the simpler level, I believed that she had seriously misrepresented much of what some useful writings had in fact maintained about the Jeffersonian Republicans and their opponents. It was also my impression— from citations, conversations, and the like—that many readers were collecting their impression of republican interpretations not from careful reading of the major works themselves but from misleading summaries by others. (If there is anything, in fact, that tends to disillusion me about our business, this would surely be the great degree to which our universal struggle to remain abreast of an exploding literature is leading to a huge amount of careless reading or to even poorer strategies for keeping up.) Thus, "Jeffersonian Ideology Revisited" was prompted partly by a wish to set the record straight and by a hope that readers might be driven back to works which it defended for a closer look at what their authors really had to say.

Throughout the early 1980s, I had been preoccupied primarily with Madison (and, more especially, with the development of Madison's ideas *before* the framing of the Constitution). Still, the argument with Appleby was not intended simply as a rear-guard action. At another level, I attempted—much as Gordon Wood has tried in several recent pieces—to suggest that arguments about the relative importance of republican and liberal ideas were not the most productive way to study the Revolutionary era.[5] Most such arguments, it seemed to me, were misconceived. They certainly seemed misconceived to the degree that scholars had forgotten that these two distinguishable traditions came into the English-speaking world together—and as allies, for the most part, rather than as foes. At some point in the nineteenth century, it may be true, American ideas and values came to be predominantly liberal and democratic; the republican concerns that had been vital to the Revolutionary generation came to be significantly overshadowed. When and how this happened—and to what degree—are questions that continue to be near the top of our research agenda. But the answers, I suggested—and I still believe—should not begin by positing an eighteenth-century war between competing classical and modern paradigms, which ended when the liberal standard swept its rival from the field. An image of this sort may hold some stirring narrative potential, but eighteenth-century people did not think that way. They blended and combined two trains of thinking that are separable for analytical objectives of our own, but usually were mixed when eighteenth-century people thought about their current problems. Accordingly, I argued that it might be better to examine the development of this distinctive combination of ideas than to imagine a dispute between its parts. Indeed, I really thought that this is what most scholars had been doing when Appleby and others mounted their critiques. The republican hypothesis, as I had always understood it, had never been intended to deny a central role in Revolutionary thinking for liberal ideas—not, at least, if "liberal" means a democratic, individualistic, and contractual conception of the origins and limits of governmental power. Rather, the republican hypothesis had always seemed to me to be an argument that Lockean or liberal ideas were only part of an

inheritance, a context, or a universe of thought which could be better understood by recognizing that it was a great deal more complex than earlier interpretations had suggested.

Here, perhaps, is where the article of 1986 was less successful. Several
readers, certainly, considered it a different sort of statement than I meant to
make, though sometimes for contrasting reasons.[6] Allow me, then, to make
another stab at this dimension of the argument and at the ways that I have
tried to build on it since then. For this, it seems to me, may still be relevant
as scholars seem to be achieving something like a general agreement that a
multiplicity of "paradigms" or ideational traditions were at work throughout
the Revolutionary age.[7]

What is the republican hypothesis most fundamentally *about?* What, if
any, are the central and enduring contributions of the "synthesis" that Shalhope named? In my conception, terms like these are handy labels for an
effort that began while I was still in college to rewrite our history to take
advantage of the rediscovery of certain strands in Revolutionary thinking
which were largely lost to national memory (and even to historical scholarship) for perhaps a century's time: ways of thinking which could be explained
as products of the influence of a set of eighteenth-century British writers who
had been essentially ignored until the later 1950s.[8] These eighteenth-century
opposition writers, to employ a neutral term, were never of a single mind.
Their early students called them by a wide variety of names: Commonwealth-
men, Old Whigs, Real Whigs, or Country critics of the Court. But whether
they were Whigs or Tories, it appeared, the most distinctive feature of their
thought was their continuing concern with values and ideas that could be
traced to a revival of a classical defense of mixed republics. Reformulated in
an English manner by the seventeenth-century opponents and supporters
of the ancient constitution, neoclassical conceptions seemed to have been
built upon by opposition writers to construct a sweeping and persistent condemnation of the eighteenth-century system of administration and finance.
In tribute to their lineage—for reasons that seemed proper at the time—
scholars soon became accustomed to referring to the opposition's values and
concerns as "classical republican" in nature (or "civic humanist" in Pocock's
monumental history of their development and influence).[9]

"Classical republican," it now appears, would prove a problem-laden
term for the tradition the enduring influence of which scholars set about to
trace. I will say more on this below. First, however, it is useful to recall that,
at the start, the striking feature of the eighteenth-century opposition writings seemed to be their constant warnings that the balanced constitution,

which supported British freedom, was increasingly endangered by the rise of standing armies, high taxation, governmental influence, and a funded debt. Emphasizing the polarities of liberty and power, independence and dependence, virtue and corruption, the militia and a standing army, opposition condemnations of the eighteenth-century system formed a long and powerful tradition. For something like a hundred years, a condemnation of a ministerial conspiracy to undermine the nation's freedom served as a consistent, necessary strategy for reconciling a persistent opposition to the government in power with a deep commitment to the mixed and balanced constitution. The republican interpretation (as it would be named by Shalhope) was, in its beginnings, nothing more—and nothing less—than the attempt to fit this "classical-republican" or "civic-humanist" or "British opposition" thinking back into our understanding of the eighteenth-century story.

Crudely speaking, a revised interpretation on these lines exploded into prominence with Bernard Bailyn's powerful analysis of the essential role of these ideas in the decisions for American independence and a republican Revolution.[10] It developed, in a manner I need not review, through Wood's outstanding history of constitutional and cultural developments to 1789 and on into attempts to reach a better understanding of political divisions in the new republic. In the aftermath of Pocock's mammoth work, the lasting influence of these civic humanist concerns became a major theme for nineteenth-century studies. Meanwhile, since it seemed apparent that republican ideas affected nearly every facet of the culture, the republican interpretation was developed in enlarging circles to rewrite our views of nearly every aspect of the Revolutionary age. These enlarging circles, as I understand it, were a major reason for Shalhope's early references to its synthetic potential. They are a major reason, too, for many of our current arguments, misunderstandings, and mistakes.

Which are which, as I conceive it? Can we separate the contributions from the errors and misunderstandings? Can a retrospect identify some faulty turnings in the work thus far, reduce confusions, and suggest some paths that might lead out of current thickets? I believe it can, and that the prospects will be best if we recur to the first, good principles with which the enterprise began.

The starting point and permanent foundation for republican interpretations is the argument that ways of thinking which derived from British opposition writers were of critical importance to the Revolutionary generation, which transmitted them to their posterity in turn, so that a recognition of their influence demands a significant rewriting of American history since that time. This argument, thus stated, does not need additional defense. When the republican hypothesis is phrased in some such terms, its contributions seem apparent and secure. At present, there are few dissenters from the view that Revolutionary history cannot be written well without according an essential place to the ideas that Pocock, Bailyn, Wood, and others called to our attention. Every year—and almost every month—brings further studies showing that republican concerns continued to exert substantial influence far into the future. From this perspective, the republican interpretation has achieved its principal objectives and continues to expand. Most of those who pioneered it could, quite fairly, simply claim a triumph on these grounds and keep repeating that they cannot help it if their critics and supporters have insisted on defining their objectives in different, more ambitious terms.

This last remark may seem outrageous in the face of sharp, continuing disputes; and yet it may prove useful to descend a moment from the heights of theoretical disputes and look a bit more closely at the ground. Certainly, it neither derogates from the achievements of revisionary work nor minimizes the legitimate objections of its critics to suggest that both the objects and the claims of most of the original proponents of republican interpretations were by no means as exclusivist as many of their critics and admirers have supposed. One fundamental problem for a major new interpretation is that it may soon acquire a superstructure grander than it can support and different, in important ways, from what its early architects may have intended.

The republican interpretation, in its current form, is not identical with books and articles that I consider central to its structure and creation. The "synthesis," as it is often called, extends to how these writings have been lumped together, built upon, extended, summarized, and criticized by others—not infrequently in ways that have been most discomforting to authors who are commonly associated with the things for which the synthesis is now supposed to stand.[11] Many current criticisms of republican interpretations do not start with what is really in its major statements but with what those statements have been taken to imply by both extenders and opponents. Recognizing this could surely help resolve some lingering misunderstandings.

These comments, to my mind, can clearly be applied to much, although by no means all, of the extended controversy over liberal and classical ideas. Almost from the start, the advocates of a republican interpretation were accused of claiming far too much. Denouncing an assumption that the reasoning of highly literate elites was shared at other levels of the population, some historians objected from the start to the consensual implications of the new interpretation.[12] Later, others argued that the theoretical assumptions of the ideological historians were seriously flawed, leaving insufficient room for intellectual innovation or for thinking which did not derive from a republican tradition.[13]

Both of these objections merit serious attention. Advocates of the republican interpretation did involve themselves in one or both of these two pitfalls to a large or small degree. Few of them, however, actually committed many of the other errors with which they are often charged. On this matter, for example, I, for one, have sometimes thought of modifying a distasteful affirmation: I do not now, nor did I ever, think of the republican tradition as a rival or alternative to a Lockean or liberal conception of the origins and limits of political society. Indeed, I do not think that any of the major architects of the republican interpretation ever claimed that revolutionary thinking could be fully understood without regard to Locke and other early modern theorists of natural rights and social compacts.[14] Neither do I think that any of them ever argued that republican ideas and values exercised a *greater* influence on the course of subsequent developments than liberal or democratic concepts.[15]

The republican interpretation, to my mind, has always been opposed to older, liberal interpretations only in so far as it insists that there is much about the Revolution and the new American Republic that cannot be understood without a comprehension of the vital role of neoclassical or civic humanist ideas—and, thus, that the American political tradition did not start with and may never have achieved a merely liberal consensus.[16] The republican interpretation is inimical to an insistence on the influence of a liberal tradition only in so far as liberal interpretations have suggested that, from the beginning of the national republic, most Americans adhered to the opinion that the public good requires no more than that the state respect the rights of all and individuals attend to little more than improving their private lives and voting their distinctive interests—only in so far as "liberalism" has been recently defined as an unqualified acceptance of acquisitive behavior, "a whole-hearted ideology of the market," redefinition of man as "*homo oeconomicus*" rather than as "*homo civicus*," or unequivocal support of an emerging commercial, industrial, and capitalistic order.[17]

Saying this, of course, is far from saying that the Revolution started from a strictly classical *and not* a modern-liberal tradition. No one, on my reading, ever made this claim. In fact, from its beginnings, the republican interpretation was, in one of its most striking aspects, an attempt to understand the great transition from an early modern to a fully modern culture, to explain the revolutionary features of the Revolution. Wood and Bailyn, as I understand them, both attributed a central role in this transition to the influence of a democratic, individualistic, natural-rights philosophy; and new interpretations of the new republic were consistently concerned, from the beginning, with the further transformation of the revolutionaries' universe of thought, not simply with the later influence of the old ideas.

This eighteenth-century universe, as I conceived it in *The Jeffersonian Persuasion*, had accustomed men to move immediately, without a consciousness of contradiction, from the concepts of a contractual origin of government and inherent individual rights to the assertions that a balanced form of government *and* sufficient virtue to preserve that form are necessary guarantees of freedom. The object of that book (and of related studies of the new republic) was by no means to deny the modern-liberal dimensions of the party's thought. It was to argue that the early party conflict could be better understood by recognizing that the founding generation had inherited a richer constellation of concerns which even the adoption of the Constitution did not rapidly or totally transform. In recent writings, I have tried to make this more explicit by suggesting that articulate Americans were liberal republicans by the beginning of the Revolution and continued to be liberal republicans until a time that I would hesitate to mark, perhaps because that time has never yet expired.[18]

"Liberal republicans," of course, is not a term that anyone was using back in 1978. In using it in recent writings, I am trying to incorporate the teachings of the leading critics of republican interpretations, to correct exaggerations and mistakes, to comment on the current state of understanding, and—for present purposes, especially—to offer some suggestions as to new directions for research. Given time and patience, I would not have competence or space to systematically consider all of the misunderstandings that republican interpretations have unleashed. These, in any case, are not the only problems. Therefore, in the space remaining, I will turn instead to some of the important misconceptions which, in my opinion, may in fact be traced to what is really in the most important works. The first requirement, if we are to get beyond the current smog, is to reduce emissions rising from misreadings. The next, however, is a critical, yet sympathetic, reconsideration of the fundamentals of the new interpretation on the chance that they might be improved. This seems to me essential if we are to take advantage of the criticisms of the 1980s and, without reverting to a pre-republican interpretation, work toward a revision that may more and more approach a valid formulation.

First, accordingly, it may be well to say again that early advocates of the republican interpretation did commit mistakes. In practice, as I see it, most of them avoided the deterministic trap to which their borrowings from social-science theory did expose them. But most of them were guilty of incautious language. In the manner of revisionists—emphasizing new materials and stressing their departures from prevailing views—most were less explicit than they might have been about received opinions they did not dispute.[19] This writer on the new republic, for example, probably did overemphasize the similarities between the Jeffersonians and eighteenth-century British oppositions. He may thus have inadvertently exaggerated "classical" at the expense of "liberal" dimensions of their thought, largely by assuming that the latter had received sufficient emphasis in the existing studies. He may thus have left an overall impression that the Jeffersonians were less progressive than was actually the case. This seemed to me a valid ground for critical objections, and errors of this sort did probably contribute to some subsequent misunderstandings.[20]

Second, it is well to note the large (and sometimes curious) misunderstandings which have followed from repeated references to "classical republican" ideas.[21] As first applied by Z. S. Fink and others, this expression seemed entirely proper. It referred to the revival of the ancient theory that a governmental mixture of the powers of the one, the many, and the few could break the never-ending cycle of decay and revolution. It referred, more broadly, to a train of thinking about citizenship and the polity which could be traced back through the Renaissance to Graeco-Roman writers. Some such term would still seem necessary to distinguish a tradition emphasizing freedom *to* participate with others in an active public life from a tradition emphasizing freedom *from* encroachments on pre-governmental rights.[22] These two traditions, usually identified as classical and modern, *do* begin with different assumptions about human nature. They may be traced to different thinkers. Logically, if not historically, they seem to us to clash, and it is therefore necessary to explore the contradictions, tensions, and confusions in the thought of those who seem to have identified with both traditions. Thus, the argument about the influence of the two traditions has improved our understanding and will certainly continue.

On the other hand, some aspects of this argument have long been fruitless; and, in part, this is because we have been tripping over terms. In the beginning, scholars who defined the "classical republican" tradition were specific as to what they meant. Pocock's vastly influential study, for example, was intensively concerned to understand how Graeco-Roman thought was *modified* by Florentine and English thinkers, *further* modified by eighteenth-century writers, and reconstructed even more completely during the American Revolution. Similarly, none of the American historians who played a central role in the construction of the republican synthesis ever believed or said that Revolutionary thought was *literally* classical in nature. Over time, however, as the synthesis was widened, some of the initial clarity was lost. Popularizers used the term more loosely, critics took it to imply a great deal more than had been said, and several of the masterworks of the interpretation came to be condemned by critics who had poorly understood them.

In the meantime, miscommunication was compounded as the argument assumed an interdisciplinary aspect, for references to "classical" ideas quite often held a different set of implications for scholars trained in political theory than they did for the American historians who used the term as shorthand for a constellation of ideas which they were perfectly aware was only distantly derived from Graeco-Roman sources. In themselves, in other words, loose references to "classical" ideas encouraged an impression that historians were saying that the thinking of the Revolutionary generation was classical *instead* of modern (in the sense that "modern" ordinarily suggests to political theorists). For the most part, the historians were saying no such thing, and reams of paper have been wasted in condemning books for what they never said or in rebuttals by their authors.[23]

None of this, I should not have to add, should be construed to mean that all of these debates have been without foundation or that theorists have not contributed importantly to better understanding.[24] Defining the republican hypothesis as I have sketched it in this essay, I am as committed to it now as when *The Jeffersonian Persuasion* was completed—maybe even more. But this is not to say that I agree with everything that has been claimed for the republican interpretation. It does not prevent me from incorporating insights by its critics. It does not suggest that I believe that even the outstanding masterworks of the republican interpretation—Bailyn's, Wood's, and Pocock's— are without substantial oversights or errors. These masterworks cannot be fairly charged, on careful reading, with many of the flaws that they are often thought to hold. Above all, in my view, they cannot be persuasively accused of arguing that Revolutionary thought was classical instead of modern.

Nevertheless, it *was* the neoclassical and not the modern-liberal influence which the pioneers of the republican interpretation set about to trace, assuming that the liberal influence was already quite well known. And for this very reason, oversights and errors did indeed get built into the very framework of republican revisions: misconceptions often present to this day whenever we discuss the "classical-republican" components of the early Revolution. Even

Wood and Pocock are imperfect; and, as imperfections really present in their work have been extended, summarized, and criticized by others, difficulties have become quite deeply seated. A third necessity for further progress, then, is to identify these imperfections and revise our image of the early Revolution in a way that might contribute to a better understanding of the Revolution's later years. This is where the "liberal" counterpoint to the republican interpretation seems to me most useful. It is where the cracks in the republican interpretation seem most likely to encourage new mistakes.

Two difficulties need particular attention. Present from the origins of the republican interpretation, they combine to help create an image of the early Revolution not as literally classical in its intentions but at least as more decidedly pre-modern than was actually the case, and such an image has some major implications for the current state of scholarship about the founding and the new republic. On the one hand, atavistic concepts of the early Revolution lend a specious plausibility to arguments that Federalist ideas (or even Revolutionary thought in general) are better understood as wholly liberal or modern: comprehensible, that is, without significant attention to a neo-classical or humanistic interest in participatory public life, without a serious consideration of the Revolutionaries' fear of rapid and intensive economic change. This Whiggish argument, I think, suggests an earlier and easier American adjustment to modernity than actually occurred and tends to reimpoverish our understanding. The opposite mistake is also being fostered by interpretations that describe the early Revolution as more decidedly pre-modern than it was. For if we see the early Revolution as decidedly pre-modern, we may also be inclined to squeeze the great transition toward a fully modern way into too brief a time, calling on developments that stretched through many decades to explain the changes of the hour.

The Creation of the American Republic, most American historians agree, is the essential starting point for current understandings of the years from 1776 through 1787. For twenty years, this modern classic has been unsurpassed as an analysis of the development of constitutional ideas between the Declaration and the launching of the federal republic. Through these years, in my opinion, Wood's interpretation of the evolution of the Constitution has successfully withstood the greater portion of his critics. Wrapped around this central narrative, however, is a broader study of the transformation of American political culture: the movement from a "Whig science of politics" toward "the end of classical politics" as eighteenth-century anglophones had once conceived them. Even here, in my opinion, Wood is nearer right than wrong; and yet this larger study is significantly more problematic.[25] While

Wood himself is far more subtle than his followers have been, the book can easily be taken to suggest that early Revolutionary talk of "virtue" *was* more literally classical (more Montesquieuan or Rousseauan, I have said) than it ever really was—and thus that Madison and other Federalists broke more decisively with early Revolutionary thinking than, in fact, they really did.[26]

A thorough recapitulation of this argument need not be offered in this place. But at the risk of oversimplifying, I can state its central points. "Virtue," it submits, was not a less important concept for the Revolutionaries than this masterwork suggests. And yet, perhaps because Wood tended to abstract the early Revolutionaries' fear of power and corruption from their general commitment to a balanced constitution, insufficient heed was paid to their assumption that it is impossible, in theory or in practice, to dissociate men's conduct from their interests. Revolutionary thinkers (and their eighteenth-century sources) knew that citizens would differ, clash, and even threaten one another's rights, especially if they were rulers. This is why they usually rejected simple forms of government and wanted bills of rights.[27] The great republican departure from the Revolutionaries' eighteenth-century sources did not lie in an assumption that republicans would constantly forswear self-interest and think only of the public. It lay in the conviction that in polities without hereditary orders, no one would possess a *permanent* self-interest different from the well-considered interest of the body of the people.

Revolutionary calls for virtue—for the sacrifice of selfish interests and commitment to the public good—were not less prominent or less significant than Wood maintained. Revolutionary fears of a decline of virtue were, indeed, as central to the course of constitutional reform as he suggested. Yet Revolutionary thinkers, I believe, had seldom hoped that individuals would not pursue their own self-interests. On the contrary, a vigorous and vigilant defense of one's own liberties and interests was widely thought of as a necessary characteristic of the citizen of a republic—his contribution of his virtue to the public. Commitment to the public good meant vigilant, continuous attention to the public life. It meant, as well, submission to the will of the community—obedience to law—and this submission had to be a conscious, voluntary act, since sound republics were assumed to be incapable of rigorous, continuing coercion. In these senses, self-immersion, if we understand that term to mean absorption in one's private life to the neglect of public duty, did appear profoundly dangerous to a republic. In these senses, individual desires and private interests *were* supposed to be subordinated to the public interest, even *sacrificed* to public needs. And in these senses, too, the individual's particular desires were certainly expected to give way to the decisions and demands of the community, which might call upon a man to sacrifice his property or, in a war, his life itself to public needs or wishes. But the sacrifice of self was to occur primarily in the submission to community decisions or in taking time from personal enjoyments to attend to public business. It would seldom happen in the *making* of political decisions, where citizens would be restrained by consciousness of others but where they neither could nor should forgo their own self-interests.

These distinctions, I believe, are critical to understanding the development of Revolutionary thinking. They suggest that Wood exaggerated the degree to which the early Revolutionaries held a truly classical (or Montesquieuan) concept of the public good in a republic, and thus that he may also have exaggerated the degree to which the Federalists rejected early-Revolutionary thinking. The central thrust of his interpretation still appears to me correct. Many Revolutionaries did begin to doubt that they were virtuous enough to manage sound republics. Still, the story of the course of Revolutionary thinking might be better understood, and needless controversies partially resolved, by clarifying what it was that late and early Revolutionaries meant by "virtue": what was classical and what was not in this conception, and what was changing over time. Wood went too far, I think, toward reading in a call for *selfless* political decisions where the early Revolutionaries really hoped for vigorous assertions of the self within a context of communal consciousness and a commitment to abide by the community's decisions. He may thus have left too little room for comprehending Madison's continuing insistence that the people's virtue was, for all of the improvements represented by the Constitution, the only ultimate security for any free regime.

This point is subject to misunderstanding, even in its more complete articulation. Let me, then, say clearly that I do not mean that virtue was a fully "modern" concept in republican opinion or that Revolutionary thought was never really neoclassical at all. Rather, I am seeking to suggest that Revolutionary thought—in 1787 as in 1776—is best conceived of as an early modern *blend* of liberal and neoclassical ideas, that a coherent mixture of the two traditions was in fact its most distinctive feature. My appeal, in short, is for a reconsideration of the ways in which these two distinguishable traditions interpenetrated and entwined for both the Revolutionaries and their eighteenth-century sources.

Popular participation is another concept that has caused no end of controversies and confusions—and ought to be restudied in this way. At the moment, I believe, there is no better source for understanding what the eighteenth-century British did denote as "virtue" than the writings of John

Pocock. Like Wood's, however, Pocock's writings are, at once, a proper starting point for further explorations and a fountainhead of difficulties that have
been compounded by his followers and critics.

Some of these confusions, we may hope, are on the way toward resolution. For example, Pocock argued that the central theme of eighteenth-
century British discourse—the fulcrum on which fundamental changes
turned—was its preoccupation with the dangers posed to virtue by the growing role of commerce. This argument became most troublesome when later
writers oversimplified what "commerce" meant in Pocock's formulation, and
much of the confusion might be ended simply by accepting his insistence
that he never said "that republican virtue was incompatible with trade and
industry."[28]

A second difficulty lies, however, in a drumbeat of complaints that Pocock's
monumental works may nonetheless portray the eighteenth century as more
completely classical than was in fact the case. In this complaint, there seems
to me more substance, though, again, a sympathetic critic must remark that
Pocock has himself insisted that his "tunnel" through the eighteenth century
does not exhaust its treasures. *The Machiavellian Moment* reaches back to
Aristotle and ahead to Richard M. Nixon, focusing throughout upon a language used by early modern civic humanists to grapple with the secular or
temporal dimensions of a polity's existence. To this language, Pocock argued,
Locke made little contribution; and the old fixation on the advent and centrality of "modern," "liberal" ideas appeared to him not merely partial but the
principal impediment to understanding that the most important changes in
eighteenth-century thought were generated by a dialogue concerning virtue
and corruption, a dialogue that Locke ignored. But Pocock's effort to construct a history *sans* Locke—a history emancipated from a single-minded,
Whiggish search for a direct, uncomplicated line into the present—seems to
many to create a new imbalance. His recent essays toward a history of two
distinctive, intertwining languages of liberty—one civic humanist, the other
civil jurisprudential—have not attempted, yet, to bring Locke back into the
picture. And despite his warnings that contemporaries did not see these languages "as distinct and ideologically" opposing, the very effort to construct
two separate tunnels may foster an impression that they were.[29] This impression, like a faulty grasp of what the Revolutionaries meant by "virtue," interferes in a variety of ways with our attempt to comprehend the Federalists'
relationship with earlier opinion.

No republic could be truly classical, as Pocock notes, once individuals
receded from a full, direct participation in the public forum and began to be

conceived of as contributing their virtue largely—or exclusively, as some elitists hoped—to the selection of their sovereign rulers. Pocock therefore joins
with Wood and others to remark that Madison accomplished an amazing feat
of intellectual and verbal daring by defining a republic as a government in
which the people *do not* "meet and exercise the government in person," but
"administer it by their representatives and agents."[30] This, these scholars have
remarked, was a direct reversal of the classical or Montesquieuan image of
republics. And, indeed, it was, for Madison not only meant to clarify a crucial difference between the new American republics and the archetypal Grecian cities, he meant to argue unequivocally for the superiority of modern
representative regimes. But still, what seems to have been wholly overlooked
in emphasizing Madison's departure from the ancients is that he departed
not at all from early Revolutionary thinking or its eighteenth-century British
sources. The English-speaking peoples, after all, had made their peace with
representation a hundred years before the American Revolution, whose leaders never thought of anything *except* a representative republic.

Again, in truly classical or Montesquieuan images of the republic, there
was little room, as critics of the Pocock-Wood interpretation sometimes
gleefully announce, for an antithesis of liberty and power. In the polis, the
community's decision had been nothing other than the product of the liberty
and virtue that every citizen contributed to public business. Yet here, again,
as neither Wood nor Pocock really fails to see, the water had been muddied years before by the acceptance of representation and by the influence of
a modern politics of natural rights. In representative, contractual republics,
liberty and power could so easily collide that an insistence on the need for
public virtue often called, more loudly than for any other thing, for vigilance
against the separate interests and ambitions of elected rulers. And for Madison, as clearly as for "Cato," Bolingbroke, or Burgh, a jealous independence of
ambitious rulers still remained a principal requirement for republics.

What may all of this imply? Most fundamentally, perhaps, that we do
not as yet possess the information, terminology, or mental tools that may be
needed to describe the transformation of the early Revolutionary universe
of thought into the thinking of the 1820s. We do not possess these things, in
part, because we cannot clearly see how we should handle the apparent mixture of distinctive modes of discourse which would seem to have been present long before the Revolution opened and, for all the intervening changes,
present also when it closed. While there are solid reasons to distinguish neoclassical and modern-liberal traditions, these would also seem to have been
shaping one another more profoundly than our usual reasoning suggests.

At present, as I understand it, scholarly debates about the modern-liberal and classical republican dimensions of early national thought are entering into a different phase. Through the middle 1980s, controversy focused on the relative importance of the two traditions in the years surrounding the adoption of the Constitution. At this writing, these disputes appear to be resulting in a general agreement (not unanimous, of course) that *both* were present in the new republic (as were other modes of thought), that both were vastly influential, and that neither should be seen as having exercised an undisputed primacy during the 1780s or 1790s.[31] Work proceeds toward understanding how the culture moved through the succeeding decades toward an ultimate predominance of liberal and democratic values, though many would insist that liberal ideas were so entangled at the Revolution with ideas deriving from a different tradition that the consequence would never be the liberal monolith that scholars once described. Ironically, however, we are entering upon this newer exploration in the midst of sharp, continuing disputes about the shape of early Revolutionary thought and, thus, of huge uncertainties about the structure that was in transition. With the starting point uncertain and the outcome in dispute, it has been proving difficult for anyone to write a satisfying history of the developments between.[32] How can we account persuasively for change when there is disagreement over nearly everything except its general direction?

We could start, I would suggest, by recognizing that the current talk of many coexisting paradigms, although a marked improvement over older formulations, is still an analytical invention of our own: useful, even necessary for demolishing inflated claims and for exploring some important topics, but nonetheless an artificial reconstruction of the Revolutionary world; a reconstruction, too, which has a strong potential to mislead because it severs what the eighteenth century joined. We might proceed, in other words, by adding questions that have not received so much attention. How did early Revolutionaries and their eighteenth-century sources manage so coherently to blend traditions which seem incompatible to us? How did later Revolutionaries grapple with this rather awkward combination?

Not long ago, John Murrin called the argument about the "Great Transition"—the movement from a "premodern" to a "modern" society and culture—"the most important controversy taking shape in recent years about early American history."[33] Murrin was referring to the controversy over whether any such transition actually occurred, for it is possible, of course, to argue that America was *always* liberal and modern. Since 1960, nevertheless, the larger portion of the most exciting work in early American history has emphasized the differentness of eighteenth-century life. Most historians, accordingly, would now accept the concept of a Great Transition. Recently, in fact, the growing interest in this transformation has been promising a massive reinterpretation of the years surrounding 1800 as a period of sweeping cultural and social change.[34] In effect, the current generation's rediscovery of the republican tradition, followed by renewed insistence on the liberating novelty of liberal ideas, has led us to perceive the early Revolution as decidedly pre-modern; and this impression has been leading us, in turn, to squeeze the Great Transition more intensively into the early national years (most commonly, into the years between the middle 1790s and the middle 1820s). Rapid social change, on these assumptions, helps account for the increasing dominance of liberal values and ideas, and rapid transformation of political beliefs is used, in turn, as evidence that social change was more intensive in this period than used to be supposed, since most of us are wary of idealist interpretations in which thinking seems to change according to its own dynamic.

Without disputing much of this interpretive thrust, it may be useful to suggest that there are several reasons for discomfort. Are we reasoning in a circle—and a circle, for that matter, which does not produce an accurate description of America at either the beginning of the Revolution or its end? How are we to weigh the impact during any span of years of "a transformation of social perceptions, political judgment, economic endeavor, and private sensibility"[35] that required at least a century for its completion? Was the force and pace of "liberalizing change," as Steven Watts describes it, so intense and so profound at any point within this period that we can pack a revolutionary transformation into any part of it that we may happen to examine— the 1780s, the 1790s, or the years between the middle nineties and the War of 1812?[36] Finally, if early Revolutionary thought was actually more modern than the masterworks of the republican interpretation would suggest, but if James Madison and others also broke less sharply with republican tradition than is commonly supposed, how should narrative historians proceed?

The principal necessity, I think, is for renewed attention to that early Revolutionary blend of modern-liberal and neoclassical concerns, a study which would have to start with further exploration of its origins in seventeenth-century England. A clearer understanding of the early modern mixture present when the Revolution opened is essential to a better understanding of its course. Such an understanding may require, as well, a different perspective on its close.

A recent article by Peter Onuf warns that we are often too inclined to link the Revolutionary reconstruction of political ideas to sweeping, sudden transformations in the social and economic context. The Constitution and the Federalist achievement, this suggests, may after all have been essentially the outcome of a crisis of the union: that is, of the specifically *political* developments connected with the founding of a federal republic.[37] It might be added that we commonly portray the Revolutionary reconstruction of political ideas, dramatic as that was, as in itself more sweeping than some further reconsiderations may support. A dozen years of grappling with James Madison has made me more and more inclined to think that Onuf is correct in calling for a stronger emphasis on the centrality of federal concerns. It has persuaded me, as well, of the advantages of thinking of the great Virginian as a liberal republican through all of his career.

Here, also, it appears, I may be forced to say repeatedly that this is *not* primarily an argument that Madison was philosophically consistent; and it is *not* an argument that his opinions never changed. Yet Madison, who is conventionally (and rightly) seen as the outstanding figure in the Federalist revision of republican ideas, did, after all, almost immediately assume the lead in the formation of the first political party. And Madison did say that after giving all due praise to constitutional contrivances for making liberty secure, "it ought . . . to be remembered that they are neither the sole nor the chief palladium of constitutional liberty. The people, who are the authors of this blessing, must also be its guardians."[38] "To suppose that any form of government will secure liberty or happiness without any virtue in the people is a chimerical idea."[39]

"Virtue," to be sure, did not connote for Madison the superhuman quality that Montesquieu had said was known to moderns "only by tradition."[40] Madison did not believe that men were angels or that the United States was any kind of Sparta. But "virtue" did connote, for Madison as clearly as for eighteenth-century critics of the British Whig regime, a jealous, vigilant commitment to the public life: continuing participation by the body of a democratic people in a politics which trusted only limited responsibilities to national rulers and demanded, even then, that these officials be continuously watched for any signs of an appearance of a separate set of interests. Slothful inattention to the public business or an enervated and debauched indulgence in a merely private life still seemed to Madison to be as dangerous to commonwealths as they had seemed to be to Bolingbroke or Burgh. And Madison insisted, too, as strongly as these British oppositionists had done, that liberty was incompatible with standing armies, overgrown executives, and swollen public debts.[41] If "virtue" did not signify for him what it had signified for Montesquieu or for the ancients, it still undoubtedly denoted most of what it had implied for eighteenth-century British oppositionists and their early Revolutionary heirs.

A better understanding of such terms may therefore be essential if we are to see that Madison did not assume a central place among the Revolutionary thinkers because he was the central figure in the substitution of a modern politics of interest for an ancient politics of virtue. Rather, Madison was most distinctive and most nearly indispensable, I think, because he stubbornly denied that it was necessary for Americans to choose between the two varieties of liberty that were, alike, supremely valued in the Revolutionaries' mixed inheritance from eighteenth-century thought.[42] The most profound of all the founders reasoned in these terms and held to values drawn from both traditions well into the 1830s, though he did so during his retirement in the face of potent tendencies to simplify his generation's thinking and to undervalue its achievements.[43] But a better understanding of the founder and of the ideas that he opposed may both require new explorations of the early modern thinking in which Madison was reared.

Notes

1. Gordon S. Wood, *The Creation of the American Republic, 1776–1787* (Chapel Hill, N.C., 1969); Lance Banning, *The Jeffersonian Persuasion: Evolution of a Party Ideology* (Ithaca, N.Y., 1978); Robert Shalhope, "Toward a Republican Synthesis: The Emergence of an Understanding of Republicanism in American Historiography," *William and Mary Quarterly* 29 (1972): 49–80.

2. Shalhope, "Republicanism and Early American Historiography," *William and Mary Quarterly* 39 (1982): 334–356.

3. Joyce Appleby, "Commercial Farming and the 'Agrarian Myth' in the Early Republic," *Journal of American History* 68 (1982): 833–849, "What Is Still American in the Political Philosophy of Thomas Jefferson?" *William and Mary Quarterly* 39 (1982): 287–309, and *Capitalism and a New Social Order: The Republican Vision of the 1790s* (New York, 1984); Isaac Kramnick, "Republican Revisionism Revisited," *American Historical Review* 87 (1982): 629–664; John Patrick Diggins, *The Lost Soul of American Politics: Virtue, Self-Interest, and the Foundations of Liberalism* (New York, 1985).

4. "Jeffersonian Ideology Revisited: Liberal and Classical Ideas in the New American Republic," *William and Mary Quarterly* 43 (1986): 3–19.

5. See, for example, "Illusions and Disillusions in the American Revolution," in Jack P. Greene, ed., *The American Revolution: Its Character and Limits* (New York, 1987), 358–361, together with the response to critics of *The Creation of the American Republic* cited in note 25 below.

6. Thus Thomas Pangle (*The Spirit of Modern Republicanism: The Moral Vision of the American Founders and the Philosophy of Locke* [Chicago, 1988], 285) read it as a waffling, obfuscating, and apologetic retraction of my earlier position, while James T. Kloppenberg ("The Virtues of Liberalism: Christianity, Republicanism, and Ethics in Early American Political Discourse," *Journal of American History* 74 [1987]: 28, note 27) saw it as excessively contentious and unyielding.

7. In addition to Kloppenberg, "The Virtues of Liberalism," see Forrest McDonald, *Novus Ordo Seclorum: The Intellectual Origins of the Constitution* (Lawrence, Kan., 1985); Kramnick, "The 'Great National Discussion': The Discourse of Politics in 1787," *William and Mary Quarterly* 45 (1988): 3–32; and the letters of Kramnick and J. G. A. Pocock in [*William and Mary Quarterly* 45 (1988)]: 817–818.

8. Four publications were especially influential in initiating the recovery of this tradition: Clinton Rossiter, *Seedtime of the Republic: The Origin of the American Tradition of Political Liberty* (New York, 1953); Caroline Robbins, *The Eighteenth Century Commonwealthman* (Cambridge, Mass., 1959); the second edition of Z. S. Fink, *The Classical Republicans* (Evanston, Ill., 1962); and J. G. A. Pocock, "Machiavelli, Harrington, and English Political Ideologies in the Eighteenth Century," *William and Mary Quarterly* 22 (1965): 549–583.

9. J. G. A. Pocock, *The Machiavellian Moment: Florentine Political Thought and the Atlantic Republican Tradition* (Princeton, 1975).

10. Bernard Bailyn, *The Ideological Origins of the American Revolution* (Cambridge, Mass., 1967).

11. As Linda Kerber put it: "thanks to Shalhope a collection of rather disparate historians have discovered that they were part of a school"; and "as republicanism has widened greatly in usage it is in danger of coming to signify too much and therefore to mean too little" ("The Republican Ideology of the Revolutionary Generation," *American Quarterly* 37 [1985]: 474, 480).

12. Shalhope, "Republicanism and Early American Historiography," is a good review of early neo-progressive and new-left criticisms.

13. The best discussions of the theoretical underpinnings of the new ideological history and of the deterministic pitfalls present in the social-science theories by which it was influenced are in three essays by Joyce Appleby: "Value and Society," in Jack P. Greene and J. R. Pole, eds., *Colonial British America: Essays in the New History of the Early Modern Era* (Baltimore, 1984), 290–316; "Republicanism and Ideology," *American Quarterly* 37 (1985): 461–473; and "Republicanism in Old and New Contexts," *William and Mary Quarterly* 43 (1986): 20–34. See also Ralph Lerner, "The Constitution of the Thinking Revolutionary," in Richard Beeman, Stephen Botein, and Edward C. Carter III, eds., *Beyond Confederation: Origins of the Constitution and American National Identity* (Chapel Hill, N.C., 1987), 38–68.

14. Pocock, in particular, has frequently been charged with making this assertion and seems to me the only major figure against whom the indictment might be made with any plausibility at all. But *The Machiavellian Moment* explicitly says that "the deem-

phasizing of Locke is for the present a tactical necessity. The historical context must be reconstructed without him before he can be fitted back into it" (424; see also 516).

15. Here, also, it is usually *The Machiavellian Moment* which is read this way. I simply do not see why. Forty-six of the 552 pages of this book are devoted to the American experience, the great majority of those to the Revolutionary and Early National periods. The relatively brief reflections on the subsequent course of American history certainly maintain that "even in America, the republic faces the problem of its own ultimate finitude . . . in space and time," and thus that there is "a dimension of historical pessimism in American thought at its most utopian, which stems from the confrontation of virtue and commerce" (541). But to assert the lasting influence of this mode of thought is not to claim that it alone is of substantial interest.

16. Thus, the standard target for the advocates of the republican tradition has been Louis Hartz, *The Liberal Tradition in America: An Interpretation of American Political Thought since the Revolution* (New York, 1955).

17. The quotations are from Kramnick, "Republican Revisionism Revisited," 661–662. The sentence also incorporates my understanding of Appleby's thesis concerning the Jeffersonian Republicans.

18. See "Some Second Thoughts on Virtue and the Course of Revolutionary Thinking," in Terence Ball and J. G. A. Pocock, eds., *Conceptual Change and the Constitution* (Lawrence, Kan., 1988), 194–212; "Quid Transit? Paradigms and Process in the Transformation of Republican Ideas," *Reviews in American History* 17 (1989): 199–204; and my review of Steven Watts, *The Republic Reborn,* in *Georgia Historical Quarterly* 42 (1988): 349–350.

19. These points are elaborated in "Jeffersonian Ideology Revisited."

20. This repetition of points from the article of 1986 may be even more subject to misunderstanding than the article as a whole. Let me add, then, that I do not see them as a flight from the position of *The Jeffersonian Persuasion.* Apart from terminology that I would not employ today, the largest problem with that book now seems to me a title which is more pretentious than the contents. Larger errors of the sort that Appleby and Lerner have discussed were made in my earlier article, "Jeffersonian Ideology and the Triumph of the Constitution, 1789 to 1793," *William and Mary Quarterly* 31 (1974): 167–188.

21. The same, of course, might well be said of references to "liberal" ideas. As Wood has noted, "liberalism," unlike "republicanism," was not a term employed during the revolutionary era; and current usage varies greatly from scholar to scholar. For example, when I write of "liberal republicans," I mean to stress both words and to associate the former with a modern philosophy of inherent individual rights. In counterrevisionary literature, however, "liberal" is often used, in addition, to refer to an ethos of possessive individualism, a bourgeois mentality, an acquisitive, materialistic, self-centered pattern of behavior, and the like. The terminology has come to be so muddled that it makes contemporary sense to write of a republican ethic in a liberal society.

22. I am influenced in this language by Hannah Arendt, *On Revolution* (New York, 1963), and J. H. Hexter, "Republic, Virtue, Liberty, and the Political Universe of J. G. A. Pocock," in *On Historians* (Cambridge, Mass., 1979), 255–303.

23. An early example was Gary J. Schmitt and Robert H. Webking, "Revolutionaries, Antifederalists, and Federalists: Comments on Gordon Wood's Understanding of the American Founding," *Political Science Reviewer* 9 (1979): 195–229. But consider, more recently, Pangle's unrestrained attack on "classical-republican" interpretations in chap. 4 of *The Spirit of Modern Republicanism*, especially his bitter condemnation of Drew R. McCoy's *The Elusive Republic: Political Economy in Jeffersonian America* (Chapel Hill, N.C., 1980). This condemnation is succeeded by a chapter (9) in which Pangle seems to me in close agreement with McCoy's essential points. Pangle's fundamental animus, I think, is more against his view of what he thinks a reference to *classical* republicanism must or should imply than against what really has been said about the new republic. McCoy and other American historians have assumed that it is less important to be clear about the philosophical position of the ancients or the nature of the ancient polis than to understand what Revolutionaries made of ancient history and sources.

24. See, for example, the superb early discussion of the differences between Pocock's civic humanists and truly classical opinions in Jean Yarbrough, "Republicanism Reconsidered: Some Thoughts on the Foundation and Preservation of the American Republic," *Review of Politics* 41 (1979): 61–95. Excellent for recent contributions by political theorists is Peter S. Onuf, "Reflections on the Founding: Constitutional Historiography in Bicentennial Perspective," *William and Mary Quarterly* 45 (1989): 341–375.

25. Most of these remarks are in accord with several of the commentaries in the helpful forum on this modern classic, "*The Creation of the American Republic, 1776–1787*: A Symposium of Views and Reviews," *William and Mary Quarterly* 44 (1987): 549–640. See especially the essays by Ruth H. Bloch, Pauline Maier, John M. Murrin, and Peter S. Onuf, together with Wood's response, "Ideology and the Origins of Liberal America."

26. See "Some Second Thoughts on Virtue," especially 200, 206–207.

27. David Hume was being neither cynical nor novel when he opened his essay "Of the Independency of Parliament" by saying: "Political writers have established it as a maxim, that, in contriving any system of government, and fixing the several checks and controuls of the constitution, every man ought to be supposed a *knave*, and to have no other end, in all his actions, than private interest." The early modern theory of mixed government—and Hume was thinking, first, of Harrington and Machiavelli—*began* from the assumption that the many and the few would each oppress the other if power rested wholly in their hands.

28. *Virtue, Commerce, and History: Essays on Political Thought and History, Chiefly in the Eighteenth Century* (Cambridge, Eng., 1985), 272.

29. See, especially, "The Varieties of Whiggism from Exclusion to Reform: A

History of Ideology and Discourse," ibid., 215–310, and "Cambridge Paradigms and Scotch Philosophers: A Study of the Relations between the Civic Humanist and the Civil Jurisprudential Interpretation of Eighteenth-Century Social Thought," in Istvan Hont and Michael Ignatieff, eds., *Wealth and Virtue: The Shaping of Political Economy in the Scottish Enlightenment* (Cambridge, 1984), 235–252, quotation at page 251.

30. Jacob E. Cooke, ed., *The Federalist* (Middletown, Conn., 1961), no. 14, page 84. See also no. 10, page 62.

31. See note 7 above.

32. "Quid Transit," cited in note 18, argues that this is a problem both for Steven Watts, *The Republic Reborn: War and the Making of Liberal America, 1790–1820* (Baltimore, 1987), and for Michael Lienesch, *New Order of the Ages: Time, the Constitution, and the Making of Modern American Political Thought* (Princeton, 1988).

33. John M. Murrin, "Self-Interest Conquers Patriotism: Republicans, Liberals, and Indians Reshape the Nation," in Greene, ed., *The American Revolution*, 225.

34. See Wood's ambitious effort to reconceptualize the period in "The Significance of the Early Republic," *Journal of the Early Republic* 8 (1988): 1–20. It is worth remarking that of all Wood's recent writings, this essay may contain the strongest stress on the "classical," anti-commercial, or anti-modern features of Revolutionary thinking (11–12). But see "Interests and Disinterestedness in the Making of the Constitution" (*Beyond Confederation*, 69–109), which also seems to me a significant revision of the position of *The Creation of the American Republic.*

35. Watts, *The Republic Reborn*, 6.

36. This may become even harder in the aftermath of Jack P. Greene, *Pursuits of Happiness: The Social Development of Early Modern British Colonies and the Formation of American Culture* (Chapel Hill, N.C., 1988), which mounts a powerful challenge to the prevailing emphasis on the differentness of eighteenth-century life and values.

37. Onuf, "Reflections on the Founding."

38. "Government of the United States," in William T. Hutchinson, Robert A. Rutland, et al., eds., *The Papers of James Madison*, 16 vols. to date (Chicago and Charlottesville, Va., 1962–), 14:218 (originally published in the *National Gazette*, February 4, 1792).

39. Speech in the Virginia Ratifying Convention of 1788, in Jonathan Elliot, ed., *The Debates in the Several State Conventions on the Adoption of the Federal Constitution . . . ,* (Washington, D.C., 1854), 5 vols., 3:536–537.

40. *The Spirit of the Laws*, bk. 3, chap. 5.

41. Before as well as after Hamilton delivered his reports on public credit. See, for example, his speech of June 29 in Max Farrand, ed., *The Records of the Federal Convention of 1787*, rev. ed., 4 vols. (New Haven, Conn., 1966), 1:464–465; *Federalist*, No. 41, 273–274; and Elliot, *Debates*, 3:382.

42. This argument, currently being developed in a book on Madison and the Founding, is sketched more fully in three essays: "James Madison and the National-

ists, 1780–1783," *William and Mary Quarterly* 40 (1983): 237–255; "The Hamiltonian Madison: A Reconsideration," *Virginia Magazine of History and Biography* 92 (1984): 3–28; and "1787 and 1776: Patrick Henry, James Madison, the Constitution, and the Revolution," in Neil L. York, ed., *Toward a More Perfect Union: Six Essays on the Constitution* (Provo, Utah, 1988), 59–89.

43. Drew R. McCoy, *The Last of the Fathers: James Madison and the Republican Legacy* (Cambridge, Eng., 1989).

Some Second Thoughts on Virtue and the Course of Revolutionary Thinking

Opponents of the Constitution, one of its supporters said, supposed that Congress would abuse its trust as often as it could.

> If this were a reasonable supposition, their objections would be good. I consider it reasonable to conclude that they will as readily do their duty as deviate from it; nor do I go on the grounds mentioned by gentlemen on the other side—that we are to place unlimited confidence in [national officials] and expect nothing but the most exalted integrity and sublime virtue. But I go on this great republican principle: that the people will have virtue and intelligence to select men of virtue and wisdom. Is there no virtue among us? If there be not, we are in a wretched situation. No theoretical checks, no form of government, can render us secure. To suppose that any form of government will secure liberty or happiness without any virtue in the people is a chimerical idea.[1]

The sentiment may sound conventional enough, but something, surely, is amiss. The stage for these remarks was the Virginia state convention. The speaker was James Madison. And it is Madison on whom we customarily rely for an insistence that the Federalists were moved by a pervasive fear of a *collapse* of virtue, Madison to whom a host of analysts have turned in order to support discussions of a new republican regime "which did not require a virtuous people for its sustenance."[2]

A little ingenuity, of course, can handle this apparent contradiction. Some interpreters might simply brush the speech aside as a debater's ploy or an anomalous intrusion of an older mode of thought into a changing situation, though they would also have to sweep aside some other statements in which Madison apparently affirms that even an enlarged republic must rest on virtue.[3] Other analysts might argue that the speech concedes no more than that the people have to know to whom they should defer, which was to drain the Revolutionary concept of its content. Here again, however, there are many passages in which Madison makes it clear that he did not envision a republic in which popular participation would be limited to choosing proper rulers.[4] A better strategy, accordingly, might follow Gordon S. Wood, who makes two subtle points that have been often overlooked. In the first place, Wood describes a Madison who was, at once, a pioneer of modern thinking and a thinker who did not depart as far from eighteenth-century patterns as some of his contemporaries did.[5] In the second, Wood observes that the depreciation of the need for virtue was as yet "sporadic," "premature," and less the current rule than the beginning "of a fundamental shift in thought."[6] Although Wood identifies the explanation and defense of the completed Constitution as a vital moment in the substitution of a politics of interest for a politics of virtue, he is well aware that this was not a moment's work. John Pocock chose his words with care when he suggested that it was "less in contradiction than in correction" (or perhaps in amplification) that I and others tracked the influence of the older values and concerns into the new republic, where Jeffersonians and Federalists continued to pursue the old antithesis of virtue and corruption.[7]

But it is not my purpose here to recapitulate the current controversy over liberal and classical dimensions of early nineteenth-century thinking.[8] Rather, I propose a tentative, decidedly preliminary effort to articulate some thoughts about another worry that has troubled me increasingly for several years. For there is yet another possibility inherent in the way that Madison's remarks seem radically at odds with dominant interpretations of the movement of republican opinion. It is possible that we have not precisely understood or have not precisely managed to convey what even early Revolutionaries meant by "virtue"—early Revolutionaries and their eighteenth-century sources. And if this is so, then we have pushed our pens into a thicket of confusions that might best be cleared away by clarifying eighteenth-century usage of this term.

Since *The Creation of the American Republic*, "virtue" has become an organizing theme for histories of Revolutionary thinking. In this masterwork itself, Wood tells us that the colonists' decision to declare their independence was related to their fear that they could not remain a free and healthy people if they continued to be bound to a corrupt and corrupting Britain. Independence was simultaneously a grim necessity, in order to defend the virtue that was threatened in a myriad of ways by the connection with Great Britain, and a revolutionary opportunity to buttress liberty and to achieve regeneration as a people by creating new republics, which would rest upon and nurture the impressive public spirit that had been displayed in the American resistance.

Americans, Wood says, did not embark upon their revolutionary enterprise without some reservations. While the people's spirited defense of liberty suggested that they were, indeed, "the stuff" of which "republicans are made," there were already many signs of "luxury and corruption"; virtue was, almost by definition, rare and constantly endangered.[9] On balance, nonetheless, the striking fact about the early Revolution was the optimistic faith with which its leaders looked to the regenerative powers of republics, trusted in the people's virtue, and anticipated countless benefits from the creation of an order in which office would depend exclusively on talent and elections. Thus, the story of the movement of elite opinion from the Declaration of Independence to the Constitution can be told, to a significant degree, in terms of a progressive testing of this faith. The disillusionment and discontents resulting from the final weary years of war and from the local legislation that was prompted by the postwar economic troubles were fundamental to the movement for a sweeping alteration of the federal system. The times seemed full of faction, indolence, extravagance, and dissipation. The failure of the people to display the public spirit on which all republics were assumed to rest produced a crisis of the Revolution. The reformers felt compelled to make and justify a new political arrangement that would guarantee good government "'even in the absence of political virtue,' . . . to establish a republican government even though the best social science of the day declared that the people were incapable of sustaining it."[10]

In *The Jeffersonian Persuasion*, I suggested, in effect, that Wood may have gone too far in his discussion of the early Revolutionary break with eighteenth-century constitutional opinion, as well as in his early dating of an end of classical concerns.[11] I nevertheless accepted—and I still accept— the fundamental thrust of his interpretation, along with most of its details. I still believe that *The Creation of the American Republic* is the proper starting point for subsequent discussions, that Wood is much more nearly right than wrong in his description of the course of Revolutionary thinking. But if he swings the pendulum too far, there may be aspects of the book that have contributed to current controversies and confusions: the paradigm may need repairs. This, indeed, now seems to me the case. There are some passages in *The Creation* that suggest—or, at the least, have frequently been taken to imply—that early Revolutionaries meant by "virtue" something more than, and different from, what I believe that most of them were saying. And especially when Wood's sophisticated presentation is compacted by his followers and critics, we can easily become entangled in a serious misunderstanding, both of early Revolutionary thought and of the Federalists' departures from new and old traditions.[12]

Wood himself is undeniably a careful, subtle analyst of "virtue"—so much so that I will often be objecting less to his discussion than to how he has been read. I do not intend, by any means, to quarrel with the burden of his comments: "Frugality, industry, temperance, and simplicity—the rustic traits of the sturdy yeoman—were the stuff that made a society strong. The virile martial qualities—the scorn of ease, the contempt of danger, the love of valor— were what made a nation great." What sickened it was luxury. "The love of refinement, the desire for distinction and elegance eventually weakened a people and left them soft and effeminate, dissipated cowards, unfit and undeserving to serve the state. 'Then slumbers that virtuous jealousy of public men and public measures, which was wont to scrutinize not only actions but motives: then nods that active zeal, which, with eagle eye watched, and with nervous arm defended the constitution.'"[13]

This paragraph repays repeated reading for the clarity with which it captures the association of "virtue" with "virility" and "vigilance," which were among its closest synonyms, and places it in opposition to a fear of softness, effeminacy, and slumber, which were antonyms attributed most commonly to the debilitating spread of luxury and refinement.[14] Every specialist has taken pains to warn against the feminine associations that "virtue" has acquired since Revolutionary times. And yet there still remains a strong temptation to associate the word with self-surrender, a temptation that is easy to give in to as we read the sentences that follow. "The sacrifice of individual interests to the greater good of the whole formed the essence of republicanism," Wood writes, "and comprehended for Americans the idealistic goal of their Revolution. . . . By 1776 the Revolution came to represent a final attempt, perhaps—given the nature of American society—even a desperate attempt, . . . to realize the traditional Commonwealth ideal of a corporate society, in which the common good would be the only objective of government." In a republic, the people were to be conceived of as

> a single organic piece . . . with a unitary concern that was the only legitimate objective of governmental policy. This common interest

was not . . . simply the sum or consensus of the particular interests that made up the community. It was rather an entity in itself,
prior to and distinct from the various private interests of groups and
individuals.

    . . . Ideally, Republicanism obliterated the individual.

    In a monarchy each man's desire to do what was right in his own
eyes could be restrained by fear or force. In a republic, however, each
man must somehow be persuaded to submerge his personal wants
into the greater good of the whole. This willingness of the individual
to sacrifice his private interests for the good of the community—
such patriotism or love of country—the eighteenth century termed
"public virtue."[15]

This language seems to me more problematic. On the one hand, it imparts
a graphic sense of the American rejection of "the base remains" of a hereditary
order, the Revolutionary faith in the capacity of democratic polities to make the
world anew.[16] Early Revolutionaries did contrast the unity of interests among
a democratic people, as well as the identity of interests between the people and
their rulers, with the divisiveness and irresponsibility of aristocrats and kings.
They did expect abundant benefits from the creation of a new political society
in which no individual or group would have either a permanent, hereditary
place in government or a persistent interest that was necessarily distinct from
that of others. On the other hand, we ought to keep it constantly and firmly
fixed in mind that eighteenth-century talk about public virtue and corruption
started—for most Anglophones at least—with a profound commitment to a
mixed or balanced constitution, a commitment that *assumed* that individuals
and groups possess potentially conflicting interests and will take advantage of
opponents if they can. Eighteenth-century British advocates of balanced constitutions did not deny that conduct will relate to selfish interests. This, they
thought, is why men need a government to start with; it is also why no government except a balanced one is likely to assure the good of all. Thus, it seems to
me that Carter Braxton's often-quoted doubt that any people could display "a
disinterested attachment to the public good, exclusive and independent of all
private and selfish interest," might best be taken to deny what very few Americans would ever have affirmed.[17] Plainly, the majority of Revolutionary leaders
disagreed with Thomas Paine's conclusion that the simplest form of government is best. Plainly, too, there was a great deal in their heritage, as well as in
the context of their lives, that warned them that it was impossible, in theory or
in practice, to dissociate men's conduct from their interests.

Remember Harrington's discussion of the serving girls and the division of the cake? In order to divide it fairly, one (who represents the few) will cut the pieces; the other (symbolizing, in this case, the many) will choose between the parts.[18] Equity results from a decision in which each *asserts* her interest but does so in the knowledge that the other must agree. Each pursues her interest knowing that she has to take the other's interest and the other's power into account. The common good emerges as a mutually respectful act of two autonomous, inherently self-interested people. Indeed, in the tradition for which Harrington was an important source, to act politically in terms of someone else's interests, rather than one's own—as servants, it was thought, would necessarily reflect the wishes of their masters—was corrupt. The citizen was self-reliant and assertive. He was expected to contribute to political decisions precisely on the basis of his independent understanding of his needs, choosing what is good for him as well as for the whole. He was not expected to *surrender* his particular self-interest. Instead, he was thought of as pursuing his particular desires while still remaining conscious of the interests of his peers and of participating in a collectivity of equals. Quoting Revolutionary sources, Wood conveys this process neatly when he writes: "Every one must consult his neighbour's happiness, as well as his own," and "each individual gives up all private interest that is not consistent with the general good, the interest of the whole body."[19] Where Wood has emphasized the sacrifice, however, I would call renewed attention to the self who must perform it.

What, then, did the Revolutionaries usually intend by their repeated calls for the sacrifice of selfish interests, for a commitment to the public good (for these were not less prominent than Wood suggests)? Not, if I am right thus far, a generally disinterested pursuit of general needs, not the continuous foreswearing of personal self-interest. On the contrary, a vigorous and vigilant defense of one's own liberties and interests, as several of the quoted sources say, was an essential characteristic of the republican citizen; it was his contribution of his virtue to the public. Far from demanding that a man forget himself and think only of the public, Revolutionary thinkers ordinarily assumed that citizens neither could nor should act selflessly.[20] The Revolutionary thinkers expected individuals to differ, clash, and even threaten one another's rights—especially if they were rulers. This helps to explain why most of them rejected simple forms of government and wanted bills of rights. The great departure that the Revolutionaries made from eighteenth-century thinking was not to call for, or expect, a conscious and continuing self-abnegation, but, instead, to conclude that in a polity that did not have legal and hereditary distinctions, no individual or group could have a *permanent* interest that was distinguishable from the well-considered interest of all. Individuals, who would inevitably assert their personal demands when making political decisions, might mistake the public good; but none could possibly escape involvement in the public fate, and none should ever forget that the public fate would be his own.

Commitment to the public good meant vigilant, continuous attention to the public life. It meant, as well, submission to the will of the community—obedience to law—and this submission had to be a conscious, voluntary act, because sound republics were assumed to be incapable of rigorous, continuing coercion.[21] In these senses, "self-immersion," if we understand that term to mean absorption in one's private goods to the neglect of public duty, *was* profoundly dangerous to a republic. In these senses, individual desires and private interests would clearly have to be "subordinated" to the public interest, even "sacrificed" to public needs. And in these senses, too, the individual's particular desires must certainly give way to the decisions and demands of the community, which might call upon a man to sacrifice his property or, in a war, his life itself, to public needs or wishes. But the sacrifice of self was to occur primarily in an individual's submission to community decisions or in taking time from personal enjoyments and pursuits in order to attend to public business. It would seldom happen in the *making* of political decisions, where citizens would be "restrained" by the consciousness of others, but where they neither should nor could "forego" their own self-interests.

These distinctions, I believe, are critical to understanding the development of Revolutionary thinking. They suggest that Wood exaggerated the degree to which the early Revolutionaries held a fully classical, perhaps a Montesquieuan, concept of the public good in a republic and that he then exaggerated the degree to which the Federalists rejected early Revolutionary thinking. In part, perhaps, because his presentation tended to abstract "the Whig science of politics"—the concerns that were most characteristic of eighteenth-century British oppositions—from the commitment to theories of balanced government, in which they were embedded, his discussion may have under-emphasized the contemporary recognition of the inherently self-interested nature of man. He may have gone too far toward reading in a call for "selflessness" where early Revolutionaries really hoped for vigorous assertions of the self within a context of communal consciousness and a willingness to live by the community's decisions. He may thus have left too little room for comprehending Madison's continued insistence on the indispensability of virtue.[22]

In none of this, again, is it my purpose to reject the central thrust of Wood's interpretation. I do not deny that Revolutionary thinking changed in much the manner that Wood describes or that the Constitution was a product of a crisis of republican convictions. I argue, rather, that this crisis can be better understood, confusions cleared away, and needless controversies partially resolved by clarifying what it was that late and early Revolutionaries meant by "virtue," what was classical and what was not classical in this conception and what was changing over time. Here I need to turn again to Pocock—always hoping, to be sure, that I have read him correctly.

Pocock says that classical republicanism and its early-modern derivatives viewed the republic as a means of associating and combining the particular virtues of distinguishable types of men in such a fashion that the particular virtues of each must contribute to a common pursuit of a general good. Each individual attains his highest good—becomes most fully human—by contributing his virtue to decisions in which he is simultaneously restrained by and aware of the power and the virtue of others. Sound republican decisions are cooperative—rather like the girls' division of the cake. They are reached in such a way that every citizen is conscious both of ruling and of being ruled, of being one of a community of equals, of contributing his fallible opinion to a process in which every judgment will be checked by others. Virtue is a matter both of an autonomous participation in community decisions and of according due authority to the virtue of others. For eighteenth-century Englishmen—indeed, for Harrington himself—this often meant electing those distinguished by their superior wisdom, talents, and public service.[23]

Persistent ambiguities or tensions, Pocock notes, were present in these concepts; and I suspect that these inherent tensions grew more tense as eighteenth-century Anglophones adjusted to the rise of commerce and incorporated a contractual component in their thinking. The individual was not a citizen, according to civic-humanist opinion, unless he was pursuing his particular good in a public forum; and yet, the subordination of the public good to his particular desires, absorption in his private interests to the point of losing sight of what was universal, was corrupt. The citizen might be conceived of, Pocock writes, either as an Athenian or as a Spartan; but the relationship between the private and the public was always problematic. Paradoxically, moreover, because the citizen was always thought of as at once deferring to and receiving deference from his fellows, as a member either of the many or of the few, and sometimes either as a ruler or as a subject, citizenship was always thought of as an equal relationship between unequals.[24]

Pocock considers Wood to be correct—and so do I—when Wood maintains that the Federalists, in completing the rejection of the concept of a people who could be qualitatively differentiated into social groups, severely modified the eighteenth-century concepts of deference and civic virtue. A civic-humanist conception of the citizen in a republic was so intimately tied to the idea of mutual deference between the many and the few, each of which possessed distinctive virtues, that demands for virtue called for something rather different as the American Revolution progressed. Democratic citizens were not expected to identify the different virtues of contrasting social groups, nor were they expected to contribute differentially according to their different social personalities—except, perhaps, in the relationship between electors and elected.[25] Thus, a truly classical conception of the virtue of the citizen broke down. "If the people could not be differentiated into separately-characterized groups," Pocock writes, "there could be no ascribing to them that higher virtue of respecting (or, if you like, deferring to) the virtues of others who in their turn defer, which is at the root of both the Polybian concept of mixed government and the Aristotelian concept of citizenship.... An undifferentiated people could not be a virtuous people" in this sense.[26]

And yet, as Pocock quickly notes, there was a great deal more to eighteenth-century talk of virtue than the concept of mutual deference between the many and the few—which itself, as Wood has recently repeated, continued to perform a central role in Federalist conceptions of relationships between the people and the sort of men who were best qualified to lead them.[27] "Deeply entrenched in eighteenth-century agrarian classicism," Pocock writes, "was an image of the human personality, at once intensely autonomous and intensely participatory," which "staked everything on a positive and civic concept of the individual's virtue."[28] "If Americans had been compelled to abandon a theory of constitutional humanism which related the personality to government directly and according to its diversities, they had not thereby given up the pursuit of a form of political society in which the individual might be free and know himself in his relation to society."[29]

We can go a good deal further, though in doing so it may be necessary to depart significantly from Pocock as well as from Wood. We might remark that even in the eighteenth century, opposition calls for virtue were seldom (at least overtly) calls for mutual deference. "'Virtue,'" Pocock writes, "consisted as much in the civic independence of the arms-bearing freeholder from private patron or governmental interest, as of his membership in one of a hierarchy of orders who respected and deferred to one another."[30] "Autonomy, and virtue, [were assumed to] rest on material as well as moral prerequisites," both of which were thought to be endangered by the instruments of oligarchic rule: standing armies, patronage, and public debts.[31] Condemnations of corruption were, in largest part, denunciations of this system: condemnations of the multiple dependencies that it forged, of its misuse of public treasure, of the degeneration of the balanced constitution, of the killing enervation and quiescence fostered by the unearned luxury with which it favored some at the expense of the impoverishment of many. In all these ways, the oligarchic system undermined the economic preconditions and the moral spirit that were necessary if the citizen was to contribute independently to public life; the system corrupted the gainers and the losers, both of whom might be "demoralized by an exclusive concern with private or group satisfactions."[32] Virtue, for the eighteenth-century British opposition, lay especially in independence from this system and in vigilance against it; and much of what the early Revolutionaries sought was the replacement of the system by a polity and a social order free from the dependencies that it entailed. Men might still be different and unequal in their faculties and possessions, but every citizen would be autonomous in his participation in the public life.

Autonomous participation in the public sphere, awareness of one's membership in a community of equals, a self-denying spirit to resist immersion in the private life of acquisition and enjoyment—all were elements of early Revolutionary or of eighteenth-century opposition talk about public virtue. But—it bears repeating—there was little in this talk that clearly called for self-effacing, totally disinterested regard for an abstracted general good, little to suggest that citizens' decisions would or should be made without consideration for their interests, and little to suggest a Spartan uniformity of individual conditions. A balanced government was necessary to control men's differences, no less than to conjoin their virtues, and a qualified assertion of self-interest was demanded even in the antithesis of virtue and corruption. The dependent man was not a citizen because it was another's interests, rather than his own, from which he had to act. Self-interest was to be restrained by a regard for the community and for one's peers. It was to be restrained, additionally, by voluntary willingness to sacrifice one's private interests to community decisions, by obedience to laws, by consciousness of being ruled as well as ruling. But it would always enter into every individual's decisions, and those decisions would be made, we need to note, within the confines of a *representative* governmental system.

All these points, it seems to me, bear stressing. All are necessary if we are to understand how different even early Revolutionary thinking was from classical conceptions of the citizen and the polis or from Montesquieu's discussion of the spirit of republics.[33] Here, however, Pocock's writings, much like Wood's, present some difficulties that have been compounded by his followers and critics. Even as Pocock's writings serve—again like Wood's—as an essential starting point for further explorations, they contain some themes that can engender serious confusion when we think about the Federalist achievement and about the Federalists' departures from prevailing modes of eighteenth-century thought.

One of these confusions, we may hope, is on its way to resolution. Pocock argued that the central theme of eighteenth-century British discourse—the fulcrum on which fundamental changes turned—was its preoccupation with the dangers posed to virtue by the growing role of commerce. This argument became most troublesome when later writers oversimplified what "commerce" means in such a formulation, and much of the confusion might be ended simply by accepting Pocock's warning that he never said "that republican virtue was [considered] incompatible with trade and industry."[34]

A second difficulty lies, however, in recurring protests that Pocock's monumental works portray the eighteenth century as more consistently and more fully classical than was in fact the case. In this complaint, there seems to me to be more substance, although we ought to bear in mind that Pocock has himself insisted that his "tunnel" through the eighteenth century does not exhaust its treasures. *The Machiavellian Moment* reaches back to Aristotle and ahead to Richard M. Nixon, focusing throughout upon a language that early-modern westerners used in order to grapple with the secular or temporal dimensions of their polities' existence. To this language, Pocock argued, Locke made little contribution, and the old fixation on the advent and centrality of "modern," "liberal" ideas appeared to him to be not merely partial but also the principal impediment to understanding that the most important changes in received ideas were generated by a dialogue concerning virtue and corruption, a dialogue that Locke ignored. But Pocock's effort to construct a history sans Locke—a history that would be emancipated from a single-minded "Whiggish" search for a direct, uncomplicated line into the present—seems to many to create a new imbalance. His recent essays toward a history of two distinctive, intertwining languages of liberty—one civic humanist, the other civil jurisprudential—have not attempted, yet, to bring Locke back into the picture. And despite his warnings that contemporaries did not see these languages "as distinct and ideologically" opposing, the very effort to construct two separate tunnels—necessary and defensible as it may be—may foster an impression that they were.[35] This impression interferes in a variety of ways with our attempt to comprehend the Federalists' relationship with earlier opinion.

No republic could be fully classical, as Pocock notes, once individuals had receded from their full, direct participation in the public forum and had begun to be conceived of as contributing their virtue largely—or exclusively, as some elitists hoped—to the selection of their sovereign rulers. Pocock therefore joins with Wood and others to remark that Madison accomplished an amazing feat of intellectual and verbal daring when he redefined republics as governments in which the people *do not* "meet and exercise the government in person" but "administer it by their representatives and agents."[36] This was to turn the classical, or Montesquieuan, image of republics nearly on its head. It not only recognized and clarified a difference between the new American republics and the archetypal Grecian cities; it opted unequivocally for the superiority of modern representative regimes.[37] And yet, what seems to have been wholly overlooked in emphasizing Madison's departure from the ancients is that he departed not at all from early Revolutionary views. The English-speaking peoples, after all, had made their peace with this concession to modernity a hundred years before the American Revolution, whose early leaders never planned on anything *except* a representative republic. And Madison, in turn, was hardly casting off the Anglophonic civic-humanist tradition when he praised this modern innovation. Thus, when we remark that Thomas Jefferson regretted the departure from the ancients far enough to sketch his scheme for ward democracies, which would allow for greater popular participation, we also ought to note that Madison's rejection of a wholly national regime, along with his elaboration of a theory in which representatives were not to be conceived of as sovereign, can also be regarded as attempts to limit the concession that modernity required.[38] It will be helpful, too, to note that even Jefferson admitted that his countrymen would never be content with Spartan portions of "a double mess of porridge."[39]

Again, in truly classical, or Montesquieuan, images of the republic, there was little room, as critics of the Pocock-Wood interpretation sometimes gleefully announce, for an antithesis of liberty and power. In the polis, the community's decision could be nothing other than the product of the liberty and the virtue that every citizen contributed to public business. But here, too, as neither Wood nor Pocock really fails to see, the water had been muddied many years before by the acceptance of representation and by the influence of a modern politics of natural rights. In representative, contractual republics, liberty and power could so easily collide that an insistence on the need for public virtue often called, more loudly than for any other thing, for vigilance against the separate interests and ambitions of elected rulers.

John Adams wrote: "Mankind have been . . . injured by insinuations that a certain celestial virtue, more than human, has been necessary to preserve liberty. . . . The best republics will be virtuous and have been so, but we may hazard a conjecture that the virtues have been the effect of the well ordered constitution rather than the cause. And perhaps it would be impossible to prove that a republic cannot exist even among highwaymen by setting one rogue to watch another; and the knaves themselves may in time be made honest men by the struggle."[40] How many times have we reverted to this passage or to Hamilton's denial of the possibility of Spartan virtue in order to explain the movement of American opinion? How often have we noted Madison's insistence on the differences between the classical democracies and modern representative republics? And yet, like Carter Braxton, Hamilton and Adams may have been rejecting concepts that few Americans had ever held; and Montesquieu's discussion of republics may have been most useful to the Revolutionaries, as they groped toward a clearer understanding of the character of citizens who might be capable of public life, while still being plainly modern. Even in the first full flush of Revolutionary optimism, I submit, only a minority of the Revolutionaries ever hoped for superhuman, self-effacing, and totally disinterested participation in political affairs—in other words, for Montesquieu's heroic virtue. On the other hand, however, the need for virtue—if we use the word without these connotations—may have been denied by just as few when the Revolutionaries faced the crisis of the postwar years.

At this point, if I am right, we should be able to revert to Madison's remarks at the Virginia state convention, prepared to understand more clearly what he had in mind. For Madison, I would suggest, the really frightening conclusions of the postwar years did not result from a discovery (or a rediscovery) that men were factious, that they are often tempted to pursue their selfish interests at other men's expense.[41] With very few exceptions, I suspect—and it is possible that these exceptions might be found primarily among New England's most enthusiastic Christians—English-speaking politicians never did count much on a disinterested attention to the public good (not, at least, among the body of the people). With few exceptions, too, most Revolutionaries knew that their societies did not suggest—and should not seek—a Spartan uniformity of interests. The crisis came, for Madison at least, when he was forced to recognize that under poorly balanced constitutions, the majority itself could be a "faction," willing and imposing policies that were persistently at odds with private rights or long-term public needs, and when an armed minority resisted the majority in Massachusetts. In Shays' Rebellion and in many other things, Madison indeed saw many signs of insufficient virtue, and these were all the more alarming at a time when liberty and union both appeared to be at risk. Too many people seemed to lack any regard for their relationship with others, to be neglectful of the public business, or to be unwilling to submit themselves to the community's decisions.[42] But the solution did not lie, as Madison conceived it, in denying the necessity of virtue or in doubting that the body of the people possessed enough virtue to maintain the Revolutionary order. The solution could be found in an enlarged compound republic, in governmental mechanisms that were calculated to impose additional restraints on passion, and in governmental policies that would correct the economic difficulties that were at the source of moral and political malaise. A flood of foreign luxuries, together with restricted foreign markets for domestic goods, was threatening the economic preconditions of a virtuous participation in the public life, making citizens incapable of looking further than their hardships or their wants. But if these constitutional and economic weaknesses could be repaired, the people's underlying virtue could be reasserted.[43]

"Virtue," to be sure, did not connote to Madison the superhuman quality that Hamilton and Adams mocked. Madison did not believe that men were angels, nor did he imagine that the United States was any kind of Sparta. But if few Americans had ever held a "Montesquieuan" concept of republican society, then Madison was rejecting early Revolutionary concepts less decisively than has been thought.

When Madison insisted on the indispensability of virtue, he plainly meant, as Wood and Pocock both suggest, a certain deference by the many to the few: a recognition of and a preference for the public-minded, wiser men who were best qualified to lead. For Madison, moreover, this elective, wholly natural aristocracy—to use a term that he himself consistently avoided—would continually defer, in turn, to popular opinion, although, again, these terms are inappropriate for representatives who were to come entirely *from* the body of the people.[44] Nor was even this the whole of what he meant when he insisted on the need for virtue. "Virtue" also meant, for Madison as clearly as for eighteenth-century critics of the British Whig regime, a jealous, vigilant commitment to the public life: continuing participation in a politics that trusted only limited responsibilities to national officials and demanded, even so, that these officials be continuously watched for any signs of an appearance of a separate set of interests. Slothful inattention to the public business and an enervated and debauched indulgence in a merely private life still seemed to Madison to be as dangerous to commonwealths as they had ever seemed to Bolingbroke or Burgh. And Madison insisted too, as strongly as these neo-Harringtonians had done, that liberty was incompatible with standing armies, overgrown executives, and swollen public debts.[45] If "virtue" did not signify for Madison what it had signified for Montesquieu, for Rousseau, or for the ancients, it still undoubtedly denoted most of what it had implied for eighteenth-century British oppositions and their early Revolutionary heirs. For most Americans, this may have been its most essential meaning all along.

Notes

I wrote this essay while a fellow at the National Humanities Center. I am deeply grateful to the center for its generous support and for the seminars and private talks in which the other fellows criticized an early draft and taught me much about republicanism in its many different contexts.

1. Jonathan Elliot, ed., *The Debates in the Several State Conventions on the Adoption of the Federal Constitution . . .* , 5 vols. (Washington, D.C., 1854), 3:536–537.

2. Gordon S. Wood, *The Creation of the American Republic, 1776–1787* (Chapel Hill: University of North Carolina Press, 1969), 475.

3. See Jacob E. Cooke, ed., *The Federalist* (Middletown, Conn.: Wesleyan University Press, 1961), no. 55, page 378; no. 57, page 387: "As there is a degree of depravity in mankind which requires a certain degree of circumspection and distrust: So there are other qualities in human nature, which justify a certain portion of esteem and confidence. Republican government presupposes the existence of these qualities in a higher degree than any other form. Were the pictures which have been drawn by the political jealousy of some among us, faithful likenesses of the human character, the inference would be that there is not sufficient virtue among men for self-government; and that nothing less than the chains of despotism can restrain them from destroying and devouring one another." What will prevent the national representatives from passing inequitous or dangerous laws? "I answer . . . above all the vigilant and manly spirit which actuates the people of America, a spirit which nourishes freedom, and in return is nourished by it. If this spirit shall ever be so far debased as to tolerate a law not obligatory on the Legislature as well as on the people, the people will be prepared to tolerate anything but liberty."

4. The clearest examples of Madison's insistence on a continuing role for popular participation and public opinion came after 1789, especially in his essays for the *National Gazette*, but I am prepared to argue that he articulated here assumptions that had guided him throughout the 1780s. See the essays on "Consolidation," "Public Opinion," "Government," "Charters," and especially "Government of the United States": "In bestowing the eulogies due to the partitions and internal checks of power, it ought not the less to be remembered, that they are neither the sole nor the chief palladium of constitutional liberty. The people, who are the authors of this blessing, must also be its guardians. Their eyes must be ever ready to mark, their voice to pronounce, and their arm to repel or repair aggressions on the authority of their constitutions." Relevant passages can be found in William T. Hutchinson, Robert A. Rutland, et al.,

eds., *The Papers of James Madison* (Chicago: University of Chicago Press, 1962–), 14:138–139, 178, 179, 192, 218; see also David F. Epstein's argument that Madison as "Publius" assumed continuous participation, in *The Political Theory of "The Federalist"* (Chicago: University of Chicago Press, 1984), 195 and passim.

5. See, esp., Wood, *Creation of the American Republic,* 411–413, 501–506.

6. Ibid., 612.

7. *The Political Works of James Harrington,* ed. J. G. A. Pocock (Cambridge, Eng.: Cambridge University Press, 1977), 150.

8. For this see Banning, "Jeffersonian Ideology Revisited: Liberal and Classical Ideas in the New American Republic," *William and Mary Quarterly,* 3d ser., 43 (1986): 3–19; Joyce Appleby, "Republicanism in Old and New Contexts," ibid., 20–34; John Ashworth, "The Jeffersonians: Classical Republicans or Liberal Capitalists?" *Journal of American Studies* 18 (1984): 425–435; and James T. Kloppenberg, "The Virtues of Liberalism: Christianity, Republicanism, and Ethics in Early American Political Discourse," *Journal of American History* 74 (1987): 9–33.

9. Wood, *Creation of the American Republic,* 93.

10. Ibid., 429. The primary quotation here is not from Madison, although the text and compound footnote may leave that impression.

11. Lance Banning, *The Jeffersonian Persuasion: Evolution of a Party Ideology* (Ithaca, N.Y.: Cornell University Press, 1978), 84–90 and chap. 4.

12. I think this may be clearly seen in John Patrick Diggins, *The Lost Soul of American Politics: Virtue, Self-Interest, and the Foundations of Liberalism* (New York: Basic Books, 1984), and in two excellent articles by John T. Agresto: "Liberty, Virtue, and Republicanism: 1776–1787," *Review of Politics* 39 (1977): 473–504, and "'A System without a Precedent'—James Madison and the Revolution in Republican Liberty," *South Atlantic Quarterly* 82 (1983): 129–144.

13. Wood, *Creation of the American Republic,* 52.

14. On this point see also Edmund S. Morgan, "The Puritan Ethic and the American Revolution," *William and Mary Quarterly,* 3d ser., 24 (1967): 1–43.

15. Wood, *Creation of the American Republic,* 53–54, 58, 61, 68.

16. "Common Sense," in *The Complete Writings of Thomas Paine,* ed. Philip S. Foner, 2 vols. (New York: 1945), 1:6–9 and below. A superb discussion of this pamphlet is Bernard Bailyn's "Common Sense," in *Fundamental Testaments of the American Revolution,* Library of Congress Symposia on the American Revolution no. 2 (Washington, D.C.: 1973), 7–22.

17. Braxton's *Address to the Convention of . . . Virginia* is quoted and discussed by Wood, *Creation of the American Republic,* 96–97.

18. "The Commonwealth of Oceana," in *Political Works of James Harrington,* 172.

19. Wood, *Creation of the American Republic,* 60–61.

20. I mean to make allowance for exceptions and for language quoted from such individuals as Samuel Adams and Benjamin Rush (ibid., 61, 118). But even Rush and Adams spoke in different terms at different times.

21. "In a republic there was no place for fear; there could be no sustained coercion from above" (ibid., 66). To trivialize a bit, consider traffic regulations: What if no one stopped on red except when fearing enforcement?

22. Carefully considered, I submit, few of the quotations in part 1 of *The Creation of the American Republic* actually suggest that many early Revolutionaries ever expected or demanded the sort of self-abnegation and disinterestedness that I am writing about. There may be some validity in this regard in the critique of Wood's subchapter on "The Public Good" in Gary J. Schmitt and Robert H. Webking, "Revolutionaries, Antifederalists, and Federalists: Comments on Gordon Wood's Understanding of the American Founding," *Political Science Reviewer* 9 (1979): 195–229. This article, however, criticizes Wood for what he never said and serves as an additional example of the way in which problems are compounded by misreadings. For a criticism more congruent with my own, as well as for a helpful argument that Pocock's civic humanists were far from strictly classical in their desires, see Jean Yarbrough, "Republicanism Reconsidered: Some Thoughts on the Foundation and Preservation of the American Republic," *Review of Politics* 41 (1979): 61–95. As I did in "Jeffersonian Ideology Revisited," which was written in ignorance of this earlier essay, Yarbrough argues that the Revolutionary generation did not *choose between* modern liberal and classical republican ideas (63).

23. See, esp., J. G. A. Pocock, *The Machiavellian Moment: Florentine Political Thought and the Atlantic Republican Tradition* (Princeton, N.J.: Princeton University Press, 1975), 71, 115–116; *Political Works of James Harrington,* 64–69.

24. Pocock, *Machiavellian Moment,* 73–74.

25. Ibid., 523–524.

26. Pocock, "Virtue and Commerce in the Eighteenth Century," *Journal of Interdisciplinary History* 3 (1972): 124–125.

27. Ibid., 124, 126, 133; Gordon S. Wood, "Interests and Disinterestedness in the Making of the Constitution," in *Beyond Confederation: Origins of the Constitution and American National Identity,* ed. Richard Beeman et al. (Chapel Hill: University of North Carolina Press, 1987), 69–109.

28. Pocock, "Virtue and Commerce," 134.

29. Pocock, *Machiavellian Moment,* 527.

30. Pocock, "Virtue and Commerce," 133.

31. *Political Works of James Harrington,* 145.

32. Pocock, "Virtue and Commerce," 121.

33. Montesquieu, in his discussion of virtue as the "spring" or fundamental principle of a republic, is less unambiguous than many American histories might suggest. He opens by associating virtue with a consciousness of membership in a community within which rules of equity apply, with a consciousness (among the magistrates as well as others) of being subject to the laws. Virtue's opposites, he writes, include ambition in the magistrates, resentment of the public treasury's demands, and "thirst of gain" in all (bk. 3, chap. 3, pages 20–22). Americans, if I am right, were saying much

the same thing and would have readily agreed when he defined the concept "as the love of the laws and of our country" (bk. 4, chap. 5, page 34). "But virtue," Montesquieu continued, "is a self-renunciation." It "requires a constant preference of public to private interest" (ibid.). Here, I am suggesting, he may well have been proceeding onto ground where relatively few Americans (or Englishmen) would follow, although it is precisely at this point that several writers introduce his influence. Montesquieu believed that a republic called for "heroic virtues which we admire in the ancients, and to us are known only by tradition" (bk. 3, chap. 5, page 23). He regarded Sparta as an archetype and made it clear that no such polity could be successfully revived without imposing a "community of goods," withdrawal from commerce (or placing it in public rather than private hands), disuse of money, and perhaps a nearly absolute equality of wealth (bk. 4, chap. 6, quotation at page 34; bk. 5, chaps. 3–5). But even Montesquieu conceded that democracies that were founded on commerce could tolerate the acquisition of great fortunes (bk. 5, chap. 6; bk. 7, chap. 2). And Americans would readily have comprehended and approved his explanation that equality "does not imply that everybody should command, or that no one should be commanded, but that we obey or command our equals." In "a well-regulated democracy, men are equal only as citizens" (bk. 8, chap. 3, page 111). Citations are to *The Spirit of the Laws*, trans. Thomas Nugent, with an introduction by Franz Neumann, "Hafner Library of Classics" (New York: Hafner, 1966; originally published in 1949).

34. Pocock, *Virtue, Commerce, and History: Essays on Political Thought and History, Chiefly in the Eighteenth Century* (Cambridge, Eng.: Cambridge University Press, 1985), 272.

35. See, esp., Pocock, "The Varieties of Whiggism from Exclusion to Reform: A History of Ideology and Discourse," ibid., 215–310, and "Cambridge Paradigms and Scotch Philosophers: A Study of the Relations between the Civic Humanist and the Civil Jurisprudential Interpretation of Eighteenth-Century Social Thought," in *Wealth and Virtue: The Shaping of Political Economy in the Scottish Enlightenment*, ed. Istvan Hont and Michael Ignatieff (Cambridge, Eng.: Cambridge University Press, 1984), 235–252. The quotation is from the latter at 251.

36. *Federalist*, No. 14, page 84; see also no. 10, page 62.

37. See Pocock, *Virtue, Commerce, and History*, 271. Other recent essays that make much of Madison's terminological legerdemain include Jean Yarbrough, "Madison and Modern Federalism," in *How Federal is the Constitution*, ed. Robert A. Goldwin and William A. Schambra (Washington, D.C.: American Enterprise Institute, 1987), 84–108; and Daniel W. Howe, "The Language of Faculty Psychology in *The Federalist Papers*," chap. 7 in this volume.

38. I do not dispute Yarbrough's valuable suggestion in "Republicanism Revisited" that Madison and the other Framers made inadequate institutional provision for popular participation and that they underestimated the enormous dangers posed to it by the enlargement of the size of the republic, in part because the context led them to assume that the perpetuation of vigorous popular involvement was the least

of their problems. I do suggest, however, not only that Madison's party building after 1789 was consciously addressed to the problem of participation but also that we should emphatically reemphasize that Madison (and most of the other Founders) consistently assumed that most political decisions would continue to be made in the states and local communities, whose governments were closer to the people. On the role of federalism in Madison's thinking, Yarbrough and I are far apart. See also her "Rethinking 'The Federalist's View of Federalism,'" Publius 15 (1985): 31–53.

39. Harold C. Syrett and Jacob E. Cooke, eds., The Papers of Alexander Hamilton, 26 vols. (New York: Columbia University Press, 1960–79), 3:103; Jefferson to John Jay, 23 Aug. 1785, in Thomas Jefferson: Writings, ed. Merrill D. Peterson (New York: Library of America, 1984), 818–820. Recent studies of the Scots, such as those in Wealth and Virtue, are making it increasingly apparent how peculiar Samuel Adams was in wishing that America could be a Christian Sparta.

40. "A Defense of the Constitutions of Government of the United States of America," in The Works of John Adams, ed. Charles Francis Adams, 10 vols. (Boston, 1850–1856), 6:219.

41. The contrary appears to be suggested by Jack N. Rakove in "The Great Compromise: Ideas, Interests, and the Politics of Constitution Making," William and Mary Quarterly, 3d ser., 44 (1987): 424–457.

42. In the early Revolutionary constitutions, Madison suggested, "a provision for the rights of persons was supposed to include of itself those of property, and it was natural [for himself as well as others, I suggest] to infer from the tendency of republican laws, that these different interests would be more and more identified." But injustices deriving from this error, together with "the multiplicity and mutability of laws" encouraged by the early constitutions, had brought into question "the fundamental principle of republican Government, that the majority who rule in such Governments, are the safest Guardians both of public Good and of private rights" ("Observations on Jefferson's Draft of a Constitution for Virginia," 15 Oct. 1788, and "Vices of the Political System of the United States," Apr. 1787, in Papers of Madison, 11:287 and 9:354).

43. "Most of our political evils may be traced up to our commercial ones, as most of our moral may to our political" (to Jefferson, 18 Mar. 1786, ibid., 8:502). On this matter see Drew R. McCoy, The Elusive Republic: Political Economy in Jeffersonian America (Chapel Hill: University of North Carolina Press, 1980), chap. 3. And note how many of the sources quoted in Wood's section on the "Political Pathology" of the 1780s (413–425) appear to be condemning the sort of self-indulgence that leads men to forget that they are citizens and parts of a community; see also the sources quoted on page 100: luxury unmans a man and renders him incapable of being vigilant or of forgoing immediate gratifications even under an immediate threat; poverty reduces men to beasts, enslaving them to want.

44. See esp., Federalist, No. 57.

45. Before as well as after Hamilton presented his reports on public credit; see,

esp., his speech of 29 June in Max Farrand, ed., *The Records of the Federal Convention of 1787,* rev. ed., 4 vols. (New Haven, Conn.: Yale University Press, 1966; originally published in 1937), 1:464–465; *Federalist,* No. 41, pages 273–274; and Elliot, *Debates in the Several State Conventions,* 3:382.

Quid Transit?

Paradigms and Process in the Transformation of Republican Ideas

Scholarly debates about the "modern-liberal" and "classical-republican" dimensions of early national thought are entering into a different phase. Through the middle 1980s, controversy focused on the relative importance of the two traditions in the years surrounding the adoption of the Constitution. At this writing, these disputes appear to have resulted in a general agreement (not unanimous, of course) that both of them were present in the new republic (as were other modes of thought), that both of them were vastly influential, and that neither should be seen as having exercised an undisputed primacy during the 1780s or 1790s.[1] In one important recent study, *The Republic Reborn* (1987), Steven Watts has argued that the liberal tradition did achieve hegemony between the early 1790s and the conclusion of the War of 1812. Michael Lienesch offers an alternative formulation. By 1800, he agrees, the thinking of the Revolutionary generation had, indeed, been fundamentally transformed, but the transition from a classical into a modern mode of thought was "inconclusive," ending in "a hybrid mixture that combined republican and liberal themes in a creative but uneasy collaboration." The founding generation, Lienesch argues, forged "a new kind of politics, one neither entirely republican nor exclusively liberal, neither classical nor modern, but a curious combination of both" (pp. 7–8). "As symbolized by the American Constitution," he maintains, "this unlikely mixture . . . has continued to characterize American politics for the last two hundred years." The tensions built into the culture at the start have proved so lasting that "the most significant fact about modern American political thought may well be that it is not entirely modern," that "as America expanded into the modern world, it carried along the baggage of the classical past" (pp. 8, 207, 206).

Thus far, my sympathies are heavily with Lienesch. Every year and almost every month, it seems, brings further demonstrations that republican ideas continued to exert a lively influence in America long after 1812, though nearly everyone agrees that the United States experienced a striking transformation of behavior and beliefs between the early Revolution and the age of Jackson. If both of these perceptions are correct, what has to be explained are ways of thinking that were changing over time—moving toward an ultimate predominance of liberal and democratic values—yet ways of thinking in which liberal ideas were so entwined with concepts coming from a different tradition that the consequence would never be the liberal monolith that scholars once described. In fairness, I should say that Watts is as aware of this as Lienesch and has given us a bigger, richer book about the complicated course of "liberalizing change." *New Order of the Ages* seems to reach the right conclusion, but it does not offer a persuasive history of the developments that it explores. Its weaknesses, in this respect, reflect the shifting and confused condition of the broader enterprise in which both authors are involved.

As the 1980s end, with books like those by Watts and Lienesch, students of the new republic are initiating what will surely prove a long discussion of the mechanisms, pace, and comprehensiveness of fundamental changes in political beliefs. Ironically, however, we are entering upon this exploration in the midst of what may also prove a serious rethinking of the shape of early Revolutionary thought and thus of new uncertainties about the structure that was in transition. With the starting point uncertain and the outcome in dispute, it has been proving difficult for anyone to write a satisfying history of the developments between. How can we account persuasively for change when there is disagreement over nearly everything except its general direction?

Not long ago, John Murrin called the argument about "the Great Transition"—the movement from a "premodern" to a "modern" society and culture—"the most important controversy taking shape in recent years about early American history."[2] Murrin was referring to the controversy over whether any such transition actually occurred, for it is possible, of course, to argue that America was *always* liberal and modern. Since 1960, nonetheless, the larger portion of the most exciting work in early American social and intellectual history has emphasized the differentness of eighteenth-century life and values. Most historians, accordingly, would now accept the concept of a Great Transition. Recently, in fact, the growing interest in this transformation has been promising a massive reinterpretation of the years surrounding 1800 as a period of sweeping cultural and social change.[3] In effect, the current generation's rediscovery of the republican tradition, followed by renewed insistence on the liberating novelty of liberal ideas, has led us to perceive the early Revolution as decidedly premodern; and this impression has been leading us, in turn, to squeeze the Great Transition more intensively into the early national years (most commonly, into the years between the middle 1790s and the middle 1820s). Rapid social change, on these assumptions, helps account for the increasing dominance of liberal values and ideas, and rapid transformation of political beliefs suggests an image of the early national period as one of more intensive social change than used to be assumed, since most of us are wary of idealist interpretations in which thinking seems to change according to its own dynamic.

Without disputing most of this interpretative thrust, it may be useful to suggest that there are several reasons for discomfort. One of them may be suggested by the incompatibility of Lienesch's account of change with the conclusions mentioned earlier in the review. The broader controversy over liberal and classical ideas has forced a general recognition that the mixture he discovers at the finish was already present early in the Revolution. If it was, it cannot be described as the synthetic product of a dialectical progression.

"Classical-republican," it now appears, has proved a troubling term for the collection of ideas—the mode of thought—whose influence scholars have been trying to recover, now, for more than twenty years. Over time, that term, which was originally employed for good and proper reasons, has encouraged an impression that the thinking of the early Revolution was considerably less "modern" than it was—less "modern," certainly, than "modern" ordinarily suggests to scholars trained in political theory. For much of the preceding decade, partly as a consequence of a confusion over terms, historians and theorists alike have often written of the "classical" and "liberal" traditions in a fashion that suggests that philosophically or analytically distinctive modes of thought—modes whose lineages and implications may be readily distinguished for some objects of our own—were also separate and competing in the minds of those we study. But early Revolutionary thinking, we may now be coming to agree, was always an amalgam of republican and liberal ideas, and liberal and classical traditions did not merely coexist or stand objectively as separate and competing choices. Rather, they were linked and blended in the minds of early modern individuals whose thinking changed as they attempted to assimilate and manage new phenomena and new events, but who were neither truly classical nor fully modern.[4] At present, we do not possess the terminology and constructs needed to describe the transformation of this early Revolutionary blend into the thinking of the 1820s. But as we recognize that it was there, it seems increasingly apparent that we should not polarize what liberal republicans combined.

Grounded on a comprehensive reading of published sermons, pamphlets, and debates, *New Order of the Ages* is a history of the appearance in the new United States of a "new way of thinking about time": the movement toward a modern view of history or change which, nonetheless, among Americans, remained "ambivalent, contradictory, and sometimes flatly paradoxical" in its insistence on combining themes of progress with persistent worries over degeneration and decline (pp. 3, 8, 205). Lienesch gives one chapter each to concepts that concerned contemporaries roughly in succession: creation, reform, development, experience, founding, posterity, and destiny.

The argument, to put it briefly, is that the Confederation years were marked by an increasing tendency among Americans to split into opposing groups according to their attitudes toward change. If this division had been perfect, it would have ranged a party of progress against a party of corruption and decline: Court against Country, advocates of commercial development against agrarian proponents of self-sufficiency and local self-control, large-republic men against proponents of a politics of virtue, and a conservative theory of balanced constitutions against a democratic theory of decline and periodic renewal. In fact, however, individuals could move from any one of these persuasions to another with greater ease than a division into parties would imply, and new developments encouraged the appearance of a growing number of "transitional" thinkers who accepted parts of opposite persuasions, hoping that virtue and commerce or expansion and republican self-government could be combined. These individuals assumed the leadership of federal reform. (John Jay or George Washington, for example, were "transitional Country" figures who combined commitments to a politics of virtue with acceptance of reform; James Madison was a "transitional Court" figure who stood between the real "agrarians" like Thomas Jefferson and those who showed no fear of commercial development.)

The framing and adoption of the Constitution saw the climax of the story. Finding little guidance from conventional conceptions of the meaning of events, relying mainly on their own experience and hopes, transitional thinkers seized direction of the Constitutional Convention. There, as Lienesch puts it, "they reached beyond precedent to create a present-oriented politics," an order aimed at "transcending time" (p. 119). Subsequently, under pressure from the Antifederalists, supporters of the Constitution built a powerfully persuasive case that their completed system could provide both permanence and progress. Winning a spectacular triumph in the battle of the minds, they next proceeded promptly and with comparable success to the creation of a "Constitutional character" or psychology: a concept of the citizen that emphasized self-regulation, a moderate pursuit of personal desires, and economic rather than political action. Here, however, the supporters of the Constitution were only partially successful. "From that time on," as the development of party politics would quickly show, "citizens would bear at least some of the attributes of modern liberalism, considering it their primary responsibility to act in the private realm, pursuing their individual interests and thereby building the country's economy." But citizens would also long retain "at least some semblance" of the classical-republican determination to do battle, when required, "against the enemies of freedom" (p. 183). And Americans would always counterbalance faith in progress with the old republican concerns about conspiracy, corruption, and decline.

As always, it is difficult to summarize a complex book. A political scientist at Chapel Hill, Lienesch writes for both historians and theorists. His central argument is tightly wrapped and certainly more subtle than my presentation may suggest. Still, the summary should be sufficient to suggest the shape of my dissatisfaction. I object to the polarities from which a synthesis is seen to have emerged. Some of them, I think, are scholarly or analytical constructions that have been transformed into real groups. In other cases, real divisions have been broadened into oppositions that were not so real. (Court and Country, for example, is a useful label for a real debate about the role of government in the economy and in promoting economic change, but it is problematic to enlarge this split in such a fashion as to pit proponents of prosperity and progress against a "Country" group that thinks exclusively in terms of corruption and historical decline.) It is suggestive, I submit, that Lienesch frequently does not succeed in finding individuals who speak unchallengeably for his extremes—especially for the "agrarian" or "classical-republican" position. It is even more instructive that he places nearly all of the important thinkers of the age among the figures in transition, that the Constitution does not really seem to flow out of the polarizing process he describes. If we suppose that most Americans were liberal republicans at the beginning of the story, it is not surprising that so many should have straddled the polarities that a division into classical and modern has imposed. The Constitution did emerge from changing views of politics and time, which its adoption speeded. But explorations of this Great Transition may be more successful if we reconsider what was present at the start. The final chapter of the book is an illuminating study of the long persistence of a politics that cannot be described as merely liberal, but the body of the work is less successful in explaining how this politics emerged.

Notes

1. See, for example, Lance Banning, "Jeffersonian Ideology Revisited: Liberal and Classical Ideas in the New American Republic," *William and Mary Quarterly*, 3rd ser., 63 (1986): 3–19; Joyce Appleby, "Republicanism in Old and New Contexts," ibid., 20–34; James T. Kloppenberg, "The Virtues of Liberalism: Christianity, Republicanism, and Ethics in Early American Political Discourse," *Journal of American History* 74 (1987): 9–33; Isaac Kramnick, "The 'Great National Discussion': The Discourse of Politics in 1787," *William and Mary Quarterly*, 3d ser., 45 (1988): 3–32; and the letters of J. G. A. Pocock and Isaac Kramnick, [*William and Mary Quarterly*, 3d ser., 45 (1988)]: 817–818.

2. John M. Murrin, "Self-Interest Conquers Patriotism: Republicans, Liberals, and Indians Reshape the Nation," in Jack P. Greene, ed., *The American Revolution: Its Character and Limits*, (1987), 225.

3. See, especially, Gordon S. Wood's ambitious effort to reconceptualize the period in his 1987 presidential address to the Society for Historians of the Early American Republic, available as "The Significance of the Early Republic," *Journal of the Early Republic* 8 (1988): 1–20.

4. For some elaboration, see Lance Banning, "Some Second Thoughts on Virtue and the Course of Revolutionary Thinking," in Terence Ball and J. G. A. Pocock, eds., *Conceptual Change and the Constitution* (1988), 194–212.

PART 3

The Constitution

Conciseness in writing is an admirable trait. "Omit needless words," as Strunk and White famously counseled. The effort to reduce large and complex subjects to the microscopic word counts required for brief essays can challenge even the most talented literary craftsmen.

But concise writing is also measured by the authorial ability to control how much material to present to readers, in what sequence, and at what length. Knowing how much readers need to know about particular subjects and presenting that information to them can be just as important as the content of information itself. When the subject matter is as capacious as the 1787 Constitutional Convention and the ratification debate, the problems of concision and authorial control become even greater.

In these essays Banning demonstrates sure-handed and admirable control over his material, bringing a deft touch and expert eye to the subject matter. Summarizing the Constitutional Convention requires constructing a narrative framework of a four-month process of ebbs and flows, patterns and rhythms, and stages into which must be fitted numerous key decisions and debates. In his account Banning provides a clear narrative arc in describing the convention but also intersperses his descriptions of debates, motions, and votes with an even-handed analysis of their meaning. By suggesting the ways in which some decisions shaped later ones, opening up some possibilities while foreclosing others, Banning brings readers a clear understanding of the significance of the developments he narrates. Readers come away from this essay with a sure sense not only of what happened in Philadelphia but also with a sound grasp of what it meant. In particular, he stresses the sheer *novelty* of the innovative system of government they created—not by preconceived design but by improvisation and innovation, as a group of smart, dedicated people working through problems together. He shows how the Constitution emerged not only as a product of compromise but as a product of creativity as well. Banning also makes it clear that the convention did not resolve every issue, nor did it draft a flawless document acceptable to all parties and interests. Resisting the urge to tie up the story too neatly, he demonstrates that for all the work the Philadelphia convention accomplished and settled, many of the debates that raged in the convention spilled over into the ratification process as well. Thus, the convention was not the be-all and end-all event in fixing Constitutional meaning.

Banning brings the same traits to his treatment of *The Federalist Papers*. Readers will find an overview of how the series came to be written and published, concise summaries of many of its key essays, and a broader consideration of the themes raised in the series as a whole. Again, Banning does not claim too much for the essays and notes that even with these skillfully written tracts, the Constitution barely achieved ratification in New York. He also explores the goals of the series, the way Alexander Hamilton came to recruit John Jay and James Madison as coauthors, and the intended audience of the authors. Mixing narrative with analysis, Banning provides readers with an able overview of the whole series as well as its place and role in the unfolding ratification debate.

The masterpiece in this section is "1787 and 1776," a piece Banning considered as good as anything he had ever written. Even at first glance, it is easy to see why he thought so. The piece is marked by his usual elegant prose and grabs readers at the outset with its arresting contrast between Patrick Henry and James Madison, between an emphasis on liberty and an emphasis on union. But as one reads this closely and digs deeper, it becomes clear that many things are going on in this rich essay. For starters, Banning develops here at some length the complexity of Madison's thinking about the Revolution and how the Constitution affected its legacy. He shows Madison to have been no less concerned with preserving Revolutionary liberty than Henry famously was. But Banning delineates subtle yet crucial differences between the two men in their understanding of liberty, union, and the meaning of the Revolution as they emerged in their debates in the Virginia ratifying convention. And he proceeds in the essay to unpack other subtleties that informed Madison's thinking about the Constitution and republican government in ways that distinguish the Virginian's own emerging conceptions from those of both Anti-Federalists like Henry and also from his fellow Federalists.

In fact, it is in this essay, perhaps for the first time, that Banning discovered and revealed what became a crucial argument of his *The Sacred Fire of*

Liberty book. Banning tells readers that Madison "assumed a very special place among the Founders . . . because he personally bridged so much of the abyss between the Revolutionary tribunes such as Henry and the aspiring consuls such as Hamilton." There seems to be a recognition that came to Banning in the writing of this piece—originally a chapter in a volume of essays—that he had found his line, his interpretive angle, his key insight that gave shape and form and focus to his larger, ongoing intellectual study of Madison.

Finally, as suggested above, Banning demonstrates how taking the words of a key figure at a particular point in history and thinking along with him as he revised and adjusted his reasoning in light of changing circumstance and concepts can clarify, in this case, Madison's way of puzzling through a conundrum to reach conclusions. Banning here takes the Madison of the Virginia ratifying convention as his subject and manages to reach important conclusions about Madison's role in that event and his thinking at that time. By doing a similar close reading and pursuing thoughtful scholarship about the rest of Madison's experience during the American founding, Banning shows also the genesis in print of what became one of the major strains of his larger book-length study. Given all that he accomplished in this piece alongside the grace and clarity with which it was written, it is little wonder that Banning considered this to be as fine a piece as any he wrote.

The Constitutional Convention

Meeting at the Pennsylvania State House (Independence Hall), the Constitutional Convention found a quorum on May 25 and sat until September 17. Fifty-five delegates participated in its work, though there were seldom more than forty in the room for any single session. Representing every state except Rhode Island, the delegates comprised a good cross-section of the early national elite. Lawyers (34), merchants (7), farmers (27), public creditors (30), and public servants (10), nearly all were wealthy men, and most had taken generally conservative positions in their states. Yet members came from a variety of local factions and from all the major regions of the several states except the west. The nation might have organized an equally impressive meeting from the ranks of leaders who did not attend. John Adams and Thomas Jefferson were representing the United States abroad in 1787. John Jay and Samuel Adams were passed over. Patrick Henry "smelt a rat" and turned down his election. Still, most states attempted to select their most experienced and best, usually with slight regard to factional considerations, and they succeeded well enough that Jefferson described the roster as a gathering of "demigods." George Washington was present. Inevitably, he was quickly chosen to preside.

Among the delegates as well was young James Madison, Jefferson's close friend, an influential member of the Annapolis Convention, and long a leading advocate of national reforms. Madison had led Virginia, which had led the other states, in organizing the convention and selecting delegates whose talents and distinguished reputations signaled a profound commitment to its work. In the weeks before the meeting, he had taken careful notes on ancient and modern confederacies and prepared a formal memorandum on the "Vices of the Political System of the United States," thinking problems through to a degree that no one else had done and urging other members of his delegation to arrive in Philadelphia in time to frame some introductory proposals with which the meeting might begin. Virginia's seven delegates assembled daily while they waited for the full convention to obtain a quorum, agreeing on a set of resolutions that might serve as a preliminary basis for discussions. Speaking for the delegation as a whole, Governor Edmund Randolph introduced these resolutions on May 29, as soon as the convention had agreed upon its rules.

Reassembling in the character of a Committee of the Whole, the meeting turned immediately to a consideration of the Randolph (or Virginia) Plan. Along with the adoption of a rigid, carefully respected rule of secrecy, which freed the members from external pressures and encouraged them to feel that they could alter their positions if discussion changed their minds, the Virginia Plan was among the great convention's most important acts. For its provisions, which were based primarily on Madison's ideas, did not propose to make the Articles of Confederation "adequate to the exigencies of the union." Rather, they envisioned the complete replacement of the current central government by a republican regime of national extent. The present, single-chamber central government would be reorganized in imitation of the balanced constitutions of the states. Based directly on the people, it would have the right "to legislate in all cases to which the separate States are incompetent, or in which the harmony of the United States may be interrupted by the exercise of individual Legislation." To guarantee the central government's supremacy wherever common measures were required, the articles of union would be ratified by state conventions chosen by the people, and federal powers would include authority "to call forth the force of the Union against any member of the Union failing to fulfill its duty" or to veto state legislation inconsistent with the federal charter.

By starting with the resolutions of May 29, the Constitutional Convention set its course from the beginning toward a thorough-going reconstruction of the present system. Meeting at least once with Pennsylvania's delegation and doubtless talking privately with others as the members trickled into town, Madison and his Virginia colleagues had correctly sensed that early sentiment was overwhelmingly opposed to patchwork, piecemeal efforts. The members opened their deliberations deeply moved by the momentousness of the occasion, as was the country as a whole. Many recognized that the convention might afford the last alternative to fragmentation of the union. Many feared, as Madison had put it in his preconvention letters, that America's republican experiment could not indefinitely survive the loss of this protective shield. Madison himself believed that popular commitment to the Revolutionary order was already flagging as the ineffectuality of the Confederation Congress reinforced a tendency in all the states toward fluctuating, ill-considered legislation which reflected slight regard for either private rights or long-term public needs. He therefore warned the other delegates that they were not assembled merely to attend to the debility of Congress. Their ultimate objective, he insisted, must be nothing less than to "perpetuate the union and redeem the honor of the republican name."

A solemn sense of high responsibility and urgent, common purpose was indispensable to the Convention's great achievement, not least because most delegates were only partially prepared for the enormous changes sketched by the Virginia Plan. Seizing the initiative for radical reform, Madison's proposals demonstrated an instinctive grasp of several broad, though hazy, understandings that would limit and direct the course of the proceedings. Leaders of a democratic Revolution, including thirty veterans of the war, the delegates had not forgotten the complaints and hopes that had propelled them into independence. Nearly all of them had come to think that an effective central government would have to have, at minimum, an independent source of revenues, authority to regulate the country's trade, and power to compel obedience to its legitimate commands. Nearly all agreed, as well, that powers that the colonies had stubbornly denied to England would have to be accompanied by careful checks against the possibility of their abuse. Many, nonetheless, were far from willing to consent to the specific kinds of checks proposed by the initial resolutions. The Pennsylvanians and Virginians were prepared from the beginning to insist that powers of this sort could be entrusted only to a well-constructed, fully representative republic. Overawed by the Virginia Plan, accepting many of its goals, and unprepared to offer comprehensive counterresolutions, dissenters were uncertain how to counter its proponents in debate. They nevertheless objected from the start that the convention was empowered only to reform the present federal system, not to overturn it. The framing of the Constitution thus became a complicated story of a fundamental conflict that occurred within the context of a common quest.

One of the finest recent studies of the Constitutional Convention calls its early weeks a period of "nationalist assault." Certainly, the members from the smaller states felt thoroughly assaulted by a plan that offered to apportion legislative seats according to the populations of the several states. George Read immediately protested that the delegates from Delaware, who were specifically instructed to insist upon the equal vote that every state had always had in Congress (as in the convention), might have to leave the meeting if the larger states were bent upon this change. Neither Read nor any of his fellows really planned to quit before the business had begun. Yet it was clear from the beginning that the smaller states anticipated total domination, even loss of their identities, in a national republic grounded on proportional representation. Nor were theirs the only worries prompted by the resolutions of May 29. No sooner was the first one taken up than Elbridge Gerry of Massachusetts and Charles C. Pinckney of South Carolina, both representing larger states, questioned whether the convention could or should propose so radical a reconstruction. The Virginia Plan not only terrified the smaller states, it also seemed to many other members to depart too far from the essential spirit of a limited confederation and to call for more participation by the people than the people were equipped to make to national affairs. By offering what Madison described as a republican corrective for the defects of democracy, as well as an extreme solution to the problems of the union, the Virginia Resolutions complicated the convention's task and multiplied the sources of contention. They entangled the convention in so many overlapping arguments that it is easy to neglect the members' early sense of common purpose. But the "miracle" at Philadelphia resulted from a complex interplay of disputation and consensus, during which the delegates collectively developed a conception of a form of government so novel that it lacked a name. To understand this process, it is necessary both to simplify a set of disagreements so complex as to defy a brief description and to recognize that these disputes were only one dimension of the story.

Between May 30 and June 13, the Committee of the Whole conducted a complete consideration of the Randolph Plan. During these two weeks, with Madison and James Wilson of Pennsylvania at their head, a brilliant group of delegates from larger states developed a compelling case for radical reform. Distinguishing between a "national" government and one "merely federal," Wilson, Madison, Randolph, George Mason (Virginia), Gouverneur Morris (Pennsylvania), and others argued that the fatal weakness of the old confederation was its unavoidable dependence on the thirteen states for revenues and for a host of intermediary actions necessary to enforce its laws and treaties. Lacking independent means to carry its decisions into action, they explained, Congress had been baffled by the states even when its measures were supported by a huge majority and undeniably were within its proper province. Paper grants of new responsibilities would only add new sources of frustration if the states retained the power to ignore or counteract the central government's decisions; and yet a federal power to compel the states might introduce a constant threat of war between the union and its members. The inescapable necessity, the nationalists maintained, was to abandon the unworkable idea of a government over governments, a sovereignty over sovereignties, and give the central government the courts and other independent means to act directly on the individual members of society. Revolutionary principles required, however, that any government possessing the authority to reach the people's lives and purses would have to represent its citizens immediately and fairly. Given the necessity for larger federal powers, the traditional equality between the states would have to be abandoned in order to preserve equality among the people and majority control.

Intellectually outclassed by men like Madison and Wilson, most members from the smaller states squirmed silently through the convention's early days. A large majority of delegates had quickly fallen in with Madison's attempts to postpone action on the most divisive resolutions until the meeting could define some common ground. But as the skeleton of the Virginia Plan acquired some flesh and as it grew increasingly more difficult to settle lesser questions while the great ones went unanswered, the confrontation that had loomed from the beginning could no longer be contained. New Jersey's delegates demanded a decision on apportioning the Congress, insisting on June 9 that proportional representation would destroy the smaller states and place the whole confederation at the mercy of a coalition of its largest members: Massachusetts, Pennsylvania, and Virginia. Ten of thirteen states, warned William Paterson, would certainly reject this scheme. If he could not defeat it in the hall, he would oppose it in his state. New Jersey would "never confederate on the plan before the committee."

Sunday intervened and tempers cooled, but not before James Wilson answered Paterson in kind. "If the small states will not confederate on this plan," he assured them, Pennsylvania and some others "would not confederate on any other." The division that would dominate proceedings for the next five weeks had burst into the open. It would prove the clearest, most dramatic, most persistent argument of the convention—the single conflict over which the gathering repeatedly approached collapse.

For all its threatening potential, nevertheless, the clash between the small states and the large cannot explain developments between May 30 and June 13. It was not the only conflict that emerged, nor can an exclusive emphasis on conflicts and divisions properly illuminate the course of the proceedings. The Constitutional Convention was successful, in the end, because its battles almost always raged in multiple dimensions, because the push-and-pull that marked its course was never *simply* a result of clashing interests, and because the men involved were more than merely clever brokers for their states. We do not need to resurrect old myths to recognize that the Constitutional Convention was, at once, a battleground for disagreeing politicians and a theater for one of the most brilliant exercises in creative statesmanship that history has ever witnessed. The famous compromises that reshaped the resolutions of May 29 into the document completed on September 17 were necessary consequences of contrasting state and sectional desires, capably advanced by representatives who were acutely conscious of competing interests. But each decision was a product, too, of a *cooperative* endeavor to achieve a better understanding of the nation's needs and to resolve its problems in accord with its ideals. Moreover, this was not the sort of meeting at which everyone arrived inflexibly committed to a set of clear objectives and compromised no more than he was forced to. It was the sort in which not even the Virginians knew exactly what they wanted at the outset, the sort from which the great majority departed rather awed by what they had achieved and with their thinking greatly changed by the collective effort.

The first two weeks of the convention seem most helpfully described as an initial exploration during which a complicated pattern of divisions rapidly emerged within a framework of evolving, general understandings. Like Madison, most delegates had come to Philadelphia as worried by conditions in the states as by the problems of the union. They readily agreed with the Virginian that the will of unrestrained majorities was often inconsistent with the rights of the minority or long-term public needs, and that the early Revolutionary constitutions had neglected dangers of this sort by trusting too much power to the lower houses of assembly, which were not effectively restrained by governmental branches less immediately responsive to majority demands. Everywhere, as Elbridge Gerry phrased it, the country seemed to suffer from "an excess of democracy." Good government appeared to have been sacrificed to revolutionary fears of unresponsive rulers.

Few members of the Constitutional Convention carried their alarm about majority misrule so far as to suggest nostalgia for aristocrats or kings. Most genuinely shared the people's fierce commitment to a democratic system. Yet nearly all were powerfully determined not to replicate the error they believed had been committed in the early Revolutionary constitutions. Here, again, the resolutions of May 29 successfully defined the boundaries of disagreement. Sound republics, they suggested, must be built upon two legislative houses: one elected by the people; the other chosen by a manner that would shield its members from the whims of the majority and thus assure continuing protection for the rights of the minority and continuing attention to the nation's long-term needs. The legislature should be counter-balanced by a forceful, separate executive, and the judiciary should be independent of them both. Through almost four months of often bitter quarrels, there was never any serious dispute about these fundamental principles of governmental structure. The Virginia Plan not only forced the meeting to consider a republican solution to the Revolutionary fear of concentrated central power, which had resulted in a general government unable to advance the nation's interests or even to fulfill its legal obligations. It also both elicited and guided a collective reconsideration of the nature of a sound republic. It did not specifically define which powers were beyond the competence of individual states. It offered only a preliminary sketch of an improved republic—not even indicating, for example, whether the executive should be a council or a single man. But it involved the delegates from the beginning in exchanges to which most contributed a determination not only to protect specific interests but also to advance a general search for principles and structural devices that could guarantee a place for governmental energy and wisdom as well as for responsiveness to popular demands.

The Virginia Plan survived its first examination fundamentally intact, its sketchy outline filling rapidly as the debates suggested and improved upon the broad agreements present from the start. As the Pennsylvanians helped elaborate the concept that the general government might act directly on the people, the Virginians dropped the resolution calling for a federal power to coerce the states, but found new reasons for their view that states should not participate directly in the choice of federal officials. Wilson, Madison, and their lieutenants made it clear that what they wanted was to build a wise and energetic central government upon a broadly popular foundation, blending a responsibility to the majority with multiple securities against an overbearing, popularly elected lower house. Impressed by their analysis of the debilities of the existing system, the convention speedily agreed to substitute a complex and authoritative central government for the present, feeble, unicameral regime. Sharing their dissatisfaction with the constitutions of the states, it worked from the beginning to establish genuinely independent, fully countervailing branches.

Through these early days, Madison and Wilson towered over the convention like a team of titans. On May 31, with only South Carolina and New Jersey voting no, and with Connecticut and Delaware divided, the Committee overwhelmingly approved the popular election of the lower house, a decision reaffirmed a few days later with the two divided delegations going opposite directions. With Madison successfully resisting a divisive argument about the scope of federal powers until some structural decisions could be made, the meeting easily decided on a three-year term for representatives, and seven years for the executive and members of the upper house. Insisting that the surest way to guarantee a safe, but firm, executive was to confer responsibility on one accountable individual, Wilson led a winning struggle for a single chief executive, though he could not prevent the fearful delegates from ruling that this magistrate could serve only a single term and was to be elected by the legislature, not the people. Both Madison and Wilson would have reinforced the veto power by involving the judiciary in the process, but Madison approved of the majority's decision that the veto was to be reversible instead of absolute. He and Wilson both were pleased, of course, by the decision on apportioning the Congress. On June 11 the Committee voted 7 states to 3, with Maryland divided and New Hampshire not yet present, for proportional representation in the lower house. Only tiny Delaware and antinational New York, where Alexander Hamilton was outvoted by Robert Yates and Jon Lansing, sided with New Jersey.

Still, the nationalist assault by no means carried everything before it. Although the smallest states seemed relatively isolated in the earliest debates and were severely beaten on the matter of the lower house, the fierce resistance vocalized by Paterson and Read became increasingly imposing as it coalesced with opposition based on different concerns. Three delegates— no more—were rigidly committed to a "merely federal" system, but Yates and Lansing could control New York while Luther Martin often managed to divide the Maryland contingent. For each obstructionist, moreover, there were several others for whom the pervasive fear of popular misrule, which made the resolutions of May 29 a universally attractive model for republican reform, could also reinforce a natural reluctance to surrender local powers to a national majority. Although the delegations from Connecticut and South Carolina were especially inclined to be distrustful of a scheme that would erect a stronger central government on greater popular involvement, almost every delegation was composed of men who differed widely in their judgments of the people's competence as well as in their willingness to shift additional responsibilities to federal hands. As the smaller states discovered partial allies, sometimes here and sometimes there, it seemed increasingly unlikely that a national republic could secure approval both from a majority of states and from the representatives of a majority of the people. Even optimistic nationalists resigned themselves to a campaign that promised to extend throughout the summer.

Confronted with so many overlapping fears, the democratic nationalists encountered rising opposition during the convention's first two weeks and suffered one decisive check. The Virginia Plan provided for election of the senate by the lower house from persons nominated by the states. On June 7, over loud objections from Madison and Wilson, majorities in every delegation disapproved this proposition in favor of election of the senate by the legislatures of the states. Nearly everyone agreed that the selection of the senate by the lower house might give the house of representatives an overweaning influence, while few were willing to entrust the choice directly to the people, as Wilson recommended. Doubting that the people were equipped to make a fit selection or insisting that a senate chosen in that way would prove unable to defend minorities against majority demands, many members saw election by the local legislatures simply as a lesser evil. Many others, though, including several delegates from larger states, were forcefully impressed by the insistence of John Dickinson (Delaware) and Roger Sherman (Connecticut) that selection by the local legislatures could collect the sense of states as states, assure a federal harmony, and offer firm securities against potential federal usurpations.

Committed nationalists were deeply disappointed. Fearing that selection of the senate by the states would build into the system exactly the flaw that was destroying the confederation, they also rightly sensed that an insistence on a federal role for states as states would reinforce demands for an equality between them. On June 11, just before the crucial votes, Sherman urged that representation in the lower house might be appointed to free population, while every state might retain an equal vote in the senate. By moving to revive an old confederation formula, which counted a slave as three-fifths of a man, Wilson promptly headed off an argument that might have split the large-state coalition. But the overwhelming vote for proportional representation in the lower house was followed by a very close decision on the senate, where Sherman's motion for equality was narrowly rejected, 6 to 5: Connecticut, New York, New Jersey, Delaware, and Maryland, aye; Massachusetts, Pennsylvania, Virginia, North Carolina, South Carolina, and Georgia, no. A combination of concerns had joined to check the nationalist momentum. Two days later the Committee of the Whole reported its amended resolutions to the House, but the convention then immediately adjourned in order to permit opponents to prepare alternatives to the Virginia Plan.

William Paterson's New Jersey Resolutions, introduced on June 15, were thrown together quickly by the coalition that had voted for an equal senate days before. This coalition was united only by its opposition to the Randolph Plan, and its proposals did not represent the real desires of any of their framers. As Dickinson suggested in a private talk with Madison, many members from the smaller states were not opposed in principle to an effective, "national" system. In order to protect themselves from large-state domination, they were willing to ally themselves with the minority who were: "we would sooner submit to a foreign power than submit to be deprived of an equality of suffrage in both branches of the legislature." But if the large-state nationalists would bend a bit, the Delawarean was hinting, both his own state and New Jersey would support a vigorous, bicameral regime. To them, the contest with the larger states was not a controversy over which responsibilities should be entrusted to the central government, not even a debate about the merits of a complex system. On both these points, their fundamental preferences were closer to the nationalists' than to their temporary allies,' and Paterson's proposals did not hide that fact. Under the New Jersey Plan, the general government would still have had the power to impose a stamp tax, postal duties, and an impost, to compel compliance with its requisitions, and to regulate the country's interstate and foreign commerce. Federal laws would still have overridden local legislation. A separate executive and federal courts would still have shared authority with Congress. For Luther Martin and the two New Yorkers, this was clearly rather much. For Dickinson and others, just as clearly, Paterson's proposal that the legislature should remain a single house, in which each state would keep its equal vote, was mainly an attempt to force concessions from the other side.

Switching back into the Committee of the Whole, the delegates debated the Virginia and New Jersey Plans on Saturday, June 16. Paterson and Lansing argued that the Randolph Resolutions would exceed the meeting's powers and could never win approval from the states. The nationalists refused to budge. Wilson argued that the gathering was free to *recommend* whatever changes it considered proper and should not consent to an enlargement of the powers of a single legislative chamber that would not derive directly from the people. Randolph pointed out again that the convention had to choose between a power to coerce the states, which would not work, and power to command the people, for which the present Congress was unfit. Alexander Hamilton monopolized the floor on Monday to suggest that even the Virginia Plan might leave excessive powers with the states, that full security against the instability inherent in a democratic system might require a closer imitation of the British constitution than anyone was willing to support. Madison concluded the discussion Tuesday morning with his longest speech to date, listing several ways in which a merely federal reform would fail to overcome specific problems and appealing to the smaller states to recognize that none had more to lose if the convention proved unable to preserve the union. The Committee of the Whole then voted 7 states to 3, with Maryland again divided, to adhere to the Virginia Plan. The delegates had needed less than three full days to reconfirm their general agreement that a purely federal reform, however thorough, could not meet the needs of union.

Little else, however, was decided by the vote of June 19, on which Connecticut had merely signaled its commitment to accommodation. As soon as the convention turned to the committee's resolutions, Lansing moved a substitute that would have vested legislative powers in a single house. Connecticut switched sides again to reproduce the characteristic 6–4–1 division: Massachusetts, Pennsylvania, and the four states south of the Potomac facing Connecticut, New York, New Jersey, and Delaware, with Maryland divided. Indeed, it soon became apparent that the conflict over representation overshadowed every lesser disagreement. The convention managed, with increasing difficulty, to confirm its preference for a bicameral regime. It voted once again for popular election of the lower house and state election of the upper. It reached agreement on a two-year term for representatives and six years for the senate. At every step, however, members fearful of a wholly national plan attempted to insert provisions that would give the states a larger role in paying or selecting federal officials. Small-state delegates attempted a variety of schemes that might disrupt the large-state coalition. Though Madison and Hamilton insisted that the small states need not fear a combination of the large, because the most important differences within the union were between the North and the South, William Samuel Johnson of Connecticut responded that a general government was being framed for states as well as people and that even Mason had admitted that the states should have some means to guarantee their rights and place within the system.

By the end of June, when the Convention voted 6–4–1 (as usual) for proportional representation in the lower house, the meeting was approaching dissolution. At this point Connecticut again proposed the compromise that Sherman had suggested weeks before, putting the proposal now in the language of an ultimatum. Remarking that the union might be "partly national," but should continue "partly federal" as well, Oliver Ellsworth said that he was not entirely disappointed that the meeting had approved proportional representation in the lower house, which would conform to national ideas and offer safety to the larger states. But he could see no ground for compromise and no alternative to the collapse of the convention and the union if the larger states would not concede an equal senate.

Madison and Wilson still refused to blink. "If the minority of the people of America refuse to coalesce with the majority on just and proper principles," the Pennsylvanian said, "a separation . . . could never happen on better grounds." Already, Madison complained, by voting that the upper house should be elected by the states, the meeting threatened to create a senate totally dependent on those bodies. If the states were also to be given equal votes, a small minority within the nation would retain the power to defeat every useful measure. Rufus King of Massachusetts also indicated his amazement that the smaller states were willing to renounce the prospect of a just and stable government "from an attachment to the ideal freedom and importance of *states*." "A government founded in a vicious principle of representation," King declared, "must be as short-lived as it would be unjust."

Gunning Bedford's sharp reply suggested that the next few days could settle the convention's fate. "*I do not, gentlemen, trust you*," the Delaware attorney said. The coalition of the large states during the convention seemed to Bedford a sufficient warning of the consequences that could follow if the smaller states submitted to the "degradation" of the Virginia Plan, and he refused to be intimidated by the prospect that the large states would permit the union to collapse. "If they do," he warned, "the small ones will find some foreign ally . . . who will take them by the hand."

Bedford soon apologized for this remark, but his apology did not diminish its effects. Adjourning over Sunday, the convention moved without additional debate on Monday, July 2, to a decision on Connecticut's proposal. The motion for an equal senate failed on an even division: Connecticut, New York, New Jersey, Delaware, and Maryland, aye; Massachusetts, Pennsylvania, Virginia, North Carolina, and South Carolina, no; Georgia now divided. With the meeting at a deadlock and the large-state coalition showing obvious internal stress, Charles C. Pinckney recommended the appointment of a grand committee to devise a compromise. Only Madison and Wilson disapproved, fearing that the tide was turning irreversibly toward an accommodation—as, indeed, it was. Voting for a member from each state, the meeting chose a grand committee that included Ellsworth, Bedford, Paterson, Yates, and Martin, but not a single member from the larger states who had not hinted at a commitment to conciliation. The convention then adjourned till Thursday to celebrate the anniversary of Independence and permit the grand committee to prepare its plan.

To Madison and Wilson, the result was not a compromise at all, but a surrender to the smaller states—and one that seriously marred the symmetry of the evolving system. In exchange for equal representation in the upper house, the smaller states accepted proportional representation in the lower *and* agreed to give the lower house exclusive authority over money bills. This last provision, Madison and Wilson argued, might rob the senate of the power to restrain the lower house on matters where restraint was needed, but it would not prevent minorities from using their position in the senate to defeat the national will. Pleading with the smaller states to give up their demand for a concession plainly incompatible with democratic principles and larger federal powers, the leading nationalists continued to oppose the compromise throughout the next two weeks. They swam against a swelling current.

During these two weeks, the meeting saw a jumble of confusing motions and appointed two additional committees to distribute seats in the first house of representatives. Regional considerations, which had lurked beneath the early 6–4–1 divisions—in which all the southern states had voted with the large-state bloc—now bubbled to the surface. In arguments about a periodic census and admission of new states, as well as in maneuvers over seats in the lower house, members hostile to the three-fifths rule or fearful of the west confronted Southerners who realized that they would be outnumbered 8 to 5 in the projected senate and insisted on provisions that would guarantee their speedy reinforcement from the west, which was a southern section at that time. The smaller northern states proved willing to concede a little on these points in order to secure their more immediate objective. Meanwhile, it became increasingly apparent that several influential members from the larger states were less and less inclined toward a continued confrontation. Not only did they realize that the convention's work would surely be rejected if the smaller states walked out, but some of them conceded that a senate that would represent the states as states might help maintain a federal equilibrium while standing at a proper distance from the lower house. Genuine consolidationists were every bit as rare in the convention as were members who were totally opposed to the replacement of the Articles of Confederation. The moderates were moving to the front. George Mason said that he would "bury his bones in this city rather than expose his country to the consequences of a dissolution of the Convention without anything being done."

Sniffing the prevailing breeze, Yates and Lansing withdrew from the convention on July 11, depriving New York of its vote. (Hamilton had left some days before and would return, as a nonvoting member, only to be present at the finish.) Three days later, Wilson, Madison, and other foes of the committee's plan delivered last appeals for an alternative that would have minimized disparities between the states without conceding equal representation in the senate. Despite the absence of New York, this was defeated 6–4. On July 16, the convention voted 5–4–1 for the committee's compromise proposal: Connecticut, New Jersey, Delaware, Maryland, North Carolina, aye; Pennsylvania, Virginia, South Carolina, Georgia, no; Massachusetts divided.

The decision of July 16, as Randolph quickly noted, was not as narrow as the margin might suggest. New York, New Hampshire, and Rhode Island were unrepresented. All would probably have favored equal representation in at least one house. In addition, several moderates from Georgia, Pennsylvania, and Virginia sympathized with those in Massachusetts, Maryland, and North Carolina, who had voted for the Connecticut plan. The large states held a caucus in the aftermath of the decision. Wilson, Madison, and others still preferred to try to face the small states down. The caucus failed to reach agreement. All the members from the larger states returned to the convention, and the smaller states were satisfied from that point forward that opponents of the compromise would make no serious attempt to countermand the vote.

Randolph also said that the decision of July 16 "embarrassed the business extremely." Every previous decision, he explained, had been directly influenced by the supposition that proportional representation would prevail in both branches of the legislature; all would have to be thought through again in light of this new ruling. The implications, for that matter, were even more profound than the Virginian immediately perceived. With the adoption of the Great (or Connecticut) Compromise, every delegate was forced to make new calculations as to how the actions of the central government might touch his state or section. Assured an equal vote in one part of the Congress, the members from the smaller middle states, as Dickinson had predicted, immediately began to favor ample federal powers. Southerners, by contrast, suddenly became more wary, especially of the enormous powers that the gathering had earlier intended for the senate. Madison and Wilson, who had disapproved not merely state equality but any role for the state legislatures in selecting national officials or making national decisions, were compelled to come to terms with the convention's ruling that the new regime would not be wholly national in structure. As Madison would put it after the convention ended, the delegates were working now to frame a government that would be neither national nor federal, but a novelty compounded of elements of both. And none of them could fully understand what this unprecedented compound would be like.

Amazingly, on first appearances at least, the members needed only ten more days to reach agreement on the basic features of the Constitution. As Randolph failed to see, however, the decision that the general government would represent both individuals and states prepared the way for resolution of more than just the conflict over representation. Both the large states and the small, the North together with the South, could now anticipate control of one part of the legislature. With every state and section armed with a capacity to counter threats to its essential interests, every delegate felt freer to address the national ills that none of them denied. Almost all the delegates had made it clear by now that they intended to define a middle ground between the ineffectuality of the confederation and excessive concentration of authority in central hands. Nearly all agreed, as well, that what they wanted in a senate was a body that would stand at a sufficient distance from the people or the lower house to check majority oppression, yet one that would be wholly democratic in its derivation. With the ruling that the upper house would represent the states, whose legislatures would select its members, the delegates had satisfied demands for more protection for states' rights. They had also reconfirmed a mode of indirect election that promised to secure the senate's independence from the lower house without provoking popular suspicions. Cutting through a thicket of entangled problems, the compromise permitted the convention to resume a path along which arguments among its members could again be guided by their general agreements.

This is not to say that the completion of the work proved quick and easy. Several complicated passages remained, and more than one debate became quite heated. Yet none of the remaining difficulties blocked the members' progress as completely as the conflict over representation, and nearly everyone appears to have assumed that the convention would succeed.

Among remaining difficulties, the most perplexing centered on the powers and selection of the chief executive. From July 17 through July 25, the convention literally revolved around these questions, which were rendered formidable because most delegates were dedicated to a complex, balanced government, yet reasoned from a heritage in which the influence and ambitions of executives had always been identified as constant dangers to a balanced system. Under the Virginia Resolutions, as modified by the Committee of the Whole, the head of the executive would be elected by the national legislature for a single term of seven years. Seconded by Morris, Wilson powerfully opposed both the election by the legislature, which might end in the executive's dependence on that body, and the ineligibility for reelection, which could remove a strong incentive to good conduct and deprive the nation of the services of an experienced and able man. The Pennsylvanians argued that election by the people might remove these difficulties. Pennsylvania was the only state, however, to favor this proposal on July 17. A large majority in the convention doubted that the people had the information or ability to make a wise selection. Many delegates, moreover, led by Mason, were concerned that a reeligible executive would prove, in practice, an executive for life. The convention reaffirmed election by the legislature, struck the

clause confining the executive to a single term, agreed that this would probably result in an improper link between the branches, moved to an election
by electors chosen by the local legislatures, and then moved back again to an
election by the Congress. By the 24th, as Gerry put it, the members seemed
"entirely at a loss."

Madison reviewed the options on the 25th. Election by the legislature, he
explained, might introduce intrigues and render the executive incapable of
acting as a check on legislative usurpations—plainly so if the executive was
eligible for reelection. Election by the local legislatures or the state executives, however, might introduce the influence of the very bodies whose "pernicious measures" the convention still intended to control. Two alternatives
remained: election by electors chosen by the people, which had been suggested on July 19 by King and Paterson, but handily defeated; or direct election by the people, which he had come to favor but which seemed to put the
smaller states, together with the South, at a considerable disadvantage. Hugh
Williamson (North Carolina) suggested that the disadvantage to the smaller
states could be corrected if the people were required to vote for more than a
single candidate. Morris added that the citizens might cast two ballots, one
of which would have to be for someone from another state. Yet, reinforced by
Gerry, Mason still insisted that the people were *least* qualified to make a good
selection. On the 26th the meeting came full circle to the proposition with
which it had started: selection by the national legislature for a single term.

Few were really satisfied with this "solution." The Pennsylvanians, who
had argued for a powerful, reeligible executive since the beginning of the
meeting, had been winning influential converts, of whom Madison was
probably the most important. The major architect of the Virginia Plan had
entered the convention sharing much of the traditional suspicion of a strong
executive. But as he listened to the Pennsylvanians and struggled to adjust
to the decision on the senate, which he considered both undemocratic and
a barrier to the pursuit of national interests, Madison supported an attempt
to switch the power to appoint ambassadors and judges from the senate to
the head of the executive, acting with concurrence of a portion of the upper
house. Discontent with state equality, fear of legislative domination, and a
wish to make it possible for an experienced executive to succeed himself,
which seemed impossible to reconcile with legislative choice, were moving Madison and other large-state nationalists toward popular election and
larger executive powers. Yet fear of an elective monarchy, distrust of popular
election, and sheer impatience to complete the meeting's tasks still counterbalanced these considerations. On July 24, the House had chosen a Com-

mittee of Detail to put its resolutions into order. Now, the members eagerly agreed to an adjournment until Monday, August 6, in order to allow ten days for this committee to report.

While Washington went fishing and visited the old encampment at Valley Forge, John Rutledge (South Carolina), Edmund Randolph, Nathaniel Gorham (Massachusetts), Oliver Ellsworth, and James Wilson assumed responsibility for much more than a careful ordering of the decisions reached in the convention by July 26. In sessions from which only fragmentary records still survive, the Committee of Detail apparently assumed—without objection from their tiring colleagues—that they were free to make significant contributions of their own. Taking note of nearly everything that had transpired in the course of the deliberations, the committee added numerous details to the convention's resolutions and offered several significant additions. Besides providing more elaborate descriptions of executive and judicial powers, their report advanced a new procedure for resolving arguments among the states and recommended that agreement by two-thirds of Congress should be necessary for admission of new states or passage of commercial regulations. It inserted prohibitions of a tax on exports or on interference with the slave trade, which Pinckney had demanded as conditions for his state's agreement. Most significant of all, it offered an enumeration of the powers of the central government, a matter that the full convention had repeatedly postponed, and introduced a range of prohibitions on the sort of local legislation that Madison had planned to counter by a federal veto on state laws, a power that the full convention had decisively refused.

All of August was consumed in close consideration of the work of the Committee of Detail, most of it on two related issues which produced quite different divisions. Reluctant to resume the tedious debate on the executive, the delegates postponed this matter until all the other articles could be considered. Assisted by their broad agreement on the nation's needs and by their general alarm about majority abuses, they reached agreement relatively quickly on the prohibitions on the states and most of the enumerated powers of the Congress. But Morris, Madison, and Wilson had objected from the start to the provision in the Connecticut Compromise that gave the lower house exclusive power over revenues; and the Committee of Detail had given in completely to the South's demands for prohibition of a tax on exports, prohibition of congressional taxation of or interference with the international slave trade, and requirement of a two-thirds vote in Congress for commercial regulations. Opposition mounted day by day to all of these concessions.

On August 8 the smaller middle states joined nationalists in Pennsylva-

nia and Virginia to strike the clause concerning money bills. Insisting that
the clause had been a valuable concession from the smaller states, denouncing the involvement in taxation of a body that would not directly represent
the people, Mason, Randolph, Williamson, and others bitterly objected,
warning that it might compel them to retract their unenthusiastic willingness to go along with state equality in the upper house. Attempting to protect
the compromise on which the hopes of the convention now depended, Caleb
Strong of Massachusetts moved that money bills might be amended by the
senate, but would have to be originated in the lower house. With many delegations thoroughly confused by the variety of questions that had come to
be encompassed in this issue, the convention narrowly decided to postpone
Strong's motion.

On August 8 all three of the New England delegations voted with the
worried Southerners to keep the clause on money bills. From that day forward, compromisers in these Yankee delegations struggled to secure the vital
interests of their section without provoking a significant secession by the
South. Seconded by Morris, Rufus King condemned the plan of the Committee of Detail as so unreasonably biased in favor of the South that Northerners
would justifiably reject it. For purposes of representation, King and Morris
pointed out, the Southerners could count three-fifths of their slaves, and it
was little consolation that the three-fifths rule would also be applied for purposes of direct taxation, which might never be employed. Hating slavery in
any case, King and Morris were infuriated by the prohibitions on congressional interference with new importations and by the ban on export taxes. The
Constitution, they protested, would commit the North to defend the South,
which would be free not only to increase the evil but to shield the products
of slave labor from taxation. Meanwhile, the requirement that two-thirds
of Congress would be necessary to impose commercial regulations would
impede the very national actions in the area of trade that were among the
most important reasons why the shipping states, with their depressed economies, favored constitutional reform.

Complicated, often heated arguments concerning these provisions dominated the convention through the second half of August. Though Madison
and Wilson joined with King and Morris to condemn the ban on export
taxes, protesting that it would deny the government an easy source of revenues and an important weapon in its efforts to compel the Europeans to relax
their navigation laws, the planting states were virtually unanimous in their
insistence on this prohibition. Georgia and the Carolinas, though opposed
by the Virginians as well as by the antislavery members from the North,

were equally insistent on prohibiting congressional restrictions on the slave trade, making this an absolute condition of their states' approval of a plan. On August 21 the compromisers from Connecticut and Massachusetts voted with the Southerners to reaffirm the prohibition of a tax on exports, 7 states to 4 (New Hampshire, New Jersey, Pennsylvania, Delaware, no). Sherman, Gerry, Ellsworth, Gorham, and their colleagues indicated, though, that they expected their conciliatory efforts to be met in kind, that they had voted to accept the South's demands in expectation that the Southerners would now prove willing to protect New England's vital interests. On August 22 Morris moved referral of the slave trade, export taxes, and commercial regulation to another grand committee, where these subjects might provide materials for a "bargain" between the North and the South. Several Southerners approved.

The August compromise between the North and the South, Massachusetts and South Carolina, was second in importance only to the bargain of July 16 to the completion of the Constitution. On August 24 the grand committee chaired by William Livingston of New Jersey reported a proposal to prohibit legislative interference with the slave trade until the year 1800, to reaffirm the ban on export taxes, but to strike the clause requiring two-thirds of Congress for the passage of commercial regulations. On August 25, Pinckney moved extension of the prohibition until 1808, Gorham seconded the motion, and the prohibition carried 7 states to 4 (New Jersey, Pennsylvania, Delaware, Virginia, no). Several Southerners continued to oppose control of trade by a majority in Congress, where they would be outvoted in both houses. This asked the South, said Mason, to "deliver themselves bound hand and foot to the Eastern states." It "would complete the deformity" of a system "so odious," objected Randolph, that he might be forced to disapprove it. Despite their fierce resistance, South Carolina abided by its bargain. A motion to reinstitute the two-thirds rule failed 4 to 7 with only Maryland, Virginia, North Carolina, and Georgia voting for it. Then, on August 31, on Sherman's motion, the convention voted to refer all postponed questions to still another grand committee. The procedure had become the members' standard strategy for handling issues too complex or too divisive for resolution by the whole.

Chaired by David Brearley of New Jersey, the Committee on Unfinished Business (or on Postponed Parts) untangled the convention's last remaining snarls, the knottiest of which was certainly the long-debated question of a sound executive. Having each secured supremacy in one house of the Congress, both the small and the large states had proved determined not to give the other a predominant advantage in selecting the chief magistrate.

Fear of legislative dominance or of corrupting links between the branches, along with the desire to make it possible for the executive to succeed himself, had seriously discredited appointment by the Congress. To this expedient, however, the convention had reluctantly returned. Although the dominance of smaller states in the projected senate had encouraged several large-state nationalists to favor more executive authority—the Committee on Unfinished Business gave the president the leading role in making treaties as well as in appointment of ambassadors and judges—fear of an elective monarchy and strong objections to election either by the people or the states had brought the meeting to an impasse. Provisions that appeared to favor the selection of an able man seemed inconsistent with his reelection. The vigor and stability demanded by the Pennsylvanians seemed incompatible to some with popular election, to others with a due republican suspicion of this branch. Theoretical disputes were complicated by the lingering suspicions of the large and smaller states.

Reporting on September 4 and drawing on the meeting's previous debates, especially on the exchanges of July 25, the Brearley committee sought to cut this knot by recommending an election for a four-year term by electors chosen in such manner as the local legislatures should direct. Each state would be entitled to as many electors as the total of its seats in Congress, and each elector would cast two ballots, at least one of which would have to be for someone from another state. If a single candidate obtained an absolute majority of the electors' votes, he would be president. If not, the president would be elected by the senate from the five who had the highest totals. (In either case, the person placing second in the voting would become vice-president, an office first suggested and defined by this committee.) Both the cumbersome procedure and the introduction of an officer who was essentially superfluous were carefully contrived to balance the demands of the larger and smaller states. Reliance on electors, as committee member Sherman soon explained, would "get rid of the ineligibility" for reelection, which had seemed inseparable from an election by Congress. In addition, Sherman might have said, opponents of election by the people and opponents of election by the states could both find solace in a mode of indirect election that might start with either, yet secure a certain independence of them both.

Some of these details proved problematic. Assuming that the college of electors would seldom show an absolute majority for any single person, most members realized that the committee's plan was meant to give the larger states the largest role in making a preliminary nomination, from which the senate, dominated by the smaller states, would make the final choice. Since the smaller states would have a disproportionate advantage even in the number of electors, several members from the larger states objected that the senate should be forced to choose from fewer nominees. Others argued that selection by the senate, whose cooperation with the president would be required for treaties and appointments, would encourage these two branches to combine against the lower house. In an excellent example of the way in which the delegates had periodically applied collective wisdom to a common problem, these difficulties were resolved by shifting final choice of the executive from the senate to the house of representatives, which would vote by states on this occasion, and by narrowing to three the individuals from among whom the selection must be made.

Several delegates were still concerned about the way in which the president and senate would combine in making treaties and appointments. On September 7, Mason, Wilson, Madison, and Dickinson all favored the revival of a privy council to assist and check the head of the executive in matters where these functions had been trusted to the senate. This was easily defeated, though the members did attempt to reconcile opponents of a senate role in framing money bills by passing Caleb Strong's suggestion of a clause requiring lower-house origination, but permitting upper-house amendment. By September 8 the House was ready to confide a finished plan to a Committee of Style. There, with help from Johnson, Hamilton, Madison, and King, Gouverneur Morris imparted final polish to the phrasing.

September 10 saw final pleas for reconsideration of some features over which several members had become increasingly alarmed. Randolph said that he had introduced "a set of republican propositions" on May 29, but that these resolutions had been so disfigured in the course of the convention that he might "dissent" from the completed plan unless the meeting would provide that state conventions could propose amendments to a second general convention, whose alterations would be final. Sharing Randolph's dread of hazy wording and majority control of commerce, together with his fear that an objectionable senate might combine with a powerful executive to overbalance the people's representatives in the lower house, Mason argued on September 12 that the convention also ought to add a bill of rights. Gerry readily agreed.

Responding partly to these fears, the members did consent to substitute two-thirds of Congress for the three-fourths previously required to override a presidential veto. But with Sherman pointing out that nothing in the Constitution would repeal state declarations or infringe the liberties that they protected, the states unanimously declined to draft a bill of rights. As the convention speedily considered the report of the Committee of Style—obviously eager to adjourn, repeatedly refusing to consider major changes—the final drama was at hand. Mason failed to win insertion of a clause requiring two-thirds of the Congress for the passage of commercial regulations until 1808 (by which date, he may have hoped, the planting states would get their reinforcements from the west). Randolph moved again for a procedure under which the plan would not be ratified until a second general convention could consider changes recommended by the state conventions, warning that he could not sign without some such provision. Concluding that the finished plan "would end either in monarchy or a tyrannical aristocracy," Mason followed with a similar pronouncement, as did Gerry. Randolph's motion was unanimously defeated. Every delegation present voted to approve the finished Constitution and to order it engrossed.

On September 17, Benjamin Franklin, who was eighty-one and so enfeebled that James Wilson read his speeches for him, intervened once more, as he had done at several anxious moments, to plead with everyone who still retained objections to "doubt a little of his own infallibility" and join in signing. Hamilton appealed for unanimity as well, observing that "no man's ideas were more remote from the plan than his own were known to be," but that he could not hesitate "between anarchy and confusion on one side and the chance of good . . . on the other." No one, to be sure, had gotten everything he wanted in the course of the convention. No one, four months earlier, had entered the convention able to conceive the sort of Constitution that the members' compromises and collective wisdom had created. No one fully understood as yet—not even Hamilton or Madison—that the collective reasoning of the convention, together with the clashing interests of its delegations, had resulted in a system that would prove not only adequate to the exigencies of union but capable of serving as a new foundation for significant revision of the theory of constitutional democracy. Of the forty-two still present on September 17, however, all but three felt able to subscribe their names to the completed work. Whereupon, as Washington confided to his diary, "the members adjourned to the City Tavern, dined together, and took a cordial leave," nearly all of them agreeing with the venerated Franklin that the emblem on the chair in which the general had presided over their deliberations—testifying by his presence to the gravity of the occasion and the possibility that great executive authority might be entrusted to great virtue—was, indeed, a *rising* sun.

The Federalist Papers

As the members of the Constitutional Convention gathered for a farewell dinner on 17 September 1787, the mood was both convivial and optimistic. Of the forty-two still present for the great Convention's final act, only three had been unwilling to affix their signatures to the unanimous agreement of the delegations present. Throughout the summer the public had been waiting patiently, yet eagerly, for the notables at Philadelphia to complete a plan of constitutional reform. The Convention had agreed to submit its work directly to the people, who would elect special ratifying conventions in their several states. Unassailable in democratic theory, this procedure also had the practical advantage of excluding the possibility of a rejection by the state legislatures, whose powers would be lessened by the plan, and whose unanimous consent had heretofore been necessary for any alteration of the Articles of Confederation. Approval by conventions in nine states would be sufficient to put the new Constitution into practice.

Several signers, nevertheless, were not allowed to rest. Almost immediately, James Madison was summoned to New York to take his seat in the Confederation Congress, where Virginia's Richard Henry Lee and others were resisting a congressional endorsement of the Convention's plan. By 28 September, when Congress agreed to refer the new Constitution to the states, newspapers in New York were filled with criticisms of the proposed reform. It was increasingly apparent that ratification was uncertain in nearly all the larger states, without which an agreement by the others might be futile.

Nowhere were the prospects poorer than in New York itself. New York City, and most other seaports, seemed to favor ratification. The country people were not so well disposed. New York enjoyed an enviable situation under the Articles of Confederation. State taxes on foreign imports drew revenues, in practice, from much of Connecticut and New Jersey as well as from New Yorkers, assuring a healthy treasury without a heavy load of internal taxation. The new Constitution placed this source of income exclusively in federal hands, threatened higher taxes, and gave New York six seats in the House of Representatives, compared to Virginia's ten. Governor George Clinton, popular and highly influential, had resisted the meeting of a constitutional convention and, over the signature "Cato," was now contributing a series of letters to the newspapers' swelling condemnation of the Constitution. Two of the state's three delegates to the Federal Convention, John Lansing and Robert Yates, had withdrawn in disgust as soon as it was clear that the Convention would not be content simply to amend the Articles of Confederation.

New York's third delegate to Philadelphia, the choice of the opponents of Clinton's popular, state-oriented politics, was, at thirty-two, one of the genuine prodigies of the American Revolution. While still a student at King's College (now Columbia), Alexander Hamilton had written one of the important revolutionary tracts of 1775. As captain of artillery, he had fought effectively at Trenton and won an appointment as an influential aide to General Washington, who later granted his request to lead the attack on the last British redoubt at Yorktown. While still in his twenties, Hamilton had helped to lead a major thrust for national reform in the Confederation Congress in 1783, and he had rapidly become the leading spokesman for conservative and Continental-minded forces in New York, where he periodically submitted persuasive essays to the press. At Annapolis in 1786 he had played a central role in bringing on the Constitutional Convention.

Repeatedly outvoted by his colleagues in the New York delegation, Hamilton had been uncharacteristically subdued through the early weeks at Philadelphia. After the departure of Lansing and Yates broke the quorum of his state, he had alternated his attendance at the Convention with his legal practice in New York, making no great contribution to the shaping of a plan of government that was considerably less powerful than he personally preferred. But despite his reservations, he returned to Philadelphia for the signing and was eloquent in urging all the delegates to join in a commitment to a reform that seemed the best the nation could achieve. Like other signers, Hamilton was willing to assume a major part in the fight for ratification. On 21 July, while the Convention was still sitting, he publicly condemned Governor Clinton's reputed predetermination to oppose whatever issued from the meeting at Philadelphia. Continuing to watch the growing opposition to the finished plan, he soon decided that the situation called for an extended and elaborate defense and explanation of the Constitution. Tradition has it that he started writing on the sloop that carried him back to New York City from the fall session of the state's supreme court at Albany. Addressed "To the People of New York" and signed "Publius," a pseudonym selected from Plutarch in order to remind readers of the hero who had given ancient Rome a stable, republican constitution, this essay was the first of the series that became America's outstanding classic on federalism and constitutional democracy.

Publication and Authorship

With the exception of the last eight numbers, the eighty-five essays that constitute *The Federalist* (often referred to as *The Federalist Papers*) originally appeared as letters in the several newspapers of New York. Numbers 1 through 7 were first printed, beginning on 27 October 1787, in the *Independent Journal,* a semi-weekly edited by John McLean. When it became apparent that the Wednesday and Saturday publication schedule of the *Independent Journal* would not permit a timely completion of the series, the plan was altered to permit original publication also in some of the other sheets that had decided to reprint the series. By 30 November, the ordinary pattern saw new numbers published on Tuesday in the *New York Packet,* on Wednesday in the *Independent Journal,* and either on Friday in the *Packet* or on Saturday in the *Journal.* (Numbers 9 and 10 were the only essays to appear first in the *Daily Advertiser.*) Finally, in the last days of March 1788, McLean published the collected newspaper essays, along with eight new numbers, in a separate, two-volume edition. McLean's edition slightly altered the sequence of the letters and divided one of the newspaper essays into two. It has become customary to follow the numbering of the McLean edition.

When Hamilton published the first of the letters of "Publius," he had already decided to seek collaborators for a work whose scope would call for much more time than he could spare from a busy legal practice and other efforts to support the Constitution. He may already have secured the cooperation of John Jay, for the first of Jay's essays, number 2 of the series, was published only four days after number 1. Hamilton also approached a merchant friend, William Duer, who prepared two essays that were judged unsuited to the series. He probably turned next to Gouverneur Morris and other longtime allies. Failing here, the brilliant young attorney looked beyond the circle of his New York friends, successfully appealing to James Madison, who had just decided to remain in the city through at least a part of the new session of the Confederation Congress.

Hamilton's appeal to Madison, whose politics were very different from his own, proved doubly fortunate. Of the three collaborators, John Jay, who was forty-two, was probably the most distinguished. The principal author of the New York constitution of 1777, which was among the most admired, Jay had also made a critical contribution to the negotiations that had brought the War for Independence to a strikingly successful end for the new United States. After Revolutionary service as peace commissioner and minister to Spain, he had returned to fill a high executive position as the Confederation's secretary for foreign affairs. Jay had scarcely undertaken the collaboration, though, when he was crippled by a severe rheumatic attack. Ultimately, he could contribute only five of the eighty-five essays. The burden of the work fell overwhelmingly on the two younger men and urged on Madison a larger part than may have been originally envisioned. Madison's experience and different views imparted new dimensions to the letters. As his participation grew, the papers gradually assumed the shape responsible for their enduring reputation.

A modest man, whose personality contrasted sharply with the vain and dashing Hamilton's, Madison was never comfortable when, late in life, he was saluted as "the father of the Constitution." The Constitution, he insisted, did not spring full-blown from any single head. This was entirely true. The Constitution was the product of a summer's difficult deliberations by the full Convention, and its provisions differed quite significantly from those that Madison might have written on his own. Of all the heads at the Convention, nevertheless, Madison's, by general agreement, had been the most important. Madison was principally responsible for the Virginia Resolutions, with which deliberations had begun. No one had given more or better thought to constitutional reform, and no one made a more important contribution to debates. Many qualified observers believed that the thirty-six-year-old Madison had no superior in his knowledge of the continent's affairs. He possessed the fullest record of the proceedings of the great Convention. He may have been the finest, most important political thinker the United States has ever produced.

Neither Madison nor Hamilton, of course, was conscious of participating in the writing of a classic. The Federalist originated as occasional pieces intended to persuade New Yorkers to support the ratification of the Constitution. Through mailings and reprintings, the letters circulated widely through the states and won quick recognition as the most important series in support of the new Constitution. Both Hamilton and Madison, however, preferred to keep their authorship a public secret, although both informed close friends of their participation. The authors were acutely conscious of The Federalist's flaws. Appearing at a rate of roughly three per week, each number approximately as long as this encyclopedia entry, the letters were a herculean feat of writing for men who did not neglect their other duties. There was seldom time for one co-author to review an essay by the other. Sometimes, Madison reported, there was not even time for the author himself to proofread copy. The printer may occasionally have set the type for the first portions of an essay while the author wrote its final paragraphs.

This rush to press, which has astounded later readers of these graceful and compelling essays, must also bear a major portion of the blame for more than a century of controversy over which man wrote which numbers. Early in the nineteenth century, as the reputation of *The Federalist* grew and publishers or friends attempted to assign each letter to the proper author, Hamilton and Madison (whose differences had long since led to a political collision) advanced conflicting claims. The authorship of the majority of the papers was never in dispute. Jay certainly wrote numbers 2–5 and 64. Hamilton wrote numbers 1, 6–9, 11–13, 15–17, 21–36, 59–61, and 65–85, fifty-one of the eighty-five letters. Madison wrote numbers 10, 14, and 37–48. On various occasions Hamilton and Madison each claimed authorship of 18–20, 49–58, and 62–63. Neither man, it is assumed, deliberately attempted to mislead. Their memories simply differed by the time the question came to seem of some importance. Missing records, carelessness, and a mistake with Roman numerals completed the confusion.

From the early nineteenth century to the present, scholars have repeatedly attempted to resolve the problem of disputed authorship by applying a variety of generally accepted tests. The content of disputed numbers has been analyzed and carefully compared both to the content of the essays whose author is known and to the other writings of both men. Surprisingly—for the philosophies of Hamilton and Madison were different enough that many scholars would maintain that "Publius" displayed a "split personality"—examinations of this sort have not been completely conclusive. The effort to defend the Constitution tended to bring out the similarities, more than the differences, in the two men's views. Their prose styles were quite similar. Each may have borrowed from the other's essays in his own numbers or in later writings. Advocates of each have been able to present close parallels between passages in the disputed essays and passages in other writings by both men. A majority of modern scholars would agree only that the internal evidence favors Madison's claim to all the disputed numbers, although the evidence is not as strong for 55–58 and 62–63 as it is for most of the other essays.

Other tests seem more conclusive. The several lists that have been traced to Hamilton contain discrepancies, whereas Madison was more consistent in his claims on different occasions. None of the lists that have been thought to derive from Hamilton would seem to represent a carefully considered claim that was undoubtedly put forward by the author himself. Alternative lists, by contrast, can be traced more certainly to Madison himself and seem to have been prepared in circumstances that permitted greater care and more deliberation. These facts, together with the balance of the internal evidence, have finally produced a scholarly consensus from which there have been few dissenters since the 1960's. The question is not absolutely closed, but modern scholars overwhelmingly agree that it is very probable that Madison wrote all of the disputed essays. Numbers 18–20, as Madison himself explained, were written after Hamilton had given him a briefer draft on the same subject; but Hamilton's materials seem to have exerted little influence. Counting 18–20 as essentially his own, Madison was probably responsible for twenty-nine of the eighty-five essays: 10, 14, 18–20, 37–58, and 62–63.

Content

Hamilton presented a preliminary outline for the series and established its essential tone in *The Federalist* number 1. Suggesting that the strongest opposition to the Constitution came from short-sighted and self-interested state politicians, some of whom preferred disruption of the American union and all of whom would see their consequence reduced by this reform, "Publius" nonetheless foreswore an appeal to passions. He promised to address the reason of his readers in a systematic consideration of the necessity of union, the inadequacy of the existing Confederation, and the propriety of the suggested Constitution, both in principle and in its particular distribution of governmental powers. Hamilton also hinted at the central themes that would suffuse the papers. "Publius" would argue, first, that the alternative to ratification of the Constitution would be the dissolution of the union, with all the damage to American prosperity, happiness, and liberty that a fracture of the Confederacy would entail. More originally and more persuasively, he would also seek to turn the principal fears of the opponents of ratification to his own advantage, insisting that the new Constitution was not merely consistent with republican principles, but necessary to secure and complete the libertarian achievements of the Revolution.

The three collaborators do not seem to have agreed at any single point on a rigid and formal division of labors. Rather, after Hamilton's first letter had defined a basic structure, each author tended to assume responsibility for topics suited to his experience and interests. Summoning his special expertise, Jay argued the superiority of union from a foreign-policy perspective in numbers 2–5, completing all but one of his contributions before Madison entered the lists. Hamilton developed the necessity of union for preventing interstate disputes in numbers 6–8. Madison's initial contribution, number 10, published on 22 November, has come to seem the most impressive of the series. Beginning with the problem of factionalism, which Hamilton had introduced in number 9, the Virginian carried readers logically from analysis of human nature through his famous argument that the liberties of all could best be reconciled with the rule of the majority in an extensive, well-constructed, federal republic, reversing the entrenched assumption that republican government was suitable only for small territories.

The history of the revolutionary states had shown, Madison reasoned, that the characteristic vices of free governments arose from the ability of a majority to pursue its special interests at the expense of other people's rights. But an enlarged republic would incorporate so many different interests that it would be extremely difficult for a majority to discover and pursue such factious goals. Madison reemphasized the value of extending the sphere of republican government in number 14. Hamilton had already demonstrated the superiority of union for commercial and financial purposes in numbers 11–13. Number 14 concluded the first section of the papers.

Having made their case for the necessity and benefits of American union (and probably having resigned themselves by now to Jay's debility), Hamilton and Madison were ready for the body of the work: a demonstration that a central government incapable of meeting national needs endangered both the union and the Revolution, followed by a systematic explanation and examination of the new Constitution, which was carefully designed to show that the Convention had devised a safe and thoroughly republican solution to the crisis posed by the imminent collapse of the Confederation. Writing, on average, a thousand words per day—an awesome demonstration of their skills and knowledge—each man worked essentially alone. Occasional and doubtless hurried conversations were sufficient to divide responsibilities and fit the pieces into a coherent whole. Each assumed the duties for which he was best equipped.

Among American statesmen, few had been as quick as Alexander Hamilton to conclude that the Articles of Confederation were irredeemably defective in their fundamental principles. None may have been more thoroughly convinced that the necessary solution to the range of ills confronting the new nation lay in a concentration of governmental powers—first in the central government, and next in the executive and judicial branches of the federal regime. Appropriately, when "Publius" initiated his analysis of the defects of the government under the Articles of Confederation and attempted to describe the basic elements of a successful remedy, it was Hamilton who took the larger role. His fifteenth *Federalist* was an eloquent description of the weaknesses of the existing union and an incisive statement of the concept that these disabilities could not be overcome unless a central government dependent on and capable of acting only through the states was replaced by one whose powers would rise directly from the people and whose courts and other agencies could compel individual obedience to its commands. Reinforced by Madison's analysis of the weaknesses of other ancient and modern confederacies in numbers 18–20, Hamilton elaborated these conclusions in numbers 16–17 and 21–36. The pen then passed to his collaborator, who opened the defense of the new Constitution.

James Madison had kept a complete record of the Philadelphia debates, missing not a single day of the deliberations. No one was better qualified to explain the key decisions in Convention. No one was more concerned to demonstrate that the new Constitution was consistent with the fundamental principles of the republican revolution. This was the central strategy of numbers 37–58 and 62–63, after which Madison departed for Virginia, leaving the completion of the long and careful, clause-by-clause defense of the Constitution in Hamilton's capable hands.

Since the Constitution opened with an article defining the legislative powers of the central government and the organization of the Congress, the clause-by-clause examination permitted each collaborator to develop his particular concerns. Madison resisted reiterated calls to hurry home for the elections to the Virginia ratifying convention until literally the final moment in order to carry his analysis through numbers 62 and 63, a point at which logic and his interests permitted his release. More sympathetic to the states than Hamilton, he undertook a rigorous definition of the federal principle in number 39 and related essays. More theoretically inclined, he offered the extended explanation of the principle of checks and balances in numbers 47–51. Numbers 62 and 63, on the theoretical advantages of a senate, completed his defense of the organization of Congress and the division of legislative powers. Jay reentered the collaboration to justify the Senate's role in treaties in number 64. Hamilton could then pursue the principal defense of the executive in numbers 67–77 and the examination of the judiciary in numbers 78–83, where he contributed importantly to the emerging concept of judicial review. Number 84 answered Antifederalist objections to which "Publius" had not yet replied, including the objection to the absence of a bill of rights, and number 85 tacitly promised the opponents of the Constitution that amendments would be added when the new government went into effect.

Contribution and Influence

The authors of *The Federalist* did not achieve their immediate objective. The voters of New York elected a convention that numbered nineteen friends and forty-six opponents of the Constitution. Assembling on 17 June 1788, the convention ratified the Constitution principally because the prior decisions of ten other states had made it clear that the new government would be put into effect with or without New York.

The immediate contribution of the letters is difficult to measure. It seems unlikely that large numbers of contemporaries read *The Federalist,* for the style and content were not intended for ordinary readers. "Publius" hoped to persuade an educated and informed elite, assuming that their influence would carry the majority. But this was not an inappropriate approach for the time and the occasion. Only a minority of voters cast ballots in the several states, many of them following the lead of local worthies; the ultimate decision on the Constitution was delivered in the state conventions by very much the sort of men to whom the essays were addressed.

The series of newspaper letters was not initiated soon enough to have much impact on the states in which conventions met before the end of 1787: Delaware, Pennsylvania, New Jersey, and Georgia. But most of these states were overwhelmingly in favor of the Constitution. Ratification depended, in the end, on the elections for and votes within the state conventions meeting after 1 January 1788. By this time thirty-two of the letters of "Publius" had appeared. It is impossible to know how many minds were influenced by the essays. In the states that ratified the Constitution after 1 January, only fourteen newspapers reprinted portions of the letters as soon as they appeared; none reprinted the whole series. On the other hand, the New York newspapers, in which the essays were originally published, were mailed throughout the country by members of Congress and other national leaders. Many voters and an even larger portion of the men whom they elected read at least a part of the series before their state conventions met. Many others heard the arguments of "Publius" repeated in the state conventions, where leaders of the ratification struggle used them as a source-book. It may not have been sheer coincidence that Federalists held firm in all the critical conventions, while a sufficient number of opponents of the

Constitution changed their minds to give the victory to the proponents of reform.

The eventual impact of the letters is beyond dispute. Within the lifetime of the authors, as the meaning of the Constitution was defined in practice, *The Federalist* rapidly assumed its place as the classic commentary on the Constitution. With the exception of the records of the Federal Convention, no document has exercised more influence on the constitutional interpretations of congressmen, scholars, and jurists. Almost immediately, moreover, Thomas Jefferson pronounced *The Federalist* the greatest work on government that he had ever read.

Jefferson exaggerated, possibly, as was his habit. *The Federalist* is repetitive and sometimes inconsistent. It carries the enduring marks of a collaborative effort by men whose clashing views, within a few years' time, would be responsible in no small part for the emergence of the warring political parties that "Publius" had feared. The letters seldom probed the fundamentals of political philosophy, assuming the importance of *justice, liberty,* and *the general welfare* without defining any of these terms. For all these flaws, however, the essays were distinguishable from the beginning from the more ephemeral polemics in which others urged the ratification of the Constitution. The Constitutional Convention had devised a new and quite distinctive form of federal association, distributing between the states and the several branches of the central government powers that were to be exerted concurrently on the individuals who made up the nation. *The Federalist* was a vital contribution to the explanation and defense of this new concept, which they helped to name. They explained why the Convention had divided powers as it did and sometimes justified or rendered more coherent decisions that the Framers made for reasons that were only partly theoretical. In doing so, they remolded and permanently revised several of the central concepts of modern constitutionalism: separation of powers, checks and balances, executive responsibility, and organic law, as well as division of authority between the federal government and the states. In the end, the letters also redefined the revolutionary ideal of a free and stable democratic order, much as their authors thought the original Publius had done for ancient Rome. In the United States and in all the modern federal republics that have been influenced by the American example, those who wish to understand these great ideas must turn, at minimum, to essays 1, 2, 9, 10, 14, 15, 17, 23, 37, 39, 47–51, 62–63, 70, 78, 84, and 85.

Bibliography

Primary Sources. Jacob E. Cooke, ed., *The Federalist* (Middletown, Conn., 1961), is the definitive scholarly edition of the text. Cooke's preface and footnotes offer precise information about publication and a superb summary discussion of the scholarly controversy over the authorship of disputed essays. Roy P. Fairfield, ed., *The Federalist,* 2nd ed. (Garden City, N.Y., 1966), contains fifty-one of the essays with excellent annotation and the most complete bibliography of editions of and writings about the classic. Clinton Rossiter, ed., *The Federalist Papers* (New York, 1961), is an inexpensive paperback edition of all eighty-five essays, based on the McLean edition of 1788 and providing a thematic table of contents and a good index of ideas.

Secondary Sources. Douglas Adair, *Fame and the Founding Fathers,* Trevor Colbourn, ed. (New York, 1974), is a collection of influential essays on the tenth *Federalist,* editions of the papers, Hamilton's use of classical pseudonyms, and the authorship of disputed numbers. Gottfried Dietze, *"The Federalist": A Classic on Federalism and Free Government* (Baltimore, 1960), is perhaps the best extended analysis. Thomas S. Engeman, *The "Federalist" Concordance* (Middletown, Conn., 1980), is a comprehensive index.

Alpheus Thomas Mason, *"The Federalist*—A Split Personality," in *American Historical Review,* 57 (1952), is a judicious discussion of similarities and differences in the views of Madison and Hamilton. Frederick Mosteller and David L. Wallace, *Inference and Disputed Authorship: "The Federalist"* (Reading, Mass., 1964), is a computer-assisted content analysis of the disputed essays. Carry Wills, *Explaining America: "The Federalist"* (Garden City, N.Y., 1981), is a recent, challenging, and debatable interpretation. Gordon S. Wood, *The Creation of the American Republic, 1776–1787* (Chapel Hill, N.C., 1969), is the most important history of the emergence of Federalist ideas.

1787 and 1776

Patrick Henry, James Madison, the Constitution, and the Revolution

Scores of patriotic speakers have reminded us, of late, that the United States enjoys the oldest written constitution in the world. As we celebrate its bicentennial, however, we might also recollect the *doubts* with which the Constitution was originally received—reservations so severe and so widespread that it was barely ratified in four of thirteen states, rejected by two more. Thomas Jefferson, John Hancock, Samuel Adams, Richard Henry Lee—a formidable corps of Revolutionary heroes—all expressed significant objections. Patrick Henry thought the Constitution might betray the democratic Revolution, and Henry spoke for fully half the voters of the union's largest state, seconded by several other Founding Fathers of Virginia. Only as these doubts were answered did the Constitution come to seem legitimate to many of our greatest Revolutionary statesmen; and there is much to gain from paying some attention to their fears, together with the way that they were countered. Nothing takes us more directly to the essence of the Founding vision, and perhaps no single source is more instructive on this subject than the record of debates in the Virginia ratifying convention, the only public meeting of the Revolutionary years for which we have a close approximation of a word-by-word account.[1]

From time to time, reality creates a situation and a cast no dramatist could top. It did so in the Old Dominion in 1788. Eight states had ratified the Constitution when Virginia's state convention met; nine were necessary to adopt it. No one doubted that the national decision was at stake, for all of the remaining states would follow the Virginians' lead in ratifying the reform or in insisting on conditions that were likely to defeat it.[2] Yet everyone agreed that the elections had resulted in a gathering too evenly divided to predict. Thomas Jefferson was still in France, his sentiments so mixed that Federalists and Antifederalists would both attempt to claim him. George Washington did not attend, knowing that his presence might have smacked of personal ambition while his known approval would exert a potent influence from behind the scenes. With these exceptions, though, the meeting brought together nearly every public man of major stature in the commonwealth that occupied about a fifth of the United States in 1788: James Madison, John Marshall, Edmund Pendleton, the brothers George and Wilson Cary Nicholas, George Mason, Patrick Henry, and James Monroe. Perhaps no other state—at this or any other time—could have assembled such a roll, and nowhere was the outcome so uncertain. When the meeting opened on June 3, the Federalists were marginally more optimistic than their foes, estimating a majority of three or four among the 160 present. But many delegates were wavering or undecided, and the Antifederalists believed that most of them could be persuaded to demand conditional amendments. The circumstances favored Patrick Henry, who had only to provoke more doubts than Federalists could put to rest and who was every bit as capable of dominating a Virginia public meeting as our national mythology suggests.[3]

History, regrettably, has been increasingly ungenerous to Henry, leaving most Americans with little more than foggy recollections that his speeches were supposed to mesmerize contemporary hearers. Words alone, however, barely hint at the authority with which he spoke. In 1765, when he was only twenty-nine and serving his initial term in the colonial assembly, this legendary country lawyer introduced the resolutions that ignited the colonial revolt against the Stamp Act. With Jefferson and Richard Henry Lee, he spurred Virginia's mounting protests through the next ten years and called the colony to arms in 1775 in words that countless children memorized for the centennial of American independence: "Give me liberty or give me death." First governor of his new state, an office to which he was reelected four more times within the next ten years, Henry was an aging patriot by 1788, when voters chose the special meeting that would ratify or disapprove the Constitution. Still, he gloried in his role as Revolutionary tribune of the people. And when he rose in the Convention to open the attack, referring to himself as "the servant of the people of this commonwealth, . . . a sentinel over their rights, liberty, and happiness," he summoned the assistance of a reputation only Washington's surpassed.[4]

The people, Henry said, "are exceedingly uneasy and disquieted" with this "alarming" plan "to change our government." Delegated to prepare amendments to the Articles of Confederation, the members of the Philadelphia Convention had instead proposed a change "as radical as that which separated us from Great Britain," a plan of government that would transform the United States from a Confederation into a national republic. "You ought to be extremely cautious," Henry warned. All "our privileges and rights are [once again] in danger." "A wrong step . . . now will plunge us into misery, and our republic will be lost."[5]

Language of this sort was not adopted merely for theatrical effect. When Henry spoke, the nation's republican experiment was barely twelve years old. It was by no means inconceivable that it could fail. The standard wisdom taught that a republic should be small enough and homogeneous enough that all its citizens would share a set of common interests and be able to maintain a jealous watch on the ambitions of their rulers. Now, suddenly, the Constitution offered to create a national republic larger than the largest European state. It sketched a central government whose powers would be greater than the British Parliament had claimed—a government, moreover, organized in striking imitation of the hated British form, where only the lower house of the legislature would be chosen in direct elections by the people. "I may be thought suspicious," Henry said, "but, sir, suspicion is a virtue [when] its object is the preservation of the public good."[6]

Having spent so much of his career resisting an encroaching, unresponsive central government, the aging firebrand was unmoved by Federalist insistence that rejection of the Constitution might destroy the union. He was unimpressed by Federalist descriptions of the benefits the nation could expect. Supporters of the Constitution seemed to fear, one of Henry's allies scoffed,

> that we shall have wars and rumors of wars, that every calamity is to attend us, and that we shall be ruined and disunited forever, unless we adopt this Constitution. Pennsylvania and Maryland are to fall upon us from the north, like the Goths and Vandals of old; the Algerines . . . are to fill the Chesapeake with mighty fleets, and to attack us on our front; the Indians are to invade us with numerous armies on our rear, in order to convert our cleared lands into hunting grounds; and the Carolinians, from the south, (mounted on alligators, I presume,) are to come and destroy our cornfields, and eat up our little children![7]

These were the mighty terrors, Henry sarcastically agreed, that would await Virginia if the Constitution was defeated. The nation was at peace, rapidly recovering from devastation and depression. He would not be terrified into an irreversible mistake when it was in Virginia's power to insist, at minimum, on alterations that might make the Constitution safer for the states and people.[8] Neither was he willing to concede that so much governmental power would produce the blessings some expected. "Those nations who have gone in search of grandeur, power, and splendor, have . . . been the victims of their own folly," he declaimed. "While they acquired those visionary blessings, they lost their freedom."[9] "You are not to inquire how your trade may be increased, nor how you are to become a great and powerful people, but how your liberties can be secured; for liberty ought to be the direct end of your government."[10]

Here the venerated Revolutionary loosed the whole of his impressive prowess. "Whither is the spirit of America gone?" he asked, the spirit that had checked the "pompous armaments" of mighty Britain. "It has gone," he feared,

> in search of a splendid government—a strong, energetic government. Shall we imitate the example of those nations who have gone from a simple to a splendid government? Are those nations more worthy of our imitation? What can make an adequate satisfaction to them for the loss they have suffered in attaining such a government—for the loss of their liberty? If we admit this consolidated government, it will be because we like a great, splendid one. Some way or other we must be a great and mighty empire; we must have an army, and a navy, and a number of things. When the American spirit was in its youth, the language of America was different: liberty, sir, was then the primary object.

"Consider what you are about to do," Henry pleaded. History was full of cautionary lessons, "instances of the people losing their liberty by their own carelessness and the ambition of a few." "A powerful and mighty empire," he insisted, "is incompatible with the genius of republicanism."[11]

Obviously, Henry was indulging in some verbal terrorism of his own. But this was not the language of an intellect that we can readily dismiss, and it does not suggest a thoughtless fear of extra-local power. Henry's sentiments had not been "antifederal" through most of his career, and they were antifederal now for well-considered reasons. Federalists believed that recent sectional collisions in the Continental Congress had predisposed the former governor to rail against whatever issued from the Constitutional Convention, and there can be no doubt that he opposed the Constitution partly out of a concern that vital local interests might be threatened by a stronger federal system. Nevertheless, the presence of these state and regional considerations, which were shared by Federalists and Antifederalists alike, does not suggest that either side was insincere when they addressed more theoretical concerns; and it does not permit us to conclude that this was "really" what the argument was all about.[12]

As a speaker, Patrick Henry used a shotgun, not a rapier, demolishing his target with scattershots that intermixed the trivial with the profound, sectional complaints with fundamental Revolutionary theory. But Henry's oratory lifted to inspiring heights because it rested on a base of penetrating, substantive objections. And while he often pressed the Federalists with state and regional concerns, his speeches also introduced a set of theoretical considerations that were shared by Antifederalists throughout the country, leading hundreds to conclude that this unprecedented plan of government was unacceptably at odds with the principles of 1776.[13] For the majority of people, Henry warned, national glory is a poor exchange for liberty and comfort. Whatever benefits the Constitution might appear to promise, it ought to be rejected—or at least substantially amended—if it would also prove oppressive for the body of the people. There seemed abundant reason for anticipating that it would.

When Henry warned that liberty was once again at risk, he meant, most obviously, that the new Constitution incorporated no specific guarantees of freedom of religious conscience, trial by jury, freedom of the press, or other privileges protected by the Revolutionary constitutions of the states.[14] The absence of a bill of rights was certainly the commonest and probably the most persuasive reason for opposition to the Constitution. The standard Federalist response—that it had not been necessary to deny the federal government powers it had not been granted in the first place—was entirely unconvincing, given the supremacy provision and the power to employ whatever measures might seem "necessary" to achieve enumerated ends. In Virginia, as in other states, the clamor for explicit guarantees was so widespread that Federalists were forced to promise that a bill of rights would be prepared by the new Congress once the Constitution was approved (which means, of course, that their descendants owe this fundamental charter of their freedoms, perhaps the plainest link between the Constitution and the Declaration, more to its opponents than its framers).

For many Antifederalists, however, the promise of a bill of rights was not enough. I should think that man "a lunatic," Henry exclaimed, "who should tell me to [adopt] a government avowedly defective, in hopes of having it amended afterwards." "Do you enter into a compact first, and afterwards settle the terms?"[15] Henry wanted his additional security while sovereignty still rested wholly in the people and the states, not least because addition of a bill of rights would not alleviate his deeper worries. Liberty, as every Revolutionary knew, was simply not reducible to any list of privileges on which a government would be forbidden to intrude. Liberty also meant a government directed and controlled by the body of a democratic people, which seemed, in any case, the only kind of government that would be likely to abide by written limitations on its power. This sort of liberty as well appeared to be profoundly threatened by the Constitution, which is why the fiery patriot initiated his attacks by warning that the "republic" might be lost. He did not believe that this new government would stay within the limits of its charter or, even if it did, that this would be sufficient to assure that it would prove responsive to the people's needs and will.

"This government is so new, it wants a name," Henry complained. Federalists might say that "it is national in this part, and federal in that part, &c. We may be amused, if we please, by a treatise of political anatomy," but for ordinary purposes of legislation the central government would act directly on the people, not the states.[16] It was to be a single, national government in this respect, and it would irresistibly become more national in time. Antifederalists were not persuaded by the Constitution's novel effort to divide what all the best-regarded theorists maintained could not be workably divided. Sovereignty, some Federalists had recently suggested, should not be thought of as residing in any government at all in a consistent Revolutionary order; sovereignty resided only in the people, who could certainly distribute portions of it to the states, portions to the general government, or even a concurrent jurisdiction to them both.[17] But holding to the standard view, which states that there had to be some agency in every governmental system that would have the final power of decision, Antifederalists could not believe that neither government would really have the final say. In its attempt to balance state and federal powers, they insisted, the Constitutional Convention had created a notorious monster: an *imperium in imperio.* "I never heard of two supreme coordinate powers in one and the same country," William Grayson said. "I cannot conceive how it can happen."[18] The state and general governments, George Mason pointed out, would both possess a power of direct taxation, and they would necessarily compete for the same sources of revenue. "These two concurrent powers cannot exist long together; the one will destroy the other; the general government being paramount to, and in every respect more powerful than the state governments, the latter must give way."[19] Sooner or later, all power would be sucked into the mighty vortex of the general government. It would be little consolation to posterity, said Henry, to know that this consolidated, unitary system had been a "mixed" one at the start.[20]

Little consolation, Henry thought, because consolidated central power would inevitably be unresponsive to the people. To many Revolutionaries this was both the clearest lesson of the colonies' rebellion against Great Britain and the irresistible conclusion of democratic logic. The size and pluralistic character of the United States were simply inconsistent with the concept of a single, national republic. George Mason, the most important framer of Virginia's state constitution, made the point in no uncertain terms. Can anyone suppose, he asked, "that one national government will suit so extensive a country, embracing so many climates, and containing inhabitants so very different in manners, habits, and customs? . . . There never was a government over a very extensive country without destroying the liberties of the people; . . . popular government can only exist in small territories. Is there a single example, on the face of the earth, to support a contrary opinion?" "Sixty-five members," Mason reasoned, referring to the number who would sit in the first House of Representatives under the proposed Constitution, "cannot possibly know the situation and circumstances of all the inhabitants of this immense continent." But "representatives ought to . . . mix with the people, think as they think, feel as they feel,—ought to be . . . thoroughly acquainted with their interest and condition." If this were not the case, the government would not be really representative at all.[21]

Antifederalists throughout the country stressed this theme, which was nearly as ubiquitous as the demand for a bill of rights. "A full and equal representation," one of their finest writers said, "is that which possesses the same interests, feelings, opinions, and views the people themselves would were they all assembled. A fair representation, therefore, should be so regulated that every order of men in the community . . . can have a share in it." And yet this federal House of Representatives would be so small that only men of great distinction could be chosen. "If we make the proper distinction between the few men of wealth and abilities and consider them . . . as the natural aristocracy of the country and the great body of the people, the middle and lower classes, as the democracy, this federal representative branch will have but very little democracy in it." With great men in the House and even greater men in the presidency and Senate, which would be chosen indirectly, all of the important powers of the nation would be lodged in "one order of men"; the many would be committed to the mercies of the few.[22]

To many Antifederalists, in short, a government was either sovereign or it was not, and genuine democracy was more than just a matter of popular elections. If the Constitution concentrated undue power in the central government (or threatened to in time), and if the powers of that government would be controlled by "representatives" unsympathetic to the needs of ordinary people, then the Constitution was profoundly flawed in its essential spirit. Insufficiently republican to start with, the structure of the general government, together with the hazy wording of its charter, would operate in practice to make it even less republican in time. First in substance, then perhaps in form as well, the system would become entirely undemocratic; the Revolution might result in nothing more than the replacement of a foreign tyranny with a domestic one. Mason had already made the point in print: "This government will commence in a moderate aristocracy; it is at present impossible to foresee whether it will, in its operation, produce a monarchy or a corrupt, oppressive aristocracy; it will most probably vibrate some years between the two and then terminate in the one or the other."[23] Grayson reinforced the argument in the Convention: "What, sir, is the present Constitution? A republican government founded on the principles of . . . the British monarchy. . . . A democratic branch marked with the strong features of aristocracy, and an aristocratic branch [the Senate] with all the impurities and imperfections of the British House of Commons, arising from the inequality of representation and want of responsibility [to the people]."[24] These were the features Henry had in mind when he denounced "that paper" as "the most fatal plan that could possibly be conceived to enslave a free people."[25]

"Plan," he said, and "plan" he meant. Through all these Antifederalist remarks there courses a profound distrust of Federalist intentions. And, indeed, in several states, the natural aristocracy was so one-sidedly in favor of the Constitution that their uniform support confirmed the popular suspicions prompted by the structure of the government itself. The Massachusetts state convention, where virtually the whole elite supported ratification, elicited a memorable expression of the underlying fear: "These lawyers, and men of learning and moneyed men, that talk so finely, and gloss over matters so smoothly, to make us poor illiterate people swallow down the pill, expect to get into Congress themselves; they expect to be managers of this Constitution, and get all the power and all the money into their own hands, and then they will swallow all us little folks like the great *Leviathan;* yes, just as the whale swallowed up Jonah!"[26] Even in Virginia, whose greatest public men were rather evenly divided by the Constitution and usually avoided charging one another with conspiratorial intentions, Antifederalists occasionally expressed distaste for some of the elitist phalanx who seemed so eager for the change. Speaking as a member of the Constitutional Convention—one of three who had refused to sign—Mason made a telling thrust: "I have some acquaintance with a great many characters who favor this government, their connections, their conduct, their political principles. . . . There are a great many wise and good men among them. But when I look round . . . and observe who are the warmest and the most zealous friends to this new government, it makes me think of the story of the cat transformed into a fine lady; forgetting her transformation, and happening to see a rat, she could not restrain herself, but sprang upon it out of the chair."[27] Who would fill the powerful and lucrative positions created by the Constitution? What did its supporters really want? These were the questions Henry posed when he warned of the ambitions of the few, when he insisted that "a powerful and mighty empire is incompatible with the genius of republicanism." They were at the quick of his demand for the "real, actual, existing danger which should lead us to . . . so dangerous" a step.[28]

The challenge was in earnest, and none of these suspicions can any longer be dismissed as groundless fantasies of fearful, local politicians. Henry and his allies knew the country's situation. Most of them conceded that the powers of the central government should be enlarged. But this did not compel them to agree that there was no alternative between the unamended Constitution and anarchy or economic ruin. Neither were they wholly wrong about the motives of many advocates of constitutional reform. Since Charles Beard demythologized the making of the Constitution, twentieth-century scholarship has overwhelmingly confirmed two leading tenets of the Antifederalist position: a dispassionate consideration of the social, cultural, and economic condition of the United States during the middle 1780s does not suggest a general crisis from which it was necessary for the country to be rescued; but even cursory examination of the movement for reform *does* reveal that it derived important impetus from much of the American elite's increasing disenchantment with democracy.[29] "The Constitution," according to the leading modern student of its sources, "was intrinsically an aristocratic document designed to check the democratic tendencies of the period." Many Federalists, Gordon Wood wrote, supported the new plan of government for the same reasons that Antifederalists opposed it: because it would forbid the sort of populistic measures many states had taken in response to a severe postwar depression; because it might deliver power to a "better sort" of people;

"because its very structure and detachment from the people would work to exclude . . . those who were not rich, well born, or prominent from exercising political power."[30]

Among these Federalists, moreover, were several influential individuals and groups whose discontent with democratic politics as practiced in the states was accompanied by dreams of national grandeur very like the ones that Henry denounced. Particularly conspicuous among the latter were the economic nationalists—who had been seeking since early in the decade to reshape the central government into an instrument of economic progress—and former Continental army officers—who associated sovereignty, stability, and national prowess with a small, professional army.[31] Rapidly emerging as a vigorous young spokesman for these groups was Alexander Hamilton of New York, who had spoken at the Constitutional Convention in favor of consolidated central power and lifetime terms of office for the presidency and Senate, who hoped to help create a thriving imperial republic, and who did undoubtedly believe that national greatness would require a close alliance between the country's men of liquid capital and national rulers capable of guiding and resisting the body of the people.[32]

Mason's cat was not a phantom. Henry's dreamers of ambitious schemes of national might and splendor were entirely real—and likely to possess important offices if the Constitution was approved. Virginia ratified the Constitution, then, in spite of rational suspicions of the antidemocratic inclinations of many of its friends. It ratified the Constitution in the face of deeply held and well-considered theoretical objections to its tendencies and structure, objections capably developed by several of the state's most honored Revolutionary heroes. How could this have happened?

Virginia ratified the Constitution, I believe, in part because the state convention's most impressive spokesmen *for* the change were men who did *not* share the vision Henry feared, men who were as conscientiously concerned with Revolutionary principles as any of their foes, men who favored the reform because they thought it was the only way to safeguard and perfect the nation's Revolutionary gains. To understand the Constitution's triumph in Virginia and the nation, we need to give renewed attention to the differences among its friends. We need to recognize that some of these were fully as alert as Henry to the dangers he denounced and not at all inclined to sacrifice democracy to national greatness and prestige.

At Richmond, Henry's principal opponents were Edmund Randolph, another of the three nonsigners present at the close of the Philadelphia Convention, and James Madison, who was more responsible than any other indi-

vidual for the distinctive shape of constitutional reform. Randolph's stand
and story, which I shall come to later, offer unexampled insight into why the
Constitution was approved despite a potent fear of counterrevolution. And
it is Madison, of course, to whom Americans have always turned to understand the Constitution as a Revolutionary act: the document that sealed the
promises of 1776. In fact, though this has not been recognized as clearly as
it should, the latter's role at Philadelphia was only the initial step in a succession of essential contributions that together justify his fame as Father of the
Constitution. Hardly less important was his explanation and defense of the
completed plan.[33]

Like Randolph, Madison responded to Henry's condemnation of the
quest for grandeur by *agreeing* that "national splendor and glory are not our
[proper] objects."[34] And when Mason said that certain clauses of the Constitution were intended to prepare the way for gradual subversion of the powers of the states, Madison immediately broke in, demanding "an unequivocal
explanation" of an insinuation that all the signers of the Constitution preferred a unitary national system.[35] "If the general government were wholly
independent of the governments of the particular states," he had already said,
"then, indeed, usurpations might be expected to the fullest extent." But the
general government, he pointed out, "derives its authority from [the state]
governments and from the same sources from which their authority derives,"
that is, from their sovereign peoples, who would certainly resist attempted
usurpations.[36] "The sum of the powers given up by the people of Virginia is
divided into two classes—one to the federal and the other to the state government," Madison explained. "Each is subdivided into three branches."[37]
In addition, "the powers of the federal government are enumerated; it can
only operate in certain cases."[38] Far from threatening a gradual absorption of
the proper powers of the people and the states, adoption of the Constitution
would "increase the security of liberty more than any government that ever
was," since powers ordinarily entrusted to a single government—and sometimes even to a single branch—would be distributed by the reform between
two sets of governments, each of which would watch the other at the same
time as its several branches served as an internal check against abuse.[39]

It is impossible to place excessive emphasis on Madison's denial that the
Constitution would result in a consolidated system *or* on his disclaimer of a
wish for national splendor. To him no less than to Henry, I hope to show, liberty and comfort, not riches or the might to rival European powers, were the
proper tests of national happiness and greatness. And liberty, to Madison as
well as his opponents, meant governments that would be genuinely respon-

sive to the people, not merely governments that would derive from popular elections and protect the people's private rights.[40] This is why he placed such stress on the enumerated powers and complicated federal structure of the system. He did not deny that too much power, placed in hands too distant from the people, would imperil republican liberty. He even spoke occasionally of the "concessions" federal reform demanded from the people and the states.[41] He understood as well as his opponents did that national representatives would be less sympathetic to the people's local needs and better shielded from their wrath or clamors than the state assemblies. Therefore, he insisted, local interests had been left in local hands, and federal representatives would be responsible only for those great and national matters—few and carefully defined—on which they *could* be trusted to reflect the people's needs and will.[42] "As long as this is the case," he reasoned, "we have no danger to apprehend."[43]

"Where power can be *safely* lodged, if it be *necessary*," Madison maintained, "reason commands its cession."[44] It was true, of course, that every grant of power carried with it the potential for abuse, and it was true as well that Revolutionary principles demanded constant scrutiny of rulers. Yet it was also possible to carry an appropriate distrust of power to extremes that would deny the very feasibility of a republic:

> Gentlemen suppose that the general legislature will do everything mischievous they possibly can and that they will omit to do everything good which they are authorized to do. If this were a reasonable supposition, their objections would be good. I consider it reasonable to conclude that they will as readily do their duty as deviate from it; nor do I go on the grounds mentioned by gentlemen on the other side—that we are to place unlimited confidence in [national officials] and expect nothing but the most exalted integrity and sublime virtue. But I go on this great republican principle: that the people will have virtue and intelligence to select men of virtue and wisdom. Is there no virtue among us? If there be not, we are in a wretched situation. No theoretical checks, no form of government, can render us secure. To suppose that any form of government will secure liberty or happiness without any virtue in the people is a chimerical idea.[45]

No American has ever given deeper thought to the machinery of government than this impressive Founder. None ever said more clearly that mechanical contrivances are not enough. Intelligent, attentive voters, he maintained, are necessary preconditions for a democratic state, and the assumption that the people will repeatedly elect only those who will betray them is really an objection to self-government itself.[46]

Apart from Mason's charge that many signers of the Constitution actually preferred a unitary system, nothing angered Madison so much as Henry's hints that only men of unsound principles or questionable ambitions could support the proposed reform. "I profess myself," he awkwardly exclaimed, "to have had a uniform zeal for a republican government. If the honorable member, or any other person, conceives that my attachment to this system arises from a different source, he is mistaken. From the first moment that my mind was capable of contemplating political subjects, I never, till this moment, ceased wishing success to a well-regulated republican government."[47] The outburst did him little credit. He ordinarily had little use for "flaming protestations of patriotic zeal." But Madison was understandably infuriated by aspersions that suggested motives nearly opposite to those he felt. For he not only thought the Constitution perfectly consistent with republican philosophy, but he questioned whether there was any other means by which the Revolution could be saved.

Henry challenged his opponents to explain the "actual, existing danger" that compelled so great a change. No one, then or later, could explain it more completely than this modest little Framer. The history of the Confederation, Madison insisted, offered "repeated unequivocal proofs . . . of the utter inutility and inefficacy" of a central government that depended on thirteen other governments for revenues and for enforcement of its laws, proofs confirmed by the experiences of other historical confederacies.[48] "The Confederation is so notoriously feeble," he continued, "that foreign nations are unwilling to form any treaties with us," for these had been "violated at pleasure by the states." Congress was "obliged to borrow money even to pay the interest of our debts," although these debts had been incurred in the sacred cause of independence.[49] It was evident, accordingly, when delegates assembled for the Constitutional Convention, that the nation could no longer trust its "happiness" and "safety" to "a government totally destitute of the means of protecting itself or its members."[50] And Revolutionary principles themselves required that independent taxing powers and independent means of compelling obedience to federal laws should rest directly on the people, not the states.[51]

But national humiliation and dishonor, disgraceful though these were, were only part of the impending peril as Madison perceived it. Members of a union were entitled to expect the general government to defend their happiness and safety, which were gravely damaged by the economic dislocations caused by British restrictions on American commerce. Nonetheless, the Continental Congress had been checked in every effort to secure a power to retaliate against the British, and states attempting independent actions had been checked by the competing laws of neighbors.[52] Discontent with the Confederation and hostility between the states had led to open talk of the replacement of the general union by several smaller confederacies, and Madison did not believe that the republican experiment could long outlive the continental union. At the Philadelphia Convention he had said:

> Let each state depend on itself for its security, and let apprehensions arise of danger from distant powers or from neighboring states, and the languishing condition of all the states, large as well as small, would soon be transformed into vigorous and high toned governments. . . . The same causes which have rendered the old world the theatre of incessant wars and have banished liberty from the face of it, would soon produce the same effects here. [The smaller states would] quickly introduce some regular military force against sudden danger from their powerful neighbors. The example . . . would soon become universal. [Great powers would be granted to executives.] A standing military force, with an overgrown executive, will not long be safe companions to liberty.[53]

Writing in *The Federalist,* he had again affirmed the warning. "Nothing short of a Constitution fully adequate to the national defense and the preservation of the Union can save America from as many standing armies" as there are states or separate confederacies, he insisted, "and from such a progressive augmentation of these establishments in each as will render them . . . burdensome to the properties and ominous to the liberties of the people." Without the general union, liberty would everywhere be "crushed between standing armies and perpetual taxes."[54] The Revolutionary order would collapse.

Henry "tells us the affairs of our country are not alarming," Madison complained. "I wish this assertion was well founded."[55] In fact, the Constitutional Convention had assembled in the midst of an immediate crisis of American union, and the union was the necessary shield for the republican experiment that Henry wanted to preserve. Nor was even this the sum of current dangers. The Convention also faced a second crisis, which Henry failed to recognize in his repeated condemnations of "the tyranny of rulers." In republics,

Madison suggested, "turbulence, violence, and abuse of power by the majority trampling on the rights of the minority . . . have, more frequently than any other cause, produced despotism." In the United States—and even in Virginia—it was not the acts of unresponsive rulers, but the follies and transgressions of the sympathetic representatives of state majorities that tempted growing numbers of the people to abandon their Revolutionary convictions. "The only possible remedy for those evils," he protested, the only one consistent with "preserving and protecting the principles of republicanism, will be found in that very system which is now exclaimed against as the parent of oppression."[56]

With these words the Framer introduced the train of reasoning that had produced another of his crucial contributions to the Founding. In every state the popular assemblies had struggled to protect their citizens from the economic difficulties of the middle 1780s. Many of their measures—paper money, laws suspending private suits for debt, postponements of taxation, or continued confiscations of the property of former Loyalists—had interfered with private contracts, endangered people's right to hold their property secure, or robbed the states of the resources necessary to fulfill their individual and federal obligations. Essentially unchecked by other parts of government, the lower houses had ignored state bills of rights and sacrificed the long-term interests of the whole community to more immediate considerations, calling into question, Madison had said, "the fundamental principle of republican government, that the majority who rule in such governments are the safest guardians both of public good and of private rights."[57]

Although Virginia managed to avoid the worst abuses of the middle eighties, Madison thought continentally. As the country moved toward constitutional reform, correspondents had alerted him to growing disillusionment with popular misgovernment—particularly in New England, where Shays's Rebellion erupted in the winter of 1786. Virginia's own immunity from popular commotions or majority misrule appeared to him in doubt. Personally revolted by the changeability, injustices, and lack of foresight of even Virginia's laws, he did not abandon his republican commitment; but he did become increasingly concerned that disenchantment with democracy, confined thus far to only a tiny (though an influential) few, could spread in time through growing numbers of the people, who might eventually prefer a despotism or hereditary rule to governments unable to secure their happiness or even to protect their fundamental rights.[58] The crisis of Confederation government, as Madison conceived it, was compounded by a crisis of republican convictions, and the interlocking dangers could be overcome only by a change that would at once "perpetuate the union and redeem the honor of the republican name."[59] He therefore went to Philadelphia to urge abandonment of the Confederation in favor of a carefully constructed great republic, which would rise directly from the people, could be trusted with effective, full, and independent powers over matters of general concern, and would incorporate so many different economic interests and religious sects that majorities would seldom form "on any other principles than those of justice and the general good."[60] Although the full Convention greatly modified his own proposals, he soon concluded that the finished Constitution was the best—and possibly the final—opportunity to reconcile democracy with private rights and public good. He even came to reason that the complicated, federal features of the finished Constitution would provide additional securities that he had not envisioned when the great Convention met.

Madison assumed a very special place among the Founders—more special, I would argue, even than is commonly believed—because he personally bridged so much of the abyss between the Revolutionary tribunes such as Henry and the aspiring consuls such as Hamilton, with whom he formed a brief and less-than-wholly-comfortable alliance. He fully shared with higher-flying Federalists not only the determination to invigorate the union, but also the emotional rejection of the early Revolutionary constitutions and the populistic politics that they permitted—what Elbridge Gerry called "an excess of democracy."[61] He believed, as Hamilton believed, that Revolutionary governments were so responsive to the wishes of unhampered, temporary state majorities that they endangered the unalienable rights that independence was intended to protect. He agreed with other Federalists that just, enduring governments demanded qualities not found in popular assemblies: protection for the propertied minority (and others); the wisdom to discern the long-term general good; and power to defend them both against more partial, more immediate considerations.

No more than Henry, though, did Madison approve the vision of a splendid, mighty future; and whatever was the case with other Federalists, his fear of the majority was always fully counterbalanced by continuing awareness of the dangers posed by unresponsive rulers or excessive central power. Hamilton and other economic nationalists hoped to use a stronger central government to speed developments that would prepare the groundwork for successful competition with the great Atlantic empires. Madison intended to "perpetuate the union" in order to *preserve* the Revolution from the European curses of professional armed forces, persistent public debts, powerful executives, and swollen taxes, as well as to invest the general government with the ability to counteract the European trading policies that seemed to him to threaten the social foundations of American democracy.[62] Some members of the Constitutional Convention may have wanted to create a system that would place as much authority as possible in rulers only distantly dependent on the people. But Madison expected to create a government that would defeat the wishes of factional majorities *without* destroying the republican "communion of interests and sympathy of sentiments" between the rulers and the ruled.[63] Although he shared the hope that large election districts would result in representatives who would resist unjust majority demands, he had been equally concerned, throughout the Constitutional Convention, to control potentially ambitious rulers and assure that they could never free themselves from their dependence on the people.[64] In *The Federalist* and in Virginia's state convention, the Constitution he defended *would* "break and control the violence" of factions and assure superior attention to the long-term good,[65] but it would *not* produce a government that would be unresponsive to the people's needs or will. Responsibility would be secured, as always, by popular elections and internal checks and balances. For the first time in the history of representative democracy, it would be further guaranteed by the enumerated limits and the compound, federal features of the reconstructed system.

Recent scholarship has not placed equal emphasis on all the vital parts of Madison's attempt to understand and justify the Constitution. It credits him, of course, with an essential role in the creation of a central government whose parts would all derive from popular elections, as well as with the most elaborate defense of its republican characteristics. It devotes elaborate attention to his argument that private rights are safer in a large than in a small republic. It leans on him, indeed—more heavily than it relies on any other individual—for its recognition that "the Constitution presented no simple choice between accepting or rejecting the principles of 1776," since the Federalists could "intelligibly picture themselves as the true defenders of the libertarian tradition."[66] In doing so, however, it commonly identifies the man too closely with the movement, makes too much of some ideas and not enough of others, and thus obscures some differences that had important consequences in Virginia and the country as a whole.

"There is something decidedly disingenuous," writes Gordon Wood, "about the democratic radicalism" of Federalist defenses of the Constitution, for behind this language lay an evident desire "for a high-toned government filled with better sorts of people, ... partisan and aristocratic purposes that belied the Federalists' democratic language."[67] For many Federalists, no doubt, this characterization is quite apt; and yet a careful effort to distinguish Madison's position from that of other key reformers—one that gives full weight to his insistence on the complicated federal structure and enumerated powers of the central government, his fear of independent rulers, and his conviction that the Constitution was a wholly democratic remedy for democratic ills—both qualifies and clarifies Wood's generalization. The Federalists did generally believe that private rights and public happiness were threatened in the states by populistic politics and poorly balanced constitutions. They looked to federal reform not only as a necessary cure for the debilities of the Confederation, but also as an opportunity to remedy those other ills; and they believed a proper remedy required both limitations on the states and the erection of a general government that would be more resistant to majority demands. Madison not only shared these wishes but he was more responsible than any other thinker for defining problems in these terms and sketching leading features of the Federalist solution. But this was only part—and not the most distinctive part—of Madison's peculiar contribution.

What distinguished Madison most clearly from all the other Framers was his early, firm, and intimate association of survival of the union with continuation of a Revolutionary enterprise he still defined, in insufficiently acknowledged ways, in early Revolutionary terms. The liberty he wished to save—the point requires repeated stress—was not just liberty defined as the inherent rights of individuals, but also liberty defined as popular self-governance.[68] Convinced that neither sort of liberty could be secure without the other, valuing them both, he worked from the beginning for a change that would restrain tyrannical majorities; and yet he never doubted that majorities should rule—or that the people *would* control the complicated structure raised by the completed Constitution. This is why he heatedly denied that he approved of a consolidated system, placed increasing emphasis on federal dimensions of the structure, and properly insisted that he had no other object than the people's liberty and comfort. He was defending a reform that he had always understood—and was still trying to define—as an attempt to rescue *both* of the ideals enunciated in the Declaration: private rights, but also popular self-rule.[69]

To fully understand his vital part in the creation of the federal republic, it is critical to see that Madison's determination to achieve a change that would secure both private rights *and* public liberty extended far beyond adjournment of the Constitutional Convention, that his effort to legitimize the Constitution from the vantage point of Revolutionary theory was nearly as important to its triumph as his contributions to its framing. Edmund Randolph's story illustrates these points, as does the rest of Madison's career.

A close associate of Madison since 1776 and governor of Virginia when the Constitutional Convention met, Randolph introduced the plan with which the Philadelphia deliberations started. Like Mason, he contributed effectively to the Convention's work but grew increasingly alarmed as the proceedings altered Madison's original proposals. Sharing Mason's doubts about a strong, reeligible executive, a Senate dominated by the smaller, northern states, the hazy wording of important clauses, and the motives of some of his colleagues, Randolph was the first of three nonsigners to declare that he could not approve the finished Constitution, hoping for the meeting of a second general convention to repair the oversights and errors of the first. Nonetheless, when the Virginia state convention met, he startled the assemblage by immediately announcing that, despite his reservations, he would unequivocally support the unamended Constitution. He took the lead, in fact, from the beginning, as a fervent foe of a conditional approval of the plan.[70]

What had happened in the intervening months to change his mind? Henry pressed him with this question to the point of personal exchanges that provided the dramatic highlight of the meeting.[71] The response was fundamentally uncomplicated but revealing. "I refused to sign," Randolph answered, "because I had, as I still have, objections to the Constitution, and wished a free inquiry into its merits." At that time, it had still seemed possible to work for previous amendments. Now, however, eight of thirteen states had ratified the unamended Constitution. In these different circumstances, to insist on previous amendments was impossible "without inevitable ruin to the Union, and . . . I will assent to the lopping of this limb [meaning his arm] before I assent to the dissolution of the Union."[72] The old Confederation, Randolph said, "is gone, whether this house says so or not. It is gone, sir, by its own weakness."[73] The eight approving states would not recede to gratify Virginia. To insist on previous amendments now could only prove "another name for rejection." "If, in this situation, we reject the Constitution, the Union will be dissolved, the dogs of war will break loose, and anarchy and discord will complete the ruin of this country."[74]

Henry feared the Revolution would be lost. "I am a child of the Revolution," Randolph replied. "I would join heart and hand in rejecting the system did I not conceive it would promote our happiness." But the Constitution offered new securities against "injustice, licentiousness, insecurity, and oppression,"[75] and Virginia could not "exist without a union with her neighbors"—not, at least, as a republic. "Those states, . . . our friends, brothers, and supporters, will, if disunited from us, be our bitterest enemies. . . . The other states have upwards of 330,000 men capable of bearing arms. . . . In case of an attack, what defense can we make? . . . Our export trade is entirely in the hands of foreigners. We have no manufactures. . . . Shall we form a partial confederacy? . . . Partial confederacies will require such a degree of force and expense as will destroy every feature of republicanism."[76]

"Is this government necessary for the safety of Virginia?" Randolph asked. For him, it was the final question, and he answered it as Madison had answered it nine months before. "Could I . . . believe that there . . . was no storm gathering," that previous amendments could really be secured, "I would concur" with Henry's plan, "for nothing but the fear of inevitable destruction would lead me to vote for the Constitution in spite of the objections I have."[77] But the approval of eight states, the governor repeated, had reduced the issue "to the single question of Union or no Union."[78] And among Virginia's vital interests, Randolph thought, none was dearer than the state's survival as a liberal republic. "When I see safety on my right, and destruction on my left, . . . I cannot hesitate to decide in favor of the former."[79]

How many moderates (or "trimmers" in contemporary parlance) reasoned much as Randolph did? It is impossible to know—and certainly impossible to say, as we can say with certainty in Randolph's case, how many were directly influenced by James Madison.[80] It is a fact, however, that in all the narrowly divided states, the ratification contest was decided in the end by a handful of uncertain, silent delegates who, at the final moment, proved unwilling to insist on previous amendments at the risk of dissolution of the union. It is not unreasonable to guess that, like the two Virginians, many of them thought that democratic liberty could only thrive within the federal hedge. Many of them may have hoped, as Madison and Randolph hoped, that private rights and public liberty would both prove more secure in an enlarged, compound republic. Madison was not, of course, the only Federalist to reason in these terms, but he was undeniably the earliest and most effective spokesman for a train of thought on which, among a Revolutionary generation, the triumph of the Constitution may have turned.[81]

The victory was narrow, to be sure, and incomplete. A motion to insist on previous amendments was defeated eighty-eight to eighty. Virginia ratified the Constitution by a margin of ten votes and recommended numerous amendments to the first new Congress.[82] Though Madison had plausibly defended every clause—and Washington, as everyone had hoped, was the unanimous selection of the first electoral college—many children of the Revolution entered on the federal experiment with all the reservations Randolph swallowed. A few proclaimed, as Patrick Henry did, that they would work with all their power "to retrieve the loss of liberty, and remove the defects of that system in a constitutional way."[83] Madison himself, however, was far from finished with his effort to define a genuinely Revolutionary, partly national, but also partly federal union. The skeptics therefore found a potent, partial ally in the Father of the Constitution, who quickly joined with Thomas Jefferson to lead most of the former Antifederalists into a party dedicated to a strict interpretation of the federal charter and a vision of the future much at odds with Hamilton's design for national glory. That Madison would take this stand should not seem so surprising as many analysts have thought.

Notes

1. We owe the record to an enterprising shorthand reporter, David Robertson, who published the proceedings later in the year. They are conveniently reprinted in Jonathan Elliot, ed., *The Debates in the Several State Conventions on the Adoption of the Federal Constitution,* 2d ed., 5 vols. (Philadelphia: J. B. Lippincott, 1901), vol. 3 [hereafter referred to as Elliot, *Debates*]. A recent article has warned that we cannot depend on Robertson's reporting with the same degree of confidence that could be placed in a modern, stenographic record, but I see little reason to believe that it is not essentially dependable for the purposes of this essay. See James H. Hutson, "The Creation of the Constitution: The Integrity of the Documentary Record," *Texas Law Review* 65 (1986): 23–24.

2. Although the news did not reach Richmond in time to influence the decision, New Hampshire ratified the Constitution on June 21, four days before Virginia. Historians agree that its approval may have made slight difference. If Virginia, North Carolina, and New York had nonetheless held out, it seems unlikely that the document could actually have gone into effect.

3. For initial estimates by leaders on both sides, see Madison to Washington, June 4, 1788, in Robert A. Rutland et al., eds., *The Papers of James Madison,* 14 vols. (Chicago: University of Chicago Press, 1975), 10:400; Robert A. Rutland, ed., *The Papers of George Mason, 1725–1792,* 3 vols. (Chapel Hill: University of North Carolina Press, 1970), 3:1040, 1044–1046; and William Wirt Henry, *Patrick Henry: Life, Correspondence, and Speeches,* 3 vols., rev. ed. (New York: Burt Franklin, 1969), 2:342–343. As everywhere, though there were numerous exceptions, the least commercial portions of the state (the Southside) tended to oppose the Constitution, the most commercial portions (e.g., the Northern Neck) tended to approve it, and the central Piedmont was divided. For the nature and closeness of the popular division, see Norman K. Risjord, *Chesapeake Politics, 1781–1800* (New York: Columbia University Press, 1978), 293–317; Risjord, "Virginians and the Constitution: A Multivariant Analysis," *William and Mary Quarterly* 31 (1974): 3:613–632; Norman K. Risjord

and Gordon DenBoer, "The Evolution of Political Parties in Virginia, 1782–1800," *Journal of American History* 60 (1974): 961–984; Robert E. Thomas, "The Virginia Convention of 1788: A Criticism of Beard's *An Economic Interpretation of the Constitution*," *Journal of Southern History* 19 (1953): 63–72; Jackson Turner Main, *Political Parties before the Constitution* (Chapel Hill: University of North Carolina Press, 1973); and Forrest McDonald, *We The People: The Economic Origins of the Constitution* (Chicago: University of Chicago Press, 1958). The best short narratives of the Convention include Gordon DenBoer, "The House of Delegates and the Evolution of Political Parties in Virginia, 1782–1792" (Ph.D. diss., University of Wisconsin, 1972), chap. 6; David John Mays, *Edmund Pendleton, 1721–1803: A Biography*, 2 vols. (Cambridge, Mass.: Harvard University Press, 1952), 2:217–272; and Jackson Turner Main, *The Antifederalists: Critics of the Constitution, 1781–1788* (Chapel Hill: University of North Carolina Press, 1961), 223–233. The fullest is still Hugh Blair Grigsby, *History of the Virginia Federal Convention of 1788*, 2 vols. (Virginia Historical Society, *Collections*, 2:9–10 [Richmond, 1890–1891]).

4. Robert Douthat Meade, *Patrick Henry*, 2 vols. (Philadelphia, 1957–1969); Richard R. Beeman, *Patrick Henry: A Biography* (New York: McGraw-Hill, 1974). The quotation is from Elliot, *Debates*, 3:21.

5. This summarizes parts of Henry's first two speeches in the Convention, from Elliot, *Debates*, 3:21–23, 44–45. Throughout the essay I have expanded abbreviations, corrected slips of the pen, and slightly modernized the punctuation and capitalization wherever this appeared to make a passage easier for twentieth-century readers.

6. Ibid., 45.

7. William Grayson, ibid., 277.

8. Ibid., 62–63.

9. Ibid., 47.

10. Ibid., 44–45.

11. Ibid., 46, 48, 53–54.

12. I have examined the Convention from this alternative perspective in "Virginia: Nation, State, and Section," a paper delivered at the conference on "Ratifying the Constitution: Ideas and Interests in the Several American States," National Humanities Center, May 21–24, 1987, in Michael Lienesch and Michael Gillespie, eds., *Ratifying the Constitution: Ideas and Interests in the Several American States* (Lawrence, Kans.: University Press of Kansas, 1988), forthcoming.

13. Antifederalist writings have recently been collected in Herbert J. Storing, ed., *The Complete Anti-Federalist*, 7 vols. (Chicago: University of Chicago Press, 1981). The most important secondary studies are the general introduction to Storing's collection, available separately as *What the Anti-Federalists Were For: The Political Thought of the Opponents of the Constitution* (Chicago: University of Chicago Press, 1981); Main, *Antifederalists*; and the introduction to Cecilia M. Kenyon, ed., *The Antifederalists* (Indianapolis: Bobbs-Merrill, 1966). For additional recent writings see

James H. Hutson, "Country, Court, and Constitution: Antifederalism and the Historians," *William and Mary Quarterly* 38 (1981): 3:337–368.

14. Elliot, *Debates,* 3:44.

15. Ibid., 176, 591.

16. Ibid., 160, 171.

17. The fullest discussion of Revolutionary changes in the concept of sovereignty is in Gordon S. Wood, *The Creation of the American Republic, 1776–1787* (Chapel Hill: University of North Carolina Press, 1969). See also Gordon S. Wood, "The Political Ideology of the Founders," in this volume.

18. Elliot, *Debates,* 3:281.

19. Ibid., 29–30.

20. Ibid., 171.

21. Ibid., 30, 32. For Mason, see Robert A. Rutland, *George Mason: Reluctant Statesman* (Williamsburg, Va.: Colonial Williamsburg, 1961), and Helen Hill Miller, *George Mason: Gentleman Revolutionary* (Chapel Hill: University of North Carolina Press, 1975).

22. Walter Hartwell Bennett, ed., *Letters from the Federal Farmer to the Republican* (University: University of Alabama Press, 1978), 10, 14, 22. See also, more largely, 47–52. Bennett writes that the evidence for the traditional attribution of these letters to Richard Henry Lee, "while strong, hardly seems sufficient to justify continuing this attribution" (20). The attribution was disputed to my satisfaction in Gordon S. Wood, "The Authorship of the *Letters from the Federal Farmer,*" *William and Mary Quarterly* 31 (1974): 3:299–308. A plausible but not compelling alternative attribution has recently been suggested in Robert H. Webking, "Melancton Smith and the *Letters from the Federal Farmer,*" *William and Mary Quarterly* 44 (1987): 510–528.

23. "Objections to the Proposed Federal Constitution," in Kenyon, *Antifederalists,* 195.

24. Elliot, *Debates,* 3:280.

25. Ibid., 176.

26. Amos Singletary, ibid., 2:102.

27. Ibid., 3:269.

28. Ibid., 23.

29. The landmark studies were Charles A. Beard, *An Economic Interpretation of the Constitution of the United States* (New York: Macmillan, 1913); Merrill Jensen, *The Articles of Confederation: An Interpretation of the Social-Constitutional History of the American Revolution, 1774–1781* (Madison: University of Wisconsin Press, 1940); and Jensen, *The New Nation: A History of the United States during the Confederation, 1781–1789* (New York: Vintage Books, 1950).

30. Wood, *Creation of the American Republic,* 513–514.

31. See especially E. James Ferguson, *The Power of the Purse: A History of American Public Finance, 1776–1790* (Chapel Hill: University of North Carolina Press, 1961); Ferguson, "The Nationalists of 1781–1783 and the Economic Interpretation

of the Constitution," *Journal of American History* 56 (1969): 241–261; and Richard H. Kohn, *Eagle and Sword: The Federalists and the Creation of the Military Establishment in America, 1783–1802* (New York: Free Press, 1975).

32. Biographies include John C. Miller, *Alexander Hamilton: Portrait in Paradox* (New York: Macmillan, 1959); Forrest McDonald, *Alexander Hamilton: A Biography* (New York: Norton, 1979); and Jacob Ernest Cooke, *Alexander Hamilton* (New York: Norton, 1982). See also Gerald Stourzh, *Alexander Hamilton and the Idea of Republican Government* (Stanford, Calif.: Stanford University Press, 1970).

33. For biographical information see Irving Brant, *James Madison*, 6 vols. (Indianapolis: Bobbs-Merrill, 1941–1961); Ralph Ketcham, *James Madison: A Biography* (New York: Macmillan, 1971); and Harold S. Schultz, *James Madison* (New York: Twayne, 1970).

34. Elliot, *Debates*, 3:135. For Randolph, see ibid., 81.

35. Mason insisted that many members of the Convention *had* desired consolidation, but that Madison had "expressed himself against it" in a private conversation and that he had never heard any Virginia delegate advocate a unitary system. Madison "declared himself satisfied," and Mason finished his speech (ibid., 517–530). Hugh Blair Grigsby, whose *History of the Virginia Federal Convention of 1788* was based in part on oral information, was being overly dramatic when he wrote that Madison "demanded reparation in a tone that menaced an immediate call to the field" (90), but there can be no doubt that the Framer sharply resented the remark. Madison was universally described as a man of remarkably "sweet" manners, who never lost his temper; but he was capable of flashes of hard anger—and an uncharacteristic breach of parliamentary decorum—when he thought himself accused of consolidationism or when someone seemed to doubt his commitment to republicanism.

36. Elliot, *Debates*, 3:96.

37. Ibid., 408–409.

38. Ibid., 95.

39. Ibid., 408–409. Madison's most elaborate explanations of the partly federal, partly national derivation and structure of the new system—and of the guarantees against a further consolidation—include his speeches of June 6 and 11, pages 94–97, 257–259, and especially *Federalist* Nos. 39, 45, 46, 51, and 62.

40. "The genius of republican liberty" demands "not only that all power should be derived from the people, but that those entrusted with it should be kept in dependence on the people." *Federalist* 37:227.

41. To Thomas Jefferson, March 19, 1787, see Rutland et al., *Papers of James Madison*, 9:318. See also his reference in the state convention in Elliot, *Debates*, 3:95, to the necessity of "submitting to the inconvenience" of greater federal power.

42. *Federalist* 10:82–83. But there are any number of indications that Madison assumed that federal representatives would reflect their constituents' will, which was a logical necessity for his argument that the large republic would defeat factious majorities. Among the clearest are *Federalist* 46:296–297, 51:325, and especially 57:350–353.

43. Elliot, *Debates*, 3:90.

44. Ibid., 394 (*emphasis* added).

45. Ibid., 536–537.

46. *Federalist* 57:350–353.

47. Elliot, *Debates*, 3:394.

48. Ibid., 128–129ff. For the experiences of other confederacies, see *Federalist* Nos. 18–20.

49. Elliot, *Debates*, 3:135–136. On the debts, see his eloquent "Address to the States" of April 26, 1783, in Rutland et al., *Papers of James Madison*, 6:494: "The citizens of the U.S. are responsible for the greatest trust ever confided to a political society. If justice, good faith, honor, gratitude, and all the other qualities which ennoble the character of a nation and fulfill the ends of government be the fruits of our [republican] establishments, the cause of liberty will acquire a dignity and lustre which it has never yet enjoyed; and an example will be set which cannot but have the most favorable influence on the rights of mankind. If, on the other side, our governments should be unfortunately blotted with the reverse of these cardinal and essential virtues, the great cause which we have engaged to vindicate will be dishonored and betrayed; the last and fairest experiment in favor of the rights of human nature will be turned against them; and their patrons and friends exposed to be insulted and silenced by the votaries of tyranny and usurpation."

50. Elliot, *Debates*, 3:129.

51. Madison's earliest sketch of a reform (to Jefferson, March 19, 1787, Rutland et al., *Papers of James Madison*, 9:318–319) suggested that an independent federal taxing power would require a reconstitution of Congress on the basis of proportional representation. Jefferson approved the power and likewise insisted that the reform must "preserve inviolate the fundamental principle that the people are not to be taxed but by representatives chosen immediately by themselves" (10:336).

52. This was clearly the problem that first led Madison to approve a thorough reconsideration of the structure of the Confederation. For elaboration and citations see Lance Banning, "James Madison and the Nationalists, 1780–1783," *William and Mary Quarterly* 40 (1983): 3:252–253.

53. Speech of June 29 in Max Farrand, ed., *The Records of the Federal Convention of 1787*, rev. ed., 4 vols. (New Haven, Conn.: Yale University Press, 1966), 1:464–465 [hereafter referred to as Farrand, *Records*].

54. *Federalist* 41:259–260, and passim. See also Elliot, *Debates*, 3:382.

55. Elliot, *Debates*, 3:399.

56. Ibid., 87–88. And see, of course, the famous, earlier elaborations of the point in *Federalist* Nos. 10 and 51: "The instability, injustice, and confusion introduced into the public councils have, in truth, been the mortal diseases under which popular governments have everywhere perished. . . . Complaints are everywhere heard from our most considerate and virtuous citizens, equally the friends of public and private faith and of public and personal liberty, that our governments are too unstable, that the

public good is disregarded in the conflicts of rival parties, and that measures are too often decided, not according to the rules of justice and the rights of the minor party, but by the superior force of an interested and overbearing majority" (10:77). "Justice is the end of government. It is the end of civil society. It ever has been and ever will be pursued until it be obtained, or until liberty be lost in the pursuit" (51:324).

57. "Vices of the Political System of the United States," April, 1787, in Rutland et al., *Papers of James Madison*, 10:354. See also "Observations on Jefferson's Draft of a Constitution for Virginia," ibid., 11:287–288. It should be noted, though, that Madison did not consider the "mutability" of laws to be pernicious to minorities alone. "Instability," says Madison in *Federalist* 62, gives an "unreasonable advantage . . . to the sagacious, the enterprising, and the moneyed few over the industrious and uninformed mass of the people. Every new regulation concerning commerce or revenue, or in any manner affecting the value of the different species of property, presents a new harvest to those who watch the change. . . . But the most deplorable effect of all is that diminution of attachment and reverence which steals into the hearts of the people towards a political system which betrays so many marks of infirmity, and disappoints so many . . . hopes" (381, 382).

58. Madison's letters to Virginia from his seat in the Confederation Congress during February and March 1787 reported widespread suspicions of a growth of pro-monarchy sentiments in New England. See, for example, the letter to Washington of February 21, Rutland et al., *Papers of James Madison*, 9:286. His fear of this phenomenon was very near the surface when he outlined his earliest ideas about reform in the letter to Jefferson of March 19 (ibid., 318), writing that "the mortal diseases of the existing constitution . . . have tainted the faith of the most orthodox republicans, and . . . challenge from the votaries of liberty every concession in favor of stable government not infringing fundamental principles as the only security against an opposite extreme of our present situation."

59. To Edmund Pendleton, February 24, 1787, in ibid., 295.

60. *Federalist* 51:325.

61. Farrand, *Records*, 1:48.

62. On the last point see Drew R. McCoy, *The Elusive Republic: Political Economy in Jeffersonian America* (Chapel Hill: University of North Carolina Press, 1980).

63. *Federalist* 57:352. This number is Madison's most complete explanation of the forces that would keep federal representatives responsive to the people.

64. Ibid., 51:321–322. For a reinterpretation of Madison's course at the Convention, see Lance Banning, "The Practicable Sphere of a Republic: James Madison, the Constitutional Convention, and the Emergence of Revolutionary Federalism," in Richard Beeman et al., eds., *Beyond Confederation: Origins of the Constitution and American National Identity* (Chapel Hill: University of North Carolina Press, 1987), 162–187.

65. *Federalist* 10:77.

66. Wood, *Creation of the American Republic*, 523–524.

67. Ibid., 562, 615.

68. *Federalist* 39:240: Only a "strictly republican" form of government "would be reconcilable with the genius of the people of America; with the fundamental principles of the revolution; or with that honorable determination which animates every votary of freedom to rest all our political experiments on the capacity of mankind for self-government."

69. I have developed many of these points at greater length in "James Madison and the Nationalists"; "The Practicable Sphere of a Republic"; and "The Hamiltonian Madison: A Reconsideration," *Virginia Magazine of History and Biography* 92 (1984): 3–28.

70. A modern biography is John J. Reardon, *Edmund Randolph: A Biography* (New York: Macmillan, 1974).

71. See especially Elliot, *Debates*, 3:187–189. Grigsby, in *History of the Virginia Federal Convention of 1788*, 165, says that in the evening after this exchange Colonel William Cabell called on Randolph as a friend of Henry, but that the Convention was relieved to learn the next morning that a reconciliation had been achieved without a recourse to the field. I doubt that there was any serious consideration of a duel, but Randolph *had* used language that one gentleman did not use to another.

72. Elliot, *Debates*, 3:24–26, 652.

73. Ibid., 84.

74. Ibid., 603.

75. Ibid., 65, 67.

76. Ibid., 72–80.

77. Ibid., 596–597.

78. Ibid., 652.

79. Ibid., 66.

80. Madison's successful effort in the months between the two conventions to persuade his friend to cooperate with the Federalists on the Massachusetts plan of recommendatory amendments can be followed in full in volumes 10–11 of Rutland et al., *Papers of James Madison*.

81. In addition to the sources cited in notes 52–54 above, see Madison's insistence, at Philadelphia as well as Richmond, that the South would be especially vulnerable in the event of a collapse of the union in Farrand, *Records*, 2:306–307, 361, 451–452; Elliot, *Debates*, 3:251, 621.

82. The recommended amendments, a bill of rights and several substantive changes in the powers and structure of the new government, are in Elliot, *Debates*, 3:657–661. The outcome would suggest (see note 3 above) that the Federalists debated their opponents to, at worst, a draw. They probably maintained and may have slightly widened the narrow margin with which they began.

83. Ibid., 652.

PART 4

James Madison

Although it touched on a variety of subjects, the bulk of Lance Banning's scholarly career was spent in the study of James Madison, culminating in his 1995 masterwork *The Sacred Fire of Liberty*. The path toward that book was a long one, initially undertaken as his first book, *The Jeffersonian Persuasion*, was being published in 1978.

Banning seems to have gotten a line on Madison very early in his research. In reviewing the scholarship on the Virginia founder, particularly the work of biographer Irving Brant, Banning was soon struck by a number of mistaken assumptions that had worked their way into the scholarly literature and taken root. Many of these interpretations cast Madison as a full-blown nationalist from the early 1780s onward who then mysteriously broke with his *Federalist* coauthor Alexander Hamilton in the 1790s and became, allegedly, a states' righter. Banning challenged this view at every turn, offering a portrait of Madison that not only broke with Brant's reigning interpretation but set forth a full-fledged revisionist understanding of the Virginian that reached its apotheosis in *Sacred Fire*.

The three writings included in this chapter provide important glimpses of that revisionist portrait that Banning was constructing in the mid-1980s. Each of them added a crucial component to his emerging reinterpretation of Madison. In "James Madison and the Nationalists, 1780–1783," Banning set forth the conventional view of Madison's nationalism only to question it repeatedly. He challenged the perception of Madison's nationalist reputation, carefully developed the parameters of Madison's subtle and unique version of nationalism, and then contrasted Madisonian nationalism with that of Hamilton, Robert Morris, and others. In doing so, Banning established the incompatibility of Madison's nationalist thinking with that of other nationalists. He shed light on the earliness of Madison's distinctive perspectives on nationalism and the way that his incompatibility with others traced to the early 1780s, not the early 1790s as so many other scholars contended.

"The Hamiltonian Madison" took the insights and implications of the previous piece and used them to explain the confusion that scholars have long had in arguing (as Hamilton himself did) that Madison had somehow deserted him after having been in agreement earlier. Banning shows that the two primary authors of "Publius" had unknowingly never been at the same point in their thinking during the 1780s when their shared desire to replace the Articles of Confederation with the Constitution overshadowed any disagreements or conflicting interpretations that they held. Only as Hamilton rolled out his program in the Washington administration did the stark differences—which Banning argues were always present—emerge, creating the sense that Madison had changed, breaking both with Hamilton and with his previous thinking. In a significant historiographical intervention, Banning cleared away the misconceptions about Madison's nationalism and the Hamiltonian version of Madison and sketched out what a "Madisonian Madison" might look like instead.

Finally, in "The Practicable Sphere of a Republic," Banning added to his emerging revisionist portrait the key point that Madison, as a founder, was changed by the founding itself—that is, by the fluid, shifting events and perceptions that took place inside the Philadelphia convention and then outside during the broader ratification debate. Rather than being a fixed and rigid thinker, consistent from start to finish, Madison's mind changed as he grappled with changing circumstances. Banning appreciates and highlights the fluidity of Madison's thinking as it was being influenced by the debate over the Constitution itself, thus further fleshing out his thesis of a Madison whose thought was ever-evolving as he considered what the new frame of government might do and how best to preserve the values he held most dear.

In all three writings, Banning displays both great subtlety and fairness. While he sides with Madison against both Hamilton and later historians, he acknowledges that Hamilton had every right to feel betrayed and deserted by Madison, even as Banning demonstrates that Hamilton was mistaken. By exploring Madison's thinking as closely as he does and by also taking Hamilton's understanding into account, Banning goes a long way toward explaining one of the great mysteries of the early republic: the breakdown of the friendship and political partnership between two of the most significant founders. Readers will encounter in these articles the earliest iterations of Banning's portrait of Madison that reached full maturity and sophistication in his book. The works in this chapter, then, allow a glimpse inside the making of his revisionist interpretation as it was in progress, emerging piecemeal in articles and book chapters such as these.

James Madison and the Nationalists, 1780–1783

In the Continental and Confederation Congresses, wrote Irving Brant, James Madison "endeavored to establish . . . national supremacy—first by a return to the original authority Congress lost when it stopped printing money and became financially dependent upon the states, next by recognition of implied powers in the Articles of Confederation, then by the vigorous exercise of powers whose validity could not be challenged, finally by amendment of the articles to confer new powers upon Congress."[1] While subsequent biographers of Madison have challenged Brant on lesser points, both they and other students of Confederation politics have generally affirmed his central theme. Current scholarship portrays the young Virginian as an eager, dedicated nationalist throughout his years of congressional service, one of a group of reformers often referred to as "the nationalists of 1781–1783."[2]

Several elements of this familiar portrait are misleading. They impede a better understanding of Madison's personal development and erect unnecessary obstacles to attempts to comprehend his later career. They also obscure some vital differences among the nationalistic reformers of the early 1780s— differences with critical implications for the more successful effort for reform that came at the decade's end.

Prevailing views do not explain that Madison first rose to prominence in Congress as a determined advocate of Virginia's special interests. For months, those interests reinforced his inclination to *resist* unauthorized extensions of congressional authority—an inclination deeply rooted in his Revolutionary creed. But a commitment to Virginia and the Revolution also called with growing urgency for change. Day by day, while British forces devastated the deep South and then turned toward Virginia, Congress groped for one expedient and then another to keep an army in the field. Victory at Yorktown put an end to the danger that the South might be torn from the Confederation, but the agonizing crawl toward peace brought difficulties nearly as severe. While Madison continued to defend his state's distinctive interests, he came increasingly to favor significant additions to the powers of Congress.

Still, Madison's acceptance of the need for fundamental change was limited and halting. Until the fall of 1782 he supported several reforms with obvious reluctance, often as a product of his alarm for Virginia or for the Revolutionary cause. Even in his final months of congressional service, when he allied himself with Robert Morris and others to push Congress toward the reforms of 1783, he proved unable to accept the ultimate objectives of his allies. James Madison was not a "nationalist" during the early 1780s—not, at least, in several of the senses commonly suggested by that term. His cooperation with the Morrisites did not reflect a concord of opinion. On the contrary, the course of the cooperation suggestively prefigured the confrontation with Alexander Hamilton that would eventually divide the Federalists of 1789 into the warring parties of the 1790s.

When Madison retired from Congress, he intended to reenter the Virginia legislature to advocate compliance with Confederation treaties and acceptance of the congressional recommendations of 1783. But he did not yet favor a complete departure from the Articles of Confederation. He had been pushed, not pulled, toward national supremacy. He had developed doubts about the program and intentions of his former allies. Developments would push him farther in a nationalistic direction in the years ahead. By the time of the Virginia Plan of 1787, he would see some very positive advantages in a program of centralizing reform. And yet the doubts he carried with him from the early 1780s would also help to shape his subsequent career. The content of Madison's nationalism was not just different from, but incompatible with, the centralizing vision of other nationalists who gathered, first, around the old Confederation's superintendent of finance and, after 1789, around the new republic's secretary of the Treasury. This incompatibility had quite important consequences, often overlooked, during the crisis of 1783. It would become explicit after a new federal government had been approved.[3]

Madison presented his credentials to the Continental Congress at a gloomy juncture in the history of the Confederation. North America was near the end of the most severe winter in a generation. At Morristown, where the continentals were enduring hardships more extreme than at Valley Forge, George Washington wondered how he could keep his hungry, unpaid troops together when their three-year enlistments began to expire. In December 1779 Congress had turned to requisitions of specific supplies to feed the army. On March 18, 1780, the day Madison arrived in Philadelphia, Congress devalued the continental dollar at a rate of forty for one and threw responsibility for generating new bills of credit on the states. Desperate as these decisions were, the long delay in reaching them had brought congressional prestige to a point as low as its power. During 1779, while precipitate inflation threatened to choke the army's supplies, Congress had erupted in bitter public controversy over peace terms, the diplomatic establishment, and the mutual accusations of Silas Deane and Arthur Lee.[4]

While Madison was aware of all these problems and had labored in particular to collect his thoughts on the financial crisis, the desperate condition of affairs hit him with redoubled force as soon as he began to view it from the central government's perspective. Soon after his arrival, he warned Gov. Thomas Jefferson that "the course of the revolution" had seen no moment "more truly critical than the present." The army was "threatened with an immediate alternative of disbanding or living on free quarter." The treasury was empty. Public credit was exhausted. Congress complained "of the extortion of the people, the people of the improvidence of Congress, and the army of both." Congress recommended measures to the states, and the states separately decided whether it was expedient to comply. "Believe me, Sir, as things now stand, if the states do not vigorously proceed in collecting the old money and establishing funds for the credit of the new, . . . we are undone."[5]

The shock that seems apparent in Madison's early letters to Virginia is a most important clue to understanding his career.[6] Forced to grapple daily with the nation's problems through the Confederation's most difficult years, he would never forget the desperation he often felt. Having occupied the station that he did, he found it impossible to see American affairs in the manner that he might have seen them had he never left Virginia. His later letters repeatedly comment on the different perspectives of those who comprehended problems from a national vantage and those who were immersed in local concerns.[7] And yet these early letters may also easily mislead. They do not justify the view that Madison attempted to extend congressional authority from the beginning of his service.

At twenty-nine, the youngest man in Congress, Madison was shy, weak-voiced, and diffident. Through his first six months of service, he made no motions and probably never entered a debate. Authorities agree that Congress was preoccupied with war and relatively free of factional division during the spring and summer of 1780, months marked by military disaster in the Carolinas, continuing depreciation of the currency, and the failure of specific supplies to meet the needs of the northern army, in which mutinies erupted in May and June. The optimism sparked by the financial reforms of

March quickly gave way to virtually unanimous alarm over the army's condition and to a general opinion that so much reliance on the states might have to be replaced by broader congressional authority.[8]

Madison plainly shared the general sense of crisis and national humiliation.[9] He seems to have agreed with Joseph Jones, his senior colleague in Virginia's delegation, that Congress had surrendered too much of its power to the states.[10] He certainly agreed that the situation demanded prompt ratification of the Articles of Confederation.[11] How much farther he might have been willing to go to strengthen the federal hand is impossible to say. But there is nothing in his surviving papers through the end of 1780 that confirms the common suggestion that he was ahead of other delegates in accepting the need for centralizing reforms. Rather, there are several hints that he persisted somewhat longer than did most in the hope that such extensive change might be unnecessary. The want of money, he protested, "is the source of all our public difficulties." One or two million guineas "would expel the enemy from every part of the United States" and "reconcile the army and everybody else to our republican forms of governments, the principal inconveniences which are imputed to these being really the fruit of defective revenues." The troops, he thought, could be as well equipped "by our governments as by any other if they possessed money enough."[12]

By the time he wrote these words, Madison had been thrust into a role of greater visibility in Congress, though hardly as an advocate of centralizing change. On September 6 he seconded a motion in which Jones presented Virginia's terms for the western cession that Congress had recommended as necessary to assure ratification of the Articles. Almost immediately, Jones, to whom the delegation had deferred on this vital issue, departed for Virginia to attend his ailing wife and to persuade the legislature to complete the cession. Appointed to the committee to consider Jones's motion, Madison shared prominently from this point on in all congressional deliberations concerning the west—not least because he feared that his remaining colleagues in Virginia's delegation, John Walker and Theodorick Bland, were not sufficiently alert to the commonwealth's long-term interests. On September 16, with Kentucky much in mind, he suddenly entered the ongoing controversy over Vermont, whose independence Bland favored, with a set of resolutions looking toward a congressional settlement that would have placed the rebellious territory firmly under the jurisdiction of either New Hampshire or New York.[13] Moreover, when Congress received the committee's report on the Virginia cession and agreed to strike a clause voiding private purchases from the Indians, Madison voted against the altered resolutions, although Bland and Walker cast the delegation's vote in favor of the committee's recommendations.[14]

For all his wish to help prepare the way for the completion of the Confederation, Madison would always stubbornly resist any cession that would not confirm his state's exclusion of the claims of the great land companies. Recognition of these claims, in his opinion, could transfer a great treasure "from the public to a few land mongers."[15] It would also imply an improper congressional jurisdiction over the northwest. Through all the months ahead, while the terms of a cession remained a periodic subject of controversy, Madison insisted that Virginia's sovereignty was absolute within the whole of its chartered bounds. He denied that Congress had a valid, independent claim to the lands northwest of the Ohio River and maintained that Congress could acquire legitimate authority only by accepting a cession on Virginia's terms.[16]

Meanwhile, Madison's preoccupation with the west and his determination to defend state interests prompted him to take a major role in deliberations over a potential treaty with Spain. With most of the delegates from the frightened South, Madison favored close cooperation with France. He quickly established close relationships with the Chevalier de La Luzerne and the secretary of the French legation, François de Barbé-Marbois.[17] He has often been identified as a member of a "French party," and French agents described him as "devoted to us." Yet La Luzerne also characterized him as "not free from prejudices in favor of the various claims of Virginia, however exaggerated they may be."[18] Certainly, these claims made Madison a difficult friend of France on the issue of America's relationship with Spain.

Aware that Spain would not complete a treaty that might threaten its position in Louisiana; French emissaries sought American flexibility on the question of a western boundary and on American pretensions to a right to navigate the Mississippi River. No one in Congress was *less* flexible on these issues than the young Virginian. The original instructions for a Spanish treaty were entirely to his liking. When the hard-pressed Georgians and South Carolinians moved to abandon Congress's original insistence on free navigation of the Mississippi, Madison forced postponement of a reconsideration despite the anxiety he suffered when his stand embroiled him in another conflict with Bland. He trusted, he told Jones, "that Congress will see the impropriety of sacrificing the acknowledged limits and claims of any state" without that state's consent.[19] And when he wrote Governor Jefferson to seek a resolution of the difference between himself and Bland, he indicated that the desperate military situation in the South had not sufficed to make him think that Virginia should agree to purchase a Spanish pact at the price of the navigation of the Mississippi or its western claims. He also asked for specific instructions as to what the delegates should do if Congress made concessions on either matter without Virginia's consent.[20]

By the end of his first year of service, Madison had become a congressman with whom his fellows reckoned. Early in 1781 he was mentioned as a candidate for the position of secretary for foreign affairs.[21] Created in January, this post was the first of four executive offices established by Congress while Virginia and Maryland were acting to complete the ratification of the Articles. Congress made these important administrative changes, culminating in the appointment of Robert Morris as superintendent of finance, without a serious division. Madison supported them, although his surviving papers are entirely silent on the subject. In the years ahead, he would become something of an administration man in Congress. He was willing to see a good deal of executive initiative, normally supported the secretaries' recommendations, and seems often to have been called upon by Morris and Robert R. Livingston, the secretary for foreign affairs, to guide their proposals through Congress.[22]

Madison's support for executive efficiency should not be confused with a determined nationalism. In close conjunction with the creation of executive departments, Congress asked the states for power to levy a 5 percent duty on foreign imports and began a broad consideration of the adequacy of the newly ratified Articles. Analyzing these deliberations of the spring and summer of 1781, most students of Confederation politics have identified Madison as one of the leaders of a nationalistic push. Failing to secure endorsement of a federal power to coerce delinquent states, it is said, Madison conducted a campaign to expand federal authority by means of a doctrine of implied congressional powers.[23] This interpretation rests on a partial reading of the evidence and smothers a deep and obvious ambivalence in Madison's position during this time of important reforms. It also raises an imposing barrier to understanding how he would arrive at the position he would occupy by 1793.

What we know of the critical decisions of 1781 can be reduced to a few essentials. On February 3 John Witherspoon moved that the states be asked to grant Congress the power to superintend the nation's commerce and an exclusive right to levy duties on imports. This motion was defeated, four states to three. Then, by the same margin, Congress approved a recommendation of power to levy a 5 percent impost. Madison and Jones overrode Bland to cast Virginia's vote *against* both proposals.[24] At some point Madison prepared a substitute resolution, which seems the best clue to his current preference: "That it be earnestly recommended to the states, as indispensably necessary to the support of public credit and the prosecution of the war, immediately to pass laws" levying a 5 percent duty on foreign imports and vesting Congress with power to collect and appropriate the funds to discharge the principal and interest of its debts. The language plainly suggests that while Madison wanted this revenue and favored congressional collection, he did not currently favor an independent congressional power to levy the tax or to use it for any purpose except to provide for the debt.[25] On this issue and on the question of congressional superintendence of commerce, he was not willing to extend congressional authority as far as many of his fellows would have liked.

Similar conclusions can be reached about the episode that may appear to offer the strongest evidence for Madison's early participation in a nationalistic thrust. During the spring and summer of 1781, a progression of three congressional committees considered ways to strengthen the Articles. Madison served on the first of these committees and wrote its report, which recommended an amendment authorizing Congress "to employ the force of the United States" to compel delinquent states to fulfill their "federal obligations."[26] Madison's biographers have correctly pointed out that he regarded the coercive power as implicit in the Articles and was quite serious about employing this formidable tool at a time when Virginians were complaining bitterly about inadequate northern support. He even wondered whether Congress, by seeking an amendment, should risk a denial by the states of power it already possessed by implication.[27] But it is equally important to recall the nature of Madison's defense of the proposed amendment. While a coercive power was implicit in the Articles, his report maintained, the absence of a more "determinate and particular provision" could lead to challenges by recalcitrant states. Moreover, it was "most consonant to the spirit of a free constitution that . . . all exercise of power should be explicitly and precisely warranted." A preference for explicit grants of power was a theme to which the Virginian would return repeatedly in the months—and, of course, the years—ahead.[28]

In 1781 Madison insisted on the existence of implied congressional powers in the case of coercion of delinquent states. He assumed the presence of implied powers—logically at least—when he moved to tighten the embargo on trade with Britain and to authorize Gen. Anthony Wayne to impress supplies on his march to Virginia. So, however, did virtually the whole of Congress, for neither of these motions generated constitutional debate. Each advocated an extension or renewal of measures that Congress had long employed. They are not sufficient grounds for concluding that Madison was engaged in a campaign to extend congressional authority. Apart from the coercion of the states, the incidents that have been cited to support the view that he was deliberately attempting to enlarge congressional authority uniformly involved measures that were obvious derivatives of the power to make war, and no one had to torture the Articles to support them.[29] Ordinarily, Madison was demonstrably wary of the doctrine of implied powers. His regard for written limitations of authority and charter boundaries between the powers of the nation and the states is clear.

Madison's position on a national bank is one of many illustrations of the point. With nearly all his colleagues, he favored the appointment of Robert Morris, conceded the financier's extraordinary conditions for acceptance, and supported the superintendent's attempts to finance the Yorktown campaign and to preserve the public credit from absolute collapse. The bank was a partial exception. Morris submitted his proposal for a bank on May 17, 1781, three days after accepting his office, two weeks after the Virginia delegates had reported the final collapse of the currency, and one week after the Virginia legislature had been forced to flee from Richmond. On May 26 Madison nevertheless distinguished himself as one of only four congressmen to oppose a resolution endorsing the superintendent's plan, believing that the Articles conferred no federal power to create a corporation. On December 31 Madison apparently acquiesced in the ordinance of incorporation itself, but not without some agony. "You will conceive the dilemma in which . . . circumstances placed the members who felt on the one side the *importance* of the institution, and on the other a want of power and an aversion to assume it," he wrote. Unwilling to frustrate the financier, disappoint the army, or break an implicit promise to subscribers, worried congressmen had felt able to do no more than insert a resolution by Edmund Randolph recommending actions by the states to give the bank's charter validity within their bounds. "As this is a tacit admission of a defect of [federal] power, I hope," Madison explained, "it will be an antidote against the poisonous tendency to precedents of usurpation."[30]

The bank was not the only issue on which Madison revealed the limits of his continentalism and his inclination to insist on strict construction of the Articles. On May 28 Congress received La Luzerne's request for a definition of its terms for peace. Through the summer and into the fall of 1781, countered at every turn by Witherspoon and opposed by the French and the frightened delegates from the deep South, Madison fought a losing battle to make the western claims of the United States—or, at minimum, the western claims of Virginia—part of the peace ultimata. Failing that, he sought to make these claims a necessary part of any commercial treaty with Great Britain.[31] During the same months he continued to worry about growing congressional sentiment in favor of independence for Vermont, not least because he suspected that "some of the little states . . . hope that such a precedent may engender a division of some of the large ones."[32] The question of western cessions was slowly working its way through a Congress hostile to Virginia's conditions.[33] Madison ended the year thoroughly angered over the congressional temperament. He counseled Virginians against despair. Congress, he explained to Jefferson, had not adopted "the obnoxious doctrine of an inherent right in the United States to the territory in question." He hoped that Jefferson would try to counteract "any intemperate measures that may be urged in the legislature." Yet he freely declared his opinion that the congressional proceedings were "ample justification" for a legislative revocation of the cession and a remonstrance against interference in Virginia's jurisdiction, as well as ample indication that the legislature should "in all their provisions for their future security, importance, and interest . . . presume that the present union will but little survive the present war."[34]

Through the spring of 1782, as he completed his second year in Congress, Madison remained preoccupied with Vermont and the western cession. He continued to work to block Vermont's admission as an independent state. He questioned congressional authority, feared the consequences of the precedent for Virginia, and resisted the addition of another state to the forces of the easterners and the landless block in Congress.[35] He also sought to force a decision on the Virginia cession, which he perceived as intimately connected to the struggle over Vermont.[36] When Congress stalled, postponing a decision indefinitely, Madison suggested to Arthur Lee that it would not be "consistent with the respect we owe to our own public characters nor with the dignity of those we serve to persist longer in fruitless applications" for a congressional decision. Instead, the delegation would request instructions from the legislature, "who will certainly be fully justified in taking any course . . . which the interest of the state shall prescribe."[37] Madison hoped the legislature would continue firm. The delegation even determined at one point to make its support for measures pressuring recalcitrant states to approve the impost "subservient to an honorable" decision on the cession.[38]

Madison's positions on the impost, on a national bank, and on the west should warn against identifying him with a group of nationalistic reformers during his first two years and more in Congress. The more closely one examines this interpretation, the larger grow the problems. H. James Henderson, for example, explicitly follows Brant in portraying the Virginian as a consistent, energetic nationalist,[39] yet Henderson's quantitative studies afford poor support for this view. The cluster-bloc analysis from 1780 places Madison in a New England-Virginia bloc on the fringes of an "Eastern Party," which was the home of most of the old radicals who remained in Congress and which voted quite differently from the Southern and New York blocs, whose members Henderson identifies with a nationalistic thrust.[40] The table for 1781 places Madison in a separate Virginia bloc, which was the most loosely attached of the four groupings within a dominant "Middle-Southern Coalition."[41] The analysis for 1782, when divisions were dominated by the issues of Vermont and the west, associates Madison with a separate Virginia group within a "Southern Party," which opposed a "Northern Party" with New England and Middle States blocs.[42] Only during 1783 does the analysis of roll calls place Madison firmly within a nationalistic coalition.

For the months between the spring of 1780 and the fall of 1782, the evidence permits few generalizations about Madison's congressional position, and these must differ markedly from the conclusions most scholars have drawn. Madison *did* consistently advocate a harmonious relationship between the United States and France, although no one in Congress was a more persistent or effective *opponent* of American concessions to French or Spanish desires on the matters of the western boundaries or the Mississippi River. By the summer of 1782, Madison's desire for close relations with the French and his appreciation of Benjamin Franklin's contribution to such relations prompted him to take a leading role in opposition to the maneuvers of his Virginia colleague Arthur Lee, whose enmity toward Franklin and suspicion of the French Madison denounced as portending a revival of the party controversies of 1779.[43] The younger man's dislike of Lee was compounded by the latter's vendetta against Robert Morris, whom Madison normally supported.[44]

Through the fall of 1782, however, Madison did not conceive of Congress as divided into pro- and anti-Morris parties, nor is it possible to identify him with a group intent on national aggrandizement. He did not vote that way across a range of issues. On the impost and the national bank he sided with the handful of congressmen most resistant to centralizing reform. Moreover, one may search in vain through his surviving papers through most of 1782 for any indication that he was even aware of a reformist push toward greater national authority, much less identified with one. Far from seeking subtle means to extend the constitutional boundaries of congressional power, he seems to have been a strict constructionist of sorts. He was not invariably consistent on the point; he consciously departed from the principle when exigencies required. But he departed from the principle with obvious reluctance and concern. Madison's fundamental inclination was to insist on charter definitions of authority, on *both* the full assertion of powers confided to the central government and genuine regard for the authority left to the states. If this could lead him to support coercion of delinquents, it could also—and more often—lead him to defend states' rights.[45]

Nowhere was this more evident than on the matter of Virginia's western claims, the issue that distinguished Madison most clearly from the majority in Congress. Historians have emphasized the young man's role in the creation of a national domain, and it is also necessary to remember that he frequently wrote home to urge adoption of the impost and compliance with other congressional recommendations. Madison was certainly no localist. Neither was he *principally* a defender of the states' constitutional preserves. Contemporaries nonetheless saw him correctly as a dedicated servant of Virginia. He was willing to subordinate his desire for the impost and the cession to his determination to exclude the speculators from the west and to defend Virginia's jurisdictional claims. He opposed congressional control of commerce. He shared with most Virginians an intense suspicion of New England and an acute resentment of the obvious congressional jealousy of the Old Dominion. When he discussed congressional divisions, he identified his foes as easterners, Pennsylvania speculators, and members from the landless states. He could not commit himself consistently to centralizing change while these remained his dominant concerns. He would not be unaffected by these feelings when his perspective changed.

In the fall of 1782, as Congress anxiously awaited news from its peace commissioners in Paris, circumstances slowly altered Madison's preoccupations. Deliberations on Vermont and the cession took turns to his liking.[46] At the same time, the Confederation government drew ever nearer to financial collapse. The superintendent of finance had completed his administrative reforms of the Department of the Treasury, put the Bank of North America into operation, enlarged the supply of usable paper by issuing the "Morris Notes," and urged a settlement of accounts between the nation and the states as the first step toward funding the general debt. But the states were increasingly in arrears on their requisitions—Virginia notoriously so. Rhode Island had not approved the impost. Pressure from unpaid public creditors was mounting, and Morris had seized the occasion of one of their memorials to deliver his most important paper on public finance. Dated July 29, 1782, this report insisted that additional general revenues must be added to receipts from the impost and the anticipated sales of western lands in order to meet current expenses and pay the interest on the debt. By fall, however, Congress had done no more than requisition additional funds for the interest due the creditors.[47]

Through the fall, Madison still served as something of an administration man in Congress. His views accorded closely with the financier's when the clamors of soldiers and civilian creditors led two states to contemplate assuming a portion of the Confederation's financial responsibilities. Reporting for a committee assigned to consider New Jersey's warning that the state might be compelled to pay its line out of funds intended for its annual quota, Madison insisted that "the federal constitution" provided that costs for the common defense be paid from the common treasury.[48] He also served with John Rutledge and Alexander Hamilton on a committee that managed to dissuade the Pennsylvania assembly from adopting a plan to pay its civilian federal creditors from state funds.[49] As before, he defended the authority confided to the general government, just as he insisted on respect for the written limitations on its power. He continued to guard Virginia's interests, not only in deliberations on the cession and Vermont, but also in early considerations of adjustments of state accounts. On the latter issue he could not agree entirely with the superintendent.[50]

Rather suddenly, the budding crisis burst. Events propelled the Virginian toward a leading role in the war years' most important effort to extend the powers of Congress. In December 1782 a deputation from the angry army arrived in Philadelphia to demand immediate pay for the private soldiers and firm assurances to the officers that they would receive the half-pay pensions promised them in 1780. Then, on Christmas Eve, a humiliated Madison was compelled to tell the fundless Congress that Virginia had rescinded its approval of the impost, destroying all remaining hope that the proposal of 1781 might provide the required relief. Soon thereafter, Robert Morris committed himself to an all-out push to win approval of his plans. The superintendent feared that the end of the war would ruin an unrepeatable opportunity for strengthening congressional authority and securing the general revenues necessary to restore public credit and promote peacetime prosperity. As rumors of a preliminary treaty of peace grew louder and unrest in the army assumed an ominous tone, a "movement for uniting the support of the public creditors—civil and military—emanated . . . from the Office of Finance."[51]

On January 6 Congress received the army's memorial. The following day a grand committee met with Morris, who informed them that the finances would not permit any payments at present or any assurances of future pay until general funds were established for the purpose. On January 9 the financier informed another committee that accounts abroad were overdrawn and secured permission for one more draft on foreign funds despite that fact. On January 17 he told the army deputation that one month's pay could be provided from this draft, but that no other provisions could be made without congressional action. At the same time, he advised Congress against further applications for foreign loans. Finally, on January 24, without warning, he submitted a letter announcing that he would resign at the end of May if permanent provision had not been made for the public debt. The superintendent declined to be "the minister of injustice."[52]

The letter from the financier jarred Congress, which began a full-scale consideration of funding the following day. Moreover, some of Morris's supporters took it as a signal for a concentrated effort to enlist extra-congressional pressure for independent federal revenues, especially from the army. For two months Congress battled over funding and commutation of the half-pay pensions amidst growing rumors that the army might refuse to disband. At camp, agitation culminated in the Newburgh Addresses of March 10 and 12, 1783.[53]

The major elements of Madison's response seem clear.[54] Through most of February, the Virginian, who served on all the key committees to confer with the army deputation and with Morris, was in close agreement with the superintendent on the measures necessary to resolve the crisis. As a guardian of Virginia's interests, he would not accept the financier's proposal that state surpluses of the old continentals be credited at the official rate of forty to one, nor would he support a tax on acreages of land. And yet, despite Virginia's instructions to oppose any departure from the present mode of apportioning taxes (which required an assessment of land values), he joined with Hamilton and James Wilson, the superintendent's closest supporters in Congress, to insist that the present rule of apportionment was unworkable and must be changed. And while he shared the general congressional resentment of Morris's threat to resign, he agreed with the financier that Congress must have both an impost and additional general revenues to meet its constitutional responsibilities.[55]

With Madison restrained by Virginia's preference for requisitions based on the Articles' rule of apportionment, Wilson and Hamilton took the early lead in advocating independent revenues collected by Congress, while Bland

and Arthur Lee led the opposition. Then, on January 28, Madison entered the debate with one of the most impressive speeches of his congressional years. It was unnecessary, he remarked, to argue the necessity of paying the public debt, since "the idea of erecting our national independence on the ruins of public faith and national honor must be horrid to every mind which retained either honesty or pride." No one, though, continued to suppose that Congress could rely on "a punctual and unfailing compliance by thirteen separate and independent governments with periodical demands of money." Nor could Congress reasonably depend on the states to make separate, permanent provisions for the debt. Innumerable occasions would arise for diversion of such funds to state uses, while the conviction of every state that others would fail to meet their obligations would ultimately stop such separate provisions completely. The situation called imperatively for "the plan of a general revenue operating throughout the United States under the superintendence of Congress." The alternative, as Pennsylvania's recent conduct showed, would be state assumptions of federal responsibilities. "What then," he asked, "would become of the Confederation?" What would be the reaction of the army? "The patience of the army has been equal to their bravery, but that patience must have its limits."

Madison denied that general revenues would contravene the principles of the Confederation. Congress was already vested with the power of the purse. "A requisition of Congress on the states for money is as much a law to them as their revenue acts, when passed, are laws to their respective citizens." The Articles authorized Congress to borrow money. If provision for the resulting debt could be made in no other way, then "a general revenue is within the spirit of the Confederation."[56]

With this speech of January 28, Madison seized a leading role in the attempt to win congressional approval of general revenues. He became, indeed, floor general of the effort, although his specific proposals could still be distinguished from those of Hamilton or Wilson by their southern flavor. Viewing the congressional support for an assessment of lands as an insuperable barrier to prior approval of general funds, Madison supported a motion to move the discussion of a mode of assessment ahead of the debate on independent revenues. Hamilton, who saw that the Virginian was trying desperately to bridge the gap between the congressional majority and Morris, quickly fell in line with Madison's attempts to untie procedural knots.

The strategy eventually misfired. By the end of January, even Lee and Bland were moving toward support of a modified impost. Madison argued quietly and effectively for a commutation of the half-pay pensions. Yet the

New England and New Jersey delegates continued to resist, provoking him, at one point, to cry out that he was "astonished to hear objections against a commutation come from states in compliance with whose objections against the half-pay itself this expedient had been substituted."[57] Even worse, Congress managed, to Madison's surprise, to agree on a method for assessing lands, although he voted consistently against the plan that was finally approved.[58] Madison had anticipated that a full discussion of the possibility of an assessment would convince others, as he was convinced, that the Articles' rule for apportioning requisitions was unworkable. Instead, Congress agreed on a procedure, and the commitment of many members to a first recourse to taxes based on such apportionments remained a major obstacle to approval of general revenues.

The problem was immediately apparent when John Rutledge and Virginia's John Frances Mercer moved to apply the proceeds from a new impost exclusively to the debt due to the army. Madison helped to defeat this proposal on February 18, only to hear Hamilton and Wilson follow with a motion that Congress open its doors to the public when matters of finance were under debate. The Virginian shared the general dislike of this surprising motion, which was greeted with adjournment, and he queried the Pennsylvania delegation privately about it. The Pennsylvanians told him that they had put themselves in a delicate position with their legislature by persuading it to drop its plans for state payments to civilian creditors and simply wished their constituents to know where they stood. "Perhaps the true reason," Madison suspected, "was that it was expected the presence of public creditors, numerous and weighty in Philadelphia, would have an influence" on congressional proceedings.[59]

Congress had already heard Hamilton urge a general revenue on grounds that worried several members. "As the energy of the federal government was evidently short of the degree necessary for pervading and uniting the states," the New Yorker had argued, "it was expedient to introduce the influence of officers deriving their emoluments from and consequently interested in supporting the power of Congress."[60] The subsequent attempt by Hamilton and Wilson to open Congress itself to a powerful lobby reinforced a gathering impression that several advocates of general funds hoped the public creditors would press both the state and federal legislatures into a grant of independent revenues to Congress.[61] Madison was obviously uncomfortable with the expression of such desires.[62]

At just this point the pressure from the army neared its peak, encouraged, if not deliberately provoked, by some of the Philadelphia advocates of general revenues. On February 19, with members openly referring to the threat from the army,[63] Rutledge renewed the motion to appropriate the impost exclusively to the soldiers' needs. Again, Hamilton "strenuously" opposed "such a partial dispensation of justice," suggesting that "it was impolitic to divide the interest of the civil and military creditors, whose joint efforts in the states would be necessary to prevail on them to adopt a general revenue." Mercer countered that he opposed "a permanent debt supported by a permanent and general revenue," believing "it would be good policy to separate instead of cementing the interest of the army and the other public creditors."[64]

On the following evening, February 20—after another day of angry debates—Madison joined Hamilton, Nathaniel Gorham, Richard Peters, and Daniel Carroll at the home of Congressman Thomas FitzSimons. Hamilton and Peters, whose military backgrounds and contacts seemed to make them best informed, told the gathering that the army had definitely decided not to lay down arms until its demands were satisfied; a public declaration would soon announce this intent, and "plans had been agitated if not formed for subsisting themselves after such a declaration," Washington, the two ex-officers announced, "was already become extremely unpopular among almost all ranks from his known dislike to any unlawful proceedings" and "many leading characters" were working industriously to replace him with Horatio Gates. Hamilton said that he had written the commander to alert him to these schemes, urging him to lead the army in any plans for redress, "that they might be moderated." If these revelations were intended to intensify the pressure for the taxes Morris wanted, the strategy could not have been more misconceived. With only Hamilton dissenting, the group of delegates agreed that the temperament of Congress made it impossible to secure any general revenues beyond the impost.[65] Several must have silently concluded that the temper of the army would permit no more delay.

The meeting at FitzSimons's was a critical event for Madison. On the morrow, he rose in Congress for a speech in which he once again defended general revenues as consistent with "the principles of liberty and the spirit of the constitution." But he "particularly disclaimed the idea of perpetuating a public debt," and he admitted that he was now convinced that Congress would have to limit its recommendations to the impost and a "call for the deficiency in the most permanent ways that could be reconciled with a revenue established within each state separately."[66] Before this speech of February 21, Madison had worked in close conjunction with Morris and his congressional spokesman. From this point forward, he was determined to construct a compromise of which they disapproved. On March 6, his alternative proposals for restoring public credit were reported from committee. Although Morris, Hamilton, and Wilson continued to resist, the proposals were accepted in amended form on April 18, and Madison was assigned to draft an address to the states. Already, on March 17, Congress had received Washington's report on the resolution of the Newburgh Affair.[67]

Madison's separation from the other advocates of general revenues has commonly been seen, when it is mentioned, as a straightforward product of his conviction that only a compromise could resolve the urgent crisis.[68] More was certainly involved. Beginning with his speech of February 21, Madison took pains to distance himself from suggestions that a "permanent" federal debt could be a useful tool for strengthening Congress and the union. He insisted that he would concur "in every arrangement that should appear necessary for an honorable and just fulfillment of the public engagements and in no measure tending to augment the power of Congress which should appear unnecessary."[69] Madison was out of sympathy, by now, with both the immediate tactics and the ultimate objectives of Hamilton, Wilson, and Morris. He was, indeed, no longer certain of the patriotism and republicanism of some of his fellow advocates of general funds.

Morris's report of July 29, 1782, had advocated general revenues adequate to meet the government's ordinary operating expenses as well as to manage the debt. These revenues would be collected by officers appointed by Congress, and they would continue as long as the debt existed. For all of Madison's insistence that such measures were within the spirit of the present constitution, no one had expressed a clearer understanding that independent federal revenues would mean a fundamental alteration in the balance of power between Congress and the states.[70] It was this fundamental change that Arthur Lee opposed and Morris, Hamilton, and Wilson found so difficult to relinquish. It was this that Madison first favored and then abandoned in his speech of February 21. He gave it up, not simply because he was more flexible than some of his allies, but because it was not for him, as it was for some of them, an object worth the risks it came to entail. He gave it up, moreover, because it had become increasingly clear that several advocates of general revenues had ulterior objectives he did not share.

All of the original supporters of general funds regarded a dependable federal revenue as essential to the restoration of public credit and probably to the very survival of the Confederation. All of them regarded a provision for regular payment of the interest on the debt as a critical test of national character and an indispensable security against the day when it might be necessary to borrow again. Not all of them, however, actually wished to see the debt retired, nor did the superintendent's plan provide for payment of the principal. Contemporary critics realized this when they condemned a "permanent" or "perpetual" debt, and historians increasingly agree that several of the advocates of general funds looked beyond the reestablishment of public credit toward management of the debt in such a fashion as to promote economic development and to advance a particular variety of political centralization. Properly funded, as Morris put it, the mass of "dead" certificates of debt could rise in value, become "a sufficient circulating medium" for the country, and provide the capital for more intensive economic development.[71] Simultaneously—to use the vivid current metaphor—the obligations of the federal government would become a new "cement" of union. Looking to Congress for their salaries, pensions, or other claims, civilian creditors, the discharged soldiers, and the officers appointed to collect federal taxes, together with merchants doing business with the national bank, would "unite the several states more closely together in one general money connection" and "give stability to government" by combining in its support.[72]

Hamilton had been thinking in similar fashion since the beginning of the decade. His private correspondence and his anonymous newspaper series, "The Continentalist," repeatedly insisted on the necessity of creating among the nation's leadership a class of influentials tied to the federal government and capable of counterbalancing the influentials currently tied to the states. Genuine federal power, he argued, required a union of the government's resources with those of a monied and office-holding class directly dependent on that government for promotion of its economic interests.[73]

Consciously seeking to replicate developments in England after the Revolution of 1689, several of the nationalists of 1783 sought to bind fragmented segments of the American elite into a single interest intimately connected with the federal government, much as it was thought that the ministers of William III had once attempted to create a "monied interest" that might counterbalance the Tory Gentry.[74] It is not a gross exaggeration to suggest that these reformers proposed to use the national debt to create a single nation—or at least an integrated national elite—where none existed in 1783. They envisioned the emergence in America of a facsimile of those linked forces of government, the military, commerce, and finance that ordinarily fell in line behind a ministry in power and lent stability to the British system—interests that the English had in mind when they referred broadly to the forces supporting the "court." Imagining a national greatness predicated on an imitation of the political and economic strengths of England, nationalists such as Hamilton and Morris were prepared to risk some further clamors from the army, if not to feed the agitation, for the sake of general funds. But Madison, who was preoccupied with the defense of a republican revolution and who would never see Great Britain as a proper model for America, was not. He did not quarrel with the Morrisites or join with Lee and Mercer. Neither was he ignorant of the implications when he disclaimed a desire for a perpetual debt.

Always sensitive about his reputation for consistency, Madison added to his record of his speech of February 21 a lengthy footnote explaining why he had earlier favored the general revenues he now saw as unattainable. This should be read with care, for it suggests the gulf between his motives and those of some of the other reformers, as well as the extent of his discomfort with their views. "Many of the most respectable people of America," he reflected—and it is hard to see whom he had in mind if these "respectable people" did not include the circle of public creditors, army officers, and congressmen that radiated from the Office of Finance—"supposed the preservation of the Confederacy essential to secure the blessings of the revolution and permanent funds for discharging debts essential to the preservation of union." If they were disappointed, he imagined, their ardor in the cause might cool, and in a "critical emergence" they might "prefer some political connection with Great Britain as a necessary cure for our internal instability." Madison himself had not been able to see how "the danger of convulsions from the army" could be obviated without general funds, which also seemed the surest method for preventing "the calamities" sure to follow from continuing disputes among the states. Without general funds "it was not likely the balances would ever be discharged. . . . The consequence would be a rupture of the Confederacy. The eastern states would at sea be powerful and rapacious, the southern opulent and weak. This would be a temptation. The demands on the southern states would be an occasion. Reprisals would be instituted. Foreign aid would be called in by first the weaker, then the stronger side, and finally both be made subservient to the wars and politics of Europe."[75] Collapse of the union would inevitably bring the collapse of the republican revolution in its wake.[76]

Concern for the republican experiment, distrust of the New Englanders, and doubts about the motives of his fellow advocates of general funds may all have contributed to Madison's original decision to support this strengthening of Congress. What is certain from the February memorandum is that all these fears contributed importantly to his decision to *abandon* general revenues in favor of a complex compromise designed to satisfy the army, put an end to the recurrent disagreements that had periodically disrupted Congress, and do these things *without* so large an alteration of the federal system. Madison did not simply conclude that it was inexpedient to delay a resolution of an urgent crisis. Rather, as he saw more clearly the directions that some of the nationalists wished to take, as he heard from credible sources the growing rumors of intrigues between the capital and the camp at Newburgh, he deliberately drew back.[77] He believed, as Washington believed, that it was profoundly dangerous to delay the satisfaction of the soldiers' demands by continuing to insist on a solution that a majority in Congress would not approve. He had also come to be uneasy at the prospect of the corollaries that Morris's solution seemed to imply. In his "Address to the States" of April 26, 1783, Madison urged the legislatures to approve the new financial plan because it was the *smallest* departure from the Articles of Confederation that could be reconciled with the necessity of providing for the debt.[78]

This was not just special pleading. Through all his years in Congress, Madison had shown a genuine regard for what he often called the "constitutional" boundaries of congressional power. Respect for written limitations of authority was near the center of his republican convictions, as was his regard for national honor. The balance of power between the federal government and the states was always, by comparison, a secondary concern. He thus stood in between the Morrisites and their opponents, genuinely swayed by what he heard from both. By 1783, some nationalists already wished for a convention that would thoroughly transform the federal system.[79] Madison was not prepared for reforms so extreme.[80] He was willing, unlike Lee or Mercer, to accept a centralizing solution to the difficulties the Confederation faced. But this was not his principal objective. He approved a tilting of the federal balance only in the sense and only to the point that he conceived it necessary for the preservation of a union without which the republican experiment could not survive. And he was not immune to fears that certain federal measures might prove incompatible with what he called the "spirit" or the "principles" of liberty.[81] He thus specifically disclaimed a wish for the sort of political centralization that other advocates of funding seemed to have in mind. In January he agreed with Morris that greater powers for Congress were necessary to resolve a crisis of the Revolution. By April he had changed his mind about how far the swing should go. He did not articulate a systematic explanation of his discontent with the emerging program of other continental-minded men to achieve political centralization by fiscal means—perhaps not even to himself. This would await developments after 1789, when their desires assumed more substantial shape. It would also require a further evolution of Madison's own views. By 1783, experience had taught him that congressional reliance on the states for revenue endangered both the character and harmony of the union. But he was not yet ready to conclude, with Hamilton, that the Articles of Confederation were irredeemably defective in their fundamental principles, and he had yet to formulate a truly nationalistic program of his own.

Madison stayed on in Congress until his term expired on October 31, 1783. Through his final months of service, with peace at hand and the financial plan on its way to the states for their decision, he was cast once more in his familiar role as servant of Virginia. Although he struggled unsuccessfully to locate the seat of the federal government on the Potomac River, he had the satisfaction to be present when his old opponents finally decided to give ground on Virginia's terms for a western cession. On September 13 deliberations opened on a compromise that was finally accepted with only Maryland and New Jersey in dissent. Madison and Jones were content, and their efforts helped secure Virginia's agreement on December 22, 1783.[82]

Madison's pleasure at the outcome of this old dispute was mixed with disappointment over his state's initial rejection of the other congressional recommendations of 1783.[83] When he retired from Congress, he intended to reenter the Virginia House of Delegates to work for the enactment of the state reforms initiated by Jefferson, who had replaced him at the seat of the federal government, and to urge the state's compliance with the Treaty of Paris and the financial proposals of 1783. Pursuing these objectives, he visited George Mason on the journey home and found the great man more favorably inclined than he had anticipated toward the measures he desired. "His heterodoxy," Madison reported, "lay chiefly in being too little impressed with either the necessity or the proper means of preserving the Confederacy.[84]

For Madison, the "proper means" had very recently come to include one significant addition to the powers sought by Congress. In fact, it was his wish for this reform that set him on the path he was to take to the Constitutional Convention. As late as the spring of 1783 he had been reluctant to deliver to the federal government extensive powers over commerce. He had resisted even a commercial treaty with Great Britain, because he feared that an agreement, eagerly desired by northern shippers, could be purchased only with concessions that would sacrifice the planting states' ability to satisfy their most essential needs. "It cannot be for the interest of" Virginia, he had written Randolph, "to preclude it from any regulations which experience may recommend for its thorough emancipation" from the British monopoly over its trade.[85] As he neared retirement, though, Madison had read with alarm the earl of Sheffield's *Observations on the Commerce of the American States,* which argued that Great Britain could maintain its dominant position in trade with the United States without dismantling its restrictive navigation laws.[86] By autumn he had seen the British proclamation of July 2, 1783, which confined most American trade with the West Indies to British bottoms.[87] "Congress," he now reported, "will probably recommend some defensive plan to the states. . . . If it fails . . . it will prove such an inefficacy in the union as will extinguish all respect for it."[88]

Madison reentered the Virginia assembly with his thoughts much occupied with the state's economic situation. In the same letter to Jefferson in which he reported on his visit with Mason, he described the Old Dominion's commercial condition as "even more deplorable than I had conceived." The note of shock is reminiscent of the note of alarm about the state of the union in his letters from Philadelphia as a beginning congressman. Detection of this note is similarly important to an understanding of his career. As Drew R. McCoy has explained, Madison conceived a proper course of economic development to be critical to the success of the republican experiment. This course required the breaching of mercantilist restrictions on American trade.[89] But the congressional request for power to retaliate against the British was denied. Madison's attempts to break the British stranglehold with new state regulations were gutted by the demands of local interests in Virginia's legislature.[90] The congressional recommendations of 1783 also failed to win approval from the states, among which tensions mounted.

By the end of 1784 Madison was willing, if not yet eager, to see a constitutional convention to amend the Articles of Confederation.[91] By August 7, 1785, if not much before, he was fully persuaded that America's commercial ills could not be corrected by state actions, such as those he had attempted in Virginia. Congressional superintendence of commerce, he now argued, was "within the reason of the federal constitution. . . . If Congress as they are now constituted cannot be trusted with the power, . . . let them be chosen oftener . . . or, if any better medium than Congress can be proposed, by which the wills of the states may be concentered, let it be substituted. . . . But let us not . . . rush on certain ruin in order to avoid possible danger."[92]

It was, in short, the obvious inability of the states to grapple separately with the economic difficulties of the postwar years that first led Madison to think in terms of a thoroughgoing alteration of the federal system. It was his profound discontent with the measures many states adopted in response to the postwar depression—measures he considered contrary to the liberal principles of the Revolution—that would complete his change of stance and lead him to assume the major role in preparing the Virginia Resolutions.[93] Before his retirement from the Confederation Congress, there had been little evidence that he would favor, much less author, such a plan.

During his years in Congress, James Madison made several major contributions to the movement to strengthen the central government. His role in the Virginia cession and his authorship of the congressional recommendations of 1783 identified him as a prominent reformer. When he retired from Congress, everyone expected him to lead the continental minded forces in his state assembly. Yet Madison had never been a nationalist by instinct, as some of the reformers of the early 1780s were. He had never shared the fascination with an English model of administration and political economy. His contributions to reform were always shaped and limited by a concern that certain centralizing changes might endanger both the interests of Virginia and the Revolution's most essential goals.

Through the years in Congress, Madison had ordinarily attributed the difficulties of the central government to the clashing interests of the different states, in which he was continuously involved, and to the disabilities that all the states experienced as a result of war. He had hoped that peace would meliorate these problems.[94] He did not deeply challenge the purposes or structure of the federal government as defined by the Articles of Confederation. He did not deeply question the republican regimes established in the states by the early Revolutionary constitutions. Only after he left Congress and went home to struggle year by year in the assembly with advocates of paper money, tax abatements, and assessments for religion, only as he grew increasingly distressed with poorly drafted and inconstant legislation, only when he could no longer hope that the parochial objectives of the states could be reconciled with the continuation of the union, was Madison compelled to reexamine the most fundamental assumptions of his republicanism. Only then did he conclude that accusations he had once dismissed as calumnies on republican government—charges of inconstancy, weakness, and oppression of minorities—were true of small republics and could be overcome only by "extending the sphere."[95]

At the Constitutional Convention, nonetheless, Madison still sought, as he insisted, a genuinely republican remedy for the ills of republican government. In 1787, as before, his fundamental purpose was to nurture and defend a Revolutionary order of society and politics. He remained, as he had always been, a nationalist at certain times, on certain issues, and within the limits of his Revolutionary hopes. Grasping this, it may seem less surprising that he quickly moved into the opposition to Alexander Hamilton's proposals for the new regime.

Hamilton may well have been "affectionately attached" to the cause of republican government.[96] As secretary of the Treasury he nevertheless attempted to "administer" the new American republic toward a future incompatible with Madison's desires.[97] Of all the nationalists of 1783, Hamilton had had the clearest vision of a nation integrated on a British model. After 1789 his foreign policy and constitutional constructions were intimately related to this vision. Both served an economic program intended to create a counterbalance to the influence of state attachments by tying the interests of a critical segment of the American elite to the fortunes of the central government. If Hamilton had seen a little deeper into the assumptions of his occasional ally, he might have been less startled when Madison rebelled.

Hamilton and Madison both understood that the United States had no equivalent of England's national elite. For Madison, this fact was an essential precondition of the promise that the new Constitution might effect a genuinely republican solution to the nation's ills. Liberty, as he conceived it, demanded both a government dependent on the body of the people and security for the fundamental rights that had been threatened in the states by majority control. The pluralistic structure of American society, which would be mirrored in the pluralistic character and conduct of its leaders, was the most important guarantee that a responsive federal government would not prove equally at odds with the protection of the civil liberties of all. For Hamilton, by contrast, pluralism was America's great weakness. A government consistent with promotion of the common good and security for private rights was not to be attained except by policies designed to overcome the centrifugal inclinations of the American order. Hamilton's economic program, calculated to encourage the appearance of a unified elite whose interests would divorce them from the localistic inclinations of the American majority, was deliberately intended to subvert the social and economic structure on which Madison believed a federal republic had to rest. In the Virginian's stands in the old Congress—his hostility to speculative gain at public expense, his profound distrust of Britain, his inclination to respect constitutional definitions of authority, and his eventual disagreement with the more determined advocates of general funds—lay several warnings that his thinking did not really share "the same point of departure" as Hamilton's own.[98] After 1789, Madison refined and made explicit principles that had already influenced him in 1783.

Notes

Mr. Banning, who is preparing a biography of Madison, is a member of the Department of History at the University of Kentucky. He wishes to thank the John Simon Guggenheim Foundation for a grant to aid research and Ralph Ketcham, Harold Schultz, Willi Paul Adams, Charles F. Hobson, and Drew R. McCoy for comments on an earlier version of the article, as well as to acknowledge benefits received between drafts from Jay Kinney, "James Madison's Nationalist Persuasion" (senior honors thesis, University of Texas at Austin, 1980).

1. Brant, *James Madison*, 6 vols. (Indianapolis, Ind., 1941–1961), vol. 2, *The Nationalist*, 418.

2. Ralph Ketcham, *James Madison: A Biography* (New York, 1971), 126–134; Merrill D. Peterson, ed., *James Madison: A Biography in His Own Words* (New York, 1974), 51, 69–71; E. James Ferguson, "The Nationalists of 1781–1783 and the Economic Interpretation of the Constitution," *Journal of American History* 56 (1969): 241–261. Important monographs identifying Madison with a group of nationalistic reformers include Merrill Jensen, *The New Nation: A History of the United States during the Confederation, 1781–1789* (New York, 1950); E. James Ferguson, *The Power of the Purse: A History of American Public Finance, 1776–1790* (Chapel Hill, N.C., 1961); H. James Henderson, *Party Politics in the Continental Congress* (New York, 1974); and Joseph L. Davis, *Sectionalism in American Politics, 1774–1787* (Madison, Wis., 1977).

3. It is not sufficient to concede, as several influential authors do, that there were differences between Madison and the nationalists from the Middle States. The caveat is commonly lost in the generalization when it is entered at all. For example, in *Power of the Purse*, 158–160, Ferguson writes that Madison "was not in the inner councils of the Morris group," at least during the Newburgh Affair. Yet Ferguson, with Brant, describes the Virginian as "an unwavering Nationalist," a phrase he usually defines in terms of Morris's objectives. The reader may fairly infer that what distinguished Madison from the inner group was that he was "less intransigent" in his insistence on a common program (ibid., 166). Other authors make no distinction between Madison and the Morrisites, sometimes with disturbing consequences. For a recent example see James H. Hutson, "Country, Court, and Constitution: Antifederalism and the Historians," *William and Mary Quarterly*, 3d ser., 38 (1981): 337–368.

4. Charles Royster, *A Revolutionary People at War: The Continental Army and American Character, 1775–1783* (Chapel Hill, N.C., 1979), 299–300; Edmund Cody Burnett, *The Continental Congress* (New York, 1941), 401–403; Jack N. Rakove, *The Beginnings of National Politics: An Interpretive History of the Continental Congress* (New York, 1979), 255–274.

5. Madison to Jefferson, Mar. 27, 1780, *The Papers of James Madison*, 14 vols. (Chicago and Charlottesville, Va., 1962–), 2:6. Hereafter cited as *Madison Papers*, vols. 1–7 were edited by William T. Hutchinson and William M. E. Rachal and vols.

8–14 by Robert A. Rutland et al. I have modernized spelling and punctuation and given abbreviations in full throughout this article.

6. As Ketcham notes in *James Madison*, 101.

7. See, especially, Madison to Edmund Randolph, May 20, 1783, *Madison Papers*, 7:59.

8. See the secondary sources cited in notes 2 and 4, together with Worthington Chauncy Ford et al., eds., *Journals of the Continental Congress, 1774–1789*, 34 vols. (Washington, D.C., 1904–1937), vols. 16–17, and Edmund C. Burnett, ed., *Letters of Members of the Continental Congress*, 8 vols. (Washington, D.C., 1921–1936), vol. 5. The latter works are hereafter cited as *Jours. Cont. Cong.* and *Letters Cont. Cong.*

9. See, especially, in Madison to Jefferson, May 6, 1780, *Madison Papers*, 2:19–20.

10. Madison to John Page, May 8, 1780, to Jefferson, June 2, 1780, and to Jones, Oct. 24, 1780, ibid., 21–22, 37–38, 145–146. On June 19, 1780, Jones wrote to Washington, "Congress have been gradually surrendering or throwing upon the several states the exercise of powers they should have retained. . . . Congress is at present little more than the medium through which the wants of the army are conveyed to the states. This body never had or at least . . . exercised powers adequate to the purposes of war" (*Letters Cont. Cong.,* 5:226–227).

11. Madison to Edmund Pendleton, Sept. 12, 1780, *Madison Papers*, 2:81–82.

12. Madison to Pendleton, Nov. 7, 1780, ibid., 166. For additional hints of his persistent hope that problems could be solved within the present structures, see Madison to Jefferson, May 6, 1780, and to John Page (?), May 8, 1780, ibid., 19–20, 21.

13. Madison, "Resolutions Respecting Vermont Lands," Sept. 16, 1780, ibid., 87–88. On Sept. 19, 1780, Madison wrote Jones that he believed a decision should be made "on principles that will effectually discountenance the erection of new governments without the sanction of proper authority" (ibid., 90). Jones's reply of Oct. 2, 1780, strengthens the impression that the Virginians, who were faced with a weak secession movement in Kentucky, had their own interest very much in view. Of the agitation for Vermont's independence, Jones said, "Such excrescences should be taken off on their first appearance. . . . We know not what may be the consequences if Congress shall countenance by precedent the dismembering of states" (ibid., 106).

14. *Jours. Cont. Cong.,* 18:916. For the issue of the western lands to this point see Thomas Perkins Abernathy, *Western Lands and the American Revolution* (New York, 1937), chap. 19, and Peter Onuf, "Toward Federalism; Virginia, Congress, and the Western Lands," *WMQ,* 3d Ser., 34 (1977): 353–374. Onuf's insistence that a resolution of this issue was, for many Virginians, a prerequisite for support of stronger federal power has been particularly helpful.

15. Madison to Jones, Oct. 17, 1780, *Madison Papers*, 2:136–137.

16. For now, Madison swallowed his "chagrin" over the decision of Oct. 10 and urged Virginians to proceed with the cession. He insisted that Virginia could still accomplish the exclusion of the companies simply by attaching to its act of cession a condition voiding private claims, perhaps even a provision that "no private claims be

complied with" in the cessions of any state (ibid.). See also Madison to Jones, Sept. 19, 1780, ibid., 89–90.

17. Jones to Madison, Oct. 9, 1780, ibid., 120–121; Madison to Jones, Oct. 24, 1780, ibid., 145; Brant, *Madison*, 2:77–79.

18. Quoted in Brant, *Madison*, 2:14.

19. Madison to Jones, Nov. 25, 1780, *Madison Papers*, 2:203. See also Madison to Jones, Dec. 5, 1780, ibid., 224.

20. Virginia Delegates in Congress to Jefferson, Dec. 13, 1780, ibid., 241–242.

21. Thomas Burke to William Bingham, Feb. 6 (?), 1781, *Letters Cont. Cong.*, 5:562–563.

22. "I have always conceived the several ministerial departments of Congress to be provisions for aiding their counsels as well as executing their resolutions" (Madison to James Monroe, Mar. 21, 1785, *Madison Papers*, 8:225–256).

23. Madison "used every stratagem to expand" congressional power "indirectly," moving to give Congress power to prohibit trade with Britain, to permit impressment of supplies, etc. (Ketcham, *James Madison*, 114). This accords closely with the longer discussion in Brant, *Madison*, vol. 2, chap. 8: Madison believed in "easy discovery of implied powers where none were expressly stated" (110). Defeated on the matter of the coercive power, he drove "to the same end by specific legislation based on implied powers" (111). "Forced by necessity, Congress adopted one specific measure after another which Madison put before it, based on implications of power" (118).

24. *Jours. Cont. Cong.*, 19:110–113.

25. Madison, "Motion on Impost," Feb. 3, 1781, *Madison Papers*, 2:303–304. At the end of May, Madison was still not as unequivocal an advocate of this independent federal revenue as he would come to be. He defended congressional collection as necessary to prevent diversion of the funds to state uses and as less disruptive of the states' internal governance than Pendleton feared. But he confessed that a congressional right to collect an impost might require a confidence in Congress "greater perhaps than many may think consistent with republican jealousy" (Madison to Pendleton, May 29, 1781, ibid., 3:140–141).

26. Madison, "Proposed Amendment of Articles of Confederation," Mar. 12, 1781, ibid., 3:17–19.

27. Madison to Jefferson, Apr. 16, 1781, ibid., 71–72, in which he argued that the grant of a coercive power was necessary because of the "shameful deficiency" of some of the "most capable" states and the "military exactions" to which others, "already exhausted," were consequently exposed. Note also the remark that a federal navy, which Madison conceived to be the proper tool of coercion, merited support for a "collateral reason." "Without it, what is to protect the southern states for many years to come against the insults and aggressions of their northern brethren?"

28. Madison's most eloquent denunciation of legislative transgressions of constitutional limitations would come in his "Memorial and Remonstrance against Religious Assessments [in Virginia]," 1785, ibid., 8:295–306.

29. The single issue on which Madison, who was frantically working to rush assistance to Virginia, might be fairly accused of torturing the Articles saw him argue that five states should be sufficient to form a quorum for ordinary business. Thomas Rodney Diary, Mar. 5, 1781, *Letters Cont. Cong.,* 6:8.

30. Madison to Pendleton, Jan. 8, 1782, *Madison Papers,* 4:22–23. See also Virginia Delegates to Benjamin Harrison, ibid., 19.

31. Ibid., 3:133; *Jours. Cont. Cong.,* 20–21, passim; Brant, *Madison,* 2:137–140, 143–146.

32. Madison to Pendleton, Aug. 14, 1781, *Madison Papers,* 3:224.

33. See Virginia Delegates to Thomas Nelson, Oct. 9, 16, 23, 1781, ibid., 281–282, 286–288, 293, and Randolph to Nelson, Nov. 7, 1781, which reported the delegation "almost worn down with motions respecting your cession. . . . Virginia is . . . not merely destitute of friends but surrounded by those who labor to retrench her territory" (*Letters Cont. Cong.,* 6:259–260).

34. Madison to Jefferson, Nov. 18, 1781, *Madison Papers,* 3:307–308.

35. With every indication of approaching hostilities between the Green Mountain men and the authorities of New Hampshire and New York, Madison groaned, it might be necessary to accept congressional interposition despite the constitutional and practical arguments against it. "It is very unhappy that such plausible pretexts, if not necessary occasions, of assuming power should occur. Nothing is more distressing to those who have a due respect for the constitutional modifications of power than to be obliged to decide on them" (Madison to Pendleton, Jan. 22, 1782, ibid., 4:38–39).

36. Madison to Pendleton, Apr. 23, 1782, ibid., 178; Madison to Randolph, May 1, 1782, ibid., 196–197. See also Madison's memorandum, "Observations Relating to the Influence of Vermont and the Territorial Claims on the Politics of Congress," May 1, 1782, ibid., 200–203.

37. Madison to Lee, May 7, 1782, ibid., 217–218.

38. Madison to Randolph, ibid., 220.

39. Henderson, *Party Politics,* 249.

40. Ibid., 250–251, and chap. 10 passim.

41. Ibid., 288–289. Indeed, if I read Henderson correctly, his reason for placing the Virginia bloc in this coalition is the link between Randolph, Jones, and some of its marginal members and the Pennsylvania-Maryland bloc, which was the core of the "Middle-Southern Coalition." This, of course, has little to do with Madison's own position, which might fairly be characterized as eccentric. Henderson sees the "Middle-Southern Coalition" of 1781 as opposed to a "New England Group" more on matters of foreign policy than on domestic issues, yet Madison often found his closest allies in the arguments over peace terms among the Massachusetts men.

42. Ibid., 295.

43. Madison to Randolph, July 23, 1782, *Madison Papers,* 4:435; Madison, "Comments on Instructions to Peace Commissioners," ibid., 436–438.

44. Madison to Randolph, June 4, 1782, ibid., 313.

45. For additional defenses of state preserves and attempts to determine "constitutional" boundaries see ibid., 195–196, 298, 391–394, 410–412, 444–445.

46. Madison, "Notes on Debates," Nov. 14, 1782, ibid., 5:273–274 (hereafter cited as "Notes"); Madison to Randolph, Sept. 10, Nov. 5, 1782, ibid., 115–116, 242–243.

47. For the evolution of and action on Morris's proposals, besides sources cited in notes 2 and 4, see Clarence L. Ver Steeg, *Robert Morris: Revolutionary Financier* (New York, 1954), chap. 5, and 123–129. Morris's report is in *Jours. Cont. Cong.*, 22:429–446.

48. Madison, "Report on Payment of New Jersey Troops," *Madison Papers*, 5:173–177.

49. "Notes," Dec. 4, 1782, ibid., 363–364.

50. Morris's advice, "in rigid adherence to his maxims of public faith," as Madison put it, was that state surpluses of old continentals be credited at the official rate of 40–1. The eastern states particularly had retired great quantities at far lower rates. Madison opposed ratios of 40–1, 75–1, 100–1, and even 150–1. "Notes," Nov. 26, 1782, ibid., 321–322; Madison to Randolph, Dec. 3, 1782, ibid., 356–357.

51. Ver Steeg, *Morris*, 166–177, 185–187, quotation on 169.

52. Ibid., 171.

53. The precise nature of the relationship between army radicals and the nationalists and public creditors supporting Morris is undiscoverable. Interpretations range from Henderson's suggestion that Hamilton and Gouverneur Morris, who was Robert's assistant at the Treasury, made "hesitant and uncoordinated" efforts to encourage continuing verbal protests from the army (*Party Politics*, 332–335), through an argument that Hamilton and both Morrises conspired to provoke a coup d'etat by the group around Gates and then to alert Washington in time to squelch it. For the latter see Richard H. Kohn, *Eagle and Sword: The Federalists and the Creation of the Military Establishment in America, 1783–1802* (New York, 1975), chap. 2, and C. Edward Skeen, "The Newburgh Conspiracy Reconsidered," With a Rebuttal by Richard H. Kohn, *WMQ*, 3d Ser., 31 (1974): 273–298. I suspect a declaration of an intent to disband was more than Hamilton or R. Morris wanted from the army, but it is clear that the Morrisites urged the army to look to Congress, not to the states, for satisfaction of its demands and used the agitation at camp to generate an atmosphere of crisis in Philadelphia. All authorities agree that Madison was not involved in contacts with the army.

54. Madison's "Notes on Debates," the single most important source for the crisis of 1783, make it possible to follow developments daily. My discussion is based primarily on these (*Madison Papers*, vol. 6, passim), and on *Jours. Cont. Cong.*, vol. 24.

55. Madison to Randolph, Jan. 22, 1783, *Madison Papers*, 6:55. For the response to Morris's letter see "Notes," Jan. 24, 1783, ibid., 120.

56. "Notes," Jan. 28, 1783, ibid., 143–147.

57. "Notes," Feb. 4, 1783, ibid., 187.

58. *Jours. Cont. Cong.*, 24:137. Madison condemned the plan as contrary to the

Articles because it required a return of population as part of the formula for making an assessment (*Madison Papers*, 6:256, 195–198, 209, 213, 215–216, 247).

59. "Notes," Feb. 18, 1783, *Madison Papers*, 6:251.

60. "Notes," Jan. 28, 1783, ibid., 143.

61. See also Nathaniel Gorham's comment, "Notes," Feb. 18, 1783, ibid., 249–250, and the famous letter of Feb. 7, 1783, in which Gouverneur Morris wrote to Gen. Henry Knox: "If you will permit me a metaphor from your own profession, after you have carried the post, the public creditors will garrison it for you" (*Letters Cont. Cong.*, 7:34n–35n).

62. Among other indications, he entered an interesting footnote to the portion of Hamilton's speech quoted above: "This remark was imprudent and injurious to the cause which it was meant to serve," since this sort of influence was precisely what made the states resist a collection by Congress. All the members who shared this fear "smiled at the disclosure." Bland and Lee said privately that Hamilton "had let out the secret" ("Notes," Jan. 28, 1783, *Madison Papers*, 6:143n).

63. FitzSimons and Williamson both said openly that they hoped the army would not disband. Williamson added, "If force should be necessary to excite justice, the sooner force were applied the better" ("Notes," ibid., 260–261).

64. Ibid., 259–261. Wilson agreed with Hamilton that "by dividing the interest of the civil from that of the military creditors provision for the latter would be frustrated."

65. "Notes," Feb. 20, 1783, ibid., 265–266.

66. "Notes," Feb. 21, 1783, ibid., 270–272.

67. Madison initially envisioned a comprehensive scheme to resolve several recurrent controversies among the states as well as to secure the revenues required by Congress. Recommendations of an import and of additional, though separate, state appropriations for servicing the debt would be linked with completion of the western cessions, a federal assumption of state debts, and an abatement of proportions owed by various states upon a settlement of accounts in favor of those states whose abilities had been most impaired by the war. Congress struck the assumption of state debts from the proposal and disjoined the various elements that Madison had meant as a package whose parts would all depend on approval of the others. After excision of assumption from the plan, Madison decided against further attempts to rejoin its parts. He feared that the final plan had "no bait for Virginia," yet hoped that "a respect for justice, good faith, and national honor" would secure the state's approval (see esp. "Notes," Feb. 26, 1783, ibid., 290–292, "Report on Restoring Public Credit," Mar. 6, 1783, ibid., 311–314, and Madison to Jefferson, May 20, 1783, ibid., 481). Morris's report on Madison's proposals approved an assumption of state debts, but preferred to turn the impost into a tariff, still insisted on the need for other congressional revenues (a land tax, a house tax, and an excise), objected to the limitation of the impost to 25 years, and urged congressional appointment of collectors. For Wilson's and Hamilton's continuing attempts to secure Morris's objectives see "Notes," Mar. 11, 20, 1783, ibid., 6:322–325, 370–372.

68. Brant, *Madison,* vol. 2, chap. 15; Ferguson, *Power of the Purse,* chap. 8, where Madison's authorship of the proposals of April 18 is not mentioned.

69. "Notes," Feb. 21, 1783, *Madison Papers,* 6:272.

70. While Congress "exercised the indefinite power of emitting money . . . they had the whole wealth and resources of the continent within their command." Since shutting the presses, they are "as dependent on the states as the king of England is on the parliament. They can neither enlist, pay, nor feed a single soldier, nor execute any other purpose but as the means are first put into their hands" (Madison to Jefferson, May 6, 1780, ibid., 2:19–20).

71. Report of July 29, 1782, *Jours. Cont. Cong.,* 22:435–437.

72. Morris to John Jay, July 13, 1781, quoted in Ferguson, *Power of the Purse,* 123–124; *Jours. Cont. Cong.,* 22:432.

73. See, especially, the letters to an unknown recipient (n.d.), to James Duane (Sept. 3, 1780), and to Robert Morris (Apr. 30, 1781) in Harold C. Syrett et al., eds., *The Papers of Alexander Hamilton,* 26 vols. (New York, 1960–1979), 2:234–251, 400–418, 604–635, together with the conclusion of "The Continentalist," ibid., 3:99–106.

74. Ferguson was first to see that the Morris nationalists understood and wished to replicate "the role of funded debt and national bank in stabilizing the regime founded in Britain after the revolution of 1689." As historians have more fully explored the character of the 18th-century British regime and the thinking of the English "court"—a term Ferguson did not employ—the implications of this desire have increasingly emerged (*Power of the Purse,* 289–290, and passim). A preliminary exploration of the course of "court" thinking in America is Lance Banning, *The Jeffersonian Persuasion: Evolution of a Party Ideology* (Ithaca, N.Y., 1978), 126–140, and passim. Since then a host of useful contributions have appeared; see particularly Drew R. McCoy, *The Elusive Republic: Political Economy in Jeffersonian America* (Chapel Hill, N.C., 1980); John M. Murrin, "The Great Inversion, or Court versus Country: A Comparison of the Revolution Settlements in England (1688–1721) and America (1776–1816)," in J. G. A. Pocock, ed., *Three British Revolutions: 1641, 1688, 1776* (Princeton, N.J., 1980), 368–453; and Pocock, "1776: The Revolution against Parliament," ibid., 265–288.

75. "Notes," Feb. 21, 1783, *Madison Papers,* 6:272.

76. Madison's fullest (and most fervent) explanation of the inseparable connection he perceived between union and the republican revolution would come in his speech of June 29, 1787, to the Constitutional Convention. Max Farrand, ed., *The Records of the Federal Convention of 1787,* rev. ed. (New Haven, Conn., 1966 [orig. publ. 1937]), 1, 464–465. Without the union, the people of every state would see their liberties crushed by powerful executives, standing armies, and high taxes—instruments, by the way, that several nationalists of the early 1780s hoped to create. See also Madison's *Federalist,* No. 41.

77. It is likely that Madison saw the letter to Jones in which Washington suggested that the first Newburgh Address was written in Philadelphia and that the agitation at

camp was ultimately attributed to Robert or, more likely, Gouverneur Morris. Madison later remarked that from "private letters from the army and other circumstances there appeared good ground for suspecting that the civil creditors were intriguing in order to inflame the army" and secure general funds ("Notes," Mar. 17, 1783, *Madison Papers*, 6:348).

78. "Address to the States by the United States in Congress Assembled," ibid., 489. Madison admitted that the plan departed from the principles of the Confederation—a point about which he was not entirely happy—yet challenged opponents to "substitute some other equally consistent with public justice and honor and more conformable to the doctrines of the Confederation" (Madison to Randolph, May 20, 1783, ibid., 7:59).

79. Hamilton drafted a congressional resolution calling for a convention shortly before he retired from Congress, then decided there was too little support to introduce it (Syrett et al., eds., *Hamilton Papers*, 3:420–426). There is disagreement among Ver Steeg, Rakove, and Ferguson as to whether Morris also hoped for a structural transformation of the system.

80. Hamilton mentioned his desire for a convention in a debate of Apr. 1, 1783 ("Notes," *Madison Papers*, 6:425). Stephen Higginson, who favored the idea, told Henry Knox in 1787 that he had "pressed upon Mr. Madison and others the idea of a special convention. . . . But they were as much opposed to this idea as I was to the measures they were then pursuing to effect, as they said the same thing" (*Letters Cont. Cong.*, 7:123n).

81. A day-by-day reading of his "Notes on Debates" is necessary for a full understanding of the antinationalists' influence on Madison and his growing anxiety for resolution of the crisis; but see particularly the "Notes" for Feb. 27, 1783. Mercer charged that commutation tended "in common with the funding of other debts to establish and perpetuate a monied interest" that "would gain the ascendance of the landed interest . . . and by their example and influence become dangerous to our republican constitutions." Madison protested that commutation was a compromise intended to conciliate those to whom pensions were obnoxious. Now opponents stigmatized commutation as well. Paying the principal of the debt at once was clearly impossible, but funding was said to be "establishing a dangerous monied interest." Madison "was as much opposed to perpetuating the public burdens as anyone," but felt that funding could not be more contrary to "our republican character and constitutions than a violation of good faith and common honesty" (*Madison Papers*, 6:297–298).

82. "Notes," June 10, 20, 1783, ibid., 7:125–126, 167–168; letters of these months to Jefferson and Randolph, ibid., passim; Abernethy, *Western Lands and the Revolution*, 270–273. On Sept. 17, and Oct. 8, 1783, two essays appeared in the *Pennsylvania Journal, and the Weekly Advertiser* (Philadelphia) over the signature "The North American." Examining the critical situation of federal affairs, these urged an alteration of state and federal constitutions that would transfer sovereignty to the central

government and render the states subordinate units. Brant drew important support for his portrait of Madison as a nationalist by arguing that the Virginian was the author and that only in these anonymous essays did he reveal the real direction of his thinking. I agree with the editors of the *Madison Papers* that this ambition was mistaken (7:319–346).

83. Madison to Randolph, June 24, 1783, *Madison Papers,* 7:191–192.

84. Madison to Jefferson, Dec. 10, 1783, ibid., 401–403, quotation on 401.

85. Madison to Randolph, May 20, 1783, ibid., 59–62, quotation on 61.

86. Madison to Randolph, Aug. 30, 1783, ibid., 295–296.

87. Madison to Randolph, Sept. 13, 1783, ibid., 314–315.

88. Ibid., 315.

89. Madison to Jefferson, Dec. 10, 1783, ibid., 401; McCoy, *Elusive Republic,* esp. chap. 3.

90. McCoy, "The Virginia Port Bill of 1784," *Virginia Magazine of History and Biography* 83 (1975), 288–303.

91. Madison to Richard Henry Lee, Dec. 25, 1784, *Madison Papers,* 8:201.

92. Madison to Monroe, ibid., 333–336.

93. Two of many passages are particularly revealing of Madison's route to the Virginia Plan. "Most of our political evils"—paper money, indulgences for debtors, etc.—"may be traced up to our commercial ones, as most of our moral may to our political" (Madison to Jefferson, Mar. 18, 1786, ibid., 502). In the Convention, June 6, 1787, Madison stated that foreign relations, national defense, and protection against interstate disputes were not the only concern; additional security for private rights was also a necessary object. "Interferences with these were evils which had more perhaps than anything else produced this convention" (Farrand, ed., *Records,* I, 134).

94. See the sketch printed in Farrand, ed., *Records,* 3:542–543.

95. *Federalist,* No. 10.

96. As he insisted in a letter to Edward Carrington, May 26, 1792 (Syrett et al., eds., *Hamilton Papers,* 11:426–445).

97. Madison's word in an interview with Nicholas P. Trist, Sept. 27, 1834 (Farrand, ed., *Records,* 3:533–534).

98. Hamilton to Carrington, May 26, 1792, Syrett et al., eds., *Hamilton Papers,* 11:426–445.

The Hamiltonian Madison

A Reconsideration

When Alexander Hamilton submitted his Report on Public Credit to the First Federal Congress, he was dismayed to learn that his proposals for funding the Revolutionary debt would be opposed by the most influential member of that body. He had accepted his position at the Treasury, he wrote, in the conviction that "a similarity of thinking" and personal good will would guarantee James Madison's support. "Aware of the intrinsic difficulties of the situation and of the powers of Mr. Madison, I do not believe I should have accepted under a different supposition."[1]

Hamilton had cause to feel betrayed and reason for concern. From their earliest acquaintance—in the Confederation Congress during the emergency of 1783—he and Madison had joined repeatedly in efforts to secure a more effective central government. The bolder, younger man had been accustomed to defer to the Virginian's talents as a parliamentary leader. His admiration was sincere, and he was not without substantial grounds for his assumption that Madison would use his talents to guide the funding and assumption plan through the House of Representatives. In 1783 James Madison had been the first public figure to propose a federal assumption of state debts. Madison's Address to the States of 26 April 1783 had defended a congressional request for new federal revenues in terms that condemned discrimination against secondary holders of the public debt. In a private conversation at the Constitutional Convention, Hamilton reported, Madison had once again endorsed assumption. In all their talks, "down to the commencement of the new government," he had never hinted at a change of mind.

Before the House of Representatives initiated its debate on the report, Hamilton approached his friend and contrasted his position of 1790 with his stance in 1783. Madison explained that massive transfers of the debt from its original to secondary holders during the years since 1783 had "essentially changed the state of the question" concerning discrimination, which he now intended to support. He also said that he had always envisioned a federal assumption of state debts, to which he was still not opposed in principle, as those debts had stood at the peace, but not as they stood in the aftermath of differential efforts by the states to retire them.

This explanation hardly satisfied the secretary of the treasury, nor has it satisfied the numerous historians who have shared Hamilton's puzzlement. An assumption of the mass of debts the states had already retired, together with the obligations not yet met, would have added enormously and unnecessarily to the federal burden, perhaps endangering the government's success. Transfers of the Revolutionary debt had been continuous since it was first incurred. Why was it only now that Madison expressed an inclination to distinguish between original and secondary holders?

Hamilton's befuddlement increased. In the congressional session following his opposition to the funding plan, Madison denounced creation of a national bank, although he had moved at Philadelphia to add a federal right to create such corporations to the enumerated powers of Congress. He also gradually revealed, in Hamilton's opinion, a "womanish attachment to France and a womanish resentment against Great Britain," which could produce an open war with the latter in six months' time. Finally, he joined with Thomas Jefferson to bring Philip Freneau to Philadelphia to establish a newspaper which consistently opposed administration measures. Indeed, as Hamilton perceived it, "in almost all the questions great and small" which arose after the first session of Congress, Madison sided with those "disposed to narrow the federal authority." His opposition to administration policies culminated in support for measures deliberately designed to drive the secretary of the treasury from office. By March of 1792, Hamilton had openly declared his intention to treat his former ally as a foe.

As the other major author of *The Federalist,* Hamilton knew that Madison had long and recently maintained that "the real danger in our system was the subversion of the national authority by the preponderancy of the state governments." After 1789, however, "all his measures have proceeded on an opposite supposition." Hamilton could not conceive how he and Madison, "whose politics had formerly so much the same point of departure," could have reasoned to such contradictory conclusions in so short a time. He could only conclude that he had been mistaken in believing that the other "Publius" was a principled and candid man.

Insisting on a concord of opinion through the first session of Congress,

Hamilton dismissed the possibility that fundamental principle could account for Madison's position of 1792. He considered other motives. He suspected that Jefferson's pernicious influence had played some part in the reversal, yet he knew that Madison's decision on the funding plan had antedated Jefferson's arrival on the scene. He decided, in the end, that Madison had been "seduced by the expectation of popularity and possibly by the calculation of advantage to the state of Virginia." After all, there had been a wave of sentiment among the people for a discrimination between original and secondary holders of the debt, a sentiment widely shared among Virginians. It was certainly a fact that Virginians overwhelmingly opposed a federal assumption of state debts. Most Virginians were wary of the new government itself. In the aftermath of the ratification contest, Virginia's legislature had refused to send Madison to the Senate. Under Patrick Henry's influence, the legislature had established congressional districts that forced him into a disagreeable campaign to win election to the House. Entirely reasonable was Hamilton's conclusion that his old ally, wishing to retain the veneration he had earned at Philadelphia and in the first session of Congress, prompted too by an insecure position in Virginia, had sacrificed his principles to the pressures of the moment.

Defeated on discrimination and assumption, blocked again in the argument over a national bank, and countered in the meantime in his efforts to secure a provision for commercial discrimination against Great Britain, Madison gradually became so thoroughly disgruntled, in Hamilton's analysis, that he would risk subversion of the government itself in order to destroy the secretary of the treasury. Principle had given way, at first, to political exigency. Then, under the frustrating influence of repeated checks, principles themselves reversed. The nationalist of the 1780s was transmuted into a proponent of states' rights. The former friend of governmental strength and wisdom became the idol of the American Jacobins. Madison grew so accustomed to "sounding the alarm with great affected solemnity at encroachments meditated on the rights of the states," to "holding up the bugbear of a faction in the government having designs unfriendly to liberty," that he eventually came to believe it. In time, he managed to convince himself that notions he had originally "sported to influence others" were actually true: There was "some dreadful combination against state government and republicanism."

Hamilton's analysis was searching and persuasive. Acknowledging the probity for which his foe was famous, the critique was so plausible that it has powerfully affected nearly everyone who has attempted to explain Madison's conduct during the 1780s and 1790s. Recent writings overwhelmingly agree that Madison reversed his course as swiftly and as completely as Hamilton maintained, probably for reasons similar to those that Hamilton suggested.[2] They do so in the face of Madison's own notorious insistence that no political figure of his time was actually less open to a charge of inconsistency.

Madison's own evaluation of his conduct should not, of course, be too readily accepted. Early in their training, historians are cautioned to beware of self-serving statements, and the crux of Hamilton's complaint was indisputably correct. As late as 1789, Madison feared that even under the new Constitution, the necessary powers of the central government would prove vulnerable to encroachments by the states. By 1792, his fears were on the other side. If Hamilton had said no more than that, his accusation would present no problem. If modern scholars said no more, this article would have no purpose. But Hamilton and Madison had never been at "the same point of departure," and Madison's intentions and assumptions were not what most historians have taken them to be.

Hamilton misunderstood his colleague. Sharing some of Hamilton's assumptions, most historians have shared to some degree in his misjudgment. Indeed, there are at least two ways in which the thrust of modern scholarship may even have compounded Hamilton's mistake. The dominant interpretation of Madison's thought and conduct during the two decades surrounding the ratification of the Constitution has come to be more "Hamiltonian" than Hamilton himself advanced. The resulting account of the great Virginian would have pained and puzzled Madison and might have seemed surprising even to his staunchest foe. It is sufficiently at odds with the perceptions of contemporaries as to demand a sympathetic reexamination of Madison's own views.

Reconsideration might begin by calling for a different set of questions. The usual inquiries are: How did Madison, the nationalist of the 1780s, become the Jeffersonian proponent of states' rights? How was the "father of the Constitution" transfigured into the author of the Virginia Resolutions of 1798? They ask for information that was vital to the secretary of the treasury and continues so for everyone who wants to understand the origins of the new government and its eventual disruption in a civil war. But these questions incorporate a bias with which Hamilton began, insisting that the most important issue of these years was a contest for power between the nation and the states, implying that resistance to the new administration's definition of the scope of federal authority must have involved a change of attitude about the new regime itself. The phrasing interjects a tangle of connected problems which impede an effort to recover Madison's intentions. The questions assume a polarity between Madison's objectives during the 1780s and during the 1790s, between his original understanding of the Constitution and his stand in 1798, that was simply not characteristic of his thought.

James Madison was never a "nationalist," not if that word is loaded with many of the connotations it has come to carry in recent histories of the 1780s.[3] Nor did his Virginia Resolutions advocate the sovereignty of the states. Even as he led the nation through the framing and ratification of the Constitution, Madison expressed a lively fear of distant, energetic government, a fear he had displayed throughout the 1780s.[4] Innovative though he was, he maintained that the purposes and powers of the central government were not so much altered by the new Constitution as were the means by which those ends could be attained.[5] As he conceived it, the fundamental flaw of the Confederation had not been a radically mistaken definition of the proper objects of the state and central governments, but ineffective mechanisms for enabling the federal government to act effectively within its proper sphere. The great accomplishment of constitutional reformers had not been a radical redistribution of responsibilities from state to federal hands, but structural reforms allowing Congress to meet the needs that it had always been intended to secure. The innovations of 1787, from this point of view, were essentially conservative in their intent. So were the arguments of 1798, with which Madison's early understanding of the Constitution was not in conflict.

From the ratification contest through the nullification controversy, which came upon the country during his retirement, Madison consistently defined the new regime as neither national nor purely confederate. Created by the bodies politic of the several united states, the Constitution, as he understood it, rendered the central government supreme within its sphere and strictly limited that sphere to needs that could not be satisfied by the separate states. The Constitution marked the proper boundaries between concurrent governments, all of which possessed a right to call attention to infractions of the charter and none of which possessed the ultimate authority to interpret the organic law.[6] In 1787 as in 1798 Madison desired a well-constructed, federal republic—not, as Hamilton did, because nothing better could be secured—but because no other form of government seemed consistent with the American Revolution. In the 1780s as in the 1790s, Madison's essential purpose was to nurture and to defend a revolutionary order of society and politics, not to widen or to contract the sphere of federal authority. His starting point for constitutional reform and his conception of the finished Constitution were never anything but incompatible with Hamilton's.

Historians, of course, have not lost sight of all of these essential differences. Several have contrasted Madison's federalism, which was friendly to the states, with Hamilton's continuing hostility to state attachments.[7] Madison's biographers do not believe that he was motivated principally by political expediency.[8] Yet Madison's defenders have been no less ready than was Hamilton to detect a quick retreat from nationalism in the years after 1789. While clearing Madison of charges of one sort of inconsistency, they have introduced an accusation that the subject might have found still more offensive: a sudden reversal from broad to strict construction of the Constitution. Meanwhile, other modern studies have increasingly relied on the tenth *Federalist* as a key to Madison's position in the years to 1789. Together these two thrusts of recent scholarship have added final touches to a current portrait of a youthful Madison who stands much closer to Alexander Hamilton than any contemporary would have believed. Certain aspects of his thought and conduct have been clarified while other aspects equally important to a balanced view have been obscured.

Modern scholarship owes an enormous debt to Irving Brant's magnificent biography. Often accused of being too defensive of his hero, Brant, nevertheless, was primarily responsible for removing Madison from the shadow cast by Thomas Jefferson and for restoring him to his contemporary standing as a major leader in his own right, both before 1787 and after 1789. While sometimes adding greatly to our knowledge, every subsequent biographer has started with Brant's masterwork, and there have been few challenges to several of his most important themes.

Brant's biases, however, pervaded his six volumes and led him to interpret Madison in ways that may persistently have misled later scholars. Brant was a New Dealer. He approved of Hamiltonian means to Jeffersonian ends. The youthful Madison, as Brant perceived him, also blended an expansive attitude toward federal authority with a commitment to civil liberties and a deep hostility to the abuse of government by special interests. From the moment when he reaches Philadelphia to take his seat in the Continental Congress, Brant's Madison is an enthusiastic leader of a persistent effort to enlarge the powers of the central government. His nationalism grows progressively more intense, culminating in the Constitutional Convention, where compromises demanded by the inflexible smaller states then engendered second thoughts. These second thoughts, in Brant's interpretation, turned into a profound change of course under the pressure of Hamilton's successes after 1789. Madison's hostility to governmental favors for the few overrode his wish for a more vigorous regime, and he became committed to a politics that forced him, for the rest of his career, to hide the fervent nationalism of his youth.

Brant's interpretation, seldom challenged in general outline and undeniably insightful, is problematic at a number of important points. Of all
these, the one that has seemed least debatable would almost certainly have
proved the most disturbing to Madison himself. Without exception, subsequent historians have followed Brant's suggestion that the Virginian moved
from broad to strict construction of the Constitution after 1789. During his
years in the Confederation Congress, Brant maintained, Madison believed in
"easy discovery" of federal powers where none were explicitly granted, conducting a deliberate campaign to expand the boundaries of federal authority
by way of a doctrine of implied congressional powers. At the Constitutional
Convention, he and other members of the committee on unfinished business
silently inserted the general welfare clause, which was a deliberate and substantive grant of power. Advancing arguments for broad construction and
implicit powers in *The Federalist* and holding to them during the first session
of the new Congress, Madison abruptly switched positions only when confronted with Hamilton's plan for a national bank.[9]

Nowhere did Brant's biases encourage a more serious misreading of his
subject. Surviving evidence conclusively suggests that Madison was always
a strict constructionist, that a profound regard for chartered limitations
of authority was as central to his thinking during the 1780s as it was after
1789.[10] Hamilton did not maintain the contrary. Nor did any other of Madison's contemporaries. Yet recent studies of the new republic uniformly say
that the Virginian was a sudden convert to a strict construction of the Constitution.[11] It has even been repeatedly suggested that Hamilton's defense of
the constitutionality of the bank was derived from Madison's argument in
Federalist No. 44.[12]

More must be said about the implications of this view below, for the Virginian's consistent strict constructionism is an indispensable, neglected starting point for better understanding. First, however, a second way in which
Madison has been forced into a mold that even Hamilton did not discern
must be described.

Of Brant's contemporaries, none added more to comprehension of the
Revolutionary generation than Douglass Adair, not least in several essays
on *The Federalist*.[13] Among their many contributions, Adair's exception-
ally fine essays added impetus to an increasing interest in *Federalist* No. 10,
which scholars since Charles Beard have seen as an especially important key
to Madison, to the Federalist movement, and to a transition from a classical to a more modern mode of political thinking. In this, there has been no
mistake. Madison's most distinctive contribution to the Federalist movement

was probably his insistence that constitutional reform address the vices of republican government within the revolutionary states as well as the debilities of the Confederation. The tenth *Federalist* was his fullest presentation of the idea—novel even if anticipated by David Hume—that enlarging the sphere of republican government might counteract the characteristic evil of a democratic system: the majority's pursuit of special interests at the expense of others' rights. Extension of the sphere may have been the most effective argument against the most persuasive criticism of the Constitution, and Madison's analysis of the relationships among a people who could not be differentiated into two social orders was a significant advance toward modern thought. The essay fully merits repeated readings.

Two difficulties nonetheless arise from our particular attention to this famous essay. It strengthens the prevailing inclination to exaggerate the author's nationalism, and it can easily result in serious misunderstanding of Madison's intentions.[14] In *Federalist* No. 10 and elsewhere, Madison maintained that the large electoral districts required by the Constitution would favor the selection of men of extensive reputation, proven talent, and magnanimous vision over petty politicians willing to flatter the voters' prejudices and devote themselves to the majority's pursuit of partial interests. He argued that large electorates were more likely to choose representatives wise enough to discern the general good and virtuous enough not to sacrifice the good of all to lesser ends. Although he scrupulously avoided any reference to a "natural aristocracy," in private letters as in published writings, he preferred a more enlightened leadership and hoped the Constitution would encourage its emergence. Madison, after all, was writing in a republican tradition which contrasted an inevitable conflict of interests between different hereditary orders with the natural identity of interests between a nonhereditary leadership and its electors. To identify the concept of a filtration of talent as the centerpiece of Madison's attempt at reconciling majority control with liberty is to misread Madison as wishing for representatives who can ignore the demands of their constituents. Thus, from the argument for an extension of the sphere is inferred that Madison's most fundamental object was to transfer power from the hands of demagogic and illiberal state politicians to this special group of federal supermen.[15] For Alexander Hamilton, the critical necessity of the 1780s and 1790s was very much a massive transfer of authority from state to federal hands—and even to the hands of federal officials least responsive to the people's immediate will. Madison's most basic wishes were quite different.

Filtration of the people's will was a secondary and subsidiary point of the tenth *Federalist*—more than an afterthought, but much less than the vital core of Madison's thinking.[16] Madison did hope for an improvement in the quality of representation and decision-making, but he neither expected nor wished for federal representatives who would not reflect the character and interests of their constituencies. The major argument of the tenth *Federalist* is that the large republic will incorporate so many different interests as to render unlikely the formation of majorities in pursuit of objects incompatible with the good of all. This reasoning would immediately collapse if the character and conduct of representatives were not assumed to mirror the variety among the people. Laws which threaten people's rights are passed by legislatures, and only if the legislators actually reflect the pluralistic structure of the great republic will the multiplicity of interests tend to check a union of a majority for factious ends.[17]

Madison emphatically did not suggest that any sort of large republic would provide superior protection for liberty. His argument for an extension of the sphere was premised on the limited authority and federal structure of the new regime. The constrained authority of federal officials seemed to him among the necessary guarantees of a continuing identity of interests between the people and their rulers, without which an extension of the sphere would not have been a democratic answer to a democratic problem. In *Federalist* No. 10, the praise of large electorates is closely followed by a major qualification: "There is a mean on both sides of which inconveniencies will be found." A small electorate is likely to elect men so thoroughly attached to local interests and perspectives as to be unfit "to comprehend and pursue great and national objects." Too large a suffrage, however, can result in representatives "too little acquainted with . . . local circumstances and lesser interests." Large electorates are therefore safe and preferable only when such local interests lie outside their province.

Madison's support for an enlarged republic as an essential safeguard for minorities was characteristically accompanied with a recognition of the danger of creating a government unresponsive to the majority. Madison recognized that too much authority in hands too distant from the people would pose the risk of tyranny. "The larger the society, *provided it lie within a practicable sphere,* the more duly capable it will be of self government. And happily for the republican cause, the practicable sphere may be carried to a very great extent, by a judicious modification and mixture of the federal principle."[18] For Madison, in short, the Constitution struck a delicate mean between an excess of democracy and the antidemocratic perils of consolidation, "the great and aggregate interests being referred to the national, the local and particular to the state legislatures," each of which would be responsible for and responsive to the needs they were particularly equipped to meet.[19]

Every part of the tenth *Federalist* must be considered in relationship to every other part and to the essay's total context. Fascination with the essay, proper in itself, too readily encourages a tendency to turn to it or even to a part of it in isolation from the other writings, including other numbers of *The Federalist,* which clarify its central concepts and qualify its place in Madison's thinking.[20] Madison considered an expanded territory to be an important barrier to formation of majority factions, but not because he hoped the result would be representatives removed from their constituents' control. Unresponsive rulers would not be republican at all. A large republic would break the force of majority interest without endangering majority rule because a large variety of concerns would be represented in a Congress whose authority would not extend beyond those national subjects on which its members would adequately reflect their constituents' desires.

Finally, Madison did not consider an extension of the sphere, important though the concept was, to be a complete solution to the difficulties suggested by the conduct of the revolutionary states. If the tenth *Federalist* had been the sum of his thinking, he need not have written twenty-eight additional numbers. With most of his contemporaries, Madison assumed that the legislature would be the dominant branch of the federal government, as the legislatures were in all the states. With an extension of the sphere, majority abuse of power would become less likely, representatives more enlightened. But majority faction would not be precluded, nor was the problem of majority abuse of power the only one with which republican statesmen had to be concerned. Madison also remained alert to the dangers of minority faction, most especially to the possibility that rulers, once independent of the people, could become the most dangerous minority of all. To *Federalist* No. 10 he therefore added several other essays on the necessity of checks and balances and on the distribution of authority between the federal government and the states. When he wrote *The Federalist,* he anticipated that state encroachments would prove the characteristic danger to the new regime. At no point, though, did he lose sight of dangers on the other side. At no time was he able to embrace the prospect of excessive concentration of authority in federal hands or in the hands of unresponsive branches of the federal government. In private letters, he was careful to make clear that the authors of *The Federalist* were not responsible for one another's numbers, hinting his discomfort with some of Hamilton's views.[21] He admitted that some advocates of the new Constitution carried their alarm with the American majority too far.[22] The

Constitution he endorsed provided for a compound, not a unitary government, a federal republic that would remain under popular control.

What difference does it make, however, if Hamilton and later critics started with assumptions, terms, or questions that might have seemed inherently misleading to Madison himself? What if we have misread or overemphasized a single essay, or come too close to thinking that Madison and Hamilton had shared "the same point of departure?" What would a more Madisonian Madison be like?

Entering the Continental Congress at age twenty-nine, Madison acquired an early reputation as a capable proponent of Virginia's distinctive desires: denial of the great land companies' claims to vast tracts beyond the mountains; treaties recognizing an American right to navigate the Mississippi River; and a Western boundary for the United States encompassing, at minimum, Virginia's western claims. As the War for Independence moved into the South, urgent problems shoved him toward support of larger powers for Congress—as, indeed, these problems pushed a large majority of delegates in the same direction. Madison was not an early or enthusiastic leader of this general shift toward centralizing change. Distrusting the New Englanders, locked constantly in bitter battles with the landless states, and theoretically inclined toward rather strict construction of the Articles of Confederation, he opposed congressional control of commerce and initially resisted both a national bank and the impost proposal of 1781. Not until the fall of 1782, when the financial crisis peaked, did he begin to work consistently with the reformers from the middle states. Even then, his differences from men of more consistent consolidating vision led him to break ranks with Hamilton and Robert Morris as the Newburgh crisis reached its climax.[23]

During his years in Congress, Madison made important contributions to the movement to strengthen the central government. Urging mutual concessions and almost instinctively inclined to associate Virginia's interests with the long-term needs of the country as a whole, he played a major role in the creation of a national domain. He repeatedly wrote home to urge attention to Confederation needs and forbearance in the face of irritating jealousies of the Old Dominion. His compromise proposals were the core of the recommendations prompted by the emergency of 1783.

Still, Madison's eventual commitment to a thoroughgoing alteration of the federal system did not rise as a response to the sort of problems the central government encountered during his years in Congress. His plan did not take a form consistent with the solutions envisioned from that time by Hamilton and Morris. While it is accurate to say, with proper cautions, that

Hamilton preferred a radical concentration of authority and attempted from the early eighties to nationalize the American system, Madison's objectives cannot be understood in similar terms. In 1783, Hamilton already wished for a general convention that would transform the federal system. Madison opposed this measure.[24] He believed that Congress could not continue to rely "on a punctual and unfailing compliance by thirteen separate and independent governments with periodical demands of money."[25] But he did not yet look, with Hamilton, toward the complete replacement of the Articles of Confederation, nor did he share in Hamilton's or Morris's desire "to achieve political centralization by fiscal reform."[26]

Madison had entered Congress a republican with a continental perspective, conditioned from his youth to look beyond Virginia for the fortunes of the Revolutionary cause. The years in Congress intensified his continentalism and confirmed his belief that the fate of the union and the fate of the Revolution were inseparably entwined. But Madison had also entered Congress a committed American Revolutionary. By 1780 he held intensely to the range of concepts identified with the Revolution's early thrust: hostility to privilege, commitment to written constitutions founded on consent, the belief that republics rest on virtue, and a concern with the social and economic foundations of virtuous conduct. These convictions, together with his role as a delegate from Virginia, shaped and limited his contributions to reform.

While in Congress, Madison usually attributed the difficulties of the central government to sectional disputes, in which he was continuously involved, or to financial disabilities resulting from the war. He hoped that peace would meliorate these problems.[27] Through these years, he quarreled neither with the central principles of the Articles of Confederation nor with the Revolutionary constitution of the several states. Only after he returned from Congress to struggle year by year in the Virginia House of Delegates with paper money, tax abatements, and assessments for religion, only as Virginia and the other states repeatedly displayed their inability to grapple separately with Britain's navigation laws, did he begin to think in terms of far more radical reform. Only then did he begin to question the republican precept that the majority is the safest repository of civil liberty, that in republics right and might are one.[28] Not until he achieved an intellectual advance linking the difficulties he had learned about in Congress with his mounting discontent as a state legislator, did he make the leap to authorship of the Virginia Plan. Even then, his early Revolutionary ardor and long experience in Congress defending Virginia's unpopular claims remained essential aspects of the context in which he shaped his brilliant and distinctive solution to the problems he perceived.

What Madison was seeking at the Constitutional Convention was far from a consolidated system. Recently—and properly—historians have emphasized the provision in the Virginia Plan for a federal veto on state laws. Madison proposed a federal veto that would reach to all state legislation, as the royal prerogative once had done. He argued strenuously for this provision, under which the central government would have exercised a power more intrusive and more plainly unacceptable to most contemporaries than anything the great convention actually proposed. He was intensely disappointed when the convention rejected even a limited veto, and this has seemed to some interpreters to be clear evidence that he would really have preferred as centralized a system as Hamilton himself desired.[29]

And yet the federal veto on state acts, as Madison conceived it, was to be a purely defensive power, wielded by a federal government whose positive authority would be of limited extent. It could not have consolidated the states into a unitary government such as the British one. Madison saw the veto as a necessary tool for checking state encroachments on the delegated powers of the central government. It seemed the only certain instrument for correcting the ills of republicanism within the several states, assuring the intervention of an impaired federal umpire whenever a local majority transgressed the bounds of justice or threatened the personal rights of a minority. The federal veto, though, was not to be an instrument with which the central government could set a positive direction. It was to be a negative on acts that breached a solemn compact or contradicted the most basic principles of a republican revolution, thereby threatening the popular commitment to a republican regime.

In the Constitutional Convention and as "Publius," Madison repeatedly insisted that America should not approve a Constitution inconsistent with revolutionary principles. The central theme of his particular contributions to The Federalist was the perfectly republican character of the proposed reform. Both there and in the private letter which contains his most complete defense of the federal negative on state laws, Madison said clearly that revolutionary principles were inconsistent with a wholly national regime.

In this famous letter, which anticipated the tenth Federalist, Madison explained to Jefferson the danger of majority oppression in republics. He suggested that the evil might be overcome by enlarging the sphere of republican government and taking in such a wide variety of different interests that a factious, oppressive majority would seldom appear. Then he immediately admitted, as he almost always did, that "this doctrine can only hold within a sphere of a mean extent." "In too extensive" a republic, he continued, a "defensive concert may be rendered too difficult against the oppression of those entrusted with the administration." A federal negative had seemed appropriate because the new government would be "sufficiently neutral" between different interests in the states "to control one part from invading the rights of another, and *at the same time* sufficiently controlled itself, from setting up an interest adverse to that of the entire society."[30] Madison called the new regime a "feudal system of republics," but fundamentally unlike a feudal system in that its head would not be "independent" of subordinate authorities, as well as limited by them, but "derived entirely from the subordinate authorities." The federal government would therefore serve as an impartial umpire of contentions between its subjects in the several states, much as a feudal monarch was supposed to be. Yet "by its dependence on the community," the central government would "be at the same time sufficiently restrained" from sacrificing the happiness of all.

In the gathering at Philadelphia, Madison sought, as he said in the tenth *Federalist,* "a republican remedy for the diseases most incident to republican government." Relying on the federal principle to help define the "practicable sphere" of the new regime, he hoped to create a central government that would secure a revolutionary American order: by conducting a foreign policy which would foster the social and economic conditions on which a healthy republican polity must rest; and by avoiding the injustices and inconstancies which were endangering the people's faith in the revolutionary experiment. In the aftermath of the convention, he speedily began to hope that the new Constitution would prove adequate despite the failure to include the federal veto. As he defended the convention's work, he overcame his early doubts. He also came to understand more clearly than he had before that the objectives he associated with the plan for constitutional reform could not be reconciled with the policies that Alexander Hamilton would soon propose.[31]

In 1789 Madison assumed a central role in putting into action the government that he had done so much to create and to defend. He helped prepare George Washington's inaugural address to Congress, wrote the House of Representatives' reply, and then helped author Washington's response. Together with his opposition to the Senate's wish for a majestic title for the president, these actions went a good way toward establishing the tone he thought essential for the new regime. He also took a major part in the creation of executive departments. At the Constitutional Convention, Madison had been convinced that only a unitary executive would prove a responsible one; now he helped defeat attempts to associate the Senate in the removal of executive officials and to place the Treasury in the hands of a commission.

He was principally responsible, as well, for quick addition to the Constitution of a Bill of Rights. Two basic goals appear to have guided him through the critical first session of the federal Congress. He wanted to complete a central government with the capacity to secure the republican revolution. He was equally determined to reconcile the host of honest men who wondered whether revolutionary principles could long survive the alteration of the federal system.

No federal initiative was more important to both ends, in Madison's opinion, than retaliatory measures against the British for their debilitating restrictions on American commerce. Madison accepted the need for radical constitutional reform when he concluded that only federal action could compel Great Britain to relax its navigation laws. He conceived this as the critical first step toward a world of freer trade which he considered indispensable to American economic independence and to sustaining America's revolutionary course.[32] Toward this end, Madison attempted in 1789 to write into the first federal tariff a discrimination against nations that had not concluded commercial treaties with the United States. He was defeated. He tried again during the winter of 1790–91. Once again, he failed. He failed, in part, because the secretary of the treasury resisted a commercial confrontation that could poison Anglo-American relations and seriously disrupt the flow of revenues on which his plans for managing the debt depended.

Hamilton had no more cause to feel betrayed when Madison opposed his plans for an assumption of state debts and for a national bank than Madison had cause to feel betrayed by Hamilton's opposition to commercial discrimination. Arguably, Hamilton had much less. From the experiences of 1783, Hamilton had reason to anticipate that Madison would oppose any federal measure patently inequitable for Virginia, as the original proposal for assumption was. Madison had also shown repeatedly that a respect for constitutional limitations of authority was central to his republican convictions. Once the Constitution had endured the gauntlet of the ratifying conventions, Madison regarded it as an organic law. As he saw it, the Federal Convention had declined to authorize creation of a national bank, and the people had not ratified a Constitution containing such a clause.

Hamilton might even have expected the Virginian's opposition to his funding plan. A persistent revulsion against speculative gains at public expense and a reiterated commitment to a social order characterized by comparative equality, honest industry, frugality, and simple manners made discrimination a natural choice for Madison.[33] He had on more than one occasion pronounced his opposition to a "prolonged" or "perpetual" debt.[34]

Nor did his proposal for discrimination really mark a complete reversal of his position of 1783. In the Confederation Congress, Madison had opposed the kind of distinction between original and secondary holders that would have involved a partial repudiation of the debt and thus a violation of national morality: revaluation of the portion of the debt that had passed out of the hands of its original holders. In 1790 Madison still insisted that the government must meet its obligations in full. His alternative to Hamilton's proposal would actually have been, in certain ways, more consistent with a scrupulous regard for public faith than the secretary's own, since it did not involve a virtually compulsory reduction of the interest that the government had promised.[35]

Many revolutionaries resisted a funding plan that would entail a massive transfer of wealth into the hands of a relative few who would depend on the government for a significant proportion of their fortunes. Madison shared the feeling that this would be poor policy for a republic. He shared the view that asking original creditors, who had been forced by a defaulting government to sell its promises for fractions of their value, to sacrifice again to pay taxes on the debt into the indefinite future would be poor justice.[36] His alternative was part of a continuing attempt to secure popular commitment to the new regime by just, republican policies. His discrimination plan was intended to keep faith with those whose sacrifices had created the national debt and may also have reflected a desire to counter all proposals hinting at a breach of contract, Hamilton's as well as those of the repudiationists in Congress.[37]

Hamilton, by contrast, had suggested that an effort to retaliate against the British would be one of the first measures of a stronger federal regime.[38] He had eloquently explained how, under the new system, the several states would retain the capacity to intervene effectively against transgressions by the federal government of the constitutional limits of its power.[39] If there was a reversal of positions after 1789, Hamilton's was clearest. And as his policies unfolded one by one, they manifestly squinted at a new American order that the other "Publius" had long since identified as incompatible with revolutionary ends. When Madison contrasted his desires for the United States with the alternatives reflected in the current state of Europe, he expressed his horror at the prospect of "corruption" on the British model, at overgrown executives, and at a people whose liberties were crushed by standing armies and high, perpetual taxes necessary to support such forces and to manage a permanent national debt.[40]

Alexander Hamilton may well have been, as he insisted in the letter with which we began, "affectionately attached" to the cause of republican government. Few revolutionary leaders had better reason to condemn a social and political order based on accidents of birth. Yet Hamilton was also committed to the view that firm executive guidance and a sizable professional army were among the necessary means to national greatness. Hamilton's financial program was consciously designed to use a long-term, funded debt to separate the interests of a critical segment of the American elite from the prevailing inclinations of the body of the people.

Hamilton and Madison were both aware that the United States had not developed any counterpart to England's national elite. To both of them this fact was fully as important as it has been said to be in recent historical efforts comparing political developments in the two countries.[41] England's political nation was virtually identical, for certain purposes, with its landed gentlemen. The gentry were a cohesive social group which sat atop an integrated social order and normally supported an administration whose patronage and economic policies linked the executive with the landed representatives in Parliament and at the same time with financial, commercial, and office-holding segments of the elite.[42] The political nation of revolutionary America was a great deal larger and, like its economy, assumed a state and regional, not a national, configuration. For Madison this was America's great strength. The pluralistic structure of American society was mirrored in the irreducibly pluralistic character of its elite. Such diversity held out the promise that a polity erected on popular participation would prove consistent with protection of the fundamental liberties of all. For Hamilton the state and regional attachments of America's elite were obstacles to the pursuit of national ends, which must be overcome by governmental inducement of a class of influentials whose economic interests would tie them to the national regime. Hamilton intended to create a practical alternative to the pluralistic structure on which Madison had grounded his great dream.[43]

Madison objected to the Hamiltonian system, as Drew McCoy has best explained, because he considered its economic and social orientation inappropriate for a republican people. He disapproved of its tendency to aggrandize the executive branch of the federal government and to give that branch influence over those inside and out of Congress whose economic fortunes would be linked to the federal treasury's.[44] He protested the funding and assumption plan for unduly favoring certain states and certain citizens at the risk of alienating others from the union. He thought congressional approval of a national bank would bend the federal charter into shapes that its creators had not meant, altering the structure of the polity in ways that would eventually endanger its republican form.

Madison's opposition to the national bank on constitutional grounds has usually been seen as a convenient screen for other motives and a sharp reversal of a hitherto expansive attitude toward federal power. It was neither. As he continued to refine a continental vision of his own—in private letters, at the Constitutional Convention, as "Publius," and in a series of letters to the *National Gazette*—Madison was more and more inclined to define a republican system in contrast to regimes in which political authority was independent of the people.[45] From 1790 forward, he saw with growing clarity that Hamiltonian measures opened the way to an exercise of influence on the federal government by special-interest factions.[46] Those policies created in the government and in its hangers-on an interest distinct from the public's as a whole.[47] With even greater perspicacity, he saw that Hamilton's construction of the Constitution allowed rulers to escape their proper dependence on society. The elective character of the government was the primary assurance of this dependence, but chartered limitations of authority and the federal structure defined in the organic law were additional supports. Madison's strict construction of the Constitution did not mark a change of course, for he had never been inclined toward any other view. His constitutional objections to Hamilton's designs were not politically convenient covers for more basic motives, not simply instrumental to his other wishes. They were integral components of a republican philosophy.

Late in life, Madison was asked why he had deserted Hamilton. He replied, "I deserted Colonel Hamilton, or, rather, Colonel Hamilton deserted me . . . from his wishing to . . . administer the government (these were Mr. Madison's very words), into what he thought it ought to be; while, on my part, I endeavored to make it conform to the Constitution as understood by the Convention that produced and recommended it, and particularly by the state conventions that *adopted* it."[48] The people, he insisted, had established a limited, federal republic. To force the federal charter into a different mold by broad construction would be to break the government's foundation in popular consent, a usurpation of the same sort as had moved the British colonies to revolution. Madison believed that usurpations were to be resisted on their first appearance, as they had been then. This one required greater seriousness of purpose because a concentration of authority in national hands would necessarily entail an end of union or a central government that must eventually approximate hereditary forms.[49]

Madison was a Virginia continentalist. This does not mean he rose in opposition to the funding and assumption plan in order to protect a faltering prestige at home; his reputation in his state and district were never that seriously at risk.[50] Nor is it very likely that he was seeking popularity, although he certainly believed that the success of the new government depended on its ability to win the veneration of the people with the equity and wisdom of its policies. He opposed assumption because he saw it as unfair to Virginia. He said as much, and said it with no feeling of embarrassment, for he believed that a representative had a duty to defend his constituents' legitimate interests. But this was not the most important way in which his stand reflected the interests and situation of his state. Unionist though he had always been—and Madison was one of the great early nationalists in his insistence on the bonds that made Americans a single people—his special kind of continentalism was a distinctive product of his experiences and perspective as a statesman of the Old Dominion.

Madison learned much from his opponents in the contest over ratification of the Constitution, but he required no help from Antifederalists to sense the dangers posed by what contemporaries called "consolidation." His comprehension of the nature of America's federal politics had been forged by several years of difficult defense of his state's particular interests in a Confederation Congress whose majority was usually unsympathetic to and jealous of Virginia. As a southern continentalist and former member of that Congress, as former leader of the Federalists in the state convention of 1788, Madison understood the depth of sectional differences in the United States. He knew that a successful union must accommodate those differences. Interests and authority were simply too diffuse in the United States, both sectionally and vertically, for there to be a viable solution to its problems along the lines suggested by the course of English history to other Federalists of 1787–89.

Early in the 1780s, as thoughts turned from the difficulties of the war years to the prospects for America in time of peace, many continental-minded men began a long retreat toward what we might describe as a conventional solution to the problems Congress faced and a conventional vision of the path toward national greatness. They wished to imitate the undeniable success of eighteenth-century British statesmen with a system of administration and political economy that had helped to raise the little island to an envied height of happiness, stability, and international prestige. As they grew increasingly disgruntled with state politics and policies, many of them also came to a conclusion that private rights and public good could not be guaranteed in the United States by anything much short of a near imitation of the British constitution. Hamilton's great speech at the convention, proposing a life term for the executive and senators and a clear subordination of the states, urged exactly that.

Through the middle 1780s, Madison shared the growing discontent with the Articles of Confederation. No one felt a more profound revulsion with state politics. Still, Madison's experiences and background made it impossible for him to share the wish for a conventional solution. As an ardent revolutionary, he could not accept the argument that any government derived from an elective process could be called republican, no matter how remote its members were from a dependence on the people. As a Virginian, he was sharply conscious of the limits beyond which the union could not push its parts. He discovered his solution in the very differences between the states and their peoples that other continental-minded men considered problems. He concluded that these differences could feed into a properly constructed great republic in a manner that would break the force of majority faction without encountering the risk of recreating a regime in which a governing minority would eventually rule.

Madison's continentalism was a newer vision, in the end, than Hamilton's. It was better grounded in American realities. Hamilton sought to override the differences between the states by forging an alternative to their existing political elites. This was both premature and out-of-date. Too many of the country's economic regions simply lacked the monied and commercial interests required by Hamilton's vision, while regions with the right materials possessed a body politic too large, too little deferential, and too irreducibly diverse for Hamilton's elite to lead them. What Hamilton succeeded in creating, as Madison insisted, was a minority faction which ruled as long as special circumstances shielded them with Washington's prestige and reinforced them with large numbers who dreaded a collapse of traditional order. Hamilton's "Court" politics were bound to fail, as Madison expected, on the impassable barrier of the new republic's social and economic structure. Meanwhile, the Virginian necessarily opposed a set of policies that threatened to upset the grand design he hoped would preclude preference of factional objectives to the common good.

Notes

Mr. Banning is an associate professor of history at the University of Kentucky. Portions of this article were read in an earlier version to the Shelby Cullom Davis Seminar at Princeton University. The author is grateful to the members of the seminar for criticisms which prompted further thinking.

1. Hamilton to Edward Carrington, 26 May 1792 (Harold C. Syrett et al., eds., *The Papers of Alexander Hamilton* [26 vols.; New York and London, 1960–79], 11:426–445). The whole of my summary of Hamilton's analysis is taken from this let-

ter. I have modernized spelling and punctuation and given abbreviations in full here and throughout the article.

2. "Madison had completely reversed his former position" on assumption and discrimination and offered a "dubious" explanation for doing so; his opposition to Hamilton's plan was "probably a tactical maneuver . . . dictated by political expediency," a move to strengthen his position in Virginia and Virginia's position in national politics (E. James Ferguson, *The Power of the Purse: A History of American Public Finance, 1776–1790* [Chapel Hill, 1961], 297–99). Ferguson's is among the most persuasive presentations of an interpretation whose shadings range from the emphasis on Madison's self-interest and hypocrisy in Forrest McDonald, *Alexander Hamilton: A Biography* (New York, 1979), 175, 177–186, 199–201, to the sympathetic explanation of Madison's constitutional reversal in the biographies cited in n. 8 below.

3. Lance Banning, "James Madison and the Nationalists, 1780–1783," *William and Mary Quarterly*, 3d ser., 40 (1983): 227–255.

4. Speech of 29 June 1787 (Max Farrand, ed., *The Records of the Federal Convention of 1787* [1911–1937; reprint ed.; 4 vols.; New Haven, 1966], 1:464–465); Jacob E. Cooke, ed., *The Federalist* (Middletown, Conn., 1961), No. 41, pages 270–275.

5. Cooke, *Federalist*, No. 45, page 314; speech of 11 June 1788 (Jonathan Elliot, ed., *The Debates in the Several State Conventions on the Adoption of the Federal Constitution . . .* , [Washington, D.C., 1854], 3:259).

6. The point is particularly well made in Edward McNall Burns, *James Madison: Philosopher of the Constitution* (New Brunswick, 1938), 178–179 and passim.

7. For example, Gottfried Dietze, *The Federalist: A Classic on Federalism and Free Government* (Baltimore, 1960), 260–264, 267–271 and passim; Alpheus Thomas Mason, "The Federalist—A Split Personality," *American Historical Review* 57 (1952), 625–643; Douglass Adair, *Fame and the Founding Fathers: Essays by Douglass Adair,* ed. Trevor Colbourn (New York, 1974).

8. Hamilton and Madison "disagreed from the outset on social and economic matters. This disagreement grew until it produced a change in Madison's political and constitutional views" (Irving Brant, *James Madison*, 6 vols. [Indianapolis, 1941–61], 2:217). Madison shifted "his view of the powers that could be safely consigned to the federal government in order to *preserve* consistency on the vastly more important matter of republican freedom" (Ralph Ketcham, *James Madison: A Biography* [New York and London, 1971], 314–15).

9. Brant, *Madison*, 2:110–111, 118; 3:chapter 10 and pages 180–181, 332–333.

10. Banning, "Madison and the Nationalists," *WMQ*, 3d ser., 40 (1983): 235–237, 239.

11. Even Harold Schultz, the biographer most resistant to describing Madison as a nationalist during the 1780s, believes that "Madison's views on specific policies came first and . . . the constitutional argument was derivative and secondary, . . . an instrumentality for blocking undesirable federal legislation" (*James Madison* [New York, 1970], 97–99).

12. Since Brant, numerous historians have pointed particularly to this number as evidence that Madison advanced a doctrine of broad construction and implied powers (Brant, *Madison*, 3:180–181; Cooke, *Federalist*, 304–305). If the often-quoted sentences are put in context, though, Madison clearly was arguing that the necessary-and-proper clause is not a grant of extensive additional powers. Madison defended the phrasing of the clause as well calculated to make it unnecessary for Congress to usurp by implication and construction authority transcending its chartered limits. Madison's numbers of *The Federalist*, not to mention his other writings, are peppered with defenses of specific grants of power on grounds that these will obviate unavoidable usurpations. He repeatedly decried a wish that the framers had written into the Constitution prohibitions that necessity would eventually have forced Congress to find a way around. These would have been "worse than in vain"; they would have planted "in the Constitution itself necessary usurpations of power, every precedent of which is a germ of unnecessary and multiplied repetitions" (see *Federalist*, No. 41, page 270; No. 42, page 280; No. 43, page 297).

13. These are conveniently reprinted in Adair, *Fame and the Founding Fathers*, ed. Colburn, 27–106, 251–258.

14. The history of modern interest in the tenth *Federalist* is too nearly a tale of the replacement of one misreading by another. Adair corrected Beard's assertion that Madison anticipated an economic interpretation of political behavior; this opinion has few current advocates. More persistent has been a "pluralist" misreading, which, in its crudest form, asserts that Madison approved a clash of special interests and identified the product of such clashes with the public good (Paul F. Bourke, "The Pluralist Reading of James Madison's Tenth *Federalist*," *Perspectives in American History* 9 [1975]: 271–95). Despite rebuttals, a subtler version of a pluralist interpretation persists among some able analysts who would regard the essay as the culmination of a long-term trend toward the acceptance of interest-group politics and an ideology of pluralistic individualism (see Kenneth A. Lockridge, "Social Change and the Meaning of the American Revolution," *Journal of Social History* 6 [1973]: 403–439). Lockridge builds on Gordon S. Wood, *The Creation of the American Republic, 1776–1787* (Chapel Hill, 1969), esp. chap. 15, "The American Science of Politics." But Lockridge neglects Wood's frequent warnings that no American of 1789, certainly not Madison himself, had fully assimilated the theory toward which their developing ideas were pointing.

15. This reading of the essay emerges most fully in Garry Wills, *Explaining America: The Federalist* (New York, 1980). Yet even Wood, who is a sensitive and cautious student of Madison, may overemphasize the centrality of this concept in Madison's own thinking if not in that of some of his allies (Wood, *Creation of the Republic*, chap. 12 passim, esp. 505).

16. The concept is not mentioned, for example, in Madison's letter to Jefferson of 24 Oct. 1787, which offered a preliminary version of the argument of the famous essay and will be discussed more fully below. The possibility of an improvement in the quality of representation is mentioned only briefly, as an "auxiliary desideratum"

of good government, in the "Vices of the Political System of the United States" (William T. Hutchinson et al., eds., *The Papers of James Madison* [Chicago and Charlottesville, 1962–], 9:357). It is clearly identified as a secondary consideration in the tenth *Federalist* itself (Cooke, *Federalist*, 63).

17. Hamilton grasped this point immediately when he first heard Madison's great speech in the convention on enlarging the sphere. "The Assembly when chosen will meet in one room if they are drawn from half the globe," he jotted, and "paper money is capable of giving a general impulse" (that is, of creating a majority faction) among the people and thus in the national legislature (Farrand, *Federal Convention*, I, 146). Among additional indications that Madison assumed that federal representatives would reflect the local interests and prejudices of their constituencies, one of the clearest is *Federalist*, No. 46 (Cooke, *Federalist*, 318–319).

18. Cooke, *Federalist*, No. 10, page 63; No. 51, page 353. My italics.

19. Ibid., No. 10, page 63; No. 51.

20. This is to reemphasize central themes of Neal Riemer, "The Republicanism of James Madison," *Political Science Quarterly*, 69(1954): 45–64, and "James Madison's Theory of the Self-Destructive Features of Republican Government," *Ethics*, 65 (1954): 34–43.

21. Madison to Jefferson, 11 Aug. 1788 (Hutchinson et al., *Papers of Madison*, 11:227). Firmer, but more suspect, was Madison's late-life statement that he and Hamilton soon dispensed with their attempt to read each other's essays prior to publication partly because neither wished "to give a positive sanction to all the doctrines and sentiments of the other; there being a known difference in the general complexion of their political theories" (Elizabeth Fleet, ed., "Madison's 'Detached Memoranda,'" *WMQ*, 3d ser., 3 [1946]: 565).

22. Madison to Philip Mazzei, 10 Dec. 1788 (Hutchinson et al., *Papers of Madison*, 11:389).

23. Elaboration and support of my discussion of Madison's years in the old Congress may be found in "Madison and the Nationalists," *WMQ*, 3d ser., 40 (1983): 227–255.

24. Syrett et al., *Papers of Hamilton*, 3:420–426; Stephen Higginson to Henry Knox, 8 Feb. 1787 (Edmund C. Burnett, ed., *Letters of Members of the Continental Congress* [Washington, D.C., 1934], 7:123 n. 4).

25. Speech of 28 Jan. 1783 (Hutchinson et al., *Papers of Madison*, 6:143–147).

26. Ferguson, *Power of the Purse*, 292.

27. See the preface for his notes on debates in the Constitutional Convention (Farrand, *Federal Convention*, 3:542–43).

28. "Vices of the Political System" (Hutchinson et al., *Papers of Madison*, 9:350–351, 354); "Observations on Jefferson's Draft of a Constitution for Virginia" (ibid., 11:287–288).

29. Charles F. Hobson, "The Negative on State Laws: James Madison, the Constitution, and the Crisis of Republican Government," *WMQ*, 3d ser., 36 (1979): 215–235.

30. Madison to Jefferson, 24 Oct. 1787 (Hutchinson et al., *Papers of Madison,* 10:214). My emphasis.

31. Ibid., 210, 214; Cooke, *Federalist,* No. 10, page 65.

32. Banning, "Madison and the Nationalists," *WMQ,* 3d ser., 40 (1983): 252–253; Drew R. McCoy, *The Elusive Republic: Political Economy in Jeffersonian America* (Chapel Hill, 1980), esp. chap. 3; McCoy, "The Virginia Port Bill of 1784," *Virginia Magazine of History and Biography* 83 (1975), 288–303.

33. This is the area of consistency emphasized by Brant and Ketcham.

34. Among other places, in the very response to Hamilton's request for his opinions about funding to which the latter referred in his complaint to Carrington.

35. In characterizing Madison's proposal of 1790 as a sharp reversal of his previous position, Ferguson, like Hamilton, does not remark these differences. Madison's proposal of 1790, like Hamilton's own, would have paid the debt at its full face value and at a full 6 percent interest. Ferguson is also misleading when he suggests that Madison explained his support for discrimination as a consequence of "speculation attending Hamilton's report." Madison actually had been referring to transfers of the debt since 1783. But Ferguson's discussion is most suggestive in some other ways (*Power of the Purse,* 293–302). See n. 37 below.

36. Lance Banning, *The Jeffersonian Persuasion: Evolution of a Party Ideology* (Ithaca and London, 1978), 141–147.

37. When Ferguson calls Madison's proposal "a false issue" and an "unrealistic alternative," he does not mean that it would have been impossible to identify the original holders to whom the Virginian wished to return a portion of the money the government owed. Rather, he means to point out that Madison's plan might have made an assumption of state debts impossible and, more importantly, that it had only very narrow support. The really popular alternative to Hamilton, he suggests, would have been revaluation of the debt. This, together with a reduction of interest, is what had been suggested to Madison by William Maclay and what was being urged in the House by Samuel Livermore, Thomas Scott, James Jackson, and Thomas Tucker. I suspect that Madison had not given close consideration to the details of a proper funding plan until after he saw Hamilton's report. Then, disliking several features of Hamilton's plan and aware of the sizable sentiment in favor of what amounted to a partial repudiation, Madison developed an alternative that might conciliate the opposition while simultaneously fulfilling the government's pledges (and thus restoring public credit) at least as faithfully as Hamilton's own.

38. Cooke, *Federalist,* No. 11.

39. Ibid., No. 28.

40. In convention on 29 June 1787, after denouncing the "vicious representation" in Britain, Madison "prayed" the smaller states "to ponder well the consequences of suffering the Confederacy to go to pieces. . . . Let each state depend on itself for security . . . and the languishing condition of all the states . . . would soon be transformed into vigorous and high-toned governments." This would prove "fatal to the internal

liberty of all. . . . A standing military force, with an overgrown executive, will not long be safe companions to liberty" (Farrand, *Federal Convention,* I, 464–465). In *Federalist,* No. 41, he insisted that "nothing short of a Constitution fully adequate to the national defense and the preservation of the union can save America from as many standing armies" as there are separate states or confederacies and thus from the fate of Rome or contemporary Europe, where liberty was everywhere "crushed between standing armies and perpetual taxes" (Cooke, *Federalist,* 272, 274).

41. John M. Murrin, "The Great Inversion, or Court versus Country: A Comparison of the Revolution Settlements in England (1688–1721) and America (1776–1816)," in *Three British Revolutions: 1641, 1688, 1776,* ed. J. G. A. Pocock (Princeton, 1980), 368–453.

42. J. G. A. Pocock, "1776: The Revolution against Parliament," in ibid., 265–288.

43. Since the early 1780s, Hamilton had argued the necessity of creating among the nation's leadership a class of influentials tied to the federal government and capable of counterbalancing the influentials currently tied to the states. Genuine federal power, he insisted, required a union of the government's resources with those of a monied and officeholding class directly dependent on that government for promotion of their economic interests. See especially Hamilton's letters to an unknown recipient, to James Duane, and to Robert Morris, together with the conclusion of "The Continentalist" (Syrett et al., *Papers of Hamilton,* 2:234–251, 400–418, 604–635; 3:99–106).

44. McCoy, *Elusive Republic;* Banning, *Jeffersonian Persuasion.*

45. On this point see also Robert J. Morgan, "Madison's Analysis of the Sources of Political Authority," *American Political Science Review* 75 (1981): 613–625.

46. In the debate on the national bank, Madison reminded colleagues of "the great and extensive influence that incorporated societies had on public affairs in Europe. They are a powerful machine, which have always been found competent to effect objects on principles, in a great measure independent of the people" (Hutchinson et al., *Papers of Madison,* 13:384).

47. Madison came as close to outrage as it was possible for him to do in response to the speculation attendant on the opening of the national bank—"a mere scramble for so much public plunder"—and on a further assumption of state debts during the summer of 1791. Such abuses, he told Jefferson, "make it a problem whether the system of the old paper under a bad government, or of the new under a good one, be chargeable with the greater substantial injustice. The true difference seems to be that by the former the few were victims to the many; by the latter the many to the few. . . . My imagination will not attempt to set bounds to the daring depravity of the times. The stock-jobbers will become the pretorian band of the government, at once its tools and its tyrant; bribed by its largesses, and overawing it by clamors and combinations" (Hutchinson et al., *Papers of Madison,* 14:43, 69).

48. Interview with Nicholas P. Trist, 27 Sept. 1834 (Farrand, *Federal Convention,* 3:533–534). Perhaps the plainest evidence that Hamilton did hope to administer the

government toward consolidation is his memorandum on the Constitution's prospects, 17–30 Sept. 1787 (Syrett et al., *Papers of Hamilton,* 4:275–277).

49. Madison's most systematic explanation of the anti-democratic consequences of consolidation would come in his report to the House of Delegates on the responses to the Virginia Resolutions of 1798 (Gaillard Hunt, ed., *The Writings of James Madison* [New York, 1906], 6:357–359).

50. In the decidedly Antifederalist state legislature, following a powerful attack on Madison's principles by an embittered and magnetic Patrick Henry, the balloting for two senators produced 98 votes for Richard Henry Lee, 86 for William Grayson, and 77 for Madison. In a congressional district deliberately gerrymandered (or henrymandered) to place Madison's county in an Antifederalist district, he defeated James Monroe 1,308 to 972, winning more than 57 percent of the vote.

The Practicable Sphere of a Republic

James Madison, the Constitutional Convention, and the Emergence of Revolutionary Federalism

James Madison made three distinctive contributions to the writing of the Constitution. Together, these distinguished him as first among the framers. He was primarily responsible for the preliminary resolutions that served throughout the summer of 1787 as the outline for reform, proposals that initiated the Constitutional Convention's transformation of the old Confederation into a republican government of national extent. In the early weeks of the deliberations, he persuasively explained why lesser changes would not work, an enterprise in which he was impressively assisted but never overshadowed by a handful of like-minded men. And most distinctively of all, he repeatedly insisted that the meeting could not limit its attention to the crisis of the Union, but must also come to terms with the vices of democratic government as these had been revealed in the Revolutionary states. Constitutional reform, he argued, would also have to overcome a crisis of republican convictions, both by placing limitations on the states and by creating a great republic free from the structural errors of the state constitutions and capable of restoring the damaged reputation of democratic rule. With the latter plea particularly, he led the Constitutional Convention to a thorough reconsideration of the proper governmental structure of a sound republic. Meanwhile, with his famous argument that private rights are safer in a large than in a small republic, he helped instill a faith that the emerging Constitution might accomplish all the ends he had in mind.

All three of Madison's distinctive contributions are well and widely understood. All three, it should be noted, came early in the course of the proceedings. Madison was first among the framers, by general agreement of historians and his peers, in part because he came to Philadelphia the best prepared. Of all the delegates, he seemed to have the most precise and comprehensive knowledge of American affairs, together with a masterful ability to place the country's situation in historical and philosophical perspective. He had thought things through to a degree that no one else had done, and it was therefore his ideas that set the course, his suggestions to which other delegates initially responded. Throughout the summer, he would speak as often and impressively as any. He would serve on most of the convention's key committees. But he was not responsible for any of the famous compromises or for any of the late additions that reshaped the resolutions of May 29 into the document completed on September 17. He earned his reputation as the father of the Constitution principally because of what he did toward the beginning of the work—then, and after the adjournment, by which time his own ideas had been significantly remolded.[1]

This essay focuses on that remolding. For we have seldom asked how Madison was influenced *by* the framing of the Constitution—not, at least, without presuming that he must have been severely disappointed. Historians are well aware that the convention thoroughly revised the resolutions of May 29 and that the finished plan reflected great defeats as well as stunning triumphs for Madison's original proposals. They have carefully assessed his victories and disappointments. But they have yet to recognize how much he *learned*, how greatly he was *changed* by his participation in the framing. Thus, a closer look at the Virginian's preparations for the meeting and an effort to approach the making of the Constitution as an episode in the development of his ideas can cast new light on the convention, on Madison's original assumptions, and on the most important framer's understanding of the finished Constitution. When we turn the ordinary questions inside out, I hope to show, we find that we have yet to reach a balanced understanding of the great Virginian's founding vision, which was influenced by the shaping of the Constitution more profoundly—and in different ways—than has before been seen.

The Constitutional Convention, as Madison eventually explained, proposed a form of government that had no precedent in history. Neither wholly national nor purely federal, this novel scheme divided political responsibilities between concurrent and interlocking state and central governments, each of which would act directly on the individuals composing the political societies from which they rose. The people of the thirteen states could be conceived as granting portions of the sovereign power to different parts of both the state and general governments while reserving certain rights, together with the ultimate authority to alter or abolish any of these governments, for themselves. The structure thus established, Madison maintained, could make the central government effective without endangering the people or the states. It offered an entirely democratic solution to the characteristic problems of democracy.[2]

This solution to the nation's problems was significantly different from the one that Madison envisioned when the great convention opened. It differed even more, though this has not been noticed, from the proposals he supported midway through the work. He stubbornly resisted some of its essential features through most of the proceedings and worried when the gathering adjourned that they would vitiate the system.[3] And yet his numbers of *The Federalist* did not defend a system that he privately regarded as severely flawed, as seems to be the dominant impression. Rather, these impressive essays, building on ideas that first occurred in course of the convention and representing his more settled views, confessed his reconciliation to decisions he had earlier opposed and outlined a position he defended through the rest of his career.

I

Shortly after its deliberations opened, the Constitutional Convention entered on an argument that polarized its members for at least the next six weeks. With Madison and James Wilson of Pennsylvania at their head, the members from the larger states confronted delegates from smaller states on the provision in the resolutions of May 29 for proportional representation in both branches of the national legislature. No part of the debates is better known. Small-state delegates insisted on the equal vote that every state had always had in Congress. Madison and Wilson attempted to convince the smaller states that differences among the large ones would guarantee security against a coalition of the giants, pleading with opponents to surrender a demand for a concession plainly incompatible with larger federal powers and majority control. The confrontation, as has been repeatedly remarked, pitted large-state nationalists against delegates who worried that the smaller states would be completely dominated in a great republic. The latter soon were reinforced by others who insisted that the states as states *should* retain a role in the general government, that states as well as individuals *should* be represented in order to preserve a federal harmony and enable the states to protect their own share of power in a mixed regime.[4]

In this phase of the convention, Madison completed the initial, most neglected phase of a significant rethinking of his suppositions. He had come to Philadelphia convinced that no extension of the central government's authority could overcome the crisis of the Union if the execution of congressional decisions continued to depend on intermediary actions by the states. The fundamental flaw of the Confederation, he believed, lay in its structure. States were necessary instruments of federal action, but they were not amenable to federal commands. The articles of union took the form of a "political constitution," but the general government lacked independent means to carry out the tasks with which it was entrusted. It was thus as ineffectual in practice as the states would be if every citizen were free to follow or ignore their laws.[5] This insight was the starting point for the Virginia Resolutions, which sought to free the general government from secondary, state decisions capable of baffling all its measures. It was Madison's first major contribution to the framing.

When the Constitutional Convention opened, nonetheless, the most important architect of the Virginia Plan had not yet formed a clear conception of fully concurrent governments, all possessing all the means required to carry out their tasks.[6] Although he insisted on the need to end the states' capacity to intervene between the making and the execution of federal decisions, he did not yet see how they could be denied all agency in executing federal commands, nor did he see how it was possible to keep the lesser legislatures from "molesting" one another or infringing private rights unless the general government could act directly on the states.[7] On the eve of the convention, Madison had written of his hope that "positive" additions to the powers of the general government—authority to regulate and tax the country's trade, together with at least a partial power of direct taxation—would render it unnecessary, *for the most part*, for Congress to compel the states.[8] He evidently still imagined, then, that on occasion the central government would still rely upon the states for requisitions or for other actions necessary to enforce its laws. And he was equally concerned to vest the central government with power to defend itself, the private rights of citizens, and peaceful relationships between the states from independent state decisions. Accordingly, while the Virginia Resolutions sought to solve the federal problem partly by removing the state governments from their direct and equal role in *making* federal decisions—by placing a republican regime on top of a confederation of republics—they also sought to guarantee the faithful execution of the central government's decisions by *compelling* the confederated states to follow federal directives, either by a federal veto on their laws or by a federal power of coercion.

As deliberations started, to put this point another way, Madison had not entirely freed himself from the assumption that the Union would remain confederal in several major respects. He had not yet firmly grasped the concept that would rapidly become the key to the convention's ultimate solution to the problem he defined. Although his thinking had been moving him in this direction (and although the resolutions of May 29 led the entire convention toward the same conclusion), the concept that the central government should act exclusively upon the people, not upon the states, is nowhere to be found in the Virginian's preconvention writings.

Language of this sort was introduced to the convention on May 30, when Gouverneur Morris contrasted a "national" government with one "merely federal" and George Mason distinguished a government acting on individuals from one acting on states. Madison, suggestively, was not as quick as others to adopt this language, which soon was heard on every side. He even pointed out that there were instances in which the present government acted directly on individuals. It seems apparent, nevertheless, that he was soon profoundly influenced by the concept.[9] It obviously strengthened and improved his earlier analysis of the Confederation's ills. It rendered more explicit what was probably the most important thrust of the Virginia Resolutions, a thrust which he had neither followed to its logical conclusion nor separated from proposals based on different ideas.

Madison had started his analysis of the Confederation's weaknesses— the point is critical to understanding the development and content of his thought—by probing the relationship between the general government and states, conscious of the need to make the central government genuinely "sovereign" in its sphere, preoccupied with the ability of the provincial governments to frustrate federal measures. This is why he had referred to rendering the states "subordinately useful," why many of the resolutions of May 29 were meant to make the states obedient to federal commands.[10] As May turned into June, however, it became increasingly apparent that the concept of a central government that would compel obedience directly from the people, if more consistently applied, might become the central premise of reform. Day by day, the delegates could see more clearly that immediate connection with the people could permit the general government to wield effective power without relying on or trying to coerce the states.

As the battle with the smaller states approached its climax, Madison's attraction to this concept grew. As the arguments of his opponents began to sway some minds and as his allies clarified their own desires, he could imagine more concretely what he wished for, and he rebutted small-state fears with rising passion. On June 29, remarking that the states must sometimes be regarded as "political societies" and sometimes only as "districts of individual citizens," William Samuel Johnson suggested that the thirteen collectivities should be represented in each of these two ways in the two different branches of the legislature. Madison agreed with Johnson "that the mixed nature of the Govt. ought to be kept in view," but he denied that this required an equal representation of the states in either house. Oliver Ellsworth then developed Johnson's point: "We were partly national; partly federal. The proportional representation in the first branch was conformable to the national principle and would secure the large States agst. the small. An equality of voices was conformable to the federal principle and was necessary to secure the Small States agst. the large. He trusted that on this middle ground a compromise would take place."[11]

Madison replied to Ellsworth on July 14 in his final plea before the crucial vote that carried the famous compromise: "It had been said that the Governt. would . . . be partly federal, partly national; that altho' in the latter respect the Representatives of the people ought to be in proportion to the people: yet in the former it ought to be according to the number of States. If there was any solidity in this distinction he was ready to abide by it." But there now seemed no solidity in the distinction as applied to the emerging system. Madison "called for a single instance in which the Genl. Govt. was not to operate on the people individually. The practicability of making laws, with coercive sanctions, for the States as political bodies, had been exploded on all hands."[12] Accepting the distinction now between a "national" government, which would act on individuals, and a "federal" government, which would act on states, Madison revealed that he had come to think of the new system as wholly "national" in its structure and operations. The system he envisioned and defended on July 14 was not the plan he had originally proposed.

This phase of the convention, though, is also highly likely to mislead us. Through these weeks, as nearly every major study has repeated, Madison appears as the magnificent titan of a "nationalist assault."[13] During these debates, he showed almost no fear of central power. Quickly read, some of his comments and proposals may suggest that he was willing to pursue consolidation of authority nearly to the point of turning states into the counties of the great republic, and analysts have sometimes said that his desires seem very similar to Alexander Hamilton's at this point in the work. But this opinion disregards the qualifying phrases or the context of his speeches. It reflects inadequate attention to the way his thinking had developed before the confrontation with the smaller states began. And it produces a misleading view of how he changed as a result of his defeat.

Madison did lead a nationalist offensive at the Constitutional Convention—provided that we use this word as delegates themselves employed it for purposes of this particular debate.[14] He entered the convention seeking national supremacy: complete, unchallengeable authority for the general government over matters of general concern. By July 14, he had come to think that national supremacy should be secured by the creation of a great republic which would rise directly from the people and possess all means required to act directly on the people to enforce its laws. He saw more clearly now than he had seen at the beginning of deliberations how the states could be removed from their intermediary role between the general government and people. He therefore struggled to the last to prevent the Connecticut Compromise. He had become a more consistent nationalist, in this respect, than he had been when the proceedings started.

Even on July 16, however, Madison can be legitimately described as a determined "nationalist" only in his quest for a structure and mode of operation that would make the general government effective and supreme *within its proper sphere,* which he consistently conceived as relatively small. He was not a "nationalist" in his conception of the duties or responsibilities that should be placed in federal hands. On this issue he remained, as he had always been, a moderate. Indeed, if he had not been so accustomed and committed to a basically conventional conception of state and federal duties, he would not have concentrated so intently and so long on ways to keep the states from baffling federal measures, from intervening in the federal sphere.

After the convention, Madison repeatedly insisted that the Constitution should be seen less as a grant of new authority than as a means of rendering effective the powers that the central government had always had.[15] Usually dismissed as an expedient response to Antifederalist objections, these statements might instead remind us of the reasoning behind the resolutions of May 29, which tells us much about the limits of their author's plans. In the writings that record his path to the convention, Madison consistently devoted very little space to powers he desired to shift from state to federal hands, for there was little that was new or controversial in what he was proposing on this subject.[16] Apart from power over trade, as he conceived it, the present constitution granted Congress positive authority to do most of the things a general government should do—even power to require the states to raise the revenues it needed.[17] The fundamental difficulty, then, was not a radically mistaken definition of the proper scope of federal responsibilities. It was the inability of the existing government to carry out the tasks that most informed Americans believed to be its proper business.[18] As he thought his way to the Virginia Plan, Madison concerned himself from the beginning, not with redivision of responsibilities between the general government and states, but with the structural and operational deficiencies of the existing system. He wanted an *effective* central government, not a vastly swollen one. In fact, he wanted a reform that would impinge on state authority only when the clear necessities of union or the fundamental liberties intended by the Revolution appeared to be endangered.[19]

Early in his preconvention thinking Madison explained to Edmund Randolph that the alternatives before the country extended, theoretically, from total independence for the thirteen states to their complete consolidation into a single, national republic. He rejected both of these extremes in favor of a "middle ground" that would provide for national supremacy where common measures were required but leave the states' authority in force where they were not.[20] He sought this "middle ground," not just because he thought a more complete consolidation could not be achieved, but because he never doubted that a fragmentation of the Union *or* excessive concentration of authority in federal hands would eventually betray the Revolution.

How did he define "excessive"? The simplest answer is that he did not attempt to frame a rigid rule that might be universally applied, and we should not attempt to do so for him. Yet if we fail to understand how firmly he rejected any option other than the "middle ground," we will mistake his purposes, misread his words, and end with an imperfect grasp of what he taught and what he learned at the Constitutional Convention. At Philadelphia, the need to win a point was sometimes incompatible with an articulation of all of a member's thoughts. Speakers might suppress one set of fears because a different set was temporarily foremost in their minds. During the convention, Madison was fierce in his determination to create a general government that would suffice for all the nation's common needs, so fixed in this intention that we readily forget those early references to "middle ground." But when he entered the convention, the powers he designed to transfer from the states to the general government were relatively few, the need for such a transfer generally conceded even by opponents of his plan. The battle with the smaller states was not essentially a contest over *how much* power should be placed in federal hands.[21]

The resolutions of May 29 suggested that the national legislature be empowered with the legislative rights already vested in the general Congress by the Articles of Confederation, together with the right to legislate "in all cases to which the separate States are incompetent, or in which the harmony

of the United States may be interrupted by the exercise of individual Legislation." "It can not be supposed that these descriptive phrases were to be left
in their indefinite extent to Legislative discretion," Madison later warned. "A
selection and definition of the cases embraced by them was to be the task of
the Convention. If there could be any doubt that this was intended, and so
understood by the Convention, it would be removed by the course of [the
subsequent] proceedings."[22]

Clearly, Madison himself had no intention of confiding plenary authority
to the new government. Two days after the Virginia Plan was introduced, he
said that he preferred enumeration of the general government's authorities,
although he might accept a general grant of power if a workable enumeration could not be achieved.[23] The context shows that he was principally concerned to keep the gathering from getting sidetracked into a debate about
the proper reach of federal powers. Later in the course of the proceedings,
Madison would act as one of the convention's most consistent advocates of
strict, though full, enumeration. Early on, he feared that a debate about specific powers could distract the meeting from a more important issue: how to
make the central government effective. But this does not suggest that he was
unconcerned to keep it safe.[24]

Madison did nothing—at any point in the convention—that is inconsistent with the view that he imagined, and consistently attempted to secure,
a new central government whose authority would be autonomous, unchallengeable, but also strictly limited to matters that the individual states could
not effectively handle on their own. The very speeches in which he was most
insistent on the evils of state intervention in the federal sphere also indicate
in passing that he sought a "mixed" regime, that he intended to "preserve the
State rights, as carefully as the trials by jury."[25] The advocates of compromise
explicitly conceded that neither he nor Wilson wanted to remold the states
as counties of a single, consolidated republic.[26] They know how central to
the contemporary mind—and certainly to Madison's—was the distinction
between a government to be created by a written constitution and a fully
national regime. Many of them understood that, from the first, the architect
of the Virginia Plan assumed that federal powers would be strictly limited to
those to be defined by the convention and the people.[27]

II

More than one mistake has followed from a failure to distinguish Madison's
determination to secure a general government whose authority would be

effective or *complete* from his opinion of the *quantity of power*, the nature of the duties, that ought to be confided to federal hands. Thus, most interpretations of the framer's conduct follow Irving Brant, his great biographer, in seeing his defeat on the apportionment of the Senate as possibly the most important watershed in Madison's political career.[28] The small-state victory, in this interpretation, initiated a retreat from an expansive view of federal powers which started in the second half of the convention, gathered new momentum during Washington's administration, and culminated in the Virginia Resolutions of 1798.[29] The dominant impression of the founder's whole career is gravely marred by an analysis that does not keep in mind the difference between his concept of the *way* in which the new regime should work and his opinion of the work it ought to do.

The small-state triumph on July 16 did, indeed, throw everything into confusion. When Madison and others failed to bring a caucus of the larger states to risk continuing the confrontation, every previous decision in convention had to be thought through again.[30] Few delegates were more alarmed than Madison himself. Nevertheless, a reconsideration of his course through the rest of the meeting will suggest that the Virginian turned in quite a different direction than is usually believed.

Madison did not "reverse his course" in consequence of the decision of July 16. He did not become "less nationalistic" than he had been during the weeks when it appeared that the convention might approve proportional representation in both branches of the legislature. It is true that he had warned that the concession to the smaller states could rob the new regime of "every effectual prerogative," making it "as impotent and short lived as the old."[31] Here, however, he predicted the effect that compromise might have on other members from the larger states, not the course he would himself pursue.

Madison had sought from the beginning to make the general government's authority complete within a sphere of limited responsibilities. He remained intent on this objective. He continued to support a federal negative on all state legislation. Unlike other southerners, he continued to support a federal power to levy export taxes. He opposed insertion of provisions requiring more than a majority of Congress for passage of commercial legislation or limiting the Senate's role in money bills. Near the close of the convention, he moved to add additional specifics to the enumerated powers of Congress. A thorough search does not identify a single power that he wanted to withhold from the general government after July 16 but would have granted had the large states won proportional representation in both branches. Madison did not retreat on the issue of the quantum of authority that should be vested in the general government. He had never assumed a more advanced position from which he found it necessary to withdraw.

The compromise did have significant effects on the Virginian, but it worked a different sort of change than has been thought. The concession to smaller states did not significantly affect his vision of the proper scope of federal power. It did almost immediately affect his view of how this power should be shared by the various parts of the new government.[32]

At the start of the convention, Madison had plainly seen the indirectly elected upper house as the branch best suited to control the passions of the people, to secure a place for wisdom and stability in the great republic, and to guard against the mutability, injustices, and multiplicity of laws that he identified as major weaknesses of democratic rule. When the proceedings opened, the role that he envisioned for the upper house contrasted sharply with his evident uncertainty, his Revolutionary fears, about the character and powers of a national executive. He planned to place enormous powers in the Senate and offered only very sketchy hints about the nature of the new executive.[33]

The decision of July 16 struck Madison as inconsistent with the rule of the majority, a barrier to the pursuit of general interests and a potential peril to the South. By this time, moreover, he was forcefully impressed by Wilson's argument that executive responsibility could be secured only by concentrating the executive authority in the hands of a single man. Together, these considerations moved him noticeably toward strengthening the executive at the expense of the Senate. This was the most obvious and most immediate effect of the Great Compromise.[34]

A second consequence, unnoticed in the standard literature, was fully as important. By July 14, Madison had come to be completely dedicated to the prospect that the great republic might be made completely national in its structure and operations. The compromise wrecked his desires. He and all the delegates were forced to readjust their thinking to accord with the decision that the general government would *not* be wholly national in structure, that the Senate would still represent the states. Madison, in fact, was among the first to make the point explicit. "The principle of [the great] compromise . . . required," he said, "that there shd. be a concurrence of two authorities, in one of which the people, in the other the states, should be represented."[35] On August 31, he even moved a complex ratification formula which would require the consent of both a majority of people and a majority of states. He was attempting, now, to form a concrete and consistent image of a system "partly national and partly federal" in structure.

Madison said nothing during the convention to suggest that he approved of this sort of hybrid. He only pointed to the logical consequences of a decision he had disagreed with and used them to advance particular objectives. Even at the close of the convention, he was not completely reconciled to the reintroduction of state agency into the federal system.[36] Still, there obviously echoed in his mind the earlier insistence of John Dickinson, George Mason, Roger Sherman, and others that it was *proper* for the states to be directly represented in the federal government, if only to protect their share of power in a mixed regime. For when he came to write *The Federalist,* he persuasively defended just this point of view. He still objected to an *equal* representation of the states, but now supported their participation as political societies in the workings of the new regime.[37] The system he defended in *The Federalist* was only partly national; and by the time of the Virginia state convention, he was saying, "If the general government were wholly independent of the governments of the particular states, then, indeed, usurpations might be expected to the fullest extent." But as the central government "derives its authority from [the state] governments, and from the same source from which their authority is derived," no usurpations need be feared. Far from threatening a general absorption of the proper powers of the states, adoption of the Constitution would "increase the security of liberty more than any government that ever was," since in America the powers ordinarily confided to a single government—and sometimes even to a single branch—would be entrusted to two sets of governments, each of which would watch the other at the same time as its several branches served as an internal check against abuse.[38]

What had caused this change of mind? Antifederalist attacks on the convention's work? *The Federalist* was obviously written to defend the Constitution from its critics, and criticism surely forced its advocates to rationalize the work of the convention, leading them to see advantages in clauses they had not especially regarded or had even disapproved.[39] That Madison responded partly to the Antifederalist critiques seems all the likelier in light of a developmental study of the framing, which challenges a very common, deep, and usually unrecognized assumption that Madison and other framers entered the convention with their thoughts essentially in order, struggled with opponents holding different ideas, and compromised no more than they were forced to. Studies of the Constitutional Convention seldom make a full allowance for truly fundamental changes of mind. Yet even the ingenious experience the same fluidity of shifting, jarring, dawning thoughts that we ourselves experience in any group endeavor. The Constitutional Convention was a learning process, an interchange of thoughts, for every member present.[40] Early in the work, the course of the deliberations forced the major author of the Virginia Resolutions to begin rethinking his original proposals. From then until adjournment, like every other delegate, he listened to his colleagues, was influenced by their thoughts, and struggled constantly to readjust his thinking to a plan whose shape was changing day by day. These changes outraced even Madison's ability to fully comprehend what was emerging. Not until he wrote *The Federalist* did he attempt a systematic rationalization of the summer's work, and his defense of the completed Constitution articulated understandings he achieved only in the course of the deliberations or even after they were through.

For Madison, moreover, Antifederalist criticisms of the Constitution were more than merely arguments that he was obligated to rebut. They were worries worthy of consideration, worries to which he himself was not immune. Like most supporters of the Constitution, he condemned most Antifederalists as men of little intellect and impure motives, but he did not regard all doubters in this way. Edmund Randolph and George Mason, for example, were colleagues he esteemed, colleagues he had listened to and learned from through the Philadelphia summer, colleagues whose anxieties and hopes he shared to a significant degree. Indeed, when we recall the limitations of his wishes during the convention, when we recognize that he was never simply on a single side of its divisions, it follows that the framing of the Constitution almost certainly affected Madison in one way modern scholarship has overlooked. It heightened his awareness of undemocratic and consolidationist opinion among his fellow framers. It taught him that among his allies in the battle with the smaller states were some who wished to carry centralization to objectionable extremes and some who were inclined to treat the document completed in convention more flexibly than he considered safe. As he reflected on the course of the proceedings and anticipated the important role that many of the framers would continue to perform, he may have recognized that his opponents of the summer had been right to seek additional assurance that the general government would stay within its proper bounds.[41]

The evidence for this effect, a critic might assert, is tenuous at best. Madison said nothing, then or later, that would indisputably confirm that he was seriously disturbed by the opinions of his allies. There may be some tantalizing hints that this was so. But there is no specific statement that would unimpeachably confirm it.[42]

But why should Madison have armed the doubters, either during the convention or as he worked to win approval of the Constitution? Perhaps we need not be surprised that his surviving writings do not prove beyond all doubt that he was worried by the centralizing, antidemocratic sentiments expressed in the convention.[43] The fact is that he did defend provisions he had earlier resisted, not only in *The Federalist* but through the rest of his career. And he defended them in language very similar to what he heard from his opponents during the convention. Perhaps he actually accorded his opponents' fears more plausibility than he admitted at the time. The records of proceedings leave no doubt that, on a spectrum which would take into account all issues faced by the convention, Madison stood almost equidistant from Hamilton and Randolph, from Mason and Gouverneur Morris. If we are open to the possibility that, standing in between, he was affected and occasionally alarmed by what he heard from both extremes, new insights will result; the framer's thought and conduct will appear less puzzling. The proof that Madison was privately alarmed by some of those who joined him in the battle with the smaller states cannot be found, so far as I can tell, in an explicit statement. But it is there, despite the absence of this sort of confirmation. It is present in the obvious progression of his thought. What did he desire at the beginning of the great convention? What did he defend when it was through? What happened in between?

Madison approached the Constitutional Convention persuaded that continuation of America's republican experiment required "concessions" from the states of part of their autonomy, "concessions" from the people sufficient to restrain the governing majority's eventual ability to have its way with additional security for private rights and long-term needs. But as he said to Thomas Jefferson, he wanted to concede *no more* to governmental vigor and stability than was consistent with the Revolution.[44] And he ended the convention knowing that his own intentions and his own evolving understanding of the Constitution were inconsistent with the hopes of several of his large-state allies. Madison intended to invigorate the Union in order to protect the Revolution from persistent public debts, swollen military forces, overpowerful executives, disillusionment with popular control, and majority contempt for constitutional protection of minority rights.[45] He searched for ways that all of this might be accomplished at minimal expense to the residual autonomy of the people in their several states. He consistently assumed that the new Constitution granted to the central government only the specific powers listed. Other framers wanted to invigorate the Union for very different ends, and only a minority shared Madison's consistent, scrupulous respect for constitutional restraints.[46]

If we think of the convention as an incident in the Virginian's education, it seems entirely likely that his numbers of *The Federalist* were written in response to friends as well as foes. They answered those who sought *more* governmental energy than he considered proper as well as those who feared the Constitution. They answered even his collaborator in the series. This is not to say that Madison already thought of Hamilton as dangerous to the Republic. The evidence does not permit us even to insist that he was consciously conducting a debate with his coauthor, though it is clear that he was less than fully comfortable with the alliance.[47] One thing, nonetheless, seems absolutely certain. For Madison, these essays represented more than an attempt to erect a theoretical justification of what the convention had done. They were also part of a continuing attempt to comprehend and publicly define a new political phenomenon, a novel instrument of government to which their author felt obliged to make a personal, emotional commitment.[48] They were part of an extended effort to revise his own ideas in light of the experience of the summer, to adjust his thought to the decisions of the Federal Convention, and thus to reassure himself as well as others that the Constitution would fulfill the Revolution. As he wrote these essays, Madison was consciously distilling from the lessons of the framing a new constitutional philosophy. That philosophy cannot be fully understood without a grasp of *all* the ways that he was changed by the convention and the plan that it proposed. *The Federalist,* in turn, illuminates his conduct through the framing.

III

Two related emphases of modern scholarship have left us with a poorly balanced understanding of Madison's founding vision. In the first place, studies of the Constitutional Convention understandably and strongly emphasize his leadership of delegates determined to replace the old Confederation with a great republic. Although this draws attention properly to the Virginian's most important contribution, it discourages a due attention to the limits of his wishes, limits which suggest important differences within the nationalist coalition and alert us to a subtle struggle which engaged the framer no less than did the battle with the smaller states.

Studies that do not distinguish Madison's variety of nationalism, which was structural, or operational, in nature, from the views of radical proponents of a concentration of authority underestimate a critical dimension of the tensions present in the Constitutional Convention. Genuine consolidationists were present. Consolidation was a potent fear, as were the antidemocratic sentiments of several framers. Madison participated in these fears. He also consciously attempted to identify the novel system shaped by the decisions in convention and to readjust his thoughts to its demands. Much of this is missed in most examinations of his conduct, and all of it was instrumental to the shaping of *The Federalist*. Only in these essays did Madison begin to demonstrate how much he had been changed by the convention and the Constitution. Here he was most careful to articulate assumptions and concerns that had continuously shaped his conduct. Here he offered a philosophy remolded by the lessons he had learned.

This brings us to the second emphasis that interferes with a better understanding of Madison's position at the founding. An imprecise description of his stand in the convention suggests that he intended to confide more power to the central government than he ever really did. This suggestion then is reinforced by an excessive emphasis on *Federalist* No. 10. Undue concentration on this single essay, Madison's most careful presentation of the argument that private rights are safer in a large than in a small republic, strengthens the impression that he planned to safeguard liberty almost exclusively by means of an "extension of the sphere" and might, therefore, have actually preferred a greater concentration of authority in central hands than the convention finally approved.

Federalist No. 10 *is* indispensable to understanding the concerns and hopes that generated the Virginia Resolutions and inspired James Madison's defense of the completed Constitution. Agonized by his perception that the rule of state majorities appeared to be persistently at odds with private rights and long-term public needs, unable to relinquish either one of his commitments, Madison attempted to escape the trap by generalizing lessons drawn from his political experience, particularly from the experience of Virginia's recent struggle over tax support for teachers of religion.[49] Had a single sect been dominant in the Old Dominion, he believed, no considerations could have blocked this measure. The multiplicity of disagreeing sects had done what no appeal to principle and public good could have accomplished. From this and other lessons, aided possibly by David Hume, he leaped to the conclusion that the democratic way to counteract the self-destructive features of a democratic system was to enlarge the size of the republic. A large enough republic would encompass such a host of sects and factions that majorities would seldom find a common purpose inimical to private rights or long-term public needs. Its large election districts would encourage the selection of representatives less likely to abandon justice or the enduring public good for "temporary or partial considerations."[50] The legislature of a great republic might even have been trusted with the task of overseeing factional disputes within the states and intervening to protect minorities when factional majorities endangered private rights.

This train of reasoning was basically complete when Madison prepared the "Vices of the Political System of the United States." He pressed it through the Constitutional Convention. It became a cornerstone of his assertion that the Constitution promised a republican solution to the vices most endemic to republics. Taken by itself, however, the argument for an extension of the sphere by no means offers a sure path to understanding Madison's entire position. Taken by itself, it leads most easily to serious distortion of his views.

This is true, particularly, if we disregard the qualifications that Madison was careful to insert in every presentation of his thesis. As he explained to Jefferson, the general government created by the Constitution might safely have been trusted even with a veto on state laws because its officers, impartial judges of contentions in the individual states, would at the same time have no interests separate from the interest of the body of the states and people.[51] Not just one, but two considerations had been present in the framer's mind throughout the shaping of the great republic. Vicious legislation, he believed, can issue either from the passions of an interested majority *or* from legislators who betray the needs of their constituents in order to pursue their personal interests and ambitions.[52] Enlargement of the size of the republic will impede formation of a factional majority, but this is only half of a solution to the problem of representative democracy. And it may increase the risk that representatives will not reflect the people's needs and will. "There is a mean," says *Federalist* No. 10, "on both sides of which inconveniencies will be found." Although small electorates may favor the selection of representatives so close to their constituents as to be unable or unwilling to pursue the general good, large electorates may choose men insufficiently "acquainted with all their local circumstances and lesser interests."[53] Extension of the sphere of the republic will therefore prove a truly democratic remedy for democratic ills "only . . . within a sphere of a mean extent." "In too extensive" a republic, Madison admitted, "a defensive concert may be rendered too difficult against the oppression of those entrusted with the administration."[54]

Majority excess had never seemed to Madison the only danger to republics—not even in the Revolutionary states. He was always equally concerned that rulers might betray the people, that power can corrupt, that men in power would attempt to free themselves from limitations in order to pursue distinct objectives of their own. He was therefore always careful to insist that framers of a constitution "must first enable the government to controul the

governed; and . . . next . . . oblige it to controul itself."⁵⁵ One of these necessities was not more vital than the other, and dependence on the people for
election did not seem to Madison a totally sufficient guarantee of the responsibility of rulers. Accordingly, his contributions to *The Federalist* were quite
particular about the special sort of great republic he defended. Essay No. 10
is full of references to "well constructed" great republics, and Madison wrote
two dozen other numbers to explain what "well constructed" means. Among
the most important was essay No. 51, whose most suggestive passage reads:
"The larger the society, provided it lie within a practicable sphere, the more
duly capable it will be of self-government. And happily for the *republican
cause,* the practicable sphere may be carried to a very great extent, by a judicious modification and mixture of the *federal principle.*"⁵⁶

There are many keys to understanding Madison's participation in the
making and defense of the new Constitution. One of the most helpful is to
see the founding as a *process* in which Madison's initial preparations, the
Philadelphia Convention, and the effort to secure adoption of the Constitution were passages of a single stream. Each passage helps explain the others
and the whole. Through all its course, this view of his participation would
suggest, Madison had been seeking "the practicable sphere of a republic,"
the "middle ground" between excessive localism (and the tyranny of unrestrained majorities) and undue concentration of authority in distant, unresponsive rulers. He found this "middle ground" only when he felt compelled
to put in print a systematic effort to relate the Constitution to the principles of the Revolution, only as he reconstructed the collective reasoning of
the convention, compared the Constitution to the hopes with which he had
begun, and readjusted his ideas in light of the experience of the summer. He
found it in the document itself: in the compound, partly federal features of
the new regime.

Madison, in 1786, was a committed, troubled unionist, persuaded that
the Union would not last without effective general government and that
an end of union would eventually entail an end of American democracy.
He concluded that the powers of the central government would have to be
extended so that they would reach all of the nation's common business and
that these powers must be rendered genuinely supreme. In the early weeks of
the convention, intent upon this object, he became increasingly determined
to remove the states entirely from their intermediary role between the general
government and people, to make the central government wholly national in
its structure and workings. Over his determined opposition, the convention
nevertheless decided that the new regime would not be wholly national in

structure; and when the gathering adjourned, he was severely disappointed. But he was quickly forced by his assumption of a leading role in the ratification contest to think his way again through every step in the creation of the Constitution, and by the time he wrote *The Federalist,* he was beginning to believe that the convention had been right to reason that a certain agency for the states as states would help maintain the equilibrium he wanted.

This acceptance of a federal role for states as states—and not a reconsideration of the proper powers of the central government—was Madison's real reversal in the aftermath of the convention's most important compromise. It is best explained by recognizing that he learned from the convention only slightly less than he had taught. "The practicable sphere of a republic," he had always thought, would be that sphere which would be large enough that it might "break and control the violence of faction," but not *so* large that it would also break the democratic bond between the rulers and the ruled, the "communion of interests and sympathy of sentiments" which bind a representative to his constituents.[57] However much he worried over the excesses of majorities, however hard he fought for national control of national affairs, Madison had always been no less concerned to guard self-government against excessive concentration of authority in rulers unresponsive to the people. In 1787, he changed his mind repeatedly about the constitutional devices most likely to achieve the proper blend of power and responsibility, but he was dedicated first to last to a *republican* solution to the nation's ills. And he defined republics as governments in which the will of the majority might be restrained, but not indefinitely denied.

Revolutionary principles, for Madison, included *both* security for private rights *and* democratic rule. Democracy, in turn, depended on perpetuation of the Union. Pressed by circumstances, other members of his generation could be tempted to conclude that one or two of these three principles might have to be severely compromised in order to preserve the others. But Madison had something in his makeup that compelled him to rebel against this choice, and this rebellion was the crux of his distinctive contribution to the founding. The critical necessity, as he conceived it, was to build a structure that would best secure them all. Such a structure, he was soon prepared to hope, had actually emerged—and not by accident alone—from the collective reasoning of the convention. Carefully respected, he maintained, the Constitution might provide as much security for all the objects of the Revolution as the nation's ingenuity could offer. Liberty, democracy, and union might prove safer in a federal system of republics than in any simpler system.[58]

In a *federal* system of republics, Madison explained, the will of the majority would be refined and purified by passing it successively through different filters. Authority would be distributed among two sets of governmental branches, state and general. Within each set, the different branches would be chosen sometimes more and sometimes less directly by the people, which would guarantee a due concern for both their short- and long-term needs. State and national representatives would each be charged with the responsibilities that they were best equipped for. Both would be denied authority to act on matters poorly suited to their character or knowledge. State representatives would not participate in national decisions, which demanded less-constricted vision. Federal officials would not intervene in matters that required a more particular familiarity with local needs and situations.[59] Thus, the product of successive distillations of the people's will would be, withal, the people's will. No branch of any part of the compound republic would be able to successfully pursue an interest different from the well-considered interest of the people as a whole. The state and general governments would help to keep each other within the proper bounds. Future generations would continue to enjoy as much self-government as human nature would allow.

This was not the system Madison had started out to build. It was not the system he had advocated at the Constitutional Convention. And yet the finished Constitution did define the sort of "middle ground" that he had always wanted. It promised an effective blend of governmental energy and freedom. It might, at once, "perpetuate the Union, and redeem the honor of the Republican name."[60] Thus, "the practicable sphere of a republic," he announced, had finally been found. Identified by the collective wisdom of the Constitutional Convention, which he was not too proud to think might be superior to his alone, it rested in the partly national but also partly federal features of the large, compound republic. It is time for us to reassert the novelty of these distinctive features, and time to recognize that Madison's defense of the completed Constitution did not have a single theme, but two: that this new government was perfectly consistent with the principles of a republican revolution, and that the Federal Constitution did not establish and would not support a consolidated national government, which he considered inconsistent with the character and needs of what was still to be a genuinely revolutionary union.

Notes

The author wishes to express his gratitude to Gordon S. Wood, E. Wayne Carp, and especially Drew McCoy for valuable comments on earlier versions of this essay. He also wishes to acknowledge a University of Kentucky Research Professorship, which made it possible to devote a year to full-time research and writing.

1. Two of many excellent attempts to measure Madison's contributions against those of his colleagues are particularly helpful on this point: Clinton Rossiter, *1787: The Grand Convention* (New York, 1966), 247–252; and Harold S. Schultz, "James Madison: Father of the Constitution?" *Quarterly Journal of the Library of Congress* 37 (1980): 215–222.

2. See Madison's numbers of *The Federalists,* ed. Jacob E. Cooke (Middletown, Conn., 1961); and Gordon S. Wood, *The Creation of the American Republic, 1776– 1787* (Chapel Hill, N.C., 1969), chaps. 13, 15. All references to *The Federalist* are to Cooke's edition.

3. "I hazard an opinion . . . that the plan . . . will neither effectually *answer* its *national object* nor prevent the local *mischiefs* which every where *excite disgusts.*" Madison to Thomas Jefferson, Sept. 16, 1787, in William T. Hutchinson et al., eds., *The Papers of James Madison* (Chicago, Charlottesville, 1962–), 10:163–164.

4. For the latter argument, see particularly the speeches of John Dickinson, George Mason, Roger Sherman, and others on June 6 and 7, in Max Farrand, ed., *The Records of the Federal Convention of 1787,* rev. ed., 4 vols. (New Haven, Conn., 1937), I, 133, 136–137, 155. See also Dickinson's "Letters of Fabius," ibid., 3:304.

5. "Vices of the Political System of the United States" (Apr. 1787), in Hutchinson et al., eds., *Papers of Madison,* 9:345–358. My arguments concerning Madison's pre-convention thoughts and original intentions are based throughout primarily on this memorandum, the "Notes on Ancient and Modern Confederacies," and letters to Jefferson (Mar. 19, 1787), Edmund Randolph (Apr. 8, 1787), and George Washington (Apr. 16, 1787), all in vol. 9.

6. Wood remarks this in *Creation of the American Republic,* 525.

7. See especially the letter to Jefferson, in Hutchinson et al., eds., *Papers of Madison,* 9:318.

8. To Washington, ibid., 385.

9. Speech of June 28, in Farrand, ed., *Records,* 1:449. Unless otherwise noted, all quotations from the convention are from Madison's notes of the debates.

As early as May 31, Madison spoke of abandoning the coercive power, referring as he had in the letter to Washington to the impracticality of applying force "to people collectively and not individually" (ibid., 54). Again, I recognize that the distinction made in the convention on May 30 was one that Madison had narrowly approached and even helped his colleagues seize. My point is simply that the other delegates helped him to complete the thought and move it further toward the center of his mind.

10. The precise dating of the memorandum on confederacies is subject to dispute, but it was almost certainly the earliest step in Madison's attempt to think his way toward the Virginia Plan. The reference to rendering the states "subordinately useful," which is frequently misunderstood, is in the letter to Randolph, in Hutchinson et al., eds., *Papers of Madison,* 9:369.

11. Farrand, ed., *Records,* 1:461, 468.

12. Ibid., 2:8–9.

13. So described the title of chap. 9 of Rossiter's *1787.*

14. During his retirement, Madison himself had more than one occasion to condemn the error of supposing "that the term, *national*" as applied "in the early stage of the Convention . . . was equivalent to *unlimited* or consolidated." It was used, he wrote, "in contradistinction to . . . a *federal* Government," which operated through requisitions and rested on the sanction of the state legislatures. The emerging system, "being a novelty and a compound, had no technical terms or phrases appropriate to it." "Old terms" had to be used "in new senses, explained by the context or by the facts of the case." To Andrew Stevenson, Mar. 25, 1826, in Farrand, ed., *Records,* 3:473–474; to N. P. Trist, Dec. 1831, in Gaillard Hunt, ed., *The Writings of James Madison,* 9 vols. (New York, 1900–1910), 9:475–477.

15. *Federalist* No. 45, page 314; Jonathon Elliot, ed., *The Debates in the Several State Conventions on the Adoption of the Federal Constitution . . . ,* 5 vols. (Washington, D.C., 1888), 3:259.

16. The central government, he wrote in his first thoughts on reform, should have the "power of regulating trade and [power over] sundry other matters in which uniformity is proper." It should have—his second effort to express it—"compleat authority in all cases where uniform measures are necessary. As in trade &c. &c." *et cetera:* for this was simply not his principal preoccupation. Madison to Jefferson, to Randolph, in Hutchinson et al., eds., *Papers of Madison,* 9:318, 370.

17. Revenue requisitions are "a law to the States" as state acts are laws to individuals (speech in the Confederation Congress, Feb. 21, 1783, ibid., 7:271).

18. "However ample the federal powers may be made, or however Clearly their boundaries may be delineated, on paper, they will be easily and continually baffled by the . . . States" unless supported by additional reforms that will make the general government "clearly paramount" to the state legislatures and capable of acting without their "intervention" (Madison to Jefferson, ibid., 9:318).

19. The obvious exception might appear to be his fierce commitment to a federal power to veto all state laws. (For an argument that Madison's support for this unwieldy and intrusive power demonstrates consolidationist desires, see Charles F. Hobson, "The Negative on State Laws: James Madison, the Constitution, and the Crisis of Republican Government," *William and Mary Quarterly,* 3d Ser., 36 [1979]: 215–235.) Yet Madison repeatedly identified the federal negative as a "defensive power," an instrument for overturning legislation incompatible with federal measures, harmony between the states, or private rights. Thinking of the veto as a better tool than judicial review for assuring state compliance with federal laws—and as the *only* tool with which the federal government could act directly to defeat injustices against minorities—he was, indeed, most stubbornly committed to the power and deeply disappointed when it was refused. But as a "negative," of course, the veto could not have been employed to make positive decisions for the states, and Madison consistently

distinguished it from "positive" additions to the Union's powers. In developmental context, the idea for such a power flowed precisely from his habit of assuming that the individual legislatures would continue to conduct most of the people's business and from his wish for a device that would secure the supremacy of the general government over matters of general concern at *minimal* expense to the autonomy of the individual states, which would continue to possess most of the power. Suggestively, Madison defended the proposal in his preconvention letters as "the least . . . abridgement of the State Sovereignties" consistent with their union, as "the least possible encroachment on the State jurisdictions." Madison to Randolph, to Washington, in Hutchinson et al., eds., *Papers of Madison,* 9:370, 383.

20. Hutchinson et al., eds., *Papers of Madison,* 9:369. The same phrase reappears in the letter to Washington, ibid., 383.

21. Before the meeting started, Madison identified two specific "positive powers" that should be transferred to the Congress: regulation of the country's trade and power to collect at least some sorts of internal taxes as well as duties on imports and exports. The New Jersey Plan would have granted powers to regulate trade and to impose a stamp tax, postal duties, and an impost. A large majority of states had ratified amendments to the Articles approving an impost and a partial federal authority to regulate commerce.

22. Farrand, ed., *Records,* 1:21; Madison to John Tyler, 1833, ibid., 3:526–527. See also Hunt, *Writings of Madison,* 9:176–177, 475, including: "The general terms of phrases used in the introductory propositions . . . were never meant to be inserted in their loose form in the text of the Constitution. Like resolutions preliminary to legal enactments it was understood by all, that they were to be reduced by proper limitations and specifications, into the form in which they were to be final and operative."

23. Farrand, ed., *Records,* I, 53. A general grant might still, of course, have been a limited one.

24. On Aug. 18, Madison moved to refer a long list of additional grants of enumerated powers to the Committee of Detail. On Sept. 14, Benjamin Franklin wished to add a congressional power to cut canals, and Madison urged extending this to permit congressional creation of corporations. These actions, like the federal negative, have usually been seen as powerful evidence of the reach of his "nationalism" at this point. I believe that, carefully considered, they are in fact among the clearest indications of its limits. The powers he proposed to add in August were far from extensive. Several of them—power over a seat of national government, to dispose of western lands, to organize western governments, and so forth—were so obviously required that I believe his motion makes it clear that he wished to leave as little to implication as possible. His motion of Sept. 14 may be understood in similar terms. In moving for a power of incorporation, he probably had internal improvements and perhaps another national bank primarily in mind. Suggestively, Rufus King argued that the grant was unnecessary, probably hinting that it was already implicit. Similarly, Gouverneur Morris suggested that the power to create a university, another of Madison's

desires, would be covered by the power over a seat of government. See Farrand, ed., *Records,* 2:324–325, 615. These maneuvers may be profitably considered in conjunction with Madison's remark in *Federalist,* No. 41, page 270, that every omission from the Constitution of grants of necessary powers would have become a ground for "necessary usurpations of power, every precedent of which is a germ of unnecessary and multiplied repetitions." See also *Federalist,* No. 42, page 280.

25. Farrand, ed., *Records,* 1:490.

26. On June 21, Dr. Johnson said that Hamilton "boldly and decisively contended for an abolition of the state governments," but that Wilson and Madison "wished to leave the States in possession of a considerable, tho' a subordinate jurisdiction" (ibid., 1:355). A more suggestive incident occurred in the Virginia ratifying convention. Speaking on June 19, George Mason said that certain clauses of the Constitution were *intended* to prepare the way for gradual subversion of the powers of the states. In an uncharacteristic breach of parliamentary decorum, Madison immediately broke in, demanding "an unequivocal explanation" of an insinuation that all the signers of the Constitution had preferred a consolidated national system. Mason insisted that many members of the convention *had* desired consolidation, but that Madison had "expressed himself against it" in a private conversation. Madison declared himself "satisfied," and Mason completed his speech (Elliot, ed., *Debates in the State Conventions,* 3:517–530). Hugh Blair Grigsby, whose *History of the Virginia Federal Convention of 1788 . . . ,* 2 vols. (Virginia Historical Society, *Collections,* 9–10 [Richmond, 1890–1891]), was based in part on oral information, was being overly dramatic when he wrote that Madison "demanded reparation in a tone that menaced an immediate call to the field" (1:97), but there can be no doubt that the framer sharply resented Mason's insinuation.

27. For an argument that Madison was a consistent strict constructionist throughout the 1780s, see Lance Banning, "James Madison and the Nationalists, 1780–1783," *WMQ,* 3d Ser., 40 (1983): 227–255. There and in "The Hamiltonian Madison: A Reconsideration," *Virginia Magazine of History and Biography* 92 (1984), 3–28, I suggest that recognition of his scrupulous respect for written constitutions is indispensable to reinterpretation of his conduct through the founding. Shortly before this essay was to go to the compositor, I encountered Michael P. Zuckert, "Federalism and the Founding: Toward a Reinterpretation of the Constitutional Convention," *Review of Politics* 48 (spring 1986): 166–210. Developed independently, this article makes several similar points about the limits of Madison's nationalism during the convention.

28. Irving Brant, *James Madison,* 6 vols. (Indianapolis, Ind., 1941–1961), vol. 3, chaps. 1–12, is the fullest and probably most influential discussion of Madison at the convention.

29. Ralph Ketcham, *James Madison: A Biography* (New York, 1971), 215, remarks that Madison's nationalism "reached its peak" in the weeks before the compromise. Irving Brant, *The Fourth President: A Life of James Madison* (Indianapolis, Ind., 1970),

170–174, argues that the Connecticut Compromise "affected at once his attitude toward federal powers."

30. See Randolph's remarks of July 16, Farrand, ed., *Records*, 2:17.

31. July 7, ibid., 1:551. Brant and others have seen these comments as foreshadowing a change of Madison's position.

32. This accords with Harold S. Schultz, *James Madison* (New York, 1970), 67–68, 73–74.

33. Madison's preconvention letters all indicate that he had yet to form any clear ideas about a proper executive. The Virginia Plan did not even decide whether the executive was to be a single person, and Madison recorded himself as entering the first day's debate on the subject only to suggest that a prior decision on executive powers might help decide the question (Farrand, ed., *Records*, 1:66–67). Rufus King's notes (ibid., 70) have Madison expressing a fear that large executive powers could produce "the Evils of elective Monarchies" and favoring an executive council from whose advice the head of the executive could depart only at his peril. Pierce's notes (ibid., 74) accord with King's.

34. Farrand, ed., *Records*, 2:80–81, 392. All of Madison's biographers have noted this effect, but it is also worth remarking that Madison retained a considerable suspicion of a strong executive. As late as Sept. 7, he supported a move to revive an executive council. He insisted on a provision for impeachment of the executive, urged that the judiciary be associated in the veto process, opposed an absolute veto, and moved to permit conclusion of treaties of peace without executive consent.

35. Ibid., 80–81.

36. There can be no doubt that his prediction that the system would not meet his objects (see n. 3 above) resulted mainly from his discontent about the Senate and his disappointment with the convention's refusal to adopt the federal veto on state laws.

37. See, particularly, *The Federalist* Nos. 39, 45, 62.

38. Elliot, ed., *Debates in the State Conventions*, 3:96, 408–409.

39. Wood, *Creation of the American Republic*, 526–532.

40. Note Madison's own undated, late-life recognition that there were few members "who did not change in the progress of discussions the opinions on important points which they carried into the Convention . . . Few who, at the close of the Convention, were not ready to admit this change as the enlightening effect of the discussions" (Farrand, ed., *Records*, 3:455). For other explicit statements that his views changed during the convention, see ibid., 497, 517, 521, 537.

41. I find suggestive a remark in a letter from Randolph: "I confess to you without reserve, that I feel great distrust of some of those, who will certainly be influential agents in the [new] government, and whom I suspect to be capable of making a wicked use of its defects. . . . I reverence Hamilton, because he was honest and open in his views," but "the management in some stages of the convention created a disgustful apprehension of the views of some particular characters" (Sept. 3, 1788, in Hutchinson et al., eds., *Papers of Madison*, 11:246–247).

42. Several of the most important hints are mentioned in the text and notes below. Explanation of some others would require a fuller study of proceedings in convention than can be provided in this space. But see n. 24 (above) for one important difference between Madison and two of his large-state allies. And note the biting wit with which he countered Morris's desire to leave the legislature free to apportion representation—condemning such implicit confidence in rulers, especially from one so strongly persuaded of "the political depravity of men" (Farrand, ed., *Records,* I, 584). Madison repeatedly objected to permitting legislative discretion in any case in which the legislators might have an interest distinct from the people's (e.g., ibid., 2:249–250). My conviction that he came to be increasingly concerned about the views of higher-flying nationalists depends to a significant degree on many indications of this sort that his extremist stand on making the central government effective was counterbalanced by a fear of making it too vigorous or freeing it too much from popular control. On issues that involved the latter question, he was on the moderate to democratic side in the convention.

43. Moreover, in the late-life writings, Madison was plainly trying both to serve as a dispassionate historian of the convention and to protect the Constitution from new threats. Concerned for the collective reputation of the framers, he spoke no ill of his dead colleagues and conscientiously attempted to give even Hamilton and Morris their full due. All of Madison's surviving writings, for that matter, are surprisingly free of aspersions on his political opponents.

44. To Jefferson, in Hutchinson et al., eds., *Papers of Madison,* 9:318.

45. Madison developed this concern most fully in his speech in convention on June 29 (Farrand, ed., *Records,* 1:464–465) and in *Federalist,* No. 41. But the argument that only an effective union could preserve the states from standing armies, overpowerful executives, swollen taxes, persistent public debts, and other consequences inconsistent with republican liberty was outlined in a speech to the Virginia legislature as early as Nov. 1785 (Hutchinson et al., eds., *Papers of Madison,* 8:431–432; see also 9:286, 294–295, 299, 318, 371).

46. It is seldom noted, but a fact, that Hamilton's speech of June 29, in which he insisted that "no Govern. could give us tranquility and happiness at home, which did not possess sufficient stability and strength to make respectable abroad" (Farrand, ed., *Records,* I, 467), immediately followed and was in part a *response* to Madison's most impassioned warning of the perils of overly energetic government.

47. When he informed Jefferson of the authorship of *The Federalist,* Madison declared that the authors "*are not mutually answerable for all the ideas of each other*" (Hutchinson et al., eds., *Papers of Madison,* 11:227). For a stronger statement—more suspect because it came later in life—see Elizabeth Fleet, ed., "Madison's Detached Memoranda," *WMQ,* 3d Ser., 3 (1946): 565. For another contemporary admission that some Federalists carried their alarm with the American majority too far, see Madison to Philip Mazzei, Dec. 10, 1788, in Hutchinson et al., eds., *Papers of Madison,* 11:389.

48. "Whatever . . . the opinions entertained in forming the Constitution, it was the duty of all to support it in its true meaning as understood *by the Nation* at the time of its ratification. No one felt this obligation more than I have done." Madison to J. G. Jackson, Dec. 27, 1821, in Farrand, ed., *Records,* 3:450.

49. I make this argument at greater length in "James Madison, the Statute for Religious Freedom, and the Crisis of Republican Convictions," paper delivered at the Bicentennial Conference on the Virginia Statute for Religious Freedom, Sept. 1985, Charlottesville, forthcoming in volume of proceedings from Cambridge University Press.

50. *Federalist,* No. 10, page 62.

51. Oct. 24, 1787, in Hutchinson et al., eds., *Papers of Madison,* 10:214.

52. "Vices of the Political System," ibid., 9:354–357.

53. *Federalist,* No. 10, pages 62–63.

54. Madison to Jefferson, Oct. 24, 1787, in Hutchinson et al., eds., *Papers of Madison,* 10:214.

55. *Federalist,* No. 51, page 349. See also "Vices of the Political System," in Hutchinson et al., eds., *Papers of Madison,* 9:357.

56. *Federalist,* No. 51, page 353.

57. Ibid., No. 10, page 56, No. 57, page 386.

58. Ibid., No. 51, page 351.

59. Ibid., No. 10, page 63.

60. Madison to Edmund Pendleton, Feb. 24, 1787, in Hutchinson et al., eds., *Papers of Madison,* 9:295.

PART 5

The First Party Conflict

If Lance Banning is best known for his study of James Madison, he first established his scholarly reputation as a close student of early American political thought and party politics. His revised dissertation became his award-winning first book, *The Jeffersonian Persuasion,* which remains in print today more than thirty-five years after its initial publication. While Banning's scholarly work went backward in time to the 1780s in his study on Madison, he never lost interest in, nor stopped thinking about, the issues and conflicts stemming from the world of politics and ideology in the 1790s and 1800s. He edited a collection of primary documents and another collection of readings, both on the first party conflict. And he still found new things to say about these established topics in his published scholarship.

These two selections show him at his best in providing a thoughtful examination of the role of political economy in the creation of the new government and the way that controversies over that role shaped so much of the conflict that followed. Banning carefully located a key element of the party conflict of the 1790s in the different visions of the country's future that were on display, if not yet recognized fully, in a 1783 dispute over congressional funding for the army. Starting with that controversy and working forward through the 1780s to the earliest years of the new federal government, Banning demonstrates how the great clashes that shaped the party conflict originated in different visions and goals. He further points out that the differences in vision between Madison and Hamilton were not yet fully developed during the 1780s, nor were they relevant or significant enough to interfere with their ability to collaborate to support the new Constitution in 1787–1788. Only with time, further reflection, and the addition of changed circumstances—Hamilton's unveiling, in his role as Treasury secretary through his great reports, of a full and mature articulation of his vision with the plans for achieving it—did Madison and others fully grasp the scope and dimensions of a program they found repugnant. In turn, Madison, Jefferson, and their allies responded to Hamilton by providing a full and mature articulation of a counter-vision and then proceeded to move into active opposition. Only by going to the past and analyzing earlier development, Banning suggests, can we make sense of the rapid rise of intense party competition in the 1790s—something that was wholly unanticipated at the time of the Constitution. And while he freely admits that disagreements over political economy were only a part of the much larger conflict, Banning makes a convincing case that because these economic issues cut so deeply, they were tremendously important. By better understanding those disputes over the proper political economy for a young federal republic, Banning suggests a way of gaining key insights into the storms that arose.

The second work here is a sweeping history of the Jeffersonian Democratic party, written for a book analyzing the history of the Democratic party on its bicentennial in 1992. In tracing the rise of the party in the 1790s as an opposition party and then following it into power after 1801, Banning found ways to summarize huge and disparate bodies of scholarship and engage in the scholarly disputes that arose while still providing a strong and clear narrative of events. Banning never forgot to get the history of events down first. In other words, although this chapter considers any number of historiographical, theoretical, and interpretive perspectives, Banning first took great care to tell the story of the past in a lucid and compelling way. While the previous essay focused on differences in political economy between the nascent Federalists and Democratic-Republicans, this essay broadens the focus to explore the other cultural, economic, ideological, domestic, and foreign policy arguments that gave rise to the first party system. Balancing considerations of ideology with a history of the politics of the age, careful not to offer simplistic interpretations of either, Banning constructs an analytical narrative of the rise of Jeffersonian opposition to the Hamiltonian program and the birth of party politics. Like in his writings on *The Federalist Papers* and the Constitutional Convention, he achieves great concision in his careful compression of a vast array of historical and historiographical material.

As points of entry into the changed and changing political landscape of the 1790s, both of these essays excel in orienting readers to the core questions and issues. For Banning himself, although he was returning in these 1990s publications to the subjects and themes of his own scholarship from two decades earlier, his writing here is clearly informed not only by his mature understanding of his own (and others') previous work, but also by careful reading and consideration of more recent scholarship and by his reflections on it all.

Political Economy and the Creation of the Federal Republic

As recently as 1980, there was little reason to expect a reinvigoration of intensive interest in the Founders' economic thinking. Federalist opinion, nearly everyone agreed, was socially conservative, yet strongly pro-developmental: determined to defend the rights of property, to create a national market, and to raise a legal framework in which private enterprise might thrive. Since 1980, much has changed, though we are just beginning to appreciate the implications. In the aftermath of a remarkable resurgence of intense investigation,[1] the enduring image of the Federalists as champions of economic liberty and growth (and of their foes as narrow-minded or heroic friends of agricultural and populistic values) has come to seem, not altogether wrong, but certainly too simple. A subtler understanding would insist that the creation of the federal republic did not represent the triumph of a single economic vision, which competed with a single Antifederalist perspective. Rather, it resulted from a temporary union of opposing views whose presence and development were central to the story of the rise and subsequent division of the movement which secured the Constitution.

The middle 1780s, recent scholarship suggests, witnessed a convergence in support of sweeping constitutional reform by men with quite distinctive views about the economic policies and circumstances necessary to secure a permanent foundation for the nation's freedom. Two conflicting visions of a sound political economy can be detected, in their embryonic forms, in a congressional dispute of 1783. Both were deeply rooted in the British thought and practice that were starting points for late-colonial opinion. Each, in different ways, expressed the highest aspirations of the Revolution. Though neither was articulated fully in the arguments of 1783—and their intrinsic incompatibility was barely glimpsed by their respective spokesmen at that time—both received a fuller formulation during the depression of the middle eighties, and both required a more effective federal system. Thus, the major architects and most impressive spokesmen for the two distinctive visions, James Madison (in his continual collaboration with Thomas Jefferson) and Alexander Hamilton (with early help from Robert Morris), were able to cooperate effectively in constitutional reform. The deepest differences between them were not among the topics which they needed to pursue in their impressive exegesis of the Constitution.

Still, for Madison and Hamilton alike, the Constitution was a means toward larger ends, not an end within itself; and shortly after its adoption, their conflicting wishes split the Federalists of 1789 into two clashing parties. Competing visions of political economy were not the only reasons for this split, but they were certainly among its most important causes. As Hamilton completed the articulation of his vision and attempted, piece by piece, to have it written into law, Madison and Jefferson responded with a more specific formulation of a program of their own. By 1792, the two conflicting visions were essentially mature; and although both would undergo important further evolution—partly in response to changing times and partly in response to other actors—the two competing programs were a central feature of political disputes until the War of 1812 produced a short-lived synthesis of elements of each. Popular opinions and the changing shape of popular divisions can be wrapped into a narrative which treats these clashing visions as essential elements of an extended argument about the founding of a liberal republic.[2]

I. Country, Court, and the Republican Revolution

In December 1782, in the midst of growing rumors that a peace agreement had been reached, a deputation from the continental army came to Philadelphia to seek immediate provision for the unpaid private troops and firm assurances from Congress that the continental officers would actually receive the peacetime pensions promised them two years before. Soon thereafter, believing that the final weeks of war might also prove the final opportunity for doing justice to the army, for restoring public credit, and for laying the foundations for the nation's post-war economic growth, Robert Morris, the Confederation's superintendent of finance, initiated an intense campaign for independent federal taxes. On 17 January, he told the deputation from the army that the funds for one month's pay could be provided by a final draft on overdrawn accounts abroad, but that additional provisions for the military and civilian creditors could not be made without approval of new taxes. Then, on 24 January, without preliminary warning, Morris threatened to resign in four months' time if no provision had been made by then for managing the federal obligations, declaring that he would not serve as "the minister of injustice." By February, when the news of a preliminary treaty was confirmed, rumblings from the army's winter camp at Newburgh were becoming truly ominous in tone; and at the seat of Congress, Morris's supporters, some of whom were widely feared to be intriguing with the army, were pressing for his program in an atmosphere of crisis. At the camp, the agitation culminated in anonymous addresses of 10 and 12 March, calling on the soldiers to refuse to be disbanded while their needs remained unmet.[3]

For Morris, the arrival of the deputation from the army was, at once, a reason and an opportunity for forcing the Confederation Congress to initiate a serious consideration of a sweeping program of reform. Since taking his position, in the spring of 1781, the superintendent had supplied the army as it marched to victory at Yorktown. He had instituted valuable administrative changes at the Office of Finance, secured creation of a national bank, and urged a settlement of the accounts between the central government and states as an initial step toward managing the public debt. But peace was not yet certain, and Rhode Island still refused to ratify the impost, a congressional request of 1781 for power to impose a modest tax on foreign imports. The states were greatly in arrears on their congressional requisitions, and the public creditors were growing ever more impatient for their pay. On 29 July 1782, Morris had delivered an important paper on the state of public credit, insisting that a whole new set of independent federal taxes would have to be combined with the receipts anticipated from the impost and from sales of western lands in order to meet current expenses and pay the interest on the debt. He recommended the addition of a land tax, a poll tax, and an excise. By fall, however, Congress had been able to agree on nothing more than further requisitions on the states.[4]

With the arrival of the deputation from the army, there was little room for long, additional delays. Congress hurriedly deputed a committee to travel to Rhode Island for a personal appeal for ratification of the impost. These delegates were barely on the road, on Christmas eve, when a humiliated Madison was forced to tell the fundless Congress that his own Virginia had rescinded its approval of the measure, destroying all remaining hope that this amendment would provide the answer to the army's pleas.[5] As Congress turned its full attention to provisions for the debt, some of Morris's supporters took his threatened resignation as a signal for a concentrated effort to enlist extra-congressional pressure for independent federal funds. Through most of February, Congress battled over Morris's proposals in an atmosphere of mounting crisis.[6]

By 28 January, when Madison assumed strategic leadership of the proponents of reform, its advocates were making modest progress. Even the Virginia delegation, which included three of Morris's most bitter foes, seemed willing to renew the recommendation of an impost; and Congress was proceeding toward a plan for commutation of the half-pay pensions, a compromise which continental officers were willing to accept in light of fixed republican hostility to lifetime grants. Still, many congressmen were willing to depart no further from the requisition system than was absolutely necessary to fulfill the federal obligations. Shortly after the receipt of news of the preliminary peace, John Rutledge (SC) and John Francis Mercer (VA) moved to apply the proceeds from a new impost (if this amendment should be ratified by all the states) exclusively to the debt due to the army. Madison helped to defeat this proposal on 18 February, only to be startled by a motion by Alexander Hamilton (NY) and James Wilson (PA), Morris's staunchest allies in the Congress, to open the deliberations to the public when the members were debating matters of finance. Sharing in the general dislike of this surprising motion, which was greeted by a quick adjournment, Madison asked his Pennsylvania colleagues to explain it. They replied that they had put themselves in a delicate position with their legislature by persuading it to drop its plans for a state assumption of a portion of the federal debt and only wanted their constituents to see that they were doing everything they could. "Perhaps the true reason," Madison suspected, was that they hoped that "public creditors, numerous and weighty in Philadelphia, would have an influence" from the galleries on the congressional proceedings.[7]

Congress had already heard one speech in which the brilliant but incautious Hamilton had urged an independent federal revenue on grounds that worried several members: "As the energy of the federal government was evidently short of the degree necessary for pervading and uniting the states, it was expedient to introduce the influence of officers deriving their emoluments from and consequently interested in supporting the power of Congress."[8] "This remark," wrote Madison, "was imprudent and injurious to the cause which it was meant to serve," since fears of just this sort of influence were among the most important reasons why the states resisted revenues that were to be collected by the officers of Congress. All the members most opposed to independent federal revenues had "smiled," Madison noted, "at the disclosure"; Arthur Lee and Theodorick Bland, two Virginia colleagues, told him privately that Hamilton "had let out the secret."[9] Now, the obvious attempt to throw the doors of Congress open to a potent lobby reenforced the gathering impression that several of the advocates of general funds were hoping that the army and the public creditors would join to pressure both the state and federal governments into a grant of independent general taxes. Madison himself was patently uneasy over what his allies seemed to have in mind.

At just this point, the pressure from the army neared its peak, encouraged, if not deliberately provoked, by some of the Philadelphia advocates of general funds. On the morning after Hamilton's attempt to open the debates, with congressmen referring openly to pressure from the army, Rutledge renewed the motion to appropriate the impost exclusively to the soldiers' needs. Hamilton again denounced "such a partial dispensation of justice," suggesting that "it was impolitic to divide the interests of the civil and military creditors, whose joint efforts in the states would be necessary to prevail on them to adopt a general revenue." Wilson seconded the young New Yorker, adding that "by dividing the interest of the civil from that of the military creditors provision for the latter would be frustrated." But Virginia's Mercer still opposed "a permanent debt supported by a permanent and general revenue." He believed that "it would be good policy to separate instead of cementing the interest of the army and the other public creditors."[10]

On the following evening, 20 February—after another day of angry debates—Madison and several others went to dinner at the home of Congressman Thomas FitzSimons. Here, Hamilton and Richard Peters, former officers whose military contacts kept them well informed about conditions in the camp, told the gathering that it was certain that the army had decided not to put away its arms until its just demands were met. A public manifesto, they revealed, would be forthcoming soon, and "plans had been agitated if not formed for subsisting themselves after such a declaration." General Washington, the two ex-officers announced, had come to be "extremely unpopular among almost all ranks from his known dislike to any unlawful proceeding," and "many leading characters" were working to replace him with the more compliant Horatio Gates. Hamilton had written the commander, he reported, in order to alert him to these schemes, urging him to lead the army in any plans for redress, "that they might be moderated."[11]

Why Hamilton and Peters chose to make these revelations at this moment is impossible to know. Perhaps the course of conversation simply led them to divulge their latest information. For if they wanted to intensify the pressure for new taxes, the strategy could not have been more misconceived. With only Hamilton dissenting, the gathering agreed that Congress was unlikely to approve any general revenues except the impost, and several of the diners seem to have concluded that the temper of the army would permit no more delay.

For Madison, there is no doubt, the dinner at FitzSimons's home was a critical event. On the morrow, he was on his feet again in Congress for a speech in which he still defended general revenues as consistent with "the principles of liberty and the spirit of the constitution." Now, however, he "particularly disclaimed the idea of perpetuating a public debt," and he admitted that he was convinced that Congress would be forced to limit its recommendations to the impost and a "call for the deficiency in the most permanent way that could be reconciled with a revenue established within each state separately and appropriated to the common treasury."[12] Before this speech, Madison had worked in close cooperation with the financier and his congressional spokesmen. From this point forward, he was bent upon a compromise of which they disapproved. On 26 February, he outlined a proposal that he hoped would end the crisis, together with a list of the responses he expected from each state.[13] By early April he believed that his proposals, reported from committee on 6 March, would be substantially approved. They were, indeed, accepted in amended form on 18 April 1783, and Madison was asked to draft an explanation to the states. Already, on 22 March, Congress had received George Washington's report on the collapse of the conspiracy at camp.[14]

Madison's departure from the other advocates of general revenues has usually been seen, when it is mentioned, as a simple consequence of his conclusion that nothing but a compromise could end an urgent crisis. More was certainly involved. In the first place, the Virginian's plan of 26 February was not intended merely to provide as permanent a fund for managing the debt as Congress and the states seemed likely to approve. Madison intended something much more comprehensive. Congress would renew its call for power to impose an impost. This amendment to the Articles, together with additional, though individual, state appropriations for the debt, would be combined with several lesser measures meant to put an end to nearly all of the recurring conflicts that had troubled Madison throughout his years in Congress, ranging landed states against the landless, small against the large, the South against New England. This was not the quickest or the simplest way to counteract the pressure from the army, but Madison believed that it might be the surest way to guarantee that all the public creditors would actually receive their dues. And he was seeking, now, not only to avert a national disgrace, not only to conciliate the soldiers, but also to repair the fundamental fractures that appeared increasingly to threaten the very survival of the union.[15]

The long and often bitter argument about the funding of the debt had sharpened nearly all of the divisions that had marked the Continental Congress through the last three years. Sectional disputes about apportioning the obligations of the states were older than the separation from Great Britain. Any general tax—and almost any mixture of a set of general taxes with an impost—still appeared to threaten unfair burdens. Jealousies between the landed and the landless states had been intensified again by news of the preliminary peace, in which America had won the West and a potential treasure-house of future revenues before Virginia and the other landed states had completed their western cessions. Moreover, the debates had made it evident that Morris and his allies aimed at something vastly broader than a firm provision for the debt; and Madison, beginning with his speech of 21 February, had quite deliberately tried to disassociate himself from Hamilton's suggestion that a funded debt could be a useful tool for strengthening the union. While he was still convinced that funding and a commutation of the half-pay pensions could not be less consistent with "our republican character and constitutions than a violation of good faith and common honesty," he insisted that he "was as much opposed to perpetuating the public burdens as anyone" in Congress.[16] He would thus concur "in every arrangement that should appear necessary for an honorable and just fulfillment of the public engagements and in no measure tending to augment the power of Congress which should appear unnecessary."[17] Madison was out of sympathy by now, not only with the tactics, but also with the ultimate objectives of Hamilton, Wilson, and Morris. As some of their opponents had suggested, those objectives seemed to squint at a conception of the future which was much at odds with many revolutionaries' thoughts about the sort of nation the United States should be.

Morris's July report had advocated general revenues that would be adequate to meet the ordinary operating costs of Congress as well as to assure the steady payment of the interest on the debt. These revenues would be collected by the officers of Congress, and they would be conterminous with the existence of the federal obligations. Though Madison insisted that such revenues accorded with "the spirit" of the Articles of Union—they would make "the federal constitution" more "efficient"—he was also perfectly aware that independent federal taxes would entail a fundamental change in the relationship between the central government and states.[18] This alteration of the federal balance was precisely what opponents disapproved, and it was just what

Morris, Hamilton, and Wilson found so difficult to relinquish. It was this that Madison first favored, then abandoned in his speech of 21 February. But he did not surrender it because he was inherently more pliable than many of his allies. He gave it up because it did not seem to him, as it did to many of them, an object worth the risks it came to entail. He gave it up because it had become apparent that the other advocates of general funds had motives and objectives he had never really shared.[19]

All of the original supporters of independent general funds regarded a dependable federal revenue as essential to the restoration of public credit and possibly to the continuation of the union. All of them regarded steady payment of the interest on the debt as a critical test of national character and an indispensable security against the day when it might be necessary to borrow again. Not all of them, however, actually wished to see the debt retired, nor did Morris's plan provide for payment of the principal as well as of the interest. Congressional opponents noticed this when they condemned a "permanent" or "perpetual" debt, and historians increasingly agree that several of the advocates of general funds were looking consciously beyond the reestablishment of public credit toward a funding plan that would promote the nation's post-war growth and foster a particular variety of political centralization. Properly funded, as Morris said in his report, the mass of "dead" certificates of debt (or paper promises too poorly backed to be exchanged on private markets) would rise in value, become "a sufficient circulating medium" for the country, and provide the capital for more intensive economic development.[20] Simultaneously, the obligations of the federal government would become a new "cement" of union. Looking to Congress rather than the states for their salaries, pensions, or other claims, civilian creditors, the discharged soldiers, and the officers appointed to collect federal taxes would join with merchants doing business with the national bank to "unite the several states more closely together in one general money connection." They would "give stability to government" by combining in its support.[21]

Hamilton, like Morris, had been thinking in this fashion for some years. His private correspondence and his anonymous newspaper series, "The Continentalist," had repeatedly insisted on the need to create among the nation's leadership a class of influentials tied to the federal government and capable of counterbalancing the influentials currently tied to the states. As he conceived it, an enduring and effective central government required the union of the general government's resources with those of a monied and officeholding class directly dependent on that government for the promotion of its economic interests.[22]

The implications of this thinking can be understood more clearly, in the light of recent scholarship, than was the case as recently as 1980. So can its opponents' reasons for alarm. Remembering the history of England in the decades following the Glorious Revolution of 1689, Hamilton and Morris and perhaps some other economic nationalists were thinking of a replication of Great Britain's path to national stability and greatness. They were thinking of combining certain segments of America's elite into a single interest intimately tied by fortune and ambition to the infant federal regime, much as standard histories said that the ministers of William III had once successfully created a "monied interest" loyal to the new succession and capable of counterbalancing the Tory gentry. It is not, in fact, a gross exaggeration to suggest that these American reformers hoped to use the national debt to build a single nation—or at least to forge a single national elite—where none was really present in 1783. They envisioned the emergence in America of a facsimile of those related interests—government, the military, commerce, and finance—which ordinarily united in support of British ministries and lent stability to that familiar system: interests that the English had in mind when they referred in general terms to the forces supporting the "court."[23] Imagining a national greatness predicated on an imitation of the economic and financial strengths of England, Hamilton and Morris were prepared to risk some further clamors from the army, if not to feed the agitation, for the sake of general funds. But Madison, who was preoccupied with the defense of a republican revolution—and who would never see Great Britain as a proper model for the new United States—was not. Although he did not quarrel with Morris's supporters or join with Rutledge, Lee, and Mercer, he knew what he implied when he deliberately disclaimed a desire to perpetuate the national debt.

Madison was not less continental-minded than the other advocates of general taxes. Educated at the College of New Jersey, he had been accustomed since his youth to thinking of the Revolution as a national movement, and the years in Congress had intensified these feelings.[24] Yet Madison had come to Congress deeply influenced by the thinking of the early Revolution, which itself was deeply influenced by a hundred years of strident criticisms of the eighteenth-century British system of administration and finance. By the seventh decade of the century, when trouble with the colonies began, condemnations of this system had become a standard tool for understanding an enormous range of national ills. And many of the most destructive of these evils seemed to have been born with the financial innovations introduced by the creators of the Modern Whig regime.[25]

Beginning in the middle 1690s, England had developed an unprecedented method of financing its involvement in recurring European wars. Central to this system was a firm commitment of specific revenues for steady payment of the interest on the national debt, together with a sinking fund which could be used for its retirement during peacetime. Tightly interwoven with this funding system were the Bank of England and the other chartered corporations, which purchased vast amounts of government certificates of debt in exchange for their exclusive right to certain sorts of trade.[26] Credit was the key to eighteenth-century warfare, and the new financial structure made it possible for tiny England to compete successfully with France in four great wars for empire. Thus, to Modern Whig defenders, the financial system seemed the very crux of national stability and international prestige.[27] But to the critics of its managers and builders—managers like Robert Walpole—the financial system seemed a vast, deliberate addition to the instruments of influence and corruption that were driving England rapidly to ruin.

British opposition thought was not intrinsically inimical to commerce, manufacturing, or liquid forms of wealth. Several of the greatest opposition writers were spokesmen for the city and its interests.[28] Yet eighteenth-century thinkers were as conscious of the new finance as of the growth of commerce strictly speaking, and opposition thinking started from a set of neoclassical assumptions that had been imported into English thought by Harrington and other thinkers of the Interregnum: that power follows property, that great extremes of poverty and wealth are incompatible with freedom, and that only those who live upon their own and do not owe their livelihoods to others are the masters of themselves and capable of virtuous participation in a healthy public life.[29] On all these counts, the new financial system and its creatures seemed inherently corrupt. Like parliamentary placemen, public pensioners, or representatives of rotten boroughs, dealers in the public funds or owners of the stock of chartered corporations were dependent on the treasury for their support. Their economic interests chained them to the will of an executive whose aims were always different from, and often hostile to, the will and interests of the body of the freemen. In Parliament, the tools of grasping ministers subverted legislative independence. Out of Parliament, the unearned wealth of creatures of the new finance spread habits of dishonesty, subservience, and waste to every corner of the kingdom. And while the placemen and the "monied interests" fattened on the public spoils, independent farmers, artisans, and tradesmen were impoverished by high taxation and demoralized by the example of the great. Under such conditions, the survival of the nation's ancient freedom seemed increasingly in doubt.

For colonials, it now seems clear, opposition accusations offered a compelling explanation of the crisis which impelled them into independence. Indeed,
to a remarkable extent, the early revolutionaries tended to define their hopes
and character as a distinctive people by contrasting their republican experiments with what the opposition writers said was wrong with eighteenth-
century Britain. America *meant* virtue rather than corruption, vigor rather
than decay. It meant a pleasing mediocrity of fortunes, citizens who lived
upon their own resources, freemen who could fight or vote according to their
own autonomous desires. It meant, in short, whatever seemed to have been
lost with the appearance of the eighteenth-century system of administration
and finance.[30]

Experience, of course, produced a certain disenchantment. Gouging,
hoarding, and a growing weariness of war reminded everyone that even
staunch republicans were human. In order to defeat the British, the militia
had to be supported by a continental army. By the time the war was won, the
powers of the central government were widely recognized to be unequal to its
tasks. Still, the dream was stronger than the disenchantment, and the recol-
lection of the evils of the old regime was too intense for many to be willing to
abide its reconstruction, even in the most attenuated form.

By 1783, a handful of the strongest continentalists believed that national
ills were so intractable that they demanded thoroughgoing reconstruction of
the current federal system.[31] Madison, like the majority in Congress, was not
prepared for a solution so extreme.[32] Though he was willing, unlike Lee or
Mercer, to accept a centralizing change, he did not regard this as a principal
objective in itself. He was willing to approve an alteration of the federal balance, but only in the sense and only to the point that he conceived it necessary for the preservation of the union; and this was not the least because he
shared the critics' fears that certain federal measures might prove incompatible with what he called the "spirit" or the "principles" of a republican revolution. Thus, he carefully distinguished his desires from Hamilton's suggestion
that a funding system might be used to foster national integration, to create
what foes of Morris's proposals saw as a corrupting link between the government and officeholding and financial interests. Although he shared the
economic nationalists' desire to reestablish public credit, Madison could not
accept a program meant "to achieve political centralization by fiscal reform."[33]
He did not articulate a systematic explanation of his disagreement with the
other advocates of funding. This would await developments after 1789, when
Hamilton's desires became the basis for a more specific program. It would
require a further evolution of Madison's own views. By 1783, experience had

taught him that congressional reliance on the states for revenues endangered both the character and the harmony of the Confederation. But he had yet to formulate a positive economic program of his own—a program incompatible, in many of its objects and assumptions, with the economic changes that Hamilton and Morris wanted to promote.

II. Commerce, Manufactures, Agriculture, and the Constitution

As the British army left New York, a new invasion was arriving. Merchants bringing British goods, on British credit, rushed to reestablish the connections broken by the war. American consumers, unsupplied for years, greeted the arriving ships with open arms and purses; the deficit in trade with Britain in the three years after the conclusion of the peace was more than £5,000,000.[34] Excluded from their most productive pre-war markets, native merchants were unable to correct this huge imbalance. Specie poured from the United States to cover the commercial obligations, but the wartime hoard was insufficient to prevent a crisis. As American importers struggled to repay their loans, pressing smaller debtors in their turn, the country entered a severe contraction.

The depth, duration, and extent of this depression have been matters for dispute, but recent findings generally suggest that it was sharper, longer, and more general than used to be believed. A downturn started in the fall of 1783 and lasted for at least two years. The impact and duration of the troubles varied greatly in the different economic regions. Suffering was slightest in the Chesapeake and greatest in New England and the lower South. Still, all along the seaboard, merchants failed, debtors were distressed, and seamen, artisans, and shipyard workers suffered unemployment. In all the northern cities, there was growing pressure for protection. Everywhere, attention focused with new urgency upon the economic needs and promises of independence.[35]

At the beginning of the war, when Congress threw American commerce open to the world, the economic vistas opened by the end of old restrictions had seemed as boundless as the prospects for political reform. Economic liberty would complement and be supported by republican ideals. America's example of free trade would revolutionize the world and bring unparalleled prosperity at home. Few other principles acquired such axiomatic status early in the Revolution. None was challenged more severely with the peace. On 2 July 1783, Orders in Council closed the British West Indies to American shippers and barred the importation there of much American produce, including salted meats and fish. Other British regulations barred the vessels of one state from bringing in the products of another, prohibited the importation into Britain of whale oil, fish, and meat, and placed prohibitive duties on American grain. Without protection from the British, the Mediterranean trade became an easy prey for pirates. Finally, in 1784, the Spanish masters of Louisiana prohibited Americans from trading down the Mississippi.[36]

The newly independent states attempted to alleviate their citizens' distress. Seven issued paper money. Eight imposed retaliatory duties on British ships or goods.[37] But states attempting separate actions of this sort were commonly defeated by the inconsistent regulations of their neighbors, paper money fell disastrously in North Carolina and Rhode Island, and American commissioners in Europe made almost no progress in their efforts to negotiate commercial treaties. By the middle of the decade, in the midst of rising animosities among the several states, sentiment was moving overwhelmingly toward granting Congress power over trade. At least in northern cities, it was also moving unmistakably toward new support for economic changes and commercial policies that early-Revolutionary thought had generally condemned.

The early-Revolutionary doctrine of free trade had nicely managed a profound, traditional ambivalence concerning commerce, which was well expressed in Adam Smith's *The Wealth of Nations,* published in the very year of independence.[38] On the one hand, commerce seemed to nearly all enlightened eighteenth-century thinkers an improving, civilizing force, the single feature which distinguished modern Europe most decisively from its medieval past and made it possible for moderns to surpass the comforts and achievements of the ancients. Carrying the bountiful productions of a modern specialization of labor, commerce softened manners, favored the refinement of the arts, promoted peaceful international relations, and supported larger populations at a higher level of material wellbeing than had any ancient civilization.[39] On these grounds, a few of its proponents carried their enthusiasm to the point of arguing that even private vices, such as selfishness and greed, promoted the collective good.[40] More commonly, however, as was true of Smith, enlightened thinkers recognized that growing commerce also had its costs. As nations moved from savagery through agriculture to the most advanced commercialization, the benefits to individuals proved dangerously unequal. Idleness and enervating luxury appeared among the rich, and independent craftsmen were replaced, as work was subdivided to its most productive point, by laborers whose narrow lives and straitened circumstances rendered them unfit as citizens or soldiers.[41] Among the British, not surprisingly, a humanistic condemnation of the growing role of commerce tended to be most pronounced among opponents of the oligarchic system of administration and finance, which favored foreign trade and manufacturing for export. Celebration of the benefits of commerce tended to be least restrained among the Modern Whig defenders of the mercantilistic system. Arguments for natural economic growth and unrestricted international exchange were something of a mean between these more extreme positions. Certainly, to Smith and to Americans alike, the "natural" policy appeared to be ideal for thriving, mostly agricultural societies that wanted the advantages of commerce, but without its social costs.[42]

Early in the Revolution, the dividing line between a civilized society and a debilitated one seemed relatively clear. Mills and shops and trading ships were not a threat to freedom. Indeed, increased domestic manufacturing of more of the necessities of life could lessen the dependence on expensive imports and promote republican simplicity and thrift, while growing native commerce would exchange America's extractive surplus for more of the amenities of life. The social fabric would be threatened only as the population grew so dense that there was no alternative to more intensive change or if the nation forced itself into a premature old age by following the mercantilistic policies of Europe.

In the post-war slump, the line began to blur. Hamilton had verged on heresy in 1782, when he denounced the "speculative" doctrine of free trade and argued that the policy of all enlightened nations was to keep the balance on their side.[43] But by the middle of the decade, nearly everyone agreed that the United States could not pursue free trade in the face of universal mercantile restrictions, and that only by united measures could the situation be improved. By then, moreover, there was growing sentiment for policies of just the sort that Hamilton had recommended in 1782, policies toward which the economic nationalists had glanced in the congressional debates of 1783.

Two changes were especially apparent. The stronger was a more insistent argument for native manufactures. Domestic manufacturing of coarser, simpler goods—from nails to homespun clothing—had long been seen as necessary to reduce dependence on expensive imports or even to produce necessities of war. Now, the advocates of manufactures added further arguments for their importance. The growth of native manufactures might provide alternative employment for the seamen, fishermen, and dockyard workers who were suffering from the collapse of foreign trade. It might enlarge the native market for the farmers whose commodities could not be shipped abroad. It might provide new objects for investors. Everywhere, as independence fostered new attention to the opportunities at home, there was a rising interest in improving roads and rivers and in building new canals. Some easterners were even thinking of the markets that would rise beyond the Alleghenies. Thus, the argument for manufactures looked increasingly beyond the current troubles toward the opportunities that their development might hold—even, it occurred, for foreign export.[44] And, with that, the case for manufactures could be fitted into a progressive, pro-developmental vision which had had few public advocates ten years before. The emergence of this pro-developmental vision was the second change encouraged by the economic troubles.

Like the argument for manufactures, uninhibited insistence on the benefits of an expanding oceanic commerce started with the postwar slump. As the depression deepened, prices fell, and specie disappeared, many revolutionaries blamed undisciplined consumers, who were running into debt and risking their autonomy by buying foreign luxuries on credit. In response, a scattering of voices blasted atavistic fears that commerce was inherently corrupting.[45] A few dispensed entirely with the old ambivalence and offered an unqualified defense of manufacturing and commerce in their highest forms, urging policies that would encourage rapid growth and arguing that even the pursuit of luxuries would further the collective good.[46]

The rise of pro-developmental sentiment was marked, and most of it supported federal reform. Indeed, until quite recently, the link between the two seemed so apparent that even those who disagreed most strongly with the Beardian interpretation of the Constitution did not doubt that constitutional reform was partly an expression of an enterprising, pro-developmental movement. Of all the forces pushing toward reform, none was stronger than the movement for a federal power over commerce. At the Federal Convention, the determination of the delegates to make America a single market—and to make that market safe for private property and private contracts—seems beyond dispute. And it has long been clear that in the contest over the adoption of the Constitution, coastal regions and the urban and commercial centers favored the reform more strongly than did the inland regions and the farmers who were less involved in raising crops for market.[47]

But visions of American development could come in a variety of forms; and recent scholarship has strongly challenged the convention which conflates these forms into a single, modernizing movement. Pro-developmental interests did support the Constitution, but it is by no means clear that all of the progressive and dynamic economic interests favored the reform.[48] And it is certain that the single most important architect of change supported it for very different reasons. For Madison, in fact, a more effective federal system was intended to *forestall* the very economic changes which a number of his allies wanted to promote.

Madison was not an early advocate of federal authority to regulate the nation's commerce. In 1781, he helped defeat a motion to amend the Articles to this effect.[49] As late as the spring of 1783, he was reluctant even to proceed with a commercial treaty with Great Britain, fearing that a pact, though eagerly desired by northern shippers, could be purchased only with concessions that would sacrifice the basic interests of the planting states.[50] Soon, however, Madison's ideas began to change. In August 1783, as he was finishing his term in Congress, he read the earl of Sheffield's *Observations on the Commerce of the American States,* which argued that Great Britain could maintain its dominant position in the trade with the United States without dismantling its restrictive navigation system.[51] By autumn, he had seen the British proclamation of July, which confined American commerce with the West Indies to British bottoms.[52] In 1784 and 1785, as the depression deepened and the states attempted futilely to counteract the British domination of their trade, Madison became increasingly committed to a federal power of retaliation.[53] Indeed, the inability of the confederated states to grapple separately with European regulations, their failure to achieve unanimous consent to federal supervision, the mutual animosities resulting from their separate legislation, and the "vicious" measures most of them pursued in order to relieve their citizens' distress were certainly the most compelling reasons for his new conclusion that nothing short of a complete reconstitution of the federal system could preserve the union and the Revolution.

To Madison, as to the great majority of revolutionary thinkers, the viability of the American experiment in popular self-governance depended on the moral fiber of the people. This, in turn, depended heavily on the conditions of their economic life, which would be prosperous or poor in close relationship to their ability to find sufficient outlets for the products of their work. Most Americans—and almost all Virginians—were agricultural producers; and as long as this was so, they either had to trade their surplus for foreign goods, stop buying foreign imports (and lapse into a primitive, subsistence mode of life), or risk their personal and even national independence by going ever deeper into debt. Lacking markets for their products, citizens could be demoralized by idleness, indebtedness, or want; and a demoralized majority could mean no end of trouble for a fragile, new republic.[54] "Most of our political evils," Madison was coming to believe—paper money, moratoriums on taxes, and laws protecting citizens from private suits for debt—"may be traced up to our commercial ones, as most of our moral may to our political."[55] Ideally, he wrote, he favored "perfect freedom" of commerce. "But before such a system will be eligible perhaps for the United States . . . all the other nations must concur." British policy especially, he pointed out, excluded American merchants from "the channels without which our trade with them must be a losing one." But how was a redress to be "extorted"? "Only by harmony in the measures of the states." Acting individually, the states could not compel the Europeans to relax their navigation laws, any more than they could "separately carry on war or separately form treaties of alliance or commerce." Thus, in 1785, when Congress proved unable to agree on a request for federal power over trade, Madison responded with his earliest admission that the crisis might require more drastic measures—even a complete replacement of the current Congress by a "medium" which might inspire more trust.[56] A few months later, when he proved unable to persuade Virginia's legislature to instruct its delegates to move again in Congress for a power to retaliate against the Europeans, he helped revive the resolution which initiated the Annapolis Convention and the course of extra-legal action leading to the Constitution.[57]

The story from this point is widely known. Responding to Virginia's call for a convention to consider better means of regulating interstate and foreign trade, delegates from Delaware, New Jersey, and Virginia, joined by one commissioner from Pennsylvania and two from New York, gathered at Annapolis early in September 1786. Though others were en route, the dozen members present waited seven days beyond the date appointed for the meeting. Then, confronted with the possibility of total failure, they unanimously agreed to turn their disappointment into yet another evidence of the necessity for bolder action, calling for a second general convention which would be empowered to consider *all* the defects of the current constitution. Spurred by Shays's Rebellion, which culminated during the succeeding months, every state except Rhode Island answered their appeal.[58]

The decision at Annapolis was once portrayed as something of a coup. A handful of committed continentalists, it was remarked, declined to wait for the arrival of the delegations from New England and recommended a procedure that could only speed the obvious decline in the authority of Congress. In fact, however, these reformers acted more in desperation than in confidence that their proposal would succeed; and careful reconstruction of the context of their resolution, which is not so well remembered as the act itself, is critical to understanding their decision. Although the fact is seldom emphasized as strongly as it should be, the Annapolis Convention met in the immediate aftermath of the most explosive sectional crisis of the Confederation years—a crisis which encompassed and exacerbated all of Madison's concerns and turned his thoughts in earnest toward the sweeping federal reforms that Hamilton had been encouraging for years.

Even at the darkest moments of the Revolutionary War, when British armies threatened Richmond and controlled two southern states, Madison had doggedly resisted motions to forgo American insistence on a right to navigate the Mississippi River if this sacrifice proved necessary to conclude a wartime pact with Spain.[59] Happily, as he conceived it, the United States did not complete a treaty of alliance with the Spanish, and Congress reinserted its insistence on a right to navigate the Mississippi in its new instructions for a post-war treaty. Still, Madison maintained an anxious watch on these negotiations. As Kentucky moved toward separation from Virginia and depression deepened in the East, the West loomed ever larger in his vision. When the masters of Louisiana closed the river to Americans in 1784, he urged both Jefferson and Lafayette to seek French intercession. The stakes, as he explained them to these friends, can help us understand the depth of his alarm when the depression influenced a majority in Congress, on the eve of the Annapolis Convention, once again to consider a surrender of this claim.

Madison had formed a special bond with Lafayette soon after learning of the closure of the river, joining the marquis for an adventure to the Iroquois negotiations on the Mohawk. If he spoke as freely to the Frenchman as he claimed, he probably repeated much of what he wrote to Jefferson before departing from Virginia. He could not believe, he said, that Spain could "be so mad as to persist" in policies that might "delay" the navigation of the Mississippi but could no more stop it, finally, "than she can stop [the current of] the river itself." The law of nations, human rights, and natural justice—all of which were "every day deriving weight from the progress of philosophy and civilization"—all suggested that the owners of a river's mouth might levy tolls on the inhabitants above, but had no right to bar their trade completely. These and other arguments, he thought, should influence France—and all of Europe—to support an open Mississippi. Certainly, they can reveal to us how indispensable the westward movement was to all of Madison's own ambitions for the nation. "By this expansion of our people," he believed, the growth of native manufactures would be long postponed, American demand for European imports would continually increase, and the production of the agricultural commodities that the United States would trade for European manufactures would continually expand. "Reverse the case," he argued, "and suppose the use of the Mississippi denied to us, and the consequence is that

many of our supernumerary hands who in the former case would [be] husbandmen on the waters of the Mississippi will on this other supposition be
manufacturers on this [side] of the Atlantic; and even those who may not be
discouraged from seating the vacant lands will be obliged by the want of vent
for the produce of the soil and of the means of purchasing foreign manufactures, to manufacture in a great measure for themselves."[60]

Many easterners, it should be noted, feared the emigration to the West
for just the reasons Madison touched on in this passage. Madison was thoroughly familiar with their thinking, deleting from the finished letter an
admission that "the only sufferers" from westward emigration would be
those who would "remain in the Atlantic states." The westward movement, he
conceded, contributed to the depopulation of the eastern states, to the depreciation of their lands, and to their slowness in developing the naval strength
"which must be their only safety in case of war."[61] Still, he never wavered in his
course. When Lafayette returned to France and wrote that many of his correspondents in Virginia (probably including Washington himself) seemed far
from eager for an open Mississippi, Madison replied that Lafayette was right
to count him "out" of those who reasoned on "very narrow and very delusive
foundations." He emphasized again that Europe had a choice between a mari-
time and manufacturing United States and growing commerce with its farmers. He warned again that the American affection for its major European ally
could be threatened if it seemed that France supported Spain.[62]

Something very like a sense of providential purpose was involved in
Madison's conception of the West. He calculated that the westward movement would increase the numbers and prosperity of all mankind. He saw the
West as a frontier for all of Western Europe, as well as for the seaboard states,
and he insisted that the Mississippi was the outlet "nature" had intended for
its produce. It mattered, to his mind, that acquiescence in the closure of the
river would be "treason" to these natural "laws."[63] It mattered, too, of course,
that the ability of the Confederation to retire the public debt was universally believed to be dependent on the value of the western lands. By themselves, however, none of these considerations seems entirely to account for
the intensity of Madison's commitment. A fuller explanation must incorporate the depth of his fraternal feelings for the westerners themselves, along
with his conviction that beyond the mountains immigrants from all of the
Atlantic states would meet and mingle and become a single people, forming
new communities to which the older ones would each be bound more tightly,
by "the ties of friendship, of marriage and consanguinity," than any of them
were to one another. "On the branches of the Mississippi," he explained to

Lafayette, there would develop not "distinct societies" but "only an expansion of the same one," not "a hostile or a foreign people" but a people who would more and more be seen as "bone of our bones, and flesh of our flesh," a people whose essential interests merited the same consideration as those of any other portion of the union.[64] A fuller explanation must return, as well, to his repeated warnings that the closure of the Mississippi could compel the West and East alike to turn from agriculture to intensive manufactures.

Madison's resistance to a turn toward manufactures may appear surprising, for there is nothing more ubiquitous in modern writings on his thought than the assertion that he was an advocate of "multiplying interests" in "an extended commercial republic."[65] Not, it seems apparent, if we are to judge by his position on the Mississippi. Here, he quite deliberately rejected much of what this language usually implies.[66] Madison agreed with the contemporary advocates of manufactures that rapid emigration to the West retarded more intensive economic change, but he supported it, in part, *precisely for this reason*. As Drew McCoy has argued, the Virginian hoped that the United States would long continue at a "middle level" of development. He dreaded the progression to the "higher" economic stage that others wanted to encourage.[67]

Madison was not an enemy of commerce—not, at least, if "commerce" meant the civilizing, comfort-raising benefits of trade, which he was doing everything within his power to encourage. But growing commerce had a second set of implications in contemporary thinking. It could also mean intensive economic change: the transformation of a largely agricultural economy into an urban, manufacturing society that could produce and even export many of the niceties and luxuries of life. And Madison, like Jefferson, responded with revulsion to the notion that the nation ought to move as rapidly as possible in this direction. Both of the Virginians knew that most Americans enjoyed a level of material prosperity that was the envy of the most "advanced" economies in Europe. Both were deeply influenced by those countervailing strands in eighteenth-century thought which warned that the transition to a manufacturing or heavily commercialized economy could render a society incapable of freedom.

It was Jefferson, of course, with his supreme ability to dress received ideas in gifted prose, who had reduced the argument to memorable phrases:

> Those who labor in the earth are the chosen people of God, if ever he had a chosen people, whose breasts he has made his peculiar deposit for substantial and genuine virtue . . . Generally speaking, the proportion which the aggregate of the other classes of citizens

bears in any state to that of its husbandmen is the proportion of
its unsound to its healthy parts, and is a good enough barometer
whereby to measure its degree of corruption. While we have land to
labor then, let us never wish to see our citizens occupied at a workbench or twirling a distaff. Carpenters, masons, smiths are wanted
in husbandry; but for the general operations of manufacture, let our
workshops remain in Europe . . . The loss by the transportation of
commodities across the Atlantic will be made up in happiness and
permanence of government. The mobs of great cities add just so
much to the support of pure government as sores do to the strength
of the human body. It is the manners and spirit of a people which
preserve a republic in vigor.[68]

Not until the early months of 1792 would Madison prepare a full equivalent
to Jefferson's discussion of the proper population for republics.[69] And yet, if
there is any doubt that the ideas expressed in 1792 already influenced his
position of the middle eighties, this should be dispelled by the reflections he
articulated in response to Jefferson's emotional denunciation of the poverty
encountered on a trip through rural France.

Jefferson attributed the "wretchedness" of the majority in France to the
excessive concentration of its landed property in great estates. Remarking
that "the earth is given as a common stock for man" and that the combination of uncultivated lands and massive unemployment was a violation of
this natural law, he recommended legislation like his own attacks on primo-
geniture and entail in Virginia, laws that would work gradually to level individual fortunes.[70] Madison's response probed deeper. "I have no doubt," he
wrote, "that the misery of the lower classes will be found to abate wherever
the government assumes a freer aspect and the laws favor a subdivision of
property." Still, the greater comfort of the mass of people in the new American republics was as much a product of their smaller populations as it was
of the "political advantages" received. "A certain degree of misery," he feared,
might be inevitable in countries "fully peopled." For wherever this was so, a
fraction of the people would suffice to raise a mighty surfeit of "subsistence,"
and there would still remain a greater number of inhabitants "by far" than
would be necessary to produce all of the other needs and even comforts of
existence. How would such societies employ their surplus people? "Hitherto,"
he answered, they had been divided into "manufacturers of superfluities, idle
proprietors of productive funds, domestics, soldiers, merchants, mariners,"
and such. Yet all of these employments had been insufficient to absorb the

surplus, and "most" of them would be reduced by the reforms that he and Jefferson desired. A better government would have less need for soldiers. "From a more equal partition of property must result a greater simplicity of manners, consequently a less consumption of manufactured superfluities and a less proportion of idle proprietors and domestics." There would thus be no exemption for republics from the pressures rising from the productivity of laborers and land. Republican ideals could speed developments that good republicans must fear.[71]

For the long run, Madison confessed, he had no answer to the problem of "a country fully peopled." Even North America would one day be as crowded as contemporary Europe, perhaps with all the misery that this implied. But this, he knew, was looking far into the future. For the present—and for years to come—the westward movement promised an escape. As long as it continued freely, the United States would not be forced to hurry toward intensive economic change. Its republics would be shielded from the inequalities and misery that more intensive changes would entail. Expansion to the West would multiply the agricultural societies that were the best foundations for republics. It would also, and continually, relieve the crowding that would otherwise propel the East into conditions that would threaten these foundations there.

But none of this would work without an open Mississippi. None of it would work without a freer trade between the old world and the new. Already at a middle level of development, Americans would never be content, as Madison explicitly admitted, to return to mere subsistence. If western farmers were unable to exchange their surplus for the comforts and conveniences of life, then either westerners would choose to manufacture for themselves or else potential migrants would remain in the Atlantic states, where growing population and a lack of foreign markets were already urging rapid economic change. The clock could only run one way, and in that way, in some respects, lay genuine improvements. Madison, accordingly, did not propose to turn it back, or even to arrest its progress. He wanted only to prevent its speeding uncontrollably toward social circumstances undesirable for liberal republics. This, however, he desired more desperately with every passing year. Afflicted by depression, all of the Atlantic states were being pressured into legislation he condemned. And with conditions in the East already weighing heavily on that imaginary clock, the closure of the Mississippi was a dangerous addition.

In 1786, the double weights combined to pull the country into crisis. As Madison was packing for his journey to New York and on to the Annapolis Convention, James Monroe reported that John Jay, the Confederation's secretary for foreign affairs, had asked to be relieved from his instructions to insist upon the right to navigate the Mississippi. Jay had been immersed in tedious negotiations with Diego de Gardoqui since the early summer of 1785. The Spanish envoy was prepared to recognize the borders claimed by the Confederation since the peace, especially if he could win a mutual guarantee of territorial possessions. He offered valuable concessions in the monarch's European ports, Spanish purchases of naval masts in the United States, and Spanish aid against the troublesome North African corsairs—all, however, only if the union would accept the closure of the Mississippi for a period of twenty-five or thirty years. On 29 May 1786, believing that these terms demanded only that the union should forbear a while from pressing its insistence on a claim of no great present consequence to the United States—a claim, in any case, that it was hopelessly unable to enforce—Jay initiated a request for new instructions.

The sectional collision sparked by Jay's request for new instructions is described in every standard study of the background of the Federal Convention.[72] Led by Massachusetts, whose representatives were eager to assist their struggling fishermen and shippers, seven northern states were willing to approve the change. But nine states were required to ratify a treaty; and marshalled by Virginia, all the planting states were bitterly opposed. As Congress deadlocked on the issue, ancient animosities between New England and the South vented in a furious eruption. Leaders on both sides began to talk about an end of continental union with an earnestness that they had never shown before.

New Englanders were understandably infuriated by the stubborn southern stand on Jay-Gardoqui. The people of the northern ports were desperately in need of markets and employment, but the southerners, it seemed, were more concerned about protecting their investments in trans-Appalachian lands.[73] Privately, some eastern politicians wondered whether it would make more sense to form a smaller, regional confederation homogeneous enough to have a set of common interests.[74] To southerners, of course, the selfishness seemed altogether on the other side. Indeed, Virginia's leading congressmen, Monroe and William Grayson, both suspected that the whole attempt to alter Jay's instructions was an eastern plot to either dominate the union or destroy it. In 1786, the West was everywhere perceived as an extension of the South. Western settlement was still almost exclusively on lands southwest of the Ohio, and as population moved increasingly into this region, it was clear that the admission to the union of new southwestern states could fundamentally affect the federal balance.[75] While Grayson warned that westerners and southerners alike would be profoundly disaffected from the union if "they saw their dearest interests sacrificed and given up [in order] to obtain a trivial commercial advantage for their brethren in the east," Monroe warned Patrick Henry that the Jay-Gardoqui project was deliberately designed to damage western growth and keep "the weight of government and population" in New England. Should they fail in that, he thought, the men behind it would not hesitate to use that failure to destroy the union.[76]

There is nothing to suggest that Madison accepted Grayson's or Monroe's analysis of Jay's maneuvers. There is every evidence, however, that he fully shared their anger and alarm. Although he knew that he would soon be leaving for New York and promised a complete communication once he had arrived, he could not restrain the fury and amazement prompted by Monroe's original report, delivering a lengthy, livid blast as soon as he received it. Congress, he insisted, had no better right to bar Virginia's western citizens from passing down the Mississippi "than to say that her eastern citizens shall not pass through the capes of Henry and Charles." He had forgiven Congress, he suggested, for considering this measure under the duress of war. But to adopt it now "would be a voluntary barter in time of profound peace of the *rights* of one part of the empire to the *interests* of another part. What would Massachusetts say to a proposition for ceding to Britain her right of fishery as the price of some stipulation in favor of tobacco?"[77] To Grayson and Monroe, the conflict was a struggle over sectional ascendancy within the union. To Madison, for whom the westward movement and the preservation of the union were alike essential if the Revolution was to be secured, the stakes were even higher.

Madison arrived in New York City early in the fourth week of July. He reached the seat of Congress just in time for some of the most serious deliberations of the summer. On 4 August, a grand committee on the state of the Confederation handed in the period's most sweeping recommendations for amendments to the Articles of Union.[78] On 3 August, however, Jay's address to Congress had initiated the debates that soon foreclosed congressional attention to any other subject. While he was in the city, Madison was thoroughly immersed in private talks on both of these great topics. What advice he gave, if any, is uncertain. What he learned is more apparent—and would deeply influence the decisions he would soon be called upon to make.

Madison returned to Philadelphia on 10 August, but as the argument in Congress neared a temporary resolution, Monroe kept him abreast of every new maneuver. He wanted Madison to probe the views of absent congressmen from Pennsylvania and "send them up" if they were likely to assist.[79] He wanted Madison's advice about a compromise designed to keep the Mississippi open as an avenue for western exports in exchange for an agreement that would close it to their imports for a time. Most of all, perhaps, he wanted Madison to understand that "Jay and his party are determined to pursue this business as far as possible, either as the means of throwing the western people and territory without the government of the U.S. and keeping the weight of population and government here or of dismembering the government itself for the purpose of a separate confederacy."[80]

Madison advised against the introduction of Monroe's compromise proposal.[81] The warning came too late. On 30 August, Monroe reported that a seven-state majority, from Pennsylvania north without a break to Massachusetts, had swept aside the southern opposition and instructed Jay to yield the right of navigation through the Spanish enclave if the claim would otherwise prevent conclusion of a treaty.[82] On 3 September, he added that the foreign secretary was determined to pursue his talks despite the dubious legality of these instructions. Everything, he wrote, would now depend on Pennsylvania and New Jersey, where the pro-Jay forces were already working to solidify their following or to prepare for a dismemberment of the Confederation on the line of the Potomac if they could not keep these states in line. Monroe expected Madison to counter these intrigues, especially among the Pennsylvanians. "If a dismemberment takes place, that state must not be added to the eastern scale. It were as well to use force to prevent it as to defend ourselves afterwards."[83] Written on the eve of Madison's departure for Annapolis, the letter reached him in that town.[84] It was a vivid, late reminder that the union tottered on the very edge of fragmentation.

The bitter schism over Jay's negotiations with Gardoqui was by no means all of what was on the minds of the commissioners at the Annapolis Convention. As Hamilton would write in the fifteenth *Federalist,* the country seemed to many of these men "to have reached almost the last stage of national humiliation . . . There is scarcely anything that can wound the pride or degrade the character of an independent nation, which we do not experience."[85] Nevertheless, to all of these reformers, the commercial and financial troubles of the middle eighties seemed a symbol and a centerpiece of most of these debilities and dangers, which were soon to take the terrifying form of Shays's Rebellion. To Hamilton, whom Isaac Kramnick has described as "the premier state-builder in a generation of state-builders,"[86] a more effective federal system had appeared for years to be a precondition for the economic and financial policies that could assure the nation's greatness. And of all the nation's needs, a federal power over trade now seemed to Madison the most essential, the more so as a proper grant would carry with it the assurance of a steady source of independent general taxes. Continental measures were the only ones that might compel the Europeans to accept the sort of world that would sustain America's new order. In their absence, ineffective separate regulations were producing rising animosities among the states and growing talk of separate regional confederations. In their absence, too, the inability to trade commodities for European imports drained the country of its scarce supply of precious metals and provided "pretexts for the pernicious substitution of paper money, for indulgences for debtors, for postponement of taxes," and for other unjust legislation in the states. The Jay-Gardoqui crisis was another—and incalculably pernicious—consequence of these commercial evils. "An alarming proof of the predominance of temporary and partial interests over . . . just and extended maxims,"[87] it struck Madison as the final evidence that liberty and union were immediately at risk and could be rescued only by a central government which could be trusted with the powers necessary to create conditions under which the nation's revolutionary promises could be fulfilled.

Madison's and Hamilton's agreements were extensive and profound. Both of them believed that proper governments originate in the consent of the society they serve and are intended to secure the people's happiness and rights. Both maintained that private rights and popular consent could be successfully combined only by establishing effective checks and balances among distinctive governmental branches. To both, the Constitution seemed a safe and necessary remedy for pressing national ills.[88] For all of this, however, revolutionary promises were different things to different men, and underlying differences between the two collaborators were as real as their agreements.[89] Since early in the decade, Hamilton had taken Britain as an archetype of national success. Thoroughly emancipated from the early-Revolutionary condemnation of the Modern Whig regime, he saw the Constitution as an instrument that would permit a vigorous administration to construct the economic and financial props of national greatness.[90] For Madison, by contrast, the Constitution was the means by which the new world could *avoid* the European curses of professional armed forces, persistent public debts, powerful executives, and other instruments or policies that Hamilton associated with effective statehood.[91] Thus, when Patrick Henry cautioned the Virginia ratifying convention that "those nations who have gone in search of grandeur, power, and splendor have . . . been the victims of their own folly," Madison agreed that "national splendor and glory are not our [proper] objects."[92] Hamilton envisioned the creation of a "modern" state. Madison intended to perpetuate the Revolution.[93]

Still, the contest over the adoption of the Constitution was not primarily, or even very visibly, an argument concerning economic fundamentals. It did not pit capitalists against anti-capitalists, modern liberals against classical republicans, or progressive against conservative economic interests. Federalists and Antifederalists alike regarded private property and private enterprise as givens. Both preferred prosperity to economic hardships. There was little opposition to the commerce powers granted by the Constitution, and little doubt that they would be employed against the Europeans' mercantile restrictions. (In *The Federalist*, in fact, Hamilton seemed every bit as sure as Madison that efforts to retaliate against the British would be among the leading objects of the first administration.)[94] Many northern artisans and merchants did believe that constitutional reform was in their economic interest. Many southern critics of the Constitution feared that it would be employed to institute a navigation system which would favor northern manufacturers and shippers at the planting states' expense.[95] But there were other reasons for supporting (or opposing) the reform, and there were other northerners and other southerners who thought in different patterns. Many enterprising Antifederalists from Pennsylvania or New York insisted that the economic prospects and conditions of the country were by no means as distressed as their opponents claimed, argued that the difficulties could be overcome by enterprise and thrift, and feared that federal powers over commerce would produce monopolies and other favors for established economic interests.[96] On the other side, in the Virginia ratifying contest, Madison maintained that temporary burdens on the planting states would be abundantly repaid by the protections offered by the Constitution and argued that, in any case, from the beginning and more certainly with every passing year, the agricultural majority within the federal Congress would protect the farming interests from commercial domination.[97] For all these reasons, it is very difficult to say to what degree the authors of *The Federalist* were conscious of the underlying incompatibility of their objectives, which had been articulated mostly in their private writings. For both of them, the prime necessity of 1788 was the adoption of the Constitution. Only later would their different visions move into the forefront of their minds and tear the Federalists apart.

III. From Collision to Consensus

Clashing visions of political economy were not the only reason for the party conflict of the 1790s. They were, however, fundamental to its origins and course, and they were tightly interwrapped with all its other aspects. On the first day of business of the first new Congress, Madison proposed discriminatory duties on the ships of nations having no commercial treaty with the union—a striking testimony to the hopes that he had had in mind throughout the course of constitutional reform.[98] Defeated in this effort, he revived it twice again, in 1790 and 1794, before a treaty with the British (which he bitterly opposed) forbade such measures for the next ten years. On both of these occasions, he was checked, in part, by Hamilton's determined opposition to a scheme that threatened to disrupt the revenues on which the funding plan depended and to end in a commercial conflict that, as he conceived it, the United States was sure to lose.[99]

Madison and Jefferson believed that the United States was capable of forcing Britain to accept a freer trade. Most American exports, as they saw it, were necessities of life: raw materials and food on which the British and their colonies in the Caribbean were vitally dependent. Most American imports, on the other hand, were "niceties" or "luxuries" that the United States could either do without or manufacture (at a shop and household level) on their own. America, accordingly, would suffer little from an economic confrontation with the British, while the British government would soon be faced with heavy pressure from the colonies and from the manufacturers and merchants who would find themselves deprived of an essential market. Independence, as the two Virginians understood it, was to be secured—for both the nation and the citizens of whom the nation was composed—by freeing trade to take its natural channels. The promise of the Revolution would be kept by opening the oceanic markets and the western lands that would preserve the mostly agricultural economy of the United States and, with it, the personal autonomy and relatively equal distribution of the nation's wealth that characterized a population overwhelmingly composed of independent farmers.[100]

Hamilton's ideas were altogether different. Influenced more by Hume and James Steuart than by Smith or eighteenth-century opposition thinkers, he believed that a developed state would win an economic confrontation with a less developed rival.[101] More than that, he reasoned from a different understanding of the current situation and the future prospects of the new republic. Though Madison and Jefferson were very much concerned with freeing oceanic commerce, their ambitions for the nation focused on the West, where the regime of liberty could be continually revitalized as it expanded over space, and on the prospect that by force of sheer example the American experiment would revolutionize the world. Hamilton's concerns were markedly more European in their flavor. A Hobbesian or Machiavellian in his conception of the world, he faced toward the Atlantic and envisioned an arena of competing empires into which America must enter much like any other state. In time, as he conceived it, the United States could take a brilliant part in this arena. But to have this kind of future, it must first possess the economic and financial preconditions for successful competition. In the meantime, it must conscientiously avoid a confrontation with Great Britain, the nation that could threaten the United States most dangerously in war or (through investments in the new republic's economic growth) assist it most impressively toward greatness. Early in the new administration, he established close relationships with Britain's ministers to the United States and used these private channels to assure that good relations were maintained. Meanwhile, taking British institutions as a model, he set about to build a modern nation.[102]

Hamilton's design for national greatness may have been complete in its essentials when as secretary of the Treasury he answered Congress's instructions to submit a plan for managing the revolutionary debt. His first Report on Public Credit, delivered on 14 January 1790, recommended that the federal government assume responsibility for the remaining obligations of the several states, as well as those of the Confederation Congress, and fund them all at par. "If all the public creditors receive their dues from one source," Hamilton argued, "their interests will be the same. And having the same interests, they will unite in support of the fiscal arrangements of government."[103] For him, as clearly as for Robert Morris, proper management could turn the revolutionary debt into a positive advantage for the nation.

Of all the nationalists of 1783, Hamilton had had the clearest vision of a nation integrated on a British model and financially and economically equipped for national greatness. Now, he meant to put that vision into practice. Thus, the funding and assumption program was intended from the first to further major economic and political, as well as narrowly financial, goals. On one side, proper funding of the state as well as federal obligations would create a counterbalance to the state attachments that had always seemed the greatest danger to the union; it would tie the economic interests of a vital segment of America's elite to the success of national institutions.[104] On the other side, the funding program would become the principal foundation for the nation's future role in global competition. Even as it reestablished the ability to borrow and attached the monied interests to the central government's success, funding would invigorate—the modern word is "monetize"—the public debt, transforming governmental obligations into liquid capital that could be multiplied again by using the certificates of debt to back the loans and notes of a new national bank. The bonds and banknotes could be used, in turn, to foster manufacturing and commerce, which would serve as pillars for the nation's economic independence. In effect, by simply pledging that specific revenues would pay the interest on its bonds, the nation could anticipate—and in the very process could assure—its future greatness. It would be capable, at once, of leaning on descendants who would benefit from its achievements and of drawing capital investments from abroad.[105]

The trouble with this magic, which did in fact accomplish much of what the secretary had in mind, was that it threatened other founders' visions of the sort of nation the United States should be. Although he planned to make the people prosperous and happy, Hamilton's concerns were focussed on the state, not upon the citizens of whom the public was composed. Although he was a champion of private liberties and economic freedom, insisting that a more complex economy would furnish "greater scope for the diversity of talents and dispositions,"[106] he was also as emancipated from traditional concerns about the civic virtue of the people as any statesman of his age. Accordingly, although he certainly believed that every group and every region would eventually enjoy the benefits of growth, he emphasized the quick development of manufacturing and commerce, which were critical to the correction of a chronic deficit of payments; and he dismissed as selfish the inevitable complaints about the temporary sectional and class inequities that would result. For Hamilton, as surely as for his opponents, the long-term goal was economic independence; but Hamilton defined this independence in a different way. He pictured a mature and largely self-sufficient economic system in which manufacturing would build a large domestic market for the farmers and the specialized activities of different economic regions would combine into a healthy whole.[107] To reach this goal, however, it was necessary in the short term to protect the revenues derived from British imports and to use these revenues in ways that favored certain men and certain regions more directly than some others. Such means were unacceptable to many; and the end itself, as it was clarified in Hamilton's succession of reports, was incompatible with Jefferson's or Madison's ideals.

Madison had favored Hamilton's appointment to his office. Hamilton had taken his position confident of Madison's support. Only gradually, as both articulated their ideas and tried to put them in the form of legislation, did the gulf between them come to seem abysmal. Madison objected from the start to the specifics of the plan for funding and assumption: to the prolongation of the debt and of the taxes necessary to support it; to the transfer of the nation's wealth from the productive to the non-productive classes; to the sheer injustice (as he saw it) of a program that did not discriminate between original and secondary holders and, in its initial version, favored certain states while risking the allegiance of some others. But Madison was overwhelmingly defeated on the issue of discrimination, and the argument about assumption was resolved by compromises that corrected the inequities with which he was especially concerned. Only as the funding plan was followed by reports suggesting the creation of a national bank (December 1790) and federal encouragement of manufactures (December 1791) did Hamilton's design assume an unmistakeable configuration. And only as he thought about the implications did Madison's uneasiness develop into thoroughgoing opposition.

From the first, the funding and assumption program stirred anxieties about corrupting links between the federal treasury and special-interest factions, together with concerns about its consequences for the distribution of the nation's wealth. The more apparent it became, however, that Hamilton was following a British model, the more opponents saw him as another Walpole: as a minister who was subverting legislative independence and endangering the social fabric by creating a corrupted following of men who lived upon the treasury at popular expense. By the fall of 1791, Madison and Jefferson believed that Hamilton intended to "administer" the new republic toward a government and a society that would, in time, subvert the revolutionary dream. At this point, they urged the revolutionary poet Philip Freneau to come to Philadelphia to start a paper that would rouse the nation to its danger. In that paper, during 1792, Madison and others built a systematic ideology of opposition.[108]

The party struggle of the middle nineties can be analyzed in a variety of ways. Like the conflicts in the old Confederation Congress, it pitted the New England states against Virginia and her neighbors. It ranged consolidationists against the principled proponents of a strict construction of the Constitution, enemies of popular disorders against the champions of popular participation in political affairs. After 1793, when revolutionary France began its twenty years of war with Britain, clashing attitudes about the European struggle intermeshed with the domestic conflict and with different judgments of the country's interests to produce the most ferocious party battle in the nation's annals. Throughout its course, however, different visions of political economy were near the center of this conflict, and conflicting economic policies contributed importantly to its directions.

Most of the American elite and most of those who lived by manufacturing or commerce had supported the adoption of the Constitution. Others had opposed it out of fear of the elite or out of a suspicion that a stronger central government would favor the commercial interests. After 1789, the apprehensions of the latter group were rapidly confirmed. The funding plan entailed enormous gains for secondary holders, mostly in the North and East, who had acquired their bonds at fractions of their value.[109] Many of these monied men were able to increase their profits once again by using their certificates to purchase bank stock. And all of this was paid for, many said, by impost duties weighing heaviest on southern planters, together with an excise tax on whiskey that provoked rebellion in Pennsylvania, Virginia, and North Carolina. It is not surprising, then, that by the end of 1792, a large majority of former Antifederalists were starting to support the Jeffersonian opposition, whose leaders were revolted by the massive transfer of the nation's wealth and thought of the perpetuation of the debt, the prolongation of the taxes necessary to finance it, and governmental privileges for special interests (typified by the creation of the bank) as policies which undermined the relative equality appropriate for a republic. These policies, Madison complained,

> make it a problem whether the system of the old paper under a bad government, or of the new under a good one, be chargeable with the greater substantial injustice. The true difference seems to be that by the former the few were victims to the many; by the latter the many to the few . . . My imagination will not attempt to set bounds to the daring depravity of the times. The stock-jobbers will become the pretorian band of the government, at once its tools and its tyrants; bribed by its largesses, and overawing it by clamors and combinations.[110]

But many of the manufacturers and merchants who had hoped to benefit from the adoption of the Constitution benefitted only indirectly, if at all, from Hamilton's financial and commercial programs. Hamilton did very little to support the master craftsmen, journeymen, and workers who were actively involved in making manufactured goods and who had clamored for protection from the flood of British imports. The funding system, in his thinking, was the indispensable foundation for political stability and economic growth. In order to maintain it, he consistently opposed protective legislation likely to disrupt the flow of (mostly British) imports. The tariff generated 90 percent of the federal revenues which paid the interest on the debt. Accordingly, the plan for manufactures advocated bounties rather than protective tariffs and was more concerned with the encouragement of large-scale manufacturing for export than with aiding handicraft production, while Hamilton's Society for the Encouragement of Useful Manufactures was an unsuccessful scheme for mobilizing large investors in a company that smaller manufacturers regarded as a threat. By the middle of the decade, hundreds of mechanics, artisans, and small, aspiring tradesmen, who were often special targets for the Federalists' contempt for "mushroom politicians," were fleeing from the party for an opposition which encouraged popular participation and condemned monopolistic corporations.[111]

By the middle of the decade, also, many merchants were enlisting in the Jeffersonian coalition. As France and Britain each attempted to deny its enemy the benefits of neutral trade, Americans were periodically at risk. Near the end of 1793, a secret Order in Council of 6 November resulted in the sudden seizure of 250 American vessels engaged in trade with the French West Indies. The Federalists responded by defeating Madison's commercial resolutions and securing a negotiated resolution of the crisis. But John Jay's treaty with the British, ratified on 24 June 1795, acquiesced in British definitions of the rights of neutrals and provoked a naval war with France. Despite these troubles, commerce burgeoned; but it burgeoned most dramatically with areas outside the British Empire, where, of course, the traders suffered most from British seizures and the quasi-war with France.[112] By 1800, many of these traders were profoundly discontented with a foreign policy that left them most at risk and seemed to render the United States commercially subservient to Britain. Merchants such as Samuel Smith of Baltimore, the Crown-inshields of Salem, James Nicholson of New York City, and John Swanwick and Stephen Girard of Philadelphia—all of whom engaged primarily in trade with Britain's foes—were staunch Republicans before the decade's end.[113]

Economic policies were not the only reason for the Federalists' defeat in 1800. They may not have been the most important. For a large proportion of the population—market farmers, shippers, and the hosts of laborers and craftsmen who were occupied in building ships, transporting goods, or packaging and finishing materials for export—the war in Europe was an economic windfall; and Hamilton may well have been correct that this prosperity would have collapsed abruptly in a confrontation with the British. After 1807, when the Jeffersonians resorted to commercial warfare, this is just what happened. Still, Hamilton's political economy *was* predicated from the first upon an intimate relationship between the federal government and well-established monied and commercial interests, which was just what many Antifederalists had feared. His policies delivered little to the handicraft producers who competed with imported manufactures. After 1793, when the financial plan encouraged a commercial policy that smacked of a subservience to Britain, it generated disaffection even in some merchants. In 1789, the Federalists had managed to appeal to an enormous range of economic interests. By 1800, much of this support had dropped away. And, naturally, as northern artisans and merchants shifted their allegiance, the Jeffersonians became a different party too.

The change within the Jeffersonians might best be seen as a beginning, not an end. Until the War of 1812, the economic policies of Jefferson's and Madison's administrations were consistent with the goals that both men had pursued since early in the 1780s: to retire the public debt; to sever the corrupting links between the federal government and special interests; to maintain the constitutional division of responsibilities between the federal government and states; and to pursue the freer trade and western growth that might perpetuate an agrarian and republican balance of property. The Jeffersonians did not dismiss their old suspicions of intensive economic change, nor did they heartily endorse the unrestrained pursuit of individual self-interest. Yet Jefferson and Madison had always thought that individual pursuits of private economic goods would harmonize most fully in a system free from governmental privileges or from "unnatural" incentives for the sorts of enterprise least suitable for a republic; and northern artisans and merchants, who were a growing portion of the party, may always have embraced the two Virginians' enmity toward privilege while never sharing fully in their reservations about rapid economic growth. After 1808, as economic warfare favored the development of native manufactures and as northern Jeffersonians and British immigrants defended economic change, the party as a party shifted even farther toward a pro-developmental stance.[114] Party leaders shifted with it.

Again, there is a danger (often run) of overemphasizing this transition. Jefferson and Madison had never stood at the agrarian extreme of opposition to the Hamiltonian system. Neither did they ever move wholeheartedly into the pro-developmental wing of Jeffersonian opinion. But changing times did foster a significant revision of the old ideas. In the crisis of 1794, many party spokesmen had objected to the building of a navy, an enormous object of expense which they believed was needed mostly to protect the carrying trade between the island colonies and Europe. Jefferson and many others long remained ambivalent about a commerce unrelated to the nation's "natural" needs and capable of dragging the United States into the European conflict. As late as 1816, Jefferson observed that "the exercise, by our own citizens, of so much commerce as may suffice to exchange our superfluities for our wants may be advantageous for the whole. But it does not follow that . . . it is the interest of the whole to become a mere city of London to carry on the business of one half of the world at the expense of eternal war with the other half . . . Our commercial dashers . . . have already cost us . . . more than their persons and all their commerce were worth."[115] Nevertheless, both Jefferson and Madison committed their administrations to protection of this commerce, and both expressed an understanding of its role in the reduction of the chronic deficit of payments.[116] Then, as economic warfare failed—in part, as Madison conceived it, because the British found in Canada and South America alternative suppliers of the needed raw materials and food—both he and Jefferson conceded the necessity of an expanded role for native manufactures.[117]

The War of 1812 taught further lessons. Armies and supplies moved poorly on the primitive communications network in the West. Without a national bank, the federal government was a financial cripple. At the peace, the fragile manufactories that had developed during the preceding years were once again endangered. Accordingly, in 1816, Madison recommended and the Republican Congress overwhelmingly approved the first protective tariff, a second national bank, and an ambitious plan for internal improvements. With these measures, in effect, the Jeffersonians admitted that America could not compel the Europeans to accept the sort of world in which the new republic could escape the dangers of intensive economic change. With these measures, they accepted an essential portion of the Hamiltonian design.

Even this, it should be noted, hardly constituted a complete surrender of the party's old ideas. Republicans still hoped that education, proper leadership, and an enormous reservoir of western lands would limit or postpone the civic evils most of them still feared. They still had no intention of committing the United States to mercantilist economics, Hamiltonian finance, or other adjuncts of the European state. And yet the choice did seem to lie between increasing self-sufficiency and national dependence on external markets which could not be guaranteed. Under proper leaders, it could now be hoped, a national bank and moderate encouragement of native manufactures need not have the threatening effects that "monocrats" had once deliberately encouraged. Land had never seemed the *only* source of personal autonomy and civic virtue, and independent artisans and merchants had repeatedly displayed their fierce attachment to the nation's freedoms. Therefore, as the Federalists collapsed, the Jeffersonians appropriated part of the design that they had once perceived as inconsistent with the health of a republic, synthesizing elements from both of the competing visions that had shaped the nation's struggles. It was, of course, a fleeting moment of agreement. It would be quickly challenged by the Panic of 1819, which would reopen many of the old debates and set them near the center of a second party conflict. But, in that, which is a different story, both the Democrats and the Whigs would argue mostly over means. The fundamental ends—independence and the founding of a federal republic—now appeared secure.

Notes

1. Scholarly landmarks include J. G. A. Pocock, *The Machiavellian Moment: Florentine Political Thought and the Atlantic Republican Tradition* (Princeton, N.J., 1975); Drew R. McCoy, *The Elusive Republic: Political Economy in Jeffersonian America* (Chapel Hill, N.C., 1980); Joyce Appleby, *Capitalism and a New Social Order: The Republican Vision of the 1790s* (New York, 1984); Gordon S. Wood, "Interests and Disinterestedness in the Making of the Constitution," in Richard Beeman et al., eds., *Beyond Confederation: Origins of the Constitution and American National Identity* (Chapel Hill, N.C., 1987), 69–109; and Cathy D. Matson and Peter S. Onuf, *A Union of Interests: Political and Economic Thought in Revolutionary America* (Lawrence, Kans., 1990).

2. This chapter's special debt to McCoy, *The Elusive Republic,* will be repeatedly apparent. It may be fairly read as an attempt to build on that and on my own earlier writings, especially *The Jeffersonian Persuasion: Evolution of a Party Ideology* (Ithaca, N.Y., 1978). It is compatible in most respects with Stanley Elkins and Eric McKitrick, *The Age of Federalism: The Early American Republic, 1788-1800* (New York, 1993), which appeared after it was written.

3. Richard H. Kohn, *Eagle and Sword: The Federalists and the Creation of the Military Establishment in America, 1783–1802* (New York, 1975), chap. 2; C. Edward Skeen, "The Newburgh Conspiracy Reconsidered," with a rebuttal by Richard H. Kohn, *WMQ* 31 (1974): 273–298; Clarence L. Ver Steeg, *Robert Morris: Revolutionary Financier* (New York, 1954), especially 166–177.

4. Morris's report is in Worthington Chauncy Ford et al., eds., *Journals of the Continental Congress, 1774-1789,* 34 vols. (Washington, 1904–1937), 22:429–446. For the general situation and the evolution of his plans, I have relied especially on Ver Steeg, *Robert Morris,* chap. 5 and pages 123–129; E. James Ferguson, *The Power of the Purse: A History of American Public Finance, 1776-1790* (Chapel Hill, N.C., 1961); id., "The Nationalists of 1781-1783 and the Economic Interpretation of the Constitution," *JAH* 41 (1969): 241–261; Edmund Cody Burnett, *The Continental Congress* (New York, 1941); H. James Henderson, *Party Politics in the Continental Congress* (New York, 1974); Jack N. Rakove, *The Beginnings of National Politics: An Interpretive History of the Continental Congress* (New York, 1979); Charles Royster, *A Revolutionary People at War: The Continental Army and American National Character, 1775-1783* (Chapel Hill, N.C., 1979); and E. Wayne Carp, *To Starve the Army at Pleasure: Continental Army Administration and American Political Culture, 1775-1783* (Chapel Hill, N.C., 1984).

5. Edmund Randolph to James Madison, 13 Dec. 1782, and "Notes on Debates," 24 Dec. 1782, in *PJM* 5:401, 441–442.

6. The crisis can be followed day by day in *Journals of the Continental Congress* and in Madison's notes on the congressional debates. My reconstruction, developed more fully in "James Madison and the Nationalists, 1780–1783," *WMQ* 40 (1983): 227–255, is based primarily on these as supplemented by the sources cited in note 4.

7. Madison, "Notes on Debates," 18 Feb. 1783, in *PJM* 6:251.

8. Madison, "Notes on Debates," 28 Jan. 1783, in ibid., 143.

9. Ibid. Entered by Madison as a long footnote to his record of Hamilton's speech.

10. Madison, "Notes on Debates," in *PJM* 6:259–261.

11. Ibid., 265–266.

12. Ibid., 270–272.

13. Ibid., 290–292.

14. Ibid., 375. Washington's report and the Newburgh Addresses themselves are in *Journals of the Continental Congress* 24:294–311.

15. Madison's plan of 26 Feb. appears as a long footnote in his "Notes on Debates." The "Report on Restoring Public Credit" as reported from the select committee of Madison, Hamilton, Gorham, FitzSimons, and Rutledge (6 March) is printed in *PJM* 6:311–314.

16. Speech of 27 Feb., "Notes on Debates," ibid., 297–298. This was in response to Mercer's charge that commutation tended "in common with the funding of other debts to establish and perpetuate a monied interest" which "would gain the ascendance of the landed interest . . . and by their example and influence become dangerous to our republican constitutions."

17. Speech of 21 Feb., ibid., 272.

18. Speech of 28 Jan., ibid., 143–147. Compare Madison to Jefferson, 6 May 1780, *PJM* 2:19–20.

19. For the full extent of Madison's discomfort with his allies, see Banning, "James Madison and the Nationalists," 249–251.

20. Report of 29 July 1782, *Journals of the Continental Congress* 22:435–437.

21. Morris to John Jay, 13 July 1781, quoted in Ferguson, *Power of the Purse*, 123–124; report of 29 July, *Journals of the Continental Congress* 22:432.

22. See, especially, the letters to an unknown recipient (n.d.), to James Duane (3 Sept. 1780), and to Robert Morris (30 April 1781), along with the conclusion of "The Continentalist," in *PAH* 2:234–251, 400–418, 604–635; 3:99–106. In the last, originally published 4 July 1782, Hamilton wrote: "The reason of allowing Congress to appoint its own officers of the customs, collectors of taxes, and military officers of every rank is to create in the interior of each state a mass of influence in favor of the federal government . . . interesting such a number of individuals in each state in support of the federal government as will be counterpoised to the ambition of others" (3:106).

23. Ferguson was first to see that the Morris nationalists understood and wished

to replicate "the role of funded debt and national bank in stabilizing the regime founded in Britain after the revolution of 1689" (*Power of the Purse*, 289–290 and passim). See, further, Banning, *The Jeffersonian Persuasion*, 126–140 and passim; McCoy, *The Elusive Republic*; John M. Murrin, "The Great Inversion, or Court versus Country: A Comparison of the Revolution Settlements in England (1688–1721) and America (1776–1816)," in J. G. A. Pocock, ed., *Three British Revolutions: 1641, 1688, 1776* (Princeton, N.J., 1980), 368–453; and Ralph Ketcham, *Presidents Above Party: The First American Presidency, 1789–1829* (Chapel Hill, N.C., 1984), 31–38 and chap. 10.

24. There are four superb biographies of nicely varied lengths: Irving Brant, *James Madison*, 6 vols. (Indianapolis, 1941–61); Ralph Ketcham, *James Madison: A Biography* (New York, 1971); Harold S. Schultz, *James Madison* (New York, 1970); and Jack N. Rakove, *James Madison and the Creation of the American Republic* (Glenview, Ill., 1990).

25. The literature on British opposition thinking is extensive, but see, as a beginning, J. G. A. Pocock, "Machiavelli, Harrington, and English Political Ideologies in the Eighteenth Century," *WMQ* 22 (1965): 549–563; id., *The Machiavellian Moment*; Isaac Kramnick, *Bolingbroke and His Circle: The Politics of Nostalgia in the Age of Walpole* (Cambridge, Mass., 1968); and Roger Durrell Parker, "The Gospel of Opposition" (Ph.D. diss., Wayne State Univ., 1975).

26. P. G. M. Dickson, *The Financial Revolution in England: A Study in the Development of Public Credit, 1688–1756* (New York, 1967); John Brewer, *The Sinews of Power: War, Money, and the English State, 1688–1783* (New York, 1989).

27. Its stabilizing role is a central theme for J. H. Plumb, *The Growth of Political Stability in England, 1675–1725* (London, 1967).

28. See [John Trenchard and Thomas Gordon], *Cato's Letters, or Essays on Liberty, Civil and Religious, and other Important Subjects*, 4 vols., 3d ed. (London, 1733; orig. pub. 1720–23) and J[ames] B[urgh], *Political Disquisitions, or an Inquiry into Public Errors, Defects, and Abuses*, 3 vols. (London, 1774–75). Tory spokesmen, led by Viscount Bolingbroke, were more inclined to express the landed gentry's discontent with rising commerce in itself.

29. J. G. A. Pocock, ed., *The Political Works of James Harrington* (Cambridge, 1977), and id., "Machiavelli, Harrington, and English Political Ideologies."

30. The masterworks on the enormous influence of this thinking on the early Revolution are Bernard Bailyn, *The Ideological Origins of the American Revolution* (Cambridge, Mass., 1967), and Gordon S. Wood, *The Creation of the American Republic, 1776–1787* (Chapel Hill, N.C., 1969). Robert Shalhope, "Toward a Republican Synthesis: The Emergence of an Understanding of Republicanism in American Historiography," *WMQ* 29 (1972): 49–80, and id., "Republicanism and Early American Historiography," ibid., 39 (1982): 334–356, provide an introduction to the rapidly growing literature. For some of the most recent contributions, see Peter S. Onuf, "Reflections on the Founding: Constitutional Historiography in Bicentennial Perspective," *WMQ* 45 (1989): 341–375.

31. Hamilton drafted a congressional resolution calling for a federal convention

shortly before he retired from Congress, then decided that there was too little support to introduce it (*PAH* 3:420–426). Ferguson, *The Power of the Purse*, believes that Morris also hoped for a structural transformation of the system, but this is doubted by Ver Steeg, *Robert Morris*, and Rakove, *Beginnings of National Politics*.

32. Stephen Higginson to Henry Knox, 1787, in Edmund C. Burnett, ed., *Letters of Members of the Continental Congress*, 8 vols. (Washington, 1921–36), 7:123n.

33. Ferguson, *Power of the Purse*, 292.

34. Curtis P. Nettels, *The Emergence of a National Economy, 1775–1815* (New York, 1962), 48–49.

35. Ibid., especially 46–63, remains the standard survey and accords with recent studies in suggesting that Progressive scholars, led by Merrill Jensen, minimized the troubles. See John J. McCusker and Russell R. Menard, *The Economy of British America, 1606–1789: Needs and Opportunities for Study* (Chapel Hill, N.C., 1985), 367–377; and Richard B. Morris, *The Forging of the Union, 1781–1789* (New York, 1987), chap. 6.

36. For the early-revolutionary enthusiasm for free trade, see McCoy, *The Elusive Republic*, 86–90, and Matson and Onuf, *A Union of Interests*, 21–26. Frederick W. Marks III, *Independence on Trial: Foreign Affairs and the Making of the Constitution* (Baton Rouge, La., 1973), chap. 2, is a convenient summary of the restrictions on American trade.

37. George Bancroft, *History of the Formation of the Constitution of the United States of America*, 2 vols. (New York, 1882), vol. 1, bk. 2, chap. 4; Nettles, *Emergence of a National Economy*, 72–75; Marks, *Independence*, 80–82. For the states' mercantile systems see, more fully, Matson and Onuf, *Union of Interests*, chap. 2, and Forrest McDonald, *Novus Ordo Seclorum: The Intellectual Origins of the Constitution* (Lawrence, Kans., 1985), 102–106.

38. On this ambivalence, I have been influenced mostly by McCoy, *The Elusive Republic*, especially chap. 1, and by Pocock, *The Machiavellian Moment*.

39. Albert O. Hirschman, *The Passions and the Interests: Political Arguments for Capitalism before Its Triumph* (Princeton, N.J., 1977); Joyce O. Appleby, *Economic Thought and Ideology in Seventeenth-Century England* (Princeton, N.J., 1978); and the introductory essay in Istvan Hont and Michael Ignatieff, eds., *Wealth and Virtue: The Shaping of Political Economy in the Scottish Enlightenment* (Cambridge, 1983), an excellent recent collection.

40. Among the English, the most notorious example was Bernard Mandeville's *The Fable of the Bees: or Private Vices, Public Benefits* (London, 1714). See the excellent brief discussions in McCoy, *The Elusive Republic*, 25–27, and McDonald, *Novus Ordo Seclorum*, 109–110, 119–128. Far more moderate in tone, but also relatively unrestrained in their defense of commerce, were David Hume's influential essays "Of Commerce," "Of Luxury," and "Of Refinement in the Arts," originally published in 1752 and available in *Essays: Moral, Political, and Literary*, ed. Eugene F. Miller (Indianapolis, 1985).

41. See, most vividly, Adam Smith, *An Inquiry into the Nature and Causes of the Wealth of Nations*, ed. Edwin Canan (New York, 1937), 734–740; McCoy's superb dis-

cussion of Smith and other Scots, *The Elusive Republic,* 19–21, 35–40; and McDonald, *Novus Ordo Seclorum,* chap. 4.

42. Smith devoted much of book 4 of *Wealth of Nations* to a condemnation of policies designed "to enrich a great nation rather by trade and manufactures than by the improvement and cultivation of land, rather by the industry of the towns than by that of the country" (591).

43. "The Continentalist" No. 5, *PAH* 3:76.

44. McCoy, *Elusive Republic,* chap. 4; Matson and Onuf, *Union of Interests,* 46–47.

45. Perhaps the most famous came in "The Continentalist" No. 6, *PAH* 3:103.

46. For the unqualified defense of commercialization in the resolutions of public meetings and in the writings of William Barton, David Daggett, and William Vans Murray, see McCoy, *Elusive Republic,* 96–100, 118–119, and Matson and Onuf, *Union of Interests,* 91–97.

47. A central theme of Progressive and neo-Progressive scholarship from Orin G. Libby, *Geographical Distribution of the Vote of the Thirteen States on the Ratification of the Federal Constitution, 1787–1788* (Madison, Wisc., 1894) to Jackson Turner Main, *Political Parties before the Constitution* (Chapel Hill, N.C., 1973).

48. For an argument that "thousands of [enterprising] ordinary traders, petty businessmen, aspiring artisans, and market farmers" opposed the Constitution, see Wood, "Interests and Disinterestedness in the Making of the Constitution," 80 and passim, together with Saul Abraham Cornell, "The Political Thought and Culture of the Anti-Federalists" (Ph.D. diss., Univ. of Pennsylvania, 1989), chaps. 5–6.

49. *Journals of the Continental Congress* 19:110–113; Banning, "James Madison and the Nationalists," 234.

50. Madison to Edmund Randolph, 20 May 1783, *PJM* 7:59–62. Compare Madison to Jefferson, 13 May 1783, ibid., 39.

51. Madison to Randolph, 30 Aug. 1783, ibid., 295–296.

52. Madison to Randolph, 13 Sept. 1783, ibid., 314–315.

53. For Madison's own, essentially unsuccessful campaign to free Virginia from British commercial domination, see Drew R. McCoy, "The Virginia Port Bill of 1784," *Virginia Magazine of History and Biography* 83 (1975): 288–303, and Robert B. Bittner, "Economic Independence and the Virginia Port Bill of 1784," in Richard A. Rutyna and Peter C. Stewart, eds., *Virginia in the American Revolution* (Norfolk, Va., 1977), 73–92.

54. McCoy, *The Elusive Republic,* 121–132.

55. Madison to Jefferson, 18 Mar. 1786, *PJM* 8:502.

56. Madison to Monroe, 7 Aug. 1785, ibid., 333–336.

57. See Madison's speech supporting a federal power (ibid., 431–432), his letters to Washington of 11 Nov. and 9 Dec. 1785 (ibid., 404, 438–439); the editorial notes and legislative drafts in ibid., 406–410, 413–415; and Madison to Jefferson, 22 Jan. 1786, ibid., 476–477.

58. Contemporary information on the Annapolis Convention is extraordinarily

scanty, which may explain the paucity and brevity of secondary studies (e.g., Burnett, *Continental Congress*, 665–668; Morris, *Forging of the Union*, 253–257). The text of the address is in *PAH* 3:686–690.

59. Banning, "Madison and the Nationalists," 232–233, and on the Mississippi more particularly, *PJM* 2:202–204, 224, 241–242, 302–303; 3:261–262.

60. Madison to Jefferson, 7 Sept. 1784, enclosing Madison to Jefferson, 20 Aug. 1784, *PJM* 8:113–114, 104–108. The adventure to Ft. Stanwix is recounted in Brant, *James Madison*, vol. 2, chap. 21.

61. Madison to Jefferson, 20 Aug. 1784, in *PJM* 8:108.

62. Madison to Lafayette, 20 Mar. 1785, ibid., 250–253. Useful background is in Madison to Jefferson, 20 Mar. 1785, ibid., 268–269.

63. Madison to Lafayette, ibid., 251.

64. Ibid.

65. These phrases are all but universal in the commentaries of contemporary political scientists, especially on *Federalist*, No. 10. They can be traced to the enormously influential essays of the late Martin Diamond, especially "Democracy and *The Federalist:* A Reconsideration of the Framers' Intent," *APSR* 53 (1959): 52–68.

66. Most explicitly, moreover, in the passage deleted from his letter to Jefferson and written before he met Lafayette. These thoughts were not developed simply for French consumption.

67. See n. 54 above.

68. Query 19 of *Notes on the State of Virginia,* written in 1781–1782 and carefully read by Madison no later than the early fall of 1785 (*PJM* 8:415–416).

69. See the *National Gazette* essays on "Republican Distribution of Citizens" (3 Mar. 1792) and "Fashion" (20 Mar. 1792), reprinted in *PJM* 14:244–246, 257–259.

70. Jefferson to Madison, 28 Oct. 1785, *PJM* 8:285–288.

71. 19 June 1786, ibid., 9:76–77. See, further, Drew R. McCoy, "Jefferson and Madison on Malthus: Population Growth in Jeffersonian Political Economy," *Virginia Magazine of History and Biography* 88 (1980): 259–276.

72. Henderson, *Party Politics*, 387–394; Burnett, *Continental Congress*, 654–659; Morris, *Forging of the Union*, 233–244; Marks, *Independence on Trial*, 24–45.

73. See, for example, Charles Thomson's report of the speech of Rufus King, 16 Aug. 1786, in *Letters of Members of Congress* 8:429.

74. Theodore Sedgwick to Caleb Strong, 6 Aug. 1786, quoted in Burnett, *Continental Congress*, 657. The best recent discussion of the widespread talk of separate regional confederations is in Matson and Onuf, *Union of Interests*, 82–90.

75. The point is powerfully developed in Drew R. McCoy, "James Madison and Visions of American Nationality in the Confederation Period," in Beeman et al., eds., *Beyond Confederation*, 226–258, which is essential for distinguishing Madison's views from those of other Virginians.

76. Thomson's report of Grayson's speech of 16 Aug. (*Letters of Members of Congress* 8:427–29) and Monroe to Governor Patrick Henry, 12 Aug. 1786 (ibid., 422–425).

77. Madison to Monroe, 21 June 1786, *PJM* 9:82–83.

78. *Journals of the Continental Congress* 31:494–497.

79. *PJM* 9:91–92.

80. 14 Aug. 1786, ibid., 104.

81. 17 Aug. 1786, ibid., 107–108.

82. Ibid., 109. Delaware was the only state unrepresented during the crisis.

83. Ibid., 113–114.

84. Madison to Monroe, 11 Sept. 1786, ibid., 121.

85. *The Federalist*, 91–92.

86. Isaac Kramnick, ed., *The Federalist Papers* (Harmondsworth, Eng., 1987), 67.

87. Madison to Monroe, 18 Mar. 1786, in *PJM* 8:502; Madison to Monroe, 5 Oct. 1786, in ibid., 9:140.

88. George W. Carey, "Publius—A Split Personality?" *Review of Politics* 46 (1984): 5–22; David F. Epstein, *The Political Theory of "The Federalist"* (Chicago, 1984); Albert Furtwangler, *The Authority of Publius: A Reading of the Federalist Papers* (Ithaca, N.Y., 1984); and Gary Wills, *Explaining America: The Federalist* (New York, 1981).

89. Some of these differences have been detected even in *The Federalist*. See Douglas Adair, "The Authorship of the Disputed Federalist Papers," in *Fame and the Founding Fathers: Essays by Douglas Adair*, ed. Trevor Colbourn (New York, 1974), 55–60; Alpheus Thomas Mason, "The Federalist—A Split Personality," *AHR* 57 (1952): 625–643; and Gottfried Dietze, *The Federalist: A Classic on Federalism and Free Government* (Baltimore, 1960), 150–151, 260–264, 267–271.

90. The most revealing document is an undated private memorandum written shortly after the adjournment of the Federal Convention: "Conjectures About the New Constitution," in *PAH* 4:275–277.

91. The critical documents here are Madison's speech of 29 June in Max Farrand, ed., *The Records of the Federal Convention of 1787*, rev. ed., 4 vols. (New Haven, Conn., 1966), 1:464–465, and *Federalist*, No. 41, 259–260.

92. Jonathan Elliot, ed., *The Debates in the Several State Conventions on the Adoption of the Federal Constitution*, 2d ed., 5 vols. (Philadelphia, 1901), 3:47, 135.

93. For more on this distinction, see my essays "The Practicable Sphere of a Republic: James Madison, the Constitutional Convention, and the Emergence of Revolutionary Federalism," in Beeman et al., eds., *Beyond Confederation*, 162–187; and "1787 and 1776: Patrick Henry, James Madison, the Constitution, and the Revolution," in Neil L. York, ed., *Toward a More Perfect Union: Six Essays on the Constitution* (Provo, Utah, 1988), 59–89.

94. *Federalist*, 66–68.

95. For the central role of this fear in the decisions of Edmund Randolph and George Mason not to sign the Constitution, and among Virginia Antifederalists in general, see Lance Banning, "Virginia: Sectionalism and the General Good," in *Ratifying the Constitution*, ed. Michael Allen Gillespie and Michael Lienesch (Lawrence, Kans., 1989), 261–299. But note that, even so, these critics almost always argued that commercial treaties and regulations should require a two-

thirds vote in Congress, not that these commercial powers should not be placed in federal hands.

96. For the stance of "bourgeois radicals" among the Antifederalists, see Cornell, "The Political Thought and Culture of the Anti-Federalists," chap. 5. A few examples might include "A Plebeian" (perhaps Melancton Smith), in Herbert J. Storing, ed., *The Complete Anti-Federalist*, 7 vols. (Chicago, 1981), 6:131–132, 140; and the essays collected in chap. 4 of W. B. Allen and Gordon Lloyd, eds., *The Essential Antifederalist* (Lanham, Md., 1985), especially "Aggrippa" at 235, 240–241, and "Centinel" at 253–254.

97. Banning, "Virginia," 274–276, 281–282; McCoy, "Madison and Visions of American Nationality," 245–248.

98. Speech of 8 Apr. 1789, in *PJM* 12:64–66; supporting speeches of 21 and 25 Apr. and 4 May in ibid., 97–103, 109–113, 125–130.

99. See, especially, the Report on Manufactures, *PAH* 10:287–290, which McCoy rightly calls "Hamilton's answer to Madison's defense of commercial discrimination" (*Elusive Republic*, 150).

100. Madison's advocacy of commercial discrimination in congressional speeches of the early 1790s is superbly summarized in McCoy, *Elusive Republic* 140–145, 162–163. The most important public expositions of his thinking came in his *National Gazette* essays on "Parties," "Republican Distribution of Citizens," and "Fashion" (*PJM* 14:197–198, 244–246, 257–259), together with his "Political Observations" of 20 Apr. 1796 (ibid., 15:511–534). For Jefferson, see Merrill Peterson, "Thomas Jefferson and Commercial Policy, 1783–1793," *WMQ* 22 (1965): 594–610. On the Jeffersonians in power, McCoy, *Elusive Republic*, chaps. 8–10, and Banning, *The Jeffersonian Persuasion*, chap. 10, should be supplemented by J. C. A. Stagg, "James Madison and the Coercion of Great Britain: Canada, the West Indies, and the War of 1812," *WMQ* 38 (1981): 3–34, and Donald R. Hickey, "American Trade Restrictions during the War of 1812," *JAH* 68 (1981): 517–538.

101. Hamilton's indebtedness to Hume was well established in John C. Miller, *Alexander Hamilton: Portrait in Paradox* (New York, 1959), 46–51 and passim, and in Gerald Stourzh, *Alexander Hamilton and the Idea of Republican Government* (Stanford, 1970), 70–75 and passim. For the influence of the Scottish mercantilist James Steuart (*An Inquiry into the Principles of Political Oeconomy* [1767]), see McDonald, *Novus Ordo Seclorum*, 119–128, 135–142, which summarizes the important, longer discussion of Hamilton's political economy in id., *Alexander Hamilton: A Biography* (New York, 1979).

102. For Hamilton's grand vision, in addition to the essential works just cited, see McCoy, *The Elusive Republic*, 146–152; Banning, *The Jeffersonian Persuasion*, 129–140. Also useful for contrasting party understandings of America's position in the world is Jerald A. Combs, *The Jay Treaty: Political Battleground of the Founding Fathers* (Berkeley, 1970). Hamilton's relationships with George Beckwith and George Hammond were not as sinister as they appear in Julian P. Boyd, *Number Seven: Alexander Hamilton's Secret Attempts to Control American Foreign Policy* (Princeton, N.J.,

1964), but it is generally agreed that they occasionally torpedoed the administration's stance in Anglo-American negotiations.

103. *PAH* 6:80–81.

104. See, further, "Notes on the Advantages of a National Bank," in *PAH* 8:223.

105. The clearest explanations of the workings of this system are in McDonald, *Alexander Hamilton,* chap. 8; id., *The Presidency of George Washington* (Lawrence, Kans., 1974), 47–65; and Ferguson, *The Power of the Purse,* 292–296. See also Donald F. Swanson, *The Origins of Hamilton's Fiscal Policies* (Gainesville, Fla., 1963).

106. Report on Manufactures, *PAH* 10:255–256.

107. Again, the Report on Manufactures, *PAH* 10:230–340, is the major text.

108. Banning, *The Jeffersonian Persuasion,* 153–155 and chap. 6; id., "The Hamiltonian Madison," 20–28.

109. Ferguson, *Power of the Purse,* 329–330; Whitney K. Bates, "Northern Speculators and Southern State Debts, 1790," *WMQ* 19 (1962): 32–34, 39.

110. Madison to Jefferson, 10 July and 8 Aug. 1791, *PJM* 14:43, 69.

111. John R. Nelson, "Alexander Hamilton and American Manufacturing: A Reexamination," *JAH* 65 (1979): 971–995; id., *Liberty and Property: Political Economy and Policymaking in the New Nation, 1789–1812* (Baltimore, 1987), 81–90; Alfred F. Young, *The Democratic Republicans of New York: The Origins, 1763–1797* (Chapel Hill, N.C., 1967).

112. Nelson, *Liberty and Property,* 10, 93.

113. Ibid., 90–96; Murrin, "The Great Inversion," 412, 419–421; and sources cited by both.

114. Here, without accepting their interpretive positions, I draw especially on Appleby, *Capitalism and a New Social Order;* Steven Watts, *The Republic Reborn: War and the Making of Liberal America, 1790–1820* (Baltimore, 1987); and Michael Durey, "Thomas Paine's Apostles: Radical Emigres and the Triumph of Jeffersonian Republicanism," *WMQ* 44 (1987): 661–686. Years ago, in *Tom Paine and Revolutionary America* (New York, 1976), Eric Foner suggested that the author of "Common Sense" and many of the artisans to whom he most appealed were sympathetic to both of the great transformations of the age: popular participation in political affairs, *and* the advent of an advanced market economy. The influence of this thinking, both democratic and profoundly pro-developmental, has only recently become a subject of close inquiry.

115. Jefferson to William H. Crawford, in *Works,* 11:537–539.

116. For the debates on the carrying trade, see McCoy, *The Elusive Republic,* 174–178, 212–216.

117. Ibid., chap. 10; Stagg, "James Madison and the Coercion of Great Britain." Madison, who had been willing even in 1790 to protect manufactories which had already emerged, though not to foster new ones, now specifically endorsed protection for some "manufacturing establishments . . . of the more complicated kind" (quoted in McCoy, *Elusive Republic,* 245). Jefferson was more reluctant. See his letter to Benjamin Austin, 9 Jan. 1816, *Works,* 11:502–505; and Merrill Peterson, *Thomas Jefferson and the New Nation* (New York, 1970), 940–941.

The Jeffersonians

First Principles

The Democratic Party—which, to the befuddlement of countless college freshmen, called itself "Republican" at first—emerged within three years of the adoption of the Constitution.[1] This was not coincidental. The Constitution marked, at once, a new beginning for the nation and a milestone in the revolutionary reconstruction which had started ten years before. In consequence, its launching led directly to the first and most ferocious party conflict in our annals. Supporters of the Constitution thought that it had saved the Union from the danger of a speedy dissolution and had armed that Union, after years of ineffectuality, with powers equal to its duties. At the same time, they were almost painfully aware that every measure of the infant federal government would set a precedent for everything to come, and that the Constitutional Convention had provided only a beginning toward a working federal system. Moreover, nearly half of those who voted on the question had opposed the Constitution, in many instances because they thought it inconsistent with the principles of 1776; and the division over the adoption of the Constitution had intensified a feeling, in its friends and foes alike, that human liberty itself might stand or fall on the decisions of the next few years.[2] The smallest actions had to be considered in an atmosphere that citizens, today, must struggle to imagine.

On the other hand, the present moment in world history may offer us an unexampled guide to understanding the conditions under which these founders went about their work. In 1789, Americans were still a revolutionary people, and the launching of the reconstructed federal government was not unlike the reconstructions going forward at this writing through the whole of Eastern Europe. As is true in Poland, Russia, or Rumania today, awesome consequences seemed to hinge on even small decisions—conse-

313

quences that contemporaries thought could literally determine if the first great democratic Revolution would survive, consequences that would certainly decide what sort of nation the United States would be. The members of the first administration and the first new Congress were confronted first with the specific problems that had wrecked the old Confederation. But beyond those problems lay the shaping of the future; and among the leading framers of the Constitution—not to mention its opponents—there were radically contrasting visions of the sort of future the United States should have. Out of these divisions, the first political parties would emerge.

First Principles

The argument began within the infant federal government itself, when Alexander Hamilton, the first Secretary of the Treasury, presented his proposals for the funding of the revolutionary debt. Including the arrears of interest, which had not been paid for years, the state and federal governments owed $80,000,000, mostly to domestic creditors who held the bonds and other promises that had financed the Revolution. Hamilton's *Report on Public Credit*, submitted to Congress on January 14, 1790, recommended that the federal government assume responsibility for the remaining obligations of the states as well as those of the Confederation Congress, and that it undertake to pay the whole, at full face value, to the current holders of the notes. Under the provisions of this plan, the old certificates of debt would be replaced by new ones paying lower interest. In exchange, the government would pledge specific revenues to steady payment of that interest, and the nation's public credit (its ability to borrow) would be instantly restored. With interest payments guaranteed, the bonds would hold their value on the private money markets, and retirement of the principal could be postponed until it was convenient for the government to act.[3]

The implications of this plan were grander than was evident upon its face, although the secretary said enough to trouble several members of the Congress. Dashing, arrogant, and absolutely brilliant—he was barely 35 but had ascended like a rocket through the Continental staff and into national politics, where he had played a central role in the adoption of the Constitution—Hamilton has been described as "the premiere state-builder in a generation of state-builders."[4] He faced toward the Atlantic and envisioned an arena of competing empires which America would have to enter much like any other state. In time, as he conceived it, the United States could take a brilliant part in this arena, and he meant to earn immortal fame as founder of its greatness.

But for America to have this kind of future, Hamilton believed, it would be necessary first for it to have the economic and financial underpinnings for successful competition: institutions similar to those that had enabled tiny England to achieve the pinnacle of international prestige.[5] It would be necessary, too, for the United States to conscientiously avoid a confrontation with Great Britain, the single nation which (with its naval power) could threaten the United States in war, or through investments in the new republic's economic growth, could aid it most impressively toward greatness. Taking British institutions as a model, Hamilton was setting out to build a modern state, a nation able to compete with European empires on the Europeans' terms.[6]

Hamilton's design for national greatness may have been essentially complete when he delivered his first report, although the whole of it was not to be apparent for at least another year. With proper management, he realized, the heavy burden of the revolutionary debt could be transformed into a positive advantage for the country. Federal funding of states' as well as national obligations could accomplish more than the establishment of public credit: it could tie the economic interests of a vital segment of America's elite to the success of national institutions and create a counterbalance to the local loyalties that Hamilton perceived as potent dangers to the Union.[7] And even as it bound the monied interests to the central government's success, the funding program would erect a framework for the nation's future role in global competition, transforming governmental obligations into liquid capital, a currency supply, that could be multiplied by using the certificates of debt to back creation of a national bank. The bonds and banknotes could be used, in turn, to foster manufacturing and commerce, whose rapid growth would lay the groundwork for the nation's economic independence. Thus, the funding program was intended from the first to further major economic and political, as well as narrowly financial, goals.[8]

The trouble with this scheme, which Hamilton unveiled in a succession of reports, was that it aided certain citizens and regions more immediately than others. More than that, it deeply threatened other founders' visions of the sort of nation the United States should be.

Both problems were immediately apparent. In the House of Representatives, the funding program instantly aroused intense anxieties about corrupting links between the federal government and special interest factions. In many cases, current holders of the debt had purchased their certificates for fractions of their value, often from disbanding, unpaid revolutionary soldiers who had sold the government's uncertain promises for ready cash. Over time, the bonds had gravitated disproportionately into the hands of monied interests in the North and East. To pay the full face value to the present holders would entail a major shift of wealth from South to North, from West to East, and from the body of the people to a few rich men whose fortunes would expand dramatically as a result of federal largesse.[9] Moreover, federal assumption of the states' remaining debts would temporarily reward the states that had done least to pay their debts at the expense of those that had done most. In addition, by demanding that the federal government impose internal taxes, the financial plan would tilt the federal balance markedly toward greater central power—which, of course, was part of what the secretary *hoped* it would accomplish. All of this, some congressmen objected, was profoundly incompatible with harmony among the nation's sections, with republican morality, and with the relatively modest gap between the rich and poor that seemed essential to a healthy representative regime.[10]

Indeed, to Hamilton's alarm, James Madison, the major architect of constitutional reform and very much the "first man" in the Congress—Hamilton's collaborator in the classic exegesis of the Constitution and the draftsman of the Bill of Rights—soon assumed the leadership of this minority of critics.[11] Disgusted by the speculative orgy sparked by Hamilton's report,[12] revolted by the prospect that the victims of the government's original default would now be victimized again, and drawing back in horror from the notion that the country would "erect the monuments of her gratitude, not to those who saved her liberties, but to those who had enriched themselves in her funds," Madison insisted that the case was so extraordinary that it had to be decided "on the great and fundamental principles of justice."[13] As an alternative to Hamilton's proposals, Madison suggested paying present holders of the debt the highest value that securities had reached on private markets, but returning the remaining portion of the full face value of the bonds to the soldiers and other original owners.

Madison was easily defeated on his plan to discriminate between original and secondary holders, which many saw as such a violent breach of preexisting contracts as to absolutely wreck the nation's credit. But Madison was not so easily defeated on the issue of a federal assumption of the states' remaining debts. Over this, a bitter battle raged for months, provoking threats of an immediate disruption of the Union, until the Secretary of the Treasury appealed to Thomas Jefferson, who had returned from France to take up duties as the first Secretary of State, to help him end the crisis.[14] With Jefferson's assistance, Madison and Hamilton resolved the impasse in an after-dinner bargain. The resulting Compromise of 1790 modified the details of assumption and traded passage of the funding legislation for an act providing that the federal government would move in 1800 to a permanent location on the Potomac River.[15]

In 1791, however, Hamilton delivered his reports proposing the creation of a national bank and federal encouragement of native manufactures. Jefferson agreed with Madison that the incorporation of a bank was not within the powers granted by the Constitution—indeed, that the creation of a national monopoly of this or any other sort amounted to a usurpation of authority that could be likened to the parliamentary encroachments that had ended in the Revolution.[16] Increasingly, the two Virginians feared that Hamilton was following a course that could result in concentrated central power, domination of the South and West by the commercial and financial East, subversion of the federal government's responsiveness to popular control, oppression of the agricultural majority of people and—in time—a threat to the survival of democracy itself.[17]

Their reasoning requires some further explanation, but should not be difficult to grasp. Already troubled by the funding program's transfer of the nation's wealth from the productive to the non-productive classes, Jefferson and Madison suspected that creation of a national bank would deepen the emerging chasm, permitting those who had already benefitted from the secretary's program to enrich themselves again by trading their certificates for bank stock, which was guaranteed to earn substantial profits.[18] Federal encouragement of manufacturing and commerce would compound this problem, while the broad construction of the Constitution used to justify these programs would accelerate the shift of power from the states to the central government and from the House of Representatives to the federal executive. The economic program and its author's disregard for constitutional restraints both seemed to center power at a level and in governmental branches least responsive to the people. At the same time, the financial program seemed to be creating in the congressmen and private citizens who were enriched by governmental payments an interest fundamentally at odds with that of the majority of people, whose direct involvement in the nation's daily politics most Federalists seemed obviously to dread. In fact, the more apparent it became that Hamilton was following a British model, the more opponents saw him as another Robert Walpole: as a minister who was subverting legislative independence and endangering the social fabric by creating a corrupted following of congressmen and other citizens who lived off of the treasury at popular expense.[19] By the fall of 1791, Madison and Jefferson believed that Hamilton intended to "administer" the new republic toward a government and a society that would subvert the revolutionary dream.[20]

They had already urged the revolutionary poet, Philip Freneau, to come to Philadelphia to start a paper that would rouse the nation to the danger. During 1792, in unsigned essays in this *National Gazette*, Madison and others built a systematic ideology of opposition and called upon the voters to support the "Republican Interest" in the fall congressional elections.[21]

The partisan division of the early 1790s can be analyzed in a variety of ways. Like many of the conflicts in the old Confederation Congress, it pitted the New England states against Virginia and her neighbors, the states that benefitted from the funding program against those that did not, commercial areas against the planting regions and the smaller farmers.[22] By 1792, however, each of the emerging parties was beginning to acquire its own adherents in every section of the country, showing that the argument involved a great deal more than simple economic interests. As supporters of a strong new government and rapid economic growth, the Federalists appealed to merchants, artisans, and market farmers—and beyond those groups, to many who believed that ordered liberty was threatened by the radical contagion started by the Revolution.[23] As opponents of a grasping central government, which seemed to shower favors on a few, the Republicans, by contrast, appealed to former Antifederalists who had insisted that a distant central government would threaten popular control, to southerners who had suspected that the Constitution would result in domination by the North and East, and to the rising democratic sentiments of countless ordinary voters, who were often special targets for the Federalists' contempt.

The two emerging parties plainly had their strongest bases in New England and the South, a consequence of their contrasting economic programs. Nevertheless, the party battle also pitted centralists against the principled proponents of a strict construction of the Constitution, enemies of popular commotions against the champions of popular participation in political affairs, and advocates of governmental guidance of the nation's economic growth against opponents of monopolies and privilege, who favored private actions and decisions. The controversy split the leading architects of constitutional reform into two groups: those who had concluded from the lessons of the 1780s that liberty was most endangered by its own excess—a group for whom the Constitution was an instrument for turning back the Revolution—and those who held, as did the two Virginians, that the Constitution was an instrument for shielding and extending revolutionary gains.[24] The disagreement penetrated to the very essence of colliding visions of America itself.

Alexander Hamilton, like most Americans, believed that proper governments are founded on consent, and are created to protect the natural liberties that citizens do not surrender when political societies are formed. But while he clearly planned to make the people prosperous and free, Hamilton's concerns were focused tightly on the state, not upon the citizens of whom the public is composed. Although he certainly believed that everyone would benefit in time from rapid economic growth, the secretary emphasized the quick development of manufacturing and commerce, which were critical to the correction of a chronic deficit of payments, and dismissed as selfish the inevitable complaints about the temporary sectional and class inequities that would result.

Madison and Jefferson, by contrast, were committed to an image of a more responsive government supported by, and nurturing, a revolutionary social order. Sound republics, they believed, must rest on relatively equal, self-directing, independent citizens whose personal autonomy would make them capable of free political decisions and assure their vigilant, continuing participation in political affairs. The great co-architects of Jeffersonian ideals were not the enemies of independent artisans and merchants, but they did oppose monopolies and other programs (like the national bank or Hamilton's Society for Establishing Useful Manufactures) which seemed to them to be creating classes who depended for their livelihoods on governmental privileges and payments. Beyond that, Madison and Jefferson resisted plans to force the country prematurely toward intensive economic change, for that could replicate the European factories and cities which divided workers from employers and confined "the lower orders" to a narrow, straitened, and dependent life that might be incompatible with freedom. The archetypal citizen, for the Virginians, was the independent farmer-owner, who produced necessities of life and who, by being free from personal dependence, would be free as well to vote or fight according to his own, autonomous desires.[25]

The French Revolution

By the summer of 1792, when Hamilton decided to confront his critics by attacking Jefferson's connection with the *National Gazette,* the clashing groups within the federal government had hurled themselves into a full-fledged public war. In anonymous but hardly secret essays in the Philadelphia *Gazette of the United Sates,* Hamilton condemned his rival for provoking popular suspicions, blasted Jefferson's original ambivalence about the Constitution, and insisted that the opposition leader should resign his post if he could not support administration programs. Jefferson's supporters answered with defenses of his record and repeated accusations that Hamilton's economic program was deliberately designed to undermine the Constitution, build a native aristocracy, and gradually reintroduce hereditary rule. (Angered by the anti-democratic tone of high society in Philadelphia and by a growing disapproval of developments in France, Jefferson had accidentally contributed to the commotion in the press and, in the process, had supplanted Madison as the symbolic leader of the opposition. An enterpriser published as a preface to *The Rights of Man*—Thomas Paine's reply to Edmund Burke's *Reflections on the Revolution in France*—a private note in which the penman of the Revolution wrote that he was pleased that something would at least be said against "the political heresies which have sprung among us.")[26] As the controversy spread from newspapers in Philadelphia to sheets throughout the country, citizens in every section were beginning to identify with one or the other of the two emerging parties.[27]

Still, as long as party conflict focused on the mysteries of Hamiltonian finance, great masses of the people were unmoved. The tiny federal government intruded little on their daily lives. George Washington was at its helm, prosperity was rising, and the implications of the economic program could be difficult to understand.

Soon, however, all of this would change. Great masses of the people were aroused. Indeed, they were aroused so strongly that the bitterness of the division has been equalled only once in American history—during the time that actually resulted in a civil war. By the later 1790s, crowds were fighting each other in the streets. Gentlemen eluded one another on the sidewalks to avoid the courtesy of tipping hats. Self-appointed agents spied on leaders of the opposition party, and a congressman was jailed for his political opinions. Party leaders on both sides considered a recourse to force.

All this happened when the clashing visions of the two emerging parties intermeshed with their colliding sympathies about the Revolution in France and with their different judgments of the country's interests as a neutral. From 1787 through 1792, Americans had followed the developments in France with general admiration. Most believed that Lafayette and other revolutionaries were inspired by the American example. Many hoped that liberty would spread from France to every part of Europe. Then the Revolution turned in much more radical directions. On February 1, 1793, 11 days after the execution of Louis XVI, the revolutionary French Republic declared war on Great Britain. On April 22, President Washington proclaimed that the United States would pursue a "friendly and impartial" conduct toward the warring powers. While almost no one wished to see the country get entangled in the war, great numbers were offended that America would not be able, at the least, to lean in the direction of republican France, with which America had a treaty of alliance since the Revolutionary War. On the other side, of course, large numbers of conservative Americans, who were increasingly alarmed about the violence in France, confiscations of aristocratic property, a very democratic constitution, and attacks upon the Church, believed that Washington was absolutely right.

The Proclamation of Neutrality divided ordinary citizens as no preceding policy had done, and the division deepened as the warring powers both began to prey on neutral shipping. As the greatest trading neutral of the time, America could not avoid entanglement in what was rapidly developing into a worldwide war; advocating different ideologies and different forms of government, the European powers were immersed in mortal combat, and each of them intended to deny the other the benefits of neutral commerce. Neither could Americans escape emotional involvement. Republican idealism and the memory of French assistance in the Revolution generated potent sympathies, on one side, for the French Republic. Others sympathized with England, the motherland of libertarian ideas, the most effective barrier to French expansion, and by far the most important trading partner of the new American Republic.

The European war divided citizens along the lines already marked by the domestic conflict. The Jeffersonian Republicans already saw themselves as champions of liberty at home, defenders of the revolutionary cause of popular self-governance against conspirators who wanted to betray it. (This, of course, is why they called themselves "Republicans" to start with.) After 1793, it was inevitable that the Republicans would see the French as champions of liberty abroad, at war with all the aristocracies and monarchies of Europe. Republicans already saw their Federalist opponents as a faction plotting to reverse the American Revolution. It was easy, now, for the Republicans to see the Federalists as reaching out toward an alliance with the European despots and, in time perhaps, toward a political reunion with the English fountainhead of Hamiltonian ideas. The Federalists, of course, were just as ready to conclude that the Republicans were seeking an alliance with the French and, probably, a second, much more violent revolution in America itself.

Here was a dispute that ordinary citizens found easier to understand. Conflicting sympathies in foreign policy distinguished the emerging parties in a way that the debate about the consequences of the economic system never had. Clashing sentiments about the second democratic revolution resonated with contrasting attitudes about the people's role at home. Growing numbers sided either with the Federalists, who called themselves the party of order and claimed to be resisting a collapse into the anarchy and violence of France, or with the Jeffersonian Republicans, who saw themselves resisting a conspiracy against equality and liberty, at home as well as overseas.

The European war absorbed American attention through most of Washington's second term, bringing an accession of popular support to both political parties. On balance, though, events between the Proclamation of Neutrality and Washington's retirement favored the opponents of administration policies, which seemed to lean increasingly toward England and against the democratic spirit of equality and popular political participation being carried to new heights in France. Thousands of Americans turned out to see the French Republic's first ambassador to the United States, "Citizen" Edmond Genet, who came ashore at Charleston and conducted a triumphal tour to Philadelphia in the spring of 1793.[28] A score of democratic-republican societies sprang up in every portion of the country, filled with "citizens" determined to support the French and to assert the people's rights at home.[29] Revolutionary songs—"The Marseillaise" and "Ca Ira"—were sung in countless towns. Hundreds donned the French cockade.

Misled by the enthusiasm, Citizen Genet encouraged violations of neutrality and put himself on a collision course with Washington's administration, which soon demanded his recall. But early in 1794, soon after Jefferson's retirement as Secretary of State, the Royal Navy suddenly seized more than 200 American vessels engaged in trade with the French West Indies. The people were enraged, and the Republicans in Congress moved for strong retaliation in the form of sharp restrictions on the British imports that dominated American trade. The Federalists preferred negotiations and increased expenditures for national defense. (Ninety percent of the revenues on which the administration's funding plan depended were derived from import duties, most of which were paid on British goods.) In March 1794, Washington appointed John Jay, Secretary for Foreign Affairs during the Confederation and now Chief Justice of the United States, special minister to England.

Jay's negotiations took almost a year, during which the party conflict rose to new extremes. By the summer of 1794, western Pennsylvania was literally in arms against the excise tax on whiskey, which had been imposed to pay for the assumption of state debts. Some 13,000 federalized militia, with Hamilton along to represent the government, were mobilized to deal with the rebellion.[30] The Republicans, who had been damaged by the violence even though they disapproved of armed resistance to the law, recovered by condemning the recourse to massive military force and by attacking Washington's denunciation of the "self-created societies" (the Democratic-Republican clubs) on which he blamed the popular resistance. All this while, moreover, Britain had continued its high-handed policies on the seas while refusing to evacuate its soldiers from a string of forts in the American Northwest, which it had occupied since Independence. Growing numbers of people were increasingly impatient with the government's inaction.

In this context, John Jay's Treaty with the British, which was not presented to the Senate until June 1795, appeared to many to confirm the opposition's charges that the Federalists would suffer any insult if it issued from the British. In exchange for a British agreement to evacuate the northwest posts and to permit small vessels to trade with the British West Indies, the United States abandoned its position on the rights of neutrals, granted Britain most-favored-nation privileges in U.S. ports, and forswore the imposition of discriminatory duties on the British. Although historians are still divided over whether the American negotiator might have achieved better terms, the popular reaction at the time was decidedly adverse.[31] Many saw the treaty as an outright sacrifice of national interests and a gross betrayal of the revolutionary French. The Senate ratified it by a single vote, and all of Washington's prestige was necessary to defeat an effort in the House of Representatives to refuse the appropriations necessary to put it into effect. Further, in the presidential election of 1796, John Adams defeated Thomas Jefferson by a margin of only three electoral votes. Under the terms of the Constitution at that time, Jefferson became vice president, a post from which he would continue to direct the opposition.

Washington had left the hapless Adams with a crisis.[32] Damaged and offended by Jay's Treaty, the French announced that they would treat American ships "in the same manner as they suffer the English to treat them." Seizures followed, and the President responded, much as Washington had done in 1794, by recommending both negotiations and increased appropriations for defense. Adams chose John Marshall of Virginia, Charles C. Pinckney of South Carolina, and Elbridge Gerry of Massachusetts for a mission to resolve the crisis. The negotiations stalled when unofficial agents of the French foreign minister—referred to in American dispatches as X, Y, and Z—informed the American commissioners that nothing could be done until they paid a bribe to Talleyrand and agreed to a large American loan to the Republic.

In April 1798, goaded by Republicans in Congress, Adams released the papers revealing the XYZ Affair. Patriotic fury of a wholly unexampled nature swept the states from end to end; and on the crest of this hysteria, which swelled into a widespread fear of treasonable plots between the French and their Republican supporters, the Federalists embarked upon a naval war with France. They also seized the opportunity to launch a program of repression consciously intended to destroy domestic opposition to their programs. French and Irish immigrants supported the Republicans and favored France in its collision with Great Britain. In June and July, in the Alien Act, Congress extended to fourteen years the period of residence required for naturalization and gave the President the power to summarily deport any alien whose residence he deemed a threat to the United States. Then, in a direct blow to the opposition, Congress passed the Sedition Act, making it a criminal offense to incite opposition to the laws or to "write, print, utter, or publish . . . any false, scandalous, and malicious writing . . . against the government of the United States, or either house of the Congress of the United States, or the President of the United States with intent to defame them or to bring them . . . into dispute."[33]

Enforced by a partisan judiciary, the Alien and Sedition Acts established a bloodless reign of terror in the country. Under the Sedition Act (or under the common law of seditious libel), every important Republican newspaper in the country was attacked. William Duane of the *Philadelphia Aurora* (which had replaced the *National Gazette* as the leading Republican sheet when the latter failed financially in 1793), Thomas Adams of the *Independent Chronicle* in Boston, and Republican pamphleteers such as Thomas Cooper and James Thompson Callender all faced prosecution. The *Time Piece* and the *Argus,* the only Republican newspapers in New York City, were forced out of business. Matthew Lyon of Vermont, a Republican congressman, was imprisoned for a publication incident to his reelection campaign in 1798. Men were prosecuted under the Sedition Act for offenses as diverse and as trivial as circulating a petition for its repeal, erecting a liberty pole, or expressing a drunken wish that a cannon ball had struck the President in his behind.

At first, Republicans were seriously disheartened. At the peak of the patriotic fever, several congressmen retreated to their states and left the Federalist majority to work its will. Jefferson and others who remained in Philadelphia were trailed by self-appointed spies, who hoped for proof of the leaders' French connections. In the elections of 1798, the Federalists made sizeable gains. To the Republicans, the quasi-war with France, the Alien and Sedition Acts, and a measure authorizing the enlistment of a provisional army of 50,000 men, which could be mobilized in the event of an invasion, seemed abundant proof that the conspiracy against the country's liberty had burst into the open. A handful of Virginians talked about secession and about preparing to defend themselves against the federal army. Yet Jefferson and other party leaders never lost their faith in their ability to bring the people to their senses.

While Albert Gallatin and Edward Livingston opposed the crisis laws in Congress, insisting that the legislation was a patent violation of the First Amendment and a potent danger to the people's underlying right to criticize official acts and change their government through free elections, Jefferson and Madison decided to arouse the states. The two Virginians each prepared a secret draft of legislative resolutions condemning the Alien and Sedition Acts. Madison, who had decided not to stand for reelection to Congress in 1796, gave his draft to John Taylor of Caroline, Virginia's agricultural thinker and the Republican party's most influential pamphleteer. Jefferson slipped his to John Breckenridge of Kentucky. On November 17, 1798, Kentucky's legislature resolved that the repressive laws were unconstitutional, "void and of no force." On December 24, Virginia voted a similar condemnation and called upon the other states to join the protests.[34]

All the other states refused to join Virginia and Kentucky on a path that led, much later, to nullification and secession. Still, the resolutions served the party leaders' more immediate objectives. For two full years, Republicans condemned the Federalists' hostility to popular control, always with the election of 1800 firmly in their minds. Victims of the federal prosecutions were portrayed as martyrs. Wartime taxes made new friends. The federal tax on lands and houses met with organized resistance from some Pennsylvania Germans, although the trouble hardly justified the name of Fries's "Rebellion." In time, the opposition even found an accidental ally in the plump and self-important person of John Adams.

The President had lost his first enthusiasm for the quasi-war before the end of 1798. While he supported naval warfare with the armed French cruisers, the Hamiltonians within his party pressed continually for a larger army, partly for its value in intimidating the domestic opposition. Sharing some of the Republican suspicion of a "standing army," which was deeply rooted in American tradition, Adams liked the larger army even less when Washington compelled him to accept "that creole bastard," Hamilton himself, as second in command.[35] Meanwhile, there were growing indications that the French had seen the folly of their course and would receive a new American ambassador with the dignity befitting the representative of a sovereign republic.[36]

On February 18, 1799, without consulting with his cabinet or the Federalists in Congress, Adams nominated William Vans Murray, ambassador to the Netherlands, to make another effort to negotiate with France. Adams's message to the Congress was a bombshell, and in no great time, his conduct shattered Federalist cohesion. In the first place, the appointment of an envoy to the French Republic signalled that the crisis could be ended short of an extension of the war. The Federalists were left with swollen military forces, higher taxes, and an unrelenting effort to suppress the opposition at a time when it was clear that any danger of a French invasion (which was always slight) had passed. Public sentiment began to swing to the Republicans again. Moreover, the reversal of the public mood went forward as the Federalists divided in a bitter intraparty war. On May 6, 1800, Adams blasted Secretary of War James McHenry, who was in the President's office on some minor business, berating him for his subservience to Hamilton and forcing him to offer his resignation. Four days later, when Timothy Pickering refused to follow McHenry's example, Adams fired the Secretary of State. With the quasi-war concluding and the presidential contest drawing near, the split among the Federalists was open and complete.

In the election of 1800, the Federalists were too distracted by their own internal quarrel to manage their Republican opponents. Immersed in intra-party plots, Hamilton was outmaneuvered in New York by his despised opponent Aaron Burr, who ran a stronger slate of candidates, worked harder in the city's wards, and carried both the legislature and the state's electoral vote for the Republican alliance. (Here, as elsewhere, artisans and laborers who had supported constitutional reform had gradually deserted from the Federalist alliance as administration measures failed to offer some protection from imported British goods, and as the local Federalists displayed an arrogant contempt for ordinary voters.)[37] Republicans, of course, delighted in their foes' internal fight, insisting all the while that the disputants were distinguished only by the Hamiltonians' subservience to England. They even managed to secure the publication of a private pamphlet in which Hamilton came close to calling the President insane. When the electoral votes were counted, Jefferson and Burr had 73 to Adams's 65.

The Federalists made one last stand. In the lame-duck, second session of the Federalist Fifth Congress, which was constitutionally required to break the awkward tie between the Republicans' first and second presidential choices, the Federalists held ranks through 35 ballots for Aaron Burr. Still, their unity and zest for party warfare had been badly shaken during the campaign, and they were never to control the national government again.

The Jeffersonians in Power

Thomas Jefferson described the victory of 1800 as "as real a revolution in the principles of our government as that of 1776 was in its form."[38] Jefferson exaggerated, as was frequently his bent, and yet the comment also captured two important truths: the party battle of the first few years of the Republic was as fierce as any in our annals, flowing as it did from radically contrasting visions of the sort of nation the United States should be; and Jefferson's inauguration did initiate as sharp a change in governmental attitudes and policies as almost any party triumph one might name.

For twelve years after Washington's inauguration, the infant federal government had been directed by a Hamiltonian design for national greatness. It was a brilliant scheme, in service to a grand ambition, and it worked in much the way that Hamilton expected (although the plan for federal encouragement of native manufactures was never written into law). A clash with Britain was avoided during the 1790s, if only at the cost of a demeaning treaty and a naval war with France. The funding program and the national bank provided capital for economic growth and placed the government's finances on a solid institutional foundation. As Europe went to war, the new Republic prospered, and prosperity attached the people to the government's success. Nevertheless, in 1798 and 1799, the Federalists were swept up in a panic that endangered fundamental liberties as we have since defined them in the federal republic. In the end, although the Federalists believed that they were certainly the wisest and the best—"natural" social leaders whose positions, educations, and experience equipped them, and perhaps entitled them, to put a vigorous new government into effect—the Federalists were always far less confident of their abilities as politicians. They expected ordinary voters to be silent and submissive in the intervals between elections, and they could never trust that, even then, the people would defer to those best qualified to lead. The upshot was a devastating loss in 1800. The presidential contest was a close one, in part because so many states decided that electors would be chosen by the legislatures rather than the voters.[39] The popular elections were a very different story, with the Federalists losing 40 seats in Congress. For the first time, the Republicans would easily control the Senate as well as the House. There would be little to prevent them from pursuing the ideas they had developed in the years of opposition.

The victory of 1800, as the Jeffersonians perceived it, rescued the Republic from a counterrevolutionary plot. Nevertheless, a change of men was not enough without a change of governmental measures. Hamilton had looked toward the Atlantic and supported rapid economic growth, envisioning the quick emergence of an integrated state in which the rise of native manufactures would provide materials for export and a large domestic market for the country's agricultural producers. The Republicans, by contrast, were more concerned about the preservation of the relatively democratic distribution of the nation's wealth. While they had always advocated freeing oceanic commerce and providing foreign markets for the farmers, their ambitions for the nation focused much more on the West, where a republic resting on the sturdy stock of independent farmer-owners could be constantly revitalized as it expanded over space. Hamilton had been intent on the creation of a potent central state. Jefferson and his lieutenants—Madison at State and Albert Gallatin at Treasury—were dedicated to restricting federal action to the limited responsibilities envisioned at the government's creation, trusting that America would make its impact on the world by sheer example of its democratic institutions. Hamilton had seen the national debt as an advantage for the nation, because it could be used to back a stable currency supply. The Jeffersonians despised it. To their minds, the interest payments on the debt enriched a non-productive few and forged a dangerous, corrupting link between the federal executive and wealthy monied interests. They would not repudiate it, to be sure, any more than they would move immediately for revocation of the charter of the national bank. The public's contracts would be kept. But they were willing to subordinate much else to the retirement of the debt as quickly as existing contracts would permit, and they were bent on doing so without resorting to internal taxes, which were better left, in peacetime, to the states.

The Jeffersonians did not dismantle all their predecessors' work. With sound Republicans in power, they assumed, the country could be eased toward change; and it would change more certainly that way. But Jefferson proclaimed the party's dedication to a major change of course in his inaugural address, announcing his commitment to "a wise and frugal government which shall restrain men from injuring one another, shall leave them otherwise free to regulate their own pursuits of industry and improvement, and shall not take from the mouth of labor the bread it has earned." This kind of government, he hinted, would be guided by a set of policies profoundly different from the Federalist design: genuine neutrality, not national subservience to Britain; rapid payment of the national debt; withdrawal of the federal government from its involvement with the nation's economic life; reliance on the state militia rather than a standing army; and a recognition that the states "in all their rights," were "the most competent administrations for our domestic concerns and the surest bulwark against anti-republican tendencies."[40]

Reform began in 1801 while Jefferson awaited the December meeting of the Seventh Congress, in which his party would control both houses. Presidential pardons went to the remaining victims of the Federalists' Sedition

Act, which had been written to expire with Adams's administration.[41] A handful of the most committed Federalists were purged from federal office, and the President appointed only sound Republicans to fill these public trusts.[42] The evolution of a partisan appointments policy was not complete enough or quick enough to satisfy some members of the party, who argued that "no enemy to democratic government [should] be provided with the means to sap and destroy any of its principles nor to profit by a government to which they are hostile in theory and practice."[43] But even radicals were satisfied when Jefferson announced his program at the opening of Congress.[44] After a review of foreign policy and Indian affairs, he recommended the repeal of all internal taxes. "The remaining sources of revenue will be sufficient," he insisted, "to provide for the support of government, to pay the interest on the public debts, and to discharge the principals in shorter periods than the laws or the general expectations had contemplated. . . . Sound principles will not justify our taxing the industry of our fellow citizens to accumulate treasure for wars we know not when, and which might not perhaps happen but from temptations offered by that treasure." Public burdens, Jefferson admitted, could be lifted only if expenditures fell too. But there was room to wonder "whether offices or officers have not been multiplied unnecessarily." The army, for example, had been swollen far beyond the numbers necessary to defend the western posts, and there was no use for the surplus. "For defense against foreign invasion, their number is as nothing; nor is it conceived needful or safe that a standing army should be kept up in time of peace." The judiciary system, packed and altered by the Federalists at the conclusion of their reign, would naturally "present itself to the contemplation of Congress." And the laws concerning naturalization might again be liberalized.[45]

The Seventh Congress, voting usually on party lines, enacted everything that Jefferson had recommended. It also gave approval to a plan by Gallatin for the complete retirement of the public debt by 1817, despite the abolition of internal taxes. Indeed, the session seemed to Jefferson so good a start toward introducing proper principles that there was little left to recommend in 1802.[46] The effort of the next few years would be to keep the course already set.[47]

"The revolution of 1800," as Jefferson described it, was amazingly successful. To the Federalists' surprise, America did not collapse into disorder. No one's property was threatened by the mob.[48] Instead, the country prospered and expanded as it never had before. In 1804, the people showed their general approval, reelecting Jefferson by a margin of 162 electoral votes to just 14 for Charles C. Pinckney while increasing the Republican majority in Congress. By that time, the President had even shown that he would not permit fine points of principle to stand between his conduct and the public good. In 1803, he authorized the purchase of Louisiana from the French despite his doubts that strict construction of the Constitution authorized the act. The Louisiana Purchase doubled the size of the United States and seemed to promise that the republic of the Jeffersonian vision—the republic of independent, landowning farmers who seemed to be ideally suited for self-governance and freedom—could continue to expand as far into the future as the men of 1803 could see.

And yet, there was a weakness in this vision, which would plague the President and his successor through the next three terms. Alexander Hamilton had always argued that the world would not permit republican idealists to dream their dreams in peace. Other powers would prevent it. And, indeed, in 1803, France and Britain resumed their titanic war. In 1805, Napoleon destroyed the European coalition and became essentially unchallengeable by land, while British Admiral Horatio Lord Nelson shattered the French fleet at the Battle of Trafalgar. At this point, the two great powers, the tiger and the shark, resorted necessarily to economic warfare, especially to dedicated efforts to deny the other the advantages of neutral commerce. As the greatest trading neutral of the age, although a minor military power, the United States was caught between these giants. By 1807, they had seized some 1,500 U.S. ships, and there were few remaining ports to which Americans could sail without the threat of seizure by one or the other of the two warring powers. Moreover, in the summer of 1807, near the mouth of the Chesapeake Bay, the British frigate "Leopard" fired upon the American warship "Chesapeake," forced it to submit to search, and pressed four sailors into British service. For years, the British had been stopping merchant ships to search them for deserters, taking naturalized Americans of British birth, and sometimes seizing native-born Americans as well. The "Chesapeake" affair was nonetheless an outrage of a different sort. To fire upon a frigate was an act of war.

War was what the people called for in a fury reminiscent of the XYZ Affair ten years before. Especially in the American Northwest—in Indiana, Michigan, and Illinois, where British officials in Canada soon began to give assistance and encouragement to Tecumseh and the Prophet, Shawnee brothers who were trying to unite the western tribes against the advance of American settlement—the demand for war rose steadily from this point on. Yet Jefferson's administration was determined to confront the troubles in the way their principles required. Both war itself and all the normal preparations for a war—higher taxes, swollen military forces, rising debts, and larger governmental powers—had always seemed a deadly peril for republics. Any of these measures would require a radical reversal of the course that the administration had been following since 1801.

In addition, Jefferson and Madison had long believed that the United States possessed a weapon that provided an alternative to war, a weapon that had proven its effectiveness during the long struggle preceding American Independence. That weapon was its trade. Most American exports, as they saw it, were necessities of life: raw materials and food on which the Europeans and their island colonies were vitally dependent. Most American imports, on the other hand, were "niceties" or "luxuries" that the United States could either do without or manufacture at a shop or household level on its own. Accordingly, in any confrontation with the Europeans (especially the British), the United States could force the enemy to terms by a denial of its commerce, and without the dangers to its government or social order that a war would necessarily entail.[49]

In 1807, Jefferson's administration answered French and British measures by placing a complete embargo on foreign trade.[50] The great embargo did impose some hardships on the Europeans. Unhappily, its consequences for America were even worse; it called for more self-sacrifice than many citizens were willing to display. All American sailings for foreign ports were halted for more than a year. The result was a depression that affected every section of the country, but was most severe in Federalist New England, whose economy was heavily dependent on its shipping. Resistance by New Englanders was fierce, and non-cooperation and illegal sailings could be countered only by enforcement measures so draconian that they endangered the Jeffersonians' reputation as defenders of civil rights.[51] The Federalists enjoyed a brief revival.

In short, the great embargo broke America before it broke the Europeans. To maintain the peace within America, the Jeffersonians—whose party vision did not change when Madison succeeded Jefferson in 1809—were forced to settle for less stringent measures. The embargo was replaced in 1809 with a measure confining nonintercourse to trade between America and the two belligerent powers, France or England.[52] In 1810, nonintercourse gave way in turn to a provision that restrictions would be reimposed on either European power if the other would respect America's neutral rights—a carrot rather than a stick. Napoleon, who realized that the removal of American restrictions could only aid the British, delivered an ambiguous announcement suggesting that he would exempt Americans from his Berlin and Milan Decrees against neutral vessels. Madison chose to interpret that announcement as fulfilling the American demands and called upon the British to repeal their Orders in Council. When the British government refused, he reimposed nonintercourse with Britain.

By the winter of 1811–1812, commercial warfare had been pressed, in one form or another, for a full four years. It had enraged the shipping center of New England and encouraged the resurgence of a party that the Jeffersonians regarded as a danger to democracy itself. The people were becoming restless under policies that damaged their own prosperity without compelling any change by Britain. The choice now seemed to lie between submission to the British and a war, and neither the people's sense of national honor nor the survival of the Republican party—a party that still believed that American liberty depended on its guidance—would permit submission. Thus, before the new Twelfth Congress met, Madison reluctantly decided on a war. In what was basically a party vote, a declaration passed the Congress on June 18, 1812.[53]

What followed was a tragedy of errors: thirty months of warfare during which it was uncertain whether the United States would manage to survive intact, followed by a peace that settled none of the essential issues over which the fighting had begun. After years of stubborn dedication to an antipreparation ideology, America embarked on war with Britain with fourteen warships and a regular army of less than 7,000 well-trained men. It entered on the conflict so divided that New England governors refused to let the country's best militia march beyond the borders of their states, and wealthy Yankees stubbornly declined to lend financial aid. Not too surprisingly, the War of 1812 brought little glory, other than some striking victories by U.S. frigates in their single-ship engagements with the British and, of course, the smashing triumph at New Orleans, where Andrew Jackson crushed the last invasion two weeks after peace had been agreed upon at Ghent in Belgium on December 24, 1814.[54] But then, the War of 1812 had not been undertaken for the sake of national glory. It had been declared to demonstrate that a republican regime could safeguard national interests and defend the country's rights. And in the minds of those who fought it, although little had been gained, nothing had been lost in a collision with the greatest power on the earth. National honor had been satisfied. The Union had endured. Republicans had learned important lessons.

The War of 1812 had major consequences for the nation. In December 1814, as Jackson was preparing to defend New Orleans, a convention met at Hartford, Connecticut, to consider New England's grievances against the nation, which had crippled the administration's effort to conduct the war.

The delegates demanded radical amendments to the Constitution to protect their region from the Jeffersonian majority in Washington, D.C., and threatened stronger actions if the changes were refused.[55] It was a classic case of dreadful timing. The manifesto from the gathering at Hartford reached the capital in close conjunction with the news of Jackson's dramatic victory at New Orleans. In consequence, New England's effort to extort concessions in the face of war appeared both foolish and disloyal. Lifted by the people's swelling pride, the Madison administration reached unprecedented heights of national prestige.[56] Simultaneously, the reputation of the Federalists was damaged beyond repair. Within four years of Madison's retirement, the triumph of the Jeffersonians was practically complete. With James Monroe's essentially unanimous election to a second term, the nation entered into a period of single-party rule.

As it did so, the Republicans adjusted to the lessons of the war and to the economic transformation it had fostered. Early in 1815, President Madison recommended a peacetime army of 20,000 men. In his last annual message, on December 5, 1815, the great co-architect of Jeffersonian ideals called also for a federal program of internal improvements, tariff protection for the infant industries that had sprung up during the war, and the creation of a new national bank (Congress having refused in 1811 to recharter the old Hamiltonian institution). All these measures were enacted by the Congress early in 1816, although the President refused to sign the bill for internal improvements until a constitutional amendment clearly authorized the federal government to act. Together, these initiatives amounted to another striking change of governmental course.

Madison's proposals, to be sure, were far from a complete surrender to the Federalists' ideas. The President still hoped that education, an enormous reservoir of western lands, and the continued leadership of the legitimate defenders of the people's Constitution would indefinitely postpone the civic evils he and Jefferson still feared. Like Jefferson, however, Madison had learned that "there exists both profligacy and power enough to exclude us from the field of interchange with other nations"; that Americans must either manufacture more of the necessities and niceties of life, accept "dependence on that foreign nation," or "be clothed in skins and . . . live like wild beasts in dens and caverns."[57] The policies of the Republican administrations—the war itself and many years of economic conflict with the British—had encouraged an explosive growth of native manufactures, which the President could not abandon at the peace. Meanwhile, as he saw it, Britain had been able to supply itself with raw materials and food from Canada and Latin America, which would continue to provide a rival source of the necessities on which commercial warfare hinged.[58] Accordingly, the aging founder hinted that the party's old ideas must now be blended with some fragments of the Hamiltonian design (although without the Hamiltonian monopolies or Federalist contempt for popular political participation). In the process, Madison legitimized the other side of a debate that had embroiled the nation since adoption of the Constitution.

The old debate did not abruptly reach a permanent conclusion. In 1819, a serious financial panic and a sectional collision over the admission of Missouri to the Union provoked new arguments about the country's economic transformation and the wisdom of the legislation of 1816. Soon, in the guise of Henry Clay's "American System," a Hamiltonian conception of a self-sufficient nation, where industrial development would build domestic markets for the farmers' surplus, and federal programs like the tariff and the bank would tie the country's sections into a harmonious whole, would revitalize the old disputes. Moreover, the United States has seldom had a less effective central government than during the years between 1820 and 1828, not least because the last of the Jeffersonian presidents, James Monroe and John Quincy Adams, did not believe in leading Congress, and Republicans did not believe in being led. Presidential leadership and presidential patronage still smelled too much of influence and corruption, as did blind allegiance to a party.[59] By the early 1820s, it was clear that the destruction of the Federalists had left Republicans too free to fight among themselves. But even as they did, the fundamental principles enunciated at the party's founding would endure as a foundation for the views of both the Democrats and Whigs, refurbished and revitalized to fit the different needs and different spirit of the age of Andrew Jackson.

Notes

1. Americans of the 1780s referred more often to their "republican" Revolution against aristocracy and monarchy than to "democracy," especially when they wanted to distinguish their representative forms of government from the direct democracies of ancient Greece. Nevertheless, "republican" and "democratic" were often used synonymously during these years, and by the late 1790s the progenitors of the modern party were sometimes called the Democratic-Republicans. Today's Republicans (the G.O.P.) did not appear until the 1850s and were not the lineal descendants of the Federalists of the early Republic.

2. See Lance Banning, "1787 and 1776: Patrick Henry, James Madison, the Constitution, and the Revolution," in *Toward a More Perfect Union: Six Essays on the*

Constitution, ed. Neil L. York (Provo: Brigham Young University Press, 1988), 58–89 together with the secondary sources cited there.

3. E. James Ferguson, *The Power of the Purse: A History of American Public Finance, 1776-1790* (Chapel Hill: University of North Carolina Press, 1961), 292–296; Forrest McDonald, *Alexander Hamilton: A Biography* (New York: Norton, 1979), chap. 8; and Donald F. Swanson, *The Origins of Hamilton's Fiscal Policies* (Gainesville: University of Florida Press, 1963).

4. *The Federalist Papers,* ed. Isaac Kramnick (Harmondsworth, England: Penguin, 1987), 67. See, more fully, 67–75.

5. P. G. M. Dickson, *The Financial Revolution in England: A Study in the Development of Public Credit, 1688-1756* (New York: St. Martin's Press, 1967).

6. For Hamilton's life and vision see, especially, John C. Miller, *Alexander Hamilton: Portrait in Paradox* (New York: Harper and Row, 1959); McDonald, *Alexander Hamilton;* and Gerald Stourzh, *Alexander Hamilton and the Idea of Republican Government* (Stanford: Stanford University Press, 1970).

7. "If all the public creditors receive their dues from one source," Hamilton's Report observed, "their interests will be the same. And having the same interests, they will unite in support of the fiscal arrangements of government." *The Papers of Alexander Hamilton,* Harold C. Syrett et al., eds., 26 vols. (New York: Columbia University Press), 6:80–81.

8. In addition to the sources cited in notes 3 and 6 above, see Drew R. McCoy, *The Elusive Republic: Political Economy in Jeffersonian America* (Chapel Hill: University of North Carolina Press, 1980), 146–152; and Lance Banning, "Political Economy and the Creation of the Federal Republic," forthcoming in *The Possession of Freedom,* ed. David T. Konig, vol. 5 of *The Making of Modern Freedom* (Stanford: Stanford University Press, 1993).

9. Ferguson, *The Power of the Purse,* 329–330, calculates that funding raised the market value of the federal debt from about $5,000,000 in 1786 to nearly $42,000,000 (including the arrears of interest) in 1791. It multiplied the value of state certificates by similar proportions. In 1789 and 1790, North Carolina and South Carolina securities sold for ten to twenty cents on the dollar, Virginia securities for twenty to thirty cents. Sixty percent of Virginia's certificates and ninety percent of North Carolina's were in the hands of large secondary holders. See Whitney K. Bates, "Northern Speculators and Southern State Debts, 1790," *William and Mary Quarterly,* 3d ser., 19 (1962): 32–34, 39.

10. In these objections, congressmen were drawing on an old and very potent Anglo-American critique of the disastrous consequences of a funded debt and mercantilist economics. The literature on the tremendous influence of this eighteenth century critique is now enormous. For an introduction, see Robert Shalhope, "Toward a Republican Synthesis: The Emergence of an Understanding of Republicanism in American Historiography," *William and Mary Quarterly,* 3d ser., 29 (1972): 49–80; Shalhope, "Republicanism and Early American Historiography," ibid., 39

(1982): 334–356; Peter S. Onuf, "Reflections on the Founding: Constitutional Historiography in Bicentennial Perspective," ibid., 45 (1989): 341–375; and Lance Banning, "The Republican Hypothesis: Retrospect and Prospect," forthcoming in American Antiquarian Society, *Proceedings* (Fall, 1992). The congressional debate on funding (February 1790) may be followed in *Annals of Congress,* 1:1180–1224, 1234–1239, 1248–1322; 2:1324–1354.

11. Irving Brant, *James Madison,* 6 vols. (Indianapolis: Bobbs-Merrill, 1941–1961); Ralph Ketcham, *James Madison: A Biography* (New York: Macmillan, 1971); and Jack N. Rakove, *James Madison and the Creation of the American Republic* (Glenview, Ill.: Scott, Foresman/Little, Brown, 1990).

12. Some congressmen and other insiders at New York hurried cash and agents to the farthest reaches of the Union to gobble up outstanding state certificates before their holders were aware of how much they would increase in value.

13. Speech of February 18, 1790, in *The Papers of James Madison,* William T. Hutchinson et al., eds. 17 vols. to date (Charlottesville: University Press of Virginia, 1962—) 13:48–49.

14. Dumas Malone, *Jefferson and His Time,* 6 vols. (Boston: Little, Brown, 1948–1981); Merrill D. Peterson, *Thomas Jefferson and the New Nation: A Biography* (London: Oxford University Press, 1970).

15. The most recent discussion is Kenneth R. Bowling, "The Compromise of 1790," chap. 7 of *The Creation of Washington, D.C.: The Idea and Location of the American Capital* (Fairfax: George Mason University Press, 1991).

16. Madison's speech on the national bank, February 2, 1791, in Hutchinson, *The Papers of James Madison,* 13:373–381; Jefferson's "Opinion on the Constitutionality of a National Bank," February 15, 1791, in *The Works of Thomas Jefferson,* ed. Paul Leicester Ford, 12 vols. (New York: Putnam, 1904), 5:284–289.

17. Lance Banning, *The Jeffersonian Persuasion: Evolution of a Party Ideology* (Ithaca: Cornell University Press, 1978), traces the development of party thought.

18. Madison came as close to outrage as it was possible for him to do in response to the "scramble for . . . public plunder" attendant on the opening of the national bank, writing Jefferson that "My imagination will not attempt to set bounds to the daring depravity of the times. The stock-jobbers will become the pretorian band of the government, at once its tools and its tyrants; bribed by its largesses, and overawing it by clamors and combinations." Hutchinson, *Papers of Madison,* 14:43, 69.

19. Jefferson warned President Washington that Hamilton's program "flowed from principles adverse to liberty and was calculated to undermine and demolish the republic by creating an influence of his department over the members of the legislature. . . . to draw all the powers of government into the hands of the general legislature, to establish means for corrupting a sufficient corps in that legislature to . . . preponderate . . . , and to have that corps under the command of the Secretary of the Treasury for the purpose of subverting step by step the principles of the Constitution, which he has so often declared a thing of nothing which must be changed."

Ford, *Works of Jefferson*, 7:138–139. Robert Walpole was prime minister of England in the second quarter of the eighteenth century and the classic villain of this well-established condemnation of the British system of administration and finance.

20. This characterization of Hamilton's course came in an interview with Madison by Nichols P. Trist, September 27, 1834. But compare Jefferson's late-life discussion in this preface to the "Anas," *Works of Jefferson*, 1:167–183.

21. Banning, *Jeffersonian Persuasion*, 153–155 and chap. 6.

22. Recent discussions of the configurations of the first party struggle include Richard Buel, Jr., *Securing the Revolution: Ideology in American Politics, 1789–1815* (Ithaca: Cornell University Press, 1972); David Hackett Fischer, *The Revolution of American Conservatism* (New York: Harper and Row, 1965), appendix 1; and Paul Goodman, "The First American Party System," in *The American Party Systems: Stages of Political Development*, eds. William Nesbit Chambers and Walter Dean Burnham (Oxford: Oxford University Press, 1967), 56–89. Among many state and local studies, two have been especially influential: Paul Goodman, *The Democratic-Republicans of Massachusetts* (Cambridge: Harvard University Press, 1964); and Alfred F. Young, *The Democratic Republicans of New York* (Chapel Hill: University of North Carolina Press, 1967).

23. See Gordon S. Wood, *The Radicalism of the American Revolution* (New York: Knopf, 1992); and—for the division between friends of liberty and friends of order—Thomas P. Slaughter, *The Whiskey Rebellion: Frontier Epilogue to the American Revolution* (New York: Oxford University Press, 1986).

24. See Banning, "1787 and 1776" for an argument that prevailing scholarly opinions do not properly distinguish Madison's objectives from those of other advocates of the Constitution and thus suggest that Madison shifted course in the years after 1789 more radically than was in fact the case.

25. Query xix of Jefferson's *Notes on the State of Virginia*, written in 1781–1782, is most often quoted: "Generally speaking, the proportion which the aggregate of other classes of citizens bears in any state to that of its husbandmen is the proportion of its unsound to its healthy parts. . . . While we have land to labor then, let us never wish to see our citizens occupied at a workbench or twirling a distaff. Carpenters, masons, smiths are wanted in husbandry; but for the general operations of manufacture, let our workshops remain in Europe. . . . The loss by the transportation of commodities across the Atlantic will be made up in happiness and permanence of government. The mobs of great cities add just so much to the support of pure government as sores do to the strength of the human body. It is the manners and spirit of a people which preserve a republic in vigor." But see also Madison's *National Gazette* essays on "Republican Distribution of Citizens" (March 3, 1792) and "Fashion" (March 20, 1792), written in response to Hamilton's report on manufactures and available in Hutchinson, *Papers of Madison*, 14:244–246, 285–288. My discussion of Republican political economy prefers McCoy, *The Elusive Republic*, to Joyce Appleby, *Capitalism and a New Social Order: The Republican Vision of the 1790s* (New York: New York University Press,

1984), but draws on Appleby as well for its insistence on the forward-looking, revolutionary enterprise of freeing individuals from hierarchical restraints and creating a harmonious society of self-directing equals. For an argument that revolutionary (or Republican) demands for public virtue seldom sought a selfless, sacrificial dedication to a larger public good, but did expect a self-assertive, vigilant participation in a politics of equals, see Lance Banning, "Some Second Thoughts on Virtue and the Course of Revolutionary Thinking," in *Conceptual Change and the Constitution,* eds. Terence Ball and J. G. A. Pocock (Lawrence: University Press of Kansas, 1988), 194–212. For the debate among historians about the character and sources of Republican ideas, see further Banning, "The Republican Hypothesis" and "Jeffersonian Ideology Revisited: Liberal and Classical Ideas in the New American Republic," *William and Mary Quarterly,* 3d ser., 43 (1986): 3–19, together with the sources cited in these essays.

26. Banning, *Jeffersonian Persuasion,* 154–155.

27. The progress of the party quarrel, with a special emphasis on the development of the Republicans' ideas, can be followed in Banning, *Jeffersonian Persuasion.* Other studies of the struggle's progress include Buel, *Securing the Revolution,* John C. Miller, *The Federalist Era, 1789–1801* (New York: Harper and Row, 1960); Joseph Charles, *The Origins of the American Party System: Three Essays* (New York: Harper and Row, 1961); and William Nesbit Chambers, *Political Parties in a New Nation* (New York: Oxford University Press, 1957). Noble E. Cunningham, *The Jeffersonian Republicans* (Chapel Hill: University of North Carolina Press, 1957), remains the best study of the development of party machinery.

28. Harry Ammon, *The Genet Mission* (New York: Norton, 1973).

29. Eugene Perry Link, *Democratic-Republican Societies, 1790–1800* (New York: Columbia University Press, 1942).

30. Slaughter, *The Whiskey Rebellion.*

31. The most respected recent studies conclude that he did: Jerald A. Combs, *The Jay Treaty* (Berkeley: University of California Press, 1970); and Charles R. Ritcheson, *Aftermath of Revolution: British Policy toward the United States, 1783–1795* (Dallas: Southern Methodist University Press, 1969), chap. 16.

32. For the administration of John Adams, Stephan G. Kurtz, *The Presidency of John Adams: The Collapse of Federalism, 1795–1800* (Philadelphia: University of Pennsylvania Press, 1957); Manning J. Dauer, *The Adams Federalists* (Baltimore: The Johns Hopkins University Press, 1953); and Ralph A. Brown, *The Presidency of John Adams* (Lawrence: University Press of Kansas, 1975), should be added to the sources cited in note 27 above. Alexander DeConde, *The Quasi-war: The Politics and Diplomacy of the Undeclared War with France, 1797–1801* (New York: Scribner, 1966), is the best source for the diplomacy discussed below.

33. James Morton Smith, *Freedom's Fetters: The Alien and Sedition Laws and American Civil Liberties* (Ithaca: Cornell University Press, 1956); and John C. Miller, *Crisis in Freedom: The Alien and Sedition Acts* (Boston: Little, Brown, 1951).

34. Adrienne Koch and Harry Ammon, "The Virginia and Kentucky Resolutions:

An Episode in Jefferson's and Madison's Defense of Civil Liberties," *William and Mary Quarterly*, 3d ser., 5 (1948): 145–176.

35. In retirement at Mt. Vernon, Washington agreed to assume active leadership of the enlarged and provisional armies only if they were required to take the field against invasion, joining with the cabinet to insist that Hamilton should head the list of major generals and thus assume effective leadership until that time. When Washington died on December 13, 1799, Hamilton, who had come to late-colonial New York from the West Indian island of Nevis and was the illegitimate son of an obscure member of a Scottish noble family, was officially in command.

36. Richard H. Kohn, *Eagle and Sword: The Beginnings of the Military Establishment in America* (New York: Free Press, 1975), chap. 12, is an excellent discussion of the pivotal role of the army question in Adams's decision. Contrast Jacob E. Cooke, "Country Above Party: John Adams and the 1799 Mission to France," in *Fame and Founding Fathers*, ed. Edmund P. Willis (Bethlehem, Pa.: Moravian College, 1967), 53–77.

37. Young, *The Democratic Republicans of New York*; John R. Nelson, "Alexander Hamilton and American Manufacturing: A Reexamination," *Journal of American History*, 65 (1979): 971–995.

38. Jefferson to Spencer Roane, September 6, 1819, in Ford, *Works of Jefferson*, 12:136.

39. Article II, Section 1 of the Constitution provides that presidential electors shall be chosen in such manner as the state legislatures direct. Until the age of Jackson, legislatures often chose the electors themselves. Constitutionally, they still could do so.

40. *Works of Jefferson*, 9:197–198.

41. When Congress met, the Federalists proposed renewal of the act, which was at least consistent with their claim that it was actually more liberal than the common law of libel. The Republicans defeated the proposal.

42. Noble E. Cunningham, *The Jeffersonian Republicans in Power: Party Operations, 1801–1809* (Chapel Hill: University of North Carolina Press, 1963), chap. 2 is a fine brief treatment of Jefferson's appointments policy. See also Carl E. Prince, "The Passing of the Aristocracy: Jefferson's Removal of the Federalists, 1801–1805," *Journal of American History*, 57 (1970): 563–575.

43. William Duane in the *Philadelphia Aurora*, February 27, 1801.

44. Duane himself described the first annual message as "an epitome of republican principles applied to practical purposes," ibid., December 18, 1801.

45. Ford, *Works of Jefferson*, 9:341–342.

46. Jefferson to Dupont de Nemours, Jan. 18, 1802, Ford, *Works of Jefferson*, 9:343–344.

47. For these years, the classic history is Henry Adams, *History of the United States during the Administrations of Thomas Jefferson and James Madison*, 9 vols. (New York: Scribner, 1889–1890), although the reader should be wary of the biases of

this descendant of John Adams. A briefer, modern overview is Marshall Smelser, *The Democratic Republic, 1801–1815* (New York: Harper and Row, 1968). See also Forrest McDonald, *The Presidency of Thomas Jefferson* (Lawrence: University Press of Kansas, 1976); Robert Allen Rutland, *The Presidency of James Madison* (Lawrence: University Press of Kansas, 1990); Noble E. Cunningham, *The Jeffersonian Republicans in Power: Party Operations, 1801–1809* (Chapel Hill: University of North Carolina Press, 1963); Cunningham, *The Process of Government under Jefferson* (Princeton: Princeton University Press, 1978); and Robert M. Johnstone, *Jefferson and the Presidency: Leadership in the Young Republic* (Ithaca: Cornell University Press, 1978).

48. These *were*, however, the very years when the contagious faith in liberty, equality, and the capacity of ordinary citizens to shape their own beliefs and institutions were transforming the religious as well as the political landscape, not the least by furious assaults on settled, well-paid clergy. See Nathan O. Hatch, *The Democratization of American Christianity* (New Haven: Yale University Press, 1989).

49. The best source for the Jeffersonian policy of commercial confrontation is McCoy, *The Elusive Republic*, chap. 9. See also Banning, "Political Economy and the Creation of the Federal Republic."

50. It does not seem certain that the President himself intended the embargo from the outset as a long-term alternative to war. But Secretary of State Madison probably did, and Jefferson himself was soon committed to that course. Gallatin did not agree. "In every point of view, privations, sufferings, revenue, effect on the enemy, politics at home, etc.," he told the President, "I prefer war to a permanent embargo." *The Writings of Gallatin*, ed. Henry Adams, 3 vols. (Philadelphia: Lippincott, 1879), 1:386. On these matters, see Burton Spivak, *Jefferson's English Crisis: Commerce, Embargo, and the Republican Revolution* (Charlottesville: University Press of Virginia, 1979).

51. *Jefferson and Civil Liberties: The Darker Side*, rev., ed. Leonard Levy (New York: Quadrangle Books, 1973).

52. The repeal occurred during the last days of Jefferson's administration and without the President's wholehearted approval. Jefferson virtually abdicated his leadership role once Madison had been elected, but he continued to believe that the experiment should be prolonged or abandoned only for a declaration of war.

53. Roger H. Brown, *The Republic in Peril: 1812* (New York: Columbia University Press, 1964).

54. Harry L. Coles, *The War of 1812* (Chicago: University of Chicago Press, 1965); J. C. A. Stagg, *Mr. Madison's War: Politics, Diplomacy, and Warfare in the Early American Republic, 1783–1830* (Princeton: Princeton University Press, 1983); and Donald R. Hickey, *The War of 1812: A Forgotten Conflict* (Urbana: University of Illinois Press, 1989).

55. James M. Banner, Jr., *To the Hartford Convention: The Federalists and the Origins of Party Politics in Massachusetts, 1789–1815* (New York: Knopf, 1970).

56. From his retirement, Adams wrote to Jefferson that "notwithstanding a thousand faults and blunders, [Madison's] administration has acquired more glory, and

established more Union, than all three predecessors, Washington, Adams, and Jefferson put together." *The Adams-Jefferson Letters,* ed. Lester Cappon, 2 vols. (Chapel Hill: University of North Carolina Press, 1959), 2:508.

57. Jefferson to Benjamin Austin, January 9, 1819, *Works of Jefferson,* 2:502–505.

58. J. C. A. Stagg, "James Madison and the Coercion of Great Britain: Canada, the West Indies, and the War of 1812," *William and Mary Quarterly,* 3d ser., 38 (1981): 3–34; Donald R. Hickey, "American Trade Restrictions during the War of 1812," *Journal of American History* 68 (1981): 517–538; and—more broadly—Steven Watts, *The Republican Reborn: War and the Making of Liberal America, 1790–1820* (Baltimore: The Johns Hopkins University Press, 1987).

59. James Sterling Young, *The Washington Community, 1800–1828* (New York: Columbia University Press, 1966), is still useful here. See also, Richard Hofstadter, *The Idea of a Party System: The Rise of Legitimate Opposition in the United States, 1780–1840* (Berkeley: University of California Press, 1969).

Acknowledgments

Some projects are hard work. Others are labors of love. A rare few may be both. Editing this collection of essays, for me, has been one of those rarities. While I put a lot of effort into this volume in a short span of time, it was also an honor to have the opportunity to collect and present my mentor's published work. I was reminded in rereading Lance Banning's work just how good and how important an historian he was. And I also had more than a few moments when I recalled conversations he and I had about these works in his office, his seminar room, or his home, and later via email. In other words, editing this collection of Lance's work was both a professional task and a deeply personal one. Likewise, there are intellectual debts to be recognized in this work and also personal and emotional debts.

It has been my great good fortune to have taken part in several tributes to Lance Banning in the years since his death in 2006. Shortly after his passing, I wrote a short reminiscence of Lance that was read in my absence at a memorial service at the University of Kentucky. At that summer's meeting of the Society for Historians of the Early American Republic (SHEAR) conference in Montreal, Lance's friend and University of Kentucky colleague Daniel Blake Smith organized a panel to pay tribute to Lance. Dan invited John Murrin, Drew McCoy, and Jack Rakove to be panelists and me to be the moderator. Next, I had the honor of directing a conference in 2008 in Lexington on Lance's scholarship for Liberty Fund, Inc., a private educational foundation with which he had a long relationship. Then, in June 2013, Robert McDonald invited me and several other former students to take part in a conference sponsored by the Sons of the American Revolution in St. Louis that was dedicated to Lance. The papers from that conference will be collected in a volume to be published by the University of Virginia Press, which will also be dedicated to him. I am grateful for all of these experiences which gave me the opportunity both to honor Lance and to think about his life, work, and legacy. The present volume, then, is the culmination of a long series of tributes to Lance of which I have been deeply honored to have been a part. And, because this volume is in print, it will be perhaps the most lasting tribute that I can offer.

Although most of Lance Banning's other Ph.D. students came along after I did at the University of Kentucky, it has been a great pleasure to get to know them over the years and to stay in contact through our special bond. I especially thank Paul Douglas Newman, John Craig Hammond, David Nichols, Michael Schwarz, Patrick Mullins, and all the others. Their support and interest in honoring Lance and his work means a great deal to me and it is always a treat to be in their company.

This project had its origin nearly two decades ago in correspondence between Lance Banning and Fred Woodward, senior editor at the University Press of Kansas. I am indebted to Fred Woodward for sharing that correspondence with me, answering questions about it, and for encouraging me to continue to work on the volume. Fred's generosity and kindness along with the tangible gift of the written materials he and Lance assembled not only made this project possible, they made possible a volume very much along the lines Lance himself intended. For all that, I am grateful to Fred.

This volume would never have come to fruition, however, without a happenstance conversation I had one summer evening over dinner in Annapolis, Maryland, with Stephen Wrinn, director of the University Press of Kentucky. From the first, Steve glimpsed the possibilities of this collection, assured me that it could work, waited patiently for the project to become available, and then worked very quickly to secure outside readers, make suggestions as to content and revisions, and move the book along, sometimes prodding me but always encouraging me. Steve's enthusiasm is contagious, and his enthusiasm for this volume never wavered. In all ways, Steve is an ideal editor. Also extremely helpful at the University Press of Kentucky is Allison Webster, executive assistant to the director, whose care, experience, efficiency, and diligence proved indispensable at many points. Finally, thanks to Derik Shelor for his outstanding work in copyediting this book.

I offer particular gratitude to the outside readers for the Press on this volume, Peter S. Onuf and Robert A. Ferguson, both close and devoted friends of Lance. Not only did both offer enthusiastic assent to the project, they replied very promptly during the summer months when they had other things to do. Most of all, both offered detailed and incisive comments on how the volume might be improved and on how Lance's essays could be best organized and presented. Their substantive comments were always at hand as I made revisions, and whatever success the book has owes much to their collegiality, careful eyes, and generous spirits.

Very special thanks go to Kathy Pfeiffer, my wife, for understanding how important this project was to me and for clearing time and space for me to complete it.

Lastly, and most of all, I wish to thank Lana Banning, Lance's widow, for entrusting this project to me. Her persistence and unwavering dedication to seeing this volume come into print are the main reasons the book is in readers' hands today. Her queries over the phone and through email led me to look into the possibility of producing this volume in the first place, and she was there throughout with encouragement, support, and patience. I hope she believes that the wait was worth it and I trust that Lana will see this book as a promise delivered upon. She already knows how much she has meant to me and all of Lance's students through the years.

Appendix

Bibliography of Published Works by Lance Banning

1974

"Republican Ideology and the Triumph of the Constitution, 1789–1793," *William and Mary Quarterly*, 3rd ser., 31 (April 1974): 167–188. Reprinted in several anthologies.

"John Adams" and "George Washington," in *Responses of the Presidents to Charges of Misconduct*, ed. C. Vann Woodward (Dell, 1974), 2–29.

Review: Richard Buel Jr., *Securing the Revolution*, in *Connecticut History Newsletter*, no. 13 (January 1974), 23–25.

Review: Pauline Maier, *From Resistance to Revolution*, in *American Political Science Review* 68 (March 1974): 284–285.

1975

Review: Forrest McDonald, *The Presidency of George Washington*, in *William and Mary Quarterly* 32 (Jan. 1975): 157–158.

Review: Daniel Sisson, *The American Revolution of 1800*, in *William and Mary Quarterly*, 32 (July 1975): 539–540.

1976

"Jeffersonian Ideology and the French Revolution," *Studies in Burke and His Time* 17 (winter 1976): 5–26.

Review: Henry Steele Commager, *Jefferson, Nationalism, and the Enlightenment*, in *The Historian* 37 (Feb. 1976): 359–360.

1977

Review: Helen Hill Miller, *George Mason: Gentleman Revolutionary,* in *The Historian* 39 (Feb. 1977): 366–367.

1978

The Jeffersonian Persuasion: Evolution of a Party Ideology (Cornell Univ. Press, 1978; paperback edition, 1980). Received the international book award of Phi Alpha Theta; nominated by the press for Pulitzer, Bancroft, and other awards; portions reprinted in various readers.

Review: Kenneth S. Lynn, *A Divided People,* in *The Historian* 40 (August 1978): 759.

1979

Review: G. S. Rowe, *Thomas McKean,* in *American Historical Review* 84 (April 1979): 545–546.

Review: Jacob E. Cooke, *Tench Coxe and the Early Republic,* in *Journal of American History* 66 (Sept. 1979): 389–390.

Review: "Faction and Party in the New Republic," *Reviews in American History* 7 (Dec. 1979): 499–503. An essay review of Norman K. Risjord, *Chesapeake Politics.*

1980

"The Moderate as Revolutionary: An Introduction to Madison's Life," *Quarterly Journal of the Library of Congress* 38 (spring 1980): 162–175.

"Tyler's Henry," an introduction to the Chelsea House edition of Moses Coit Tyler, *Patrick Henry* (New York, 1980).

Review: Burton Spivak, *Jefferson's English Crisis: Commerce, Embargo, and the Republican Revolution,* in *American Historical Review* 85 (April 1980): 459–460.

Review: John Zvesper, *Political Philosophy and Rhetoric: A Study of the Origins of American Party Politics,* in *Bulletin of the Society for Historians of the Early American Republic* 1 (spring 1980): 6–8.

Review: W. Robert Higgins, *The Revolutionary War in the South,* in *The Historian* 42 (Nov. 1980): 139–140.

Review: Noble E. Cunningham, *The Process of Government under Jefferson,* in *Journal of Interdisciplinary History* 11 (autumn 1980): 332–333.

1981

Review: Steven R. Boyd, *The Politics of Opposition: Antifederalists and the Acceptance of the Constitution,* in *William and Mary Quarterly* 38 (Jan. 1981): 123–124.

Review: Drew R. McCoy, *The Elusive Republic: Political Economy in Jeffersonian America,* in *Journal of American History* 68 (June 1981): 123–124.

Review: Milton Lomask, *Aaron Burr,* in *Register of the Kentucky Historical Society* 79 (winter 1981): 82–83.

Review: William Winslow Crosskey and William Jeffrey Jr., *Politics and the Constitution in the History of the United States,* vol. 3, in *American Historical Review* 86 (Dec. 1981): 1147–1148.

1982

Review: Garry Wills, *Explaining America: The Federalist,* in *Journal of American History* 68 (March 1982): 923.

1983

"James Madison and the Nationalists, 1780–1783," *William and Mary Quarterly* 40 (April 1983): 237–255; reprinted in *The New American Nation, 1776–1815,* ed. Peter S. Onuf (Garland, 1992).

Review: Herbert J. Storing, *What the Antifederalists were FOR,* in *Register of the Kentucky Historical Society* 81 (winter 1983): 87–88.

Review: Rhys Isaac, *The Transformation of Virginia, 1740–1790,* in *Register of the Kentucky Historical Society* 81 (summer 1983): 314–316.

1984

"The Hamiltonian Madison: A Reconsideration," *Virginia Magazine of History and Biography,* 92 (January 1984), 3–28; reprinted in *The New American Nation.*

"The Federalist Papers," in *Encyclopedia of American Political History,* ed. Jack P. Greene (Charles Scribner's Sons, 1984).

Review: J. R. Pole, *The Gift of Government: Political Responsibility from the English Restoration to American Independence,* in *Georgia Historical Quarterly* 68 (spring 1984): 83–84.

Review: "Image of a Phantom," *Reviews in American History* 12 (June 1984): 211–214. An essay review of Janice Potter, *The Liberty We Seek: Loyalist Ideology in Colonial New York and Massachusetts.*

Review: Daniel P. Jordan, *Political Leadership in Jefferson's Virginia*, in *Virginia Magazine of History and Biography* 92 (July 1984), 354–355.
Review: Ronald L. Hatzenbuehler and Robert L. Ivie, *Congress Declares War: Rhetoric, Leadership, and Partisanship in the Early Republic*, in *American Historical Review* 89 (Dec. 1984): 1391.

1985

"From Confederation to Constitution: The Revolutionary Context of the Great Convention," *this Constitution*, no. 6 (spring 1985): 12–18; reprinted in *this Constitution: Our Enduring Legacy* (Congressional Quarterly, 1986), 23–35, and in various readers.
Review: Jan Lewis, *The Pursuit of Happiness: Family and Values in Jefferson's Virginia*, in *Register of the Kentucky Historical Society* 82 (winter 1985): 401–403.
Review: Garry Wills, *Cincinnatus: George Washington and the Enlightenment*, in *Journal of Southern History* 51 (Aug. 1985): 430–431.
Review: Richard K. Matthews, *The Radical Politics of Thomas Jefferson: A Revisionist View*, in *American Historical Review* 90 (Oct. 1985): 1007–1008.

1986

"Jeffersonian Ideology Revisited: Liberal and Classical Ideas in the New American Republic," *William and Mary Quarterly* 43 (Jan. 1986): 3–19; reprinted in *After the Constitution*.
"James Madison," in *Encyclopedia of the American Constitution*, ed. Leonard W. Levy (Macmillan, 1986); reprinted in a slightly different version as "James Madison: The Revolutionary Moderate as Founding Father," in *The David A. Sayre History Symposium: Collected Lectures, 1985–1989* (Sayre School, 1991), 91–99.
Review: John R. Alden, *George Washington: A Biography*, in *The Historian* 48 (Nov. 1986): 607–608.

1987

"James Madison and the Dynamics of the Constitutional Convention," *Political Science Reviewer* 17 (fall 1987): 5–48.
"The Practicable Sphere of a Republic: James Madison, the Constitutional Convention, and the Emergence of Revolutionary Federalism," in *Beyond Confederation: Origins of the Constitution and American National Identity*, ed. Richard Beeman, Stephen Botein, and Edward C. Carter II (Univ. of North Carolina Press, 1987), 162–187.

"The Problem of Power: Parties, Aristocracy, and Democracy in Revolutionary Thought," in *The American Revolution: Its Character and Limits*, ed. Jack P. Greene (New York Univ. Press, 1987), 104–123.

"The Constitutional Convention," in *The Constitution: A History of Its Framing and Ratification*, ed. Leonard W. Levy and Dennis J. Mahoney (Macmillan, 1987), 112–131; reprinted in the D. C. Heath "Major Problems" series.

"James Madison, the Statute for Religious Freedom, and the Crisis of Republican Convictions," in *The Virginia Statute for Religious Freedom: Its Evolution and Consequences in American History*, ed. Merrill D. Peterson and Robert C. Vaughan (Cambridge Univ. Press, 1987), 109–138.

"To Secure These Rights: Patrick Henry, James Madison, and the Revolutionary Legitimacy of the Constitution," in *To Secure the Blessings of Liberty: First Principles of the Constitution*, ed. Sarah Baumgartner Thurow (Univ. Press of America, 1987), 280–304. A revision of "To Secure These Rights" has appeared in abbreviated versions in the *National Humanities Center Newsletter* and *The History Teacher*.

Review: Merrill D. Peterson, ed., *Thomas Jefferson: A Reference Biography*, in *Journal of American History* 74 (June 1987): 163–164.

1988

"Some Second Thoughts on 'Virtue' and the Course of Revolutionary Thinking," in *Conceptual Change and the Constitution*, ed. Terence Ball and J. G. A. Pocock (Univ. Press of Kansas, 1988), 194–212.

"1787 and 1776: Patrick Henry, James Madison, the Constitution and the Revolution," in *Toward a More Perfect Union: Six Essays on the Constitution*, ed. Neil L. York (Brigham Young Univ. Press, 1988), 59–89.

Review: Steven Watts, *The Republic Reborn: War and the Making of Liberal America, 1790–1820*, in *Georgia Historical Quarterly* 62 (summer 1988): 349–350.

Review: John R. Nelson Jr., *Liberty and Property: Political Economy and Policymaking in the New Nation, 1789–1812*, in *Georgia Historical Quarterly* 62 (fall 1988): 545–547.

1989

After the Constitution: Party Conflict in the New Republic (Wadsworth, 1989). A 450-page anthology of secondary writings on the first party struggle.

"Virginia: Sectionalism and the General Good," in *Ratifying the Constitution:*

Ideas and Interests in the Several American States, ed. Michael Lienesch and Michael Gillespie (Univ. Press of Kansas, 1989), 261–299.

Review: "Quid Transit? Paradigms and Process in the Transformation of Republican Ideas," in *Reviews in American History* 17 (1989): 199–204. An essay review of Michael Lienesch, *New Order of the Ages.*

1992

"Federalists," in *Encyclopedia of the American Constitution,* supplement, ed. Leonard W. Levy (Macmillan, 1992).

"The Republican Interpretation: Retrospect and Prospect," published jointly in the American Antiquarian Society's *Proceedings* 102 (1992): 155–179 and in *The Republican Synthesis Revisited: Essays in Honor of George Athan Billias,* ed. Milton M. Klein et al. (Univ. Press of Virginia, 1992), 91–117.

"The Jeffersonians in Power, 1801–1824," in *Of the People: The 200-Year History of the Democratic Party* (General Publishing Group, 1992), 35–47.

"The Jeffersonians: First Principles," in *Democrats and the American Idea: A Bicentennial Appraisal,* ed. Peter B. Kovler (Center for National Policy Press, 1992), 1–27.

"Election, Presidential, 1788," and "Election, Presidential, 1792," in *Encyclopedia of the American Presidency,* ed. Leonard W. Levy and Louis Fischer (Simon and Schuster, 1992).

Review: Helen E. Veit, Kenneth R. Bowling, and Charlene Bangs Bickford, eds., *Creating the Bill of Rights: The Documentary Record from the First Federal Congress,* in *Journal of Southern History* 58 (1992): 707–708.

1993

"The First Party Struggle," in *Instructor's Manual for James Henretta, et al., America's History* (Worth, 1993).

Review: William Lee Miller, *The Business of May Next: James Madison and the Founding,* in *Journal of Southern History* 59 (1993): 531–532.

Review: Peter S. Onuf, ed., *Jeffersonian Legacies,* in *William and Mary Quarterly* 50 (1993): 787–790.

Review: J. C. A. Stagg et al., eds., *The Papers of James Madison,* vols. 16 and 17, in *Journal of American History* 80 (1993): 1075–1076.

1994

"Federalist Papers," "Hamilton, Alexander," "Kentucky and the Western Country," "Republicanism," and "States' Rights," in *James Madison and the American Nation, 1751–1838: An Encyclopedia,* ed. Robert A. Rutland (Simon and Schuster, 1994).

Feature Review of Stanley Elkins and Eric McKitrick, *The Age of Federalism,* and James Roger Sharp, *American Politics in the Early Republic,* in *Journal of American History* 81 (1994): 1262–1265.

Review: Herman Belz et al., eds., *To Form a More Perfect Union: The Critical Ideas of the Constitution,* in *Journal of Southern History* 60 (1994): 121–122.

Review: Doron S. Ben-Atar, *The Origins of Jeffersonian Commercial Policy and Diplomacy,* in *Journal of the Early Republic* 14 (1994): 414–415.

1995

Jefferson and Madison: Three Conversations from the Founding (Madison House, 1995; paperback edition, 1996).

The Sacred Fire of Liberty: James Madison and the Founding of the Federal Republic (Cornell Univ. Press, 1995; paperback edition, 1998). Merle Curti Award in Intellectual History (O.A.H.), Phi Alpha Theta International Book Award, Pulitzer Prize Finalist.

"Political Economy and the Creation of the Federal Republic," in *Devising Liberty: Preserving and Creating Freedom in the New American Republic,* ed. David Thomas Konig, vol. 5 of *A History of Modern Freedom* (Stanford Univ. Press, 1995), 11–49.

"From Confederation to Constitution, 1781–1789," in *Historia Stanaow Zjednoczonyck Ameryki* (an authoritative history of the United States for Poland and Eastern Europe), vol. 1, *1607–1848,* ed. Michael Rozbicki and Imina Wawrzyczek (PWN, 1995), 33–62.

Review: Joyce Appleby, *Liberalism and Republicanism in the Historical Imagination,* in *Journal of Modern History* 67 (1995): 104–105.

Review: Norman K. Risjord, *Thomas Jefferson,* in *American Historical Review* 100 (1995): 1293–1294.

1996

Review: James Morton Smith, *The Republic of Letters: The Correspondence between Thomas Jefferson and James Madison,* in *Journal of Southern History* 62 (1996): 568–570.

1997

American Journey: The Constitution and the Supreme Court, ed. Lance Banning, Kermit L. Hall, and Jack N. Rakove (Primary Source Media, 1997). A CD-ROM research tool for college and secondary AP courses.

Review: Jack N. Rakove, *Original Meanings: Politics and Ideas in the Making of the Constitution,* in *William and Mary Quarterly,* 3rd ser., 54 (1997): 444–446.

Review: "The First Congressional Gridlock," in *Reviews in American History* 25 (1997): 44–48. An essay review of Calvin Jillson and Rick K. Wilson, *Congressional Dynamics: Structure, Coordination, and Choice in the First American Congress, 1774–1789.*

1998

"Jefferson, Thomas," in *The Encyclopedia of Political Revolutions,* ed. Jack A. Goldstone (Congressional Quarterly, 1998).

1999

"Madison, James," in *American National Biography,* ed. John A. Garraty and Mark C. Carnes (Oxford Univ. Press, 1999).

"James Madison: Memory, Service, and Fame," in *The Noblest Minds: Fame, Honor, and the American Founding,* ed. Peter McNamara (Rowman and Littlefield, 1999), 121–140.

2000

Review: Joseph M. Lynch, *Negotiating the Constitution: The Earliest Debates over Original Intent,* in *American Historical Review* 105 (Oct. 2000): 1300.

Review: "A Last Fatal Interview," in *Times Literary Supplement,* Dec. 1, 2000, 6–7. A joint review of Roger G. Kennedy, *Burr, Hamilton, and Jefferson,* and Thomas Fleming, *Duel: Aaron Burr, Alexander Hamilton, and the Future of America.*

2001

"Revolution and Constitution, Era of" and "Liberty," in *The Oxford Companion to United States History,* ed. Paul S. Boyer (Oxford Univ. Press, 2001), 664–666, 442–443.

"Thomas Jefferson and Sally Hemings: Case Closed?" *Claremont Review* 1 (summer 2001): 18–19.

Review: Joseph J. Ellis, *Founding Brothers: The Revolutionary Generation,* in *Journal of American History* 83 (Dec. 2001): 1057–1058.

2002

Review: Stuart Leibiger, *Founding Friendship: George Washington, James Madison, and the Creation of the American Republic,* in *Pennsylvania History* 69 (winter 2002): 104–106.

Review: "Popularizing the Founding: A Review Essay," in *Register of the Kentucky Historical Society* 100 (spring 2002): 153–157. A joint review of Joseph Ellis, *Founding Brothers,* and David McCullough, *John Adams.*

Review: "Honor and the Democratic Revolution," in *Reviews in American History* 30 (Sept. 2002): 389–392. An essay review of Joanne B. Freeman, *Affairs of Honor.*

2004

Conceived in Liberty: The Struggle to Define the New Republic, 1789–1793 (Rowman and Littlefield, 2004). A revision of the 2001 Leverhulme Lectures.

Liberty and Order: The First American Party Struggle (Liberty Fund, 2004). A four hundred–page anthology of primary sources.

"James Madison," *Oxford Dictionary of National Biography* (Oxford Univ. Press, 2004).

"Jeffersonian Republican Party" and "Madison, James," in *Americans at War: Society, Culture, and the Homefront,* ed. John Phillips Resch (Macmillan, 2004).

Review: "Three-Fifths Historian," *Claremont Review of Books* 4 (fall 2004): 54–56. A review of Gary Wills, *"Negro President": Thomas Jefferson and the Slave Power.*

2005

Review: Max M. Edling, *A Revolution in Favor of Government: Origins of the U.S. Constitution and the Making of the American State,* in *American Historical Review* 110 (February 2005): 132–133.

Review: R. B. Bernstein, *Thomas Jefferson,* in *Journal of American History* 91 (March 2005): 1435–1436.

2006

"Federalism, Constitutionalism, and Republican Liberty: The First Constructions of the Constitution," in *Liberty and American Experience in the Eighteenth Century,* ed. David Womersley (Liberty Fund Press, 2006), 388–424.

Copyrights and Permissions

Index

War of 1812, 14, 302–3, 333–34
Washington, George, 111, 132, 320,
   323, 327
Wilson, James, 114–15, 117–18, 121–
   22, 128, 131–32
Wilson, Major, 46

Wood, Gordon S., vii–ix, 3, 6, 9, 34,
   40, 47, 58, 60, 62–63, 65, 83–89,
   92, 94, 153–54, 161
Woodward, Fred, 9, 10, 344

XYZ Affair, 323–24, 330

CPSIA information can be obtained at www.ICGtesting.com
Printed in the USA
BVOW04*2118211114

375902BV00002B/2/P